Materialism and Sensations

.

Published with assistance from the
Kingsley Trust Association Publication Fund
established by the Scroll and Key Society of Yale College.

Library of Congress catalog card number: 75–151570
International standard book number: 0–300–01250–0

Designed by John O. C. McCrillis
and set in Times Roman type.
Printed in the United States of America by
Colonial Press, Inc., Clinton, Massachusetts.

Distributed in Great Britain, Europe, and Africa by
Yale University Press, Ltd., London; in Canada by
McGill-Queen's University Press, Montreal; in Mexico
by Centro Interamericano de Libros Académicos,
Mexico City; in Central and South America by Kaiman
& Polon, Inc., New York City; in Australasia by
Australia and New Zealand Book Co., Pty., Ltd.
Artarmon, New South Wales; in India by UBS Publishers'
Distributors Pvt., Ltd., Delhi; in Japan by John
Weatherhill, Inc., Tokyo.

Acknowledgment is gratefully made to the following journals and publishers for permission to use material by James W. Cornman:

"Categories, Grammar, and Semantics," *Theoria* 13 (1970): 297–307.

"Mental Terms, Theoretical Terms, and Materialism," *Philosophy of
Science* 35 (1968): 45–63.

"On the Elimination of 'Sensations' and Sensations," *The Review of
Metaphysics* 22 (1968): 15–35.

Philosophical Problems and Arguments, with K. Lehrer (New York:
Macmillan, 1968).

"Private Languages and Private Entities," *Australasian Journal of Philosophy* 46 (1968): 117–26.

"Sellars, Scientific Realism, and Sensa," *The Review of Metaphysics* 23
(1970): 417–51.

"Strawson's 'Person'," *Theoria* 30 (1964): 145–56.

"Types, Categories, and Nonsense," *American Philosophical Quarterly
Monograph Series* 2 (1968): 73–97. *73-07*

Materialism and Sensations

by James W. Cornman

New Haven and London: Yale University Press

1971

Contents

Preface

It is often difficult for a philosopher to resist believing that he has finally, once and for all, disposed of a philosophical problem that has survived for centuries. When in rational moments I resist the temptation, I can state that my aim in this book, as in all else I do in philosophy, is to push understanding of the issues with which I deal significantly beyond previous understanding. Of course I hope that all my conclusions are correct, but I have enough inductive evidence to indicate that some are not. My rational hope is that those of my conclusions that are wrong are at least instructive.

This seemingly pessimistic view of philosophical progress is not merely an induction from observing that many philosophical problems have continually defied solution, it is also a conclusion that follows from my thesis about the nature of these problems. In my book, *Metaphysics, Reference, and Language* (New Haven: Yale University Press, 1966), I argue that metaphysical problems are external rather than internal to the linguistic frameworks of the terms used to formulate them. What I mean by linguistic frameworks and questions internal and external to them can be understood by comparing language with chess. The two are similar in that certain moves are permitted or forbidden by rules. This network of permitted and forbidden linguistic moves is what I call the framework of language. Furthermore, there are two kinds of questions which language and chess have in common, namely, those whose answers are under the jurisdiction of the rules, either completely or partially, and those whose answers are not. Using Carnap's terminology in a modified way, I call the former internal questions and the latter external questions.

Nonphilosophers' questions are internal, but the metaphysical questions asked by philosophers are external. They are about what there is regardless of the requirements of the linguistic framework employed; they are questions about the nature of the referents of the expressions which are used within the framework to formulate the metaphysical problems. A nonphilosopher's question about what an expression refers to, however, is answered from within the framework by means of other expressions of the framework which refer to the same thing or which mean the same. If these answers will not help, he can always be shown ostensibly what the expressions refer to. Such answers enable the nonphilosopher to understand how to use the expressions of a language without becoming involved in the external problem of just what it is these expressions refer to. In other words, the nonphilosopher need only know the ways in which his own linguistic framework allows him to produce a satisfactory description of what there is. Unlike the philosopher, he need not consider the ontological question of whether the terms of his framework or perhaps those of some other provide the best, most accurate description of the way things actually are. He need not consider, for example, whether the physical-object, observation terms of his ordinary, common-sense framework describe what there is better than sense-data terms or the pure theoretical terms of science. The philosopher, who is searching for the correct ontology, however, is faced with that task, and so he cannot rest content with the answers that satisfy nonphilosophers.

On this interpretation of metaphysical problems, a philosopher is put in the most precarious position of trying to resolve external problems. His predicament is that he cannot get outside the jurisdiction of all linguistic frameworks and compare them with reality to see which, if any, he should use to construct the most accurate description of what there is. The most he can do is to search for internal clues to external questions from within some linguistic framework. Because of this, the reasons available to him confer at most plausibility upon his answers. None will settle the issue once and for all.

The prime example I have used to illustrate my thesis about an enduring, metaphysical, and therefore external problem is the mind–body problem. In particular, I have concentrated on the theory that each sensation is identical with some brain process. This identity theory has been widely debated for several years. Many people have argued that it is easily refuted because it involves clear cases of conceptual confusion. Others have claimed that we have only to wait for further development of physiology and psychology until it is finally confirmed. However, both my examination of the theory and my thesis about metaphysical problems lead me to believe that both views are wrong. Neither final refutation nor ultimate confirmation is forthcoming, let alone easy to provide. It is, in part, to test this belief against those opposed to it that I wrote this book.

Many people have helped me avoid mistakes and forced me to make corrections. Three graduate students at the University of Pennsylvania were particularly helpful: Vicki Levine, Philip Ostien, and Gary Rogers. Raymond Martin must be especially thanked for his many clear and precise comments that helped so much.

Early work on this book was done under an Andrew Mellon Postdoctoral Fellowship at the University of Pittsburgh, 1965–66. Most of the later work was done under National Science Foundation grant GS-2083. The time these grants made available for long periods of uninterrupted work was an important factor in the completion of this book.

J.W.C.

University of Pennsylvania
January 1971

Introduction to Materialism

The metaphysical doctrine of materialism is attractive to many philosophers, especially those impressed with the physical sciences and the obvious advances in knowledge resulting from them. It often seems to such philosophers that science is advancing toward a state where physics will be not only the basic science upon which all other sciences are erected, but also the one science to which all other sciences are reduced. This is the view, then, that in the scientific millennium there will be a unified science in which physics will be sufficient for the purposes of explaining and predicting the behavior of everything, including persons. The contemplation of this "future" state has led many, but not all, philosophers to materialism.

Nevertheless, despite whatever optimism about the future unification of sciences is justified, there are now, as there have been for centuries, difficult problems confronting the materialist. Perhaps the crucial problem concerns the status of sensations, a problem clearly evident as far back as Hobbes, who said that sense is "some internal motion in the sentient, generated by some internal motion of the parts of the object, and propagated through all the media to the innermost part of the organ." [1] Here Hobbes reduces sense to physical motion. But he is also found to say that sense is not motion, but "in all cases, is nothing else but original fancy," or, he says elsewhere, "phantasms" caused by internal motions.[2] He is then directly faced with the problem of reconciling appearances and sensations with his avowed materialism. Neither Hobbes nor any one else has solved this problem, and to many it seems to be obviously insoluble.

Materialism must either deny that there are any nonmaterial mental objects, events, and states, or claim that while there are some entities classified as mental, each one is actually not only identical with but reducible to purely material phenomena, usually said to be certain brain processes. But both the denial and the claim seem, initially, to contradict obvious truths. It seems obvious that we are directly aware of certain mental phenomena,

1. *Hobbes Selections,* F. Woodbridge, ed., (New York: Scribner's, 1930), p. 107.
2. Ibid., p. 140.

such as pains, afterimages, hallucinatory images, and sensory experiences, and, therefore, there clearly are such entities. Furthermore, it seems equally evident that these entities are not identical with brain processes, because each has properties the other lacks. Pains are intense, unbearable, nagging, and throbbing; afterimages are yellow, dim, fading, and circular. But physical processes lack these properties and have others that pains and afterimages lack, such as being publicly observable, spatially located, swift, and irreversible. Consequently, by the principle of the identity of indiscernibles, we can quickly conclude that sensations such as pains and afterimages are not identical with and thus not reducible to such physical phenomena. It seems, then, that the problem sensations raise for materialists is fatal. Sensations can be neither reduced to what is material nor eliminated, and that refutes materialism.

Is materialism so quickly refuted? Many people think not. Indeed, many think it can be quickly established. Clearly, both contentions, quite common today, cannot be true. In fact, they are, I shall claim, both false. Either to refute or to establish materialism is at best a complex and difficult task. To show just how difficult this is, is one of the aims of this book. In so doing I shall concentrate on materialism and sensations.

It is my contention that the problem that sensations present for materialists is their most difficult, although by no means their only one. There are also the problems that intentional states, such as thinking, doubting, and intending raise. Just as sensations are not, preanalytically, amenable to a materialistic ontology, neither are beliefs, thoughts, and doubts that people have, nor are their intentions, purposes, and wants. Accommodating such entities is difficult enough for materialists, but there is an important difference between them and sensations that makes the latter the most difficult to handle. Sensations such as pains seem to have directly presented phenomenal properties, properties we seem to experience clearly and indubitably. But, misusing a phrase of W. V. Quine, thoughts and intentions are "creatures of darkness," that is, their properties, and also the properties of intentional states of thinking and intending, are not phenomenologically present and manifest in the same way. It is because of this that the theories which construe intentional states as either functional states or central states and then reduce them to physical states, are quite reasonable. It is when sensations are construed this way that serious problems arise.

Functional states are characterized by their functional relationships to other states; central states are characterized as causal intermediaries between stimulus and resulting behavior.[3] For both sorts of states, what they turn out to be—what has the function or is the cause—is left to be discovered by science. Thus whatever nonfunctional, intrinsic properties the realizations of these states have, depends on the properties discovered and postulated by science. It is because all the intrinsic properties uncovered in this way may be purely physical that intentional states seem not to pose a serious problem for a materialist. On the other hand, we surely seem to experience intrinsic properties of sensations which are phenomenal. It is this that casts so much doubt upon reducing sensations to "Hobbesian internal motions." [4] If a materialist can resolve his problem with sensations, then I believe he can also resolve the problems with intentional states. For the above reasons, I take the converse of this to be false.

I have talked above as if it is perfectly clear just what the thesis of materialism is. I have found, however, that none of the usual formulations succeed and that attempts to amend them also fail. The usual problem is that these formulations do not distinguish materialism from other ontological theses about persons that are incompatible with it. Because of this, we have the difficult task, preliminary to the main one of the book, to provide an adequate definition of 'materialism.' In addition to

3. For a functional state theory, see H. Putnam, "Psychological Predicates," in W. Capitan and D. Merrill, eds., *Art, Mind and Religion* (Pittsburgh: University of Pittsburgh Press, 1967). For central state theories, see D. Armstrong, *A Materialist Theory of Mind* (London: Routledge and Kegan Paul, 1968); and D. Lewis, "An Argument for the Identity Theory," *Journal of Philosophy* LXII (1966): 17–25.
4. For a more detailed reason for this, see p. 119f. See also W. Sellars, *Science, Perception and Reality* (London: Routledge and Kegan Paul, 1963), pp. 32–37 for a similar claim about the crucial difference between thoughts and sensations that results in its being plausible to identify thoughts but not sensations with brain states. For Sellars' more detailed views on identifying thoughts and brain states, see "Notes on Intentionality," *Journal of Philosophy* 61 (1964): 655–65.

helping us better understand the thesis with which we shall be concerned throughout the rest of the book, this will also provide an introduction to those theories that are opposed to materialism.

A DEFINITION OF 'MATERIALISM'

One way to begin our search for an adequate characterization of materialism is by considering some of those proposed by other philosophers. D. Williams, a defender of materialism, claims that it

> is the doctrine that the whole of what exists is constituted of matter and its local motions . . . and is hence 'physical' in the literal sense that all its constituents are among the subject matter of physics. . . . In the entire universe, including the knowing mind itself, there is nothing which could not be destroyed (or repaired) by a spatio-temporal redisposition of its components.[5]

This is a helpful beginning but there are reasons for rejecting it as the final version. First, there is the minor objection that this definition implies that everything has components. If there are scientifically basic particles, then there are some things that have no components. This would falsify the definition but not materialism. We can avoid this by rewriting the definition as follows:

> Materialism is the doctrine that everything that exists (a) consists of physical matter and its local motions, and (b) if it has components, then it can be destroyed (or repaired) by a spatiotemporal redistribution of its components, all of which are among the subject matter of physics.

As we shall see later, much depends on how the term 'physical' is defined, but we need not consider that yet to find fatal objections.

As it stands, the preceding definition is compatible with two theories that are incompatible with materialism. Consider first an epiphenomenalistic theory which states that every object or individual thing that exists is physical but that there are certain nonphysical, mental *events,* such as feeling dizzy, that are by-

5. D. Williams, "Naturalism and the Nature of Things," *Philosophical Review* 53 (1944): 418.

products of certain physical processes. The only objects which are constituents in these events are persons and other physical objects. Thus, although there are mental events, there are no mental objects and nothing has mental objects as constituents. This theory is consistent with condition (a), because persons would have and *only* have as constituents physical particles in motion, even though certain (perhaps emergent) events involving persons are not physical. The theory would also be consistent with (b) because persons on this, and indeed on any epiphenomenalistic theory, are functions of their physical components. The definition is also compatible with a Strawsonian theory which takes persons to be ontologically basic, that is, not consisting of something more basic, such as minds and bodies (see the discussion of Strawson's argument in Chap. 1), and which agrees with the previous epiphenomenalist theory that there are no mental objects. The definition must be amended to rule out these theories. It would seem we must exclude mental events and states, as well as mental objects.

A definition which considers events can be derived from C. J. Ducasse's definition of 'the material world':

> Materialism is the doctrine that every object, event, property, and relation (a) either is or can be publicly observable by normal observers under normal conditions, or (b) is existentially implicit in, i.e., is a constituent of, those which are normally publicly observable.[6]

Unfortunately this formulation is also compatible with theories not compatible with materialism. First, if, as some identity theorists claim, sensations such as pains are identical with certain brain phenomena, and these entities have both the phenomenal properties of sensations and the physical properties of brain phenomena, then some form of a double aspect or neutral theory would be correct. That is, there would be certain entities that are neither purely physical nor purely mental. This theory is incompatible with materialism but not with the definition, because if sensations are identical with brain phenomena, then, depending on the sort of brain phenomena with which they are identical, they are either publicly observable themselves or at

6. See C. J. Ducasse, *Nature, Mind, and Death* (La Salle, Ill.: Open Court, 1951), pp. 222–23.

least the brains of which they are constituents are publicly observable.

A similar problem arises with a Berkeleian idealistic theory, which is clearly incompatible with materialism. Tables are publicly observable, but if tables are bundles of sensory ideas or sense-data, as Berkeleians would maintain, then because these sense-data are constituents of tables, this idealistic theory is compatible with the definition of 'materialism.' This definition would also allow the existence of sense-data, contrary to materialism, if, for example, an event of someone feeling the texture of a fabric is publicly observable and includes tactile sensations as constituents. Another problem, at least as devastating, is that the definition seems compatible with a Cartesian dualism, that is, the view that a person consists of a mental substance and a physical substance which causally interact. But a person is publicly observable and, on the Cartesian view, a mind is a constituent of a person. Thus the existence of Cartesian egos is compatible with the definition, but not with materialism. This is also true for any parallelistic view such as the preestablished harmony theory of Leibniz and Malebranche's occasionalism.

One reaction to the failure of these two attempts is to try to amend them, but another is to begin anew with the simple definition that materialism is the thesis that every object or individual has a property only if it is a physical property. It will be noted that this definition, unlike the preceding one, does not mention events, processes, and states. It might seem, therefore, to be open to objections like those that confronted the first definition. The present one, however, by mentioning properties of individuals avoids such objections if we assume, as we shall here, a universe of individuals. Thus all events, processes, and states involve individuals, and are covered when construed as consisting of individuals having properties of or relations among individuals. Another objection might seem to arise because the definition limits properties but not relations, and thus seems to be compatible with something having the relation of being mentally pictured by someone, contrary to materialism. This problem can be avoided by using 'property' to stand for both properties and relations. (For convenience I shall continue to do this.

Where it is important to distinguish I shall talk of nonrelational properties and relations.)

Even with the two preceding problems avoided, two others remain. Materialists are not committed to denying the existence of abstract entities such as classes, propositions, universals, and numbers, but the preceding definition prohibits these because they have properties that are not physical. This problem is not as easy to avoid as it might seem. For example, we cannot limit the objects mentioned in the definition to those that are a part of the physical universe or to those which are among the subject matter of empirical sciences. The former would be consistent with the existence of minds, as would the latter if the subject matter of all sciences concerned with human beings was to become fixed as human behavior. The best I think we can do is to limit the properties and relations mentioned to what I shall call "a posteriori" properties, where one of these, roughly, is a property or relation it is reasonable to claim entities have or lack, only if there is some experiential evidence or theoretical scientific reason sufficient to support the claim. We can also call an object, or an individual, a posteriori just in case it is reasonable to claim it exists or does not exist only if there is some experiential evidence or theoretical scientific reason sufficient to support the claim.[7]

The second problem is that some individuals, namely persons, seem to have certain properties and relations which on many interpretations are not physical, but which do not disprove materialism. If there are "nonnatural" (non-a-posteriori) ethical and aesthetic properties, then some persons have such nonrelational properties, e.g. being good or beautiful, and such relations, e.g. being better than or more beautiful than Mary. There are also other properties of persons that are not physical but which materialists can allow, such as being self-identical and being a member of some set. This problem can be resolved by having a materialist allow not only physical properties, but also any other properties that are neutral with respect to materialism.

7. How difficult it is to be precise here is evidenced by the seemingly insuperable problems for defining 'empirical verifiability.' See J. Cornman, "Empirically Verifiable: Everything or Nothing," *Philosophical Studies* 18 (1967): 49–55.

Many properties that are normative, mathematical, or logical, and others, such as the property of occurring over a period of time, are neutral in the sense that they can be properties both of entities that are physical and of entities that are not physical. We can call these properties "physical-neutral." More generally, we can say that a property is Φ-neutral just in case there are conditions in which it would be a property of entities that are Φ, and there are conditions in which it would be a property of entities that are not Φ.[8]

The definition we have reached expresses a sufficient condition for materialism, but not a necessary condition. The problem is that it does not capture what is meant when a materialist claims that something such as a pain or afterimage, which seems to have properties which are neither physical nor physical-neutral, are reducible to or nothing but purely physical entities. That is, we need to include in the definition what it is to claim that one entity is reduced to or is nothing but another. What are we claiming when we say that water, which is observable, is nothing but conglomerations of H_2O molecules, which is theoretical, or that the temperature of a gas, which is observable, is nothing but the mean kinetic energy of the molecules of the gas, or that a pain is nothing but a firing of the C-fibers in a brain? In general, how can we analyze that claim that e is nothing but (is reducible to) r, where r, but usually not e, is Φ? One necessary condition is that e be identical with r, but this is not sufficient, for identity is a symmetrical relation and reduction is not. If e is to be reduced to r, which is Φ, it must be that r would have only Φ and Φ-neutral properties if it were not identical with e, although, initially at least, e may seem to have some properties which keep it from being Φ. The core question for reduction is how these troublesome properties, such as the observable properties of water and temperature and the phenomenal properties of pains and afterimages, can be handled. I claim that if all the particular instances of the properties of e which are not Φ, such as the particular throbbing of my present pain, and the particular yellow color of a certain afterimage, are nothing but instances of properties which are Φ or Φ-neutral, and e is identical with r, then e is reduced to or is nothing but r.

8. Cf. J. J. C. Smart, "Sensations and Brain Processes," *Philosophical Review* 68 (1959): 149–50, where he mentions topic-neutral words.

Notice that it is not the reduction of these troublesome properties that is required, but only the reduction of all their instances. As discussed in Chapter 3, I would claim the two reductions are different and only the latter is necessary for reducing individuals. In this account, the reduction of individuals depends on the reduction of the instances of certain troublesome properties. We are left, then, with the problem of understanding what it is for an instance of one property to be reduced to or nothing but an instance of a different property which is Φ or Φ-neutral. Clearly, each reduced instance must be identical with its reducing instance, and it must have the correct sort of properties. We can express this here, although a minor revision will be required later (see p. 61), by saying that an instance *i* of a property *P* is nothing but an instance *j* of a property *Q* which is Φ or Φ-neutral just in case *i* is identical with *j* and all properties of *i* are Φ or Φ-neutral. With this accomplished, we can state what I believe is a satisfactory definition of 'materialism':

> Materialism = $_{\text{df.}}$ For each a posteriori property *P* of an existing individual *I*, (a) *P* is physical or physical-neutral, or (b) each instance of *P* is nothing but an instance of a physical or physical-neutral property.

TOWARD A DEFINITION OF 'PHYSICAL PROPERTY'

Intuitively the preceding definition may seem acceptable, but whether it is depends on how 'physical property' is defined. Unfortunately, I find this task to be more difficult than defining 'materialism.' Once again, many definitions that have been proposed are of little help. Certain of them are too broad and others are too narrow. Consider the claim of R. Taylor: "For something to count as a physical property of something it is sufficient, and necessary, that the thing in question is a physical object." [9] This leaves us with 'physical object,' which I have found no way to define without first defining 'physical property.' This is not true of Taylor who claims "a man is a physical—that is, a visible and palpable—being." [10] Using this, it is easy for Taylor to accomplish his aim: to bury the mind–body problem—alive,

9. R. Taylor, "How to Bury the Mind–Body Problem," *American Philosophical Quarterly* 6 (1969): 139.
10. Ibid., p. 142.

I might add. All properties of men, such as thinking, dreaming, willing, having sensations, are properties of physical objects, and are, therefore, physical properties. But, of course, being physical in this sense is compatible with Cartesian dualism, Berkeleian idealism, and a Strawsonian theory, and so the problem lives on. For example, if it is minds that think and men are embodied minds, then because such individuals are visible and palpable, thinking done by men would be physical by Taylor's definition.

While Taylor's definition is too broad, other proposals are too narrow. In general they face one of two problems: they saddle materialism either with a reduction of everything to entities explainable by one basic science and thus with the unity of science, or with some form of determinism such as mechanism. Materialism is compatible with the nonreducibility of, for example, neurophysiology to physics and with scientifically unexplainable and uncaused physical events. Consider the following derived from W. Sellars' definition of what he calls "physical$_2$ predicates":

> P is a physical property $=$ $_{df.}$ P is a property that is expressed by one of a set of predicates adequate to a theoretical description of non-living matter.[11]

Because of the phrase 'theoretical description,' it is not clear how to interpret this definition. But I think it is reasonable to construe it so that a set of predicates adequate to a theoretical description of nonliving matter is a set of predicates that provides a description of nonliving matter that is *minimally* adequate for a scientific theoretical explanation of the behavior of nonliving matter.[12] There are several problems with this interpretation. First, if 'matter' is construed as 'material entities' and to be material is to be construed in terms of being physical, then

11. Sellars, "The Identity Approach to the Mind–Body Problem," *Review of Metaphysics* 18 (1965), sec. 45.

12. We must interpret 'adequate' as 'minimally adequate' here. If we do not, then if a set $(P_1 \ldots P_n)$ is adequate to explain something, then so is any consistent set $(P_1 \ldots P_{n+1})$ and any property consistent with such a set of explanatory properties would be physical. A set $(P_1 \ldots P_n)$ is minimally adequate to explain something if and only if $(P_1 \ldots P_n)$ is adequate to explain it and no proper subset of $(P_1 \ldots P_n)$ is adequate to explain it.

the definition is circular; but if 'matter' is merely construed as 'subject matter,' then abstract properties required by theoretical descriptions of abstract entities such as numbers would be physical. We can correct this by again using the concept of a posteriori property. Also, this definition implies that there are no physical properties if science fails to explain adequately non-living matter, and this is surely mistaken. There are physical properties whether or not science succeeds—even if there were no science. The definition, however, is useful as a first approximation in characterizing properties attributed to entities in the physical sciences. These properties will be discussed later and, for convenience, called "scientific properties" (see Chap. 7).

Finally, there is a problem that arises in two different ways depending on whether or not we restrict what affects the behavior of nonliving matter for the purposes of the definition. If there is no restriction, then if there are minds and they affect nonliving entities in ways that require mind-terms for theoretical descriptions, then minds would be physical. This cannot be allowed. But if we restrict what affects this behavior to nonliving entities, then neurophysiological predicates that describe living brains would not be required for the relevant theoretical descriptions, and thus the properties they express would not be physical, unless reducible in some way to properties of nonliving entities. But it seems that they should be called physical whether or not reducible. We must try a different tack.

For the sake of simplicity I shall limit the definition to physical properties of individuals, where by individuals I mean objects rather than events, states, or properties. Parallel definitions can be given for properties of each of the other kinds of entities. As a helpful advance, consider the following:

> *P* is a physical property of individuals = df. *P* is an a posteriori property that, under certain conditions, would be a nonrelational property of or a relation among spatiotemporal individuals which are neither living individuals nor parts (i.e. *attached* parts) of living individuals.

This definition avoids circularity, the implication of scientific explainability of all nonliving phenomena, and the result that mental phenomena, if necessary for theoretical explanation, are physical. It does have two bothersome consequences, however. The first is that if some complex computer, such as a Turing machine, actually were to have thoughts, or if some detached brain placed in vitro were to have sensations, then both these thoughts and sensations would be physical by the preceding definition. For some people, such cases seem so absurd that they are logically or conceptually impossible, but I think an adequate definition of 'physical property' should guard against such cases. We can do this by amending the preceding definition as follows:

P is a physical property of individuals = df.

(1) P is an a posteriori property that, under certain conditions, would be a nonrelational property of or a relation among spatiotemporal individuals which are neither living individuals nor attached parts of living individuals, *and*

(2) P is not a property or relation that a spatiotemporal individual, which is living or is a part of a living individual, would have only if it or what it is part of were living.

Because living beings and their attached spatiotemporal parts think and have sensations only when the beings are living, then even if computers and detached brains in vitro think and have sensations, it would not follow that thinking and having sensations are physical. Of course, whether they are *nothing but* something physical is another matter.

The second consequence we should consider is that no properties peculiar to living individuals or their parts are physical. For example, if there are properties that the brain, or other bodily parts of a person, would have only when the person is living, then under this definition they would not be physical properties. For example, if a nerve impulse in brains took a specific route, *r,* only when the brains were part of living persons, perhaps because of the unique effect of a mental phenomenon on certain nerve synapses in the brains, then according to this definition, the property of taking route *r* would not be physical, even though it took a very similar route when in vitro and stimulated in a certain way.

What is obvious about this counterexample is that, although the specific physical property in question fails to meet the definition, it is a species of a property that does meet the definition, that is, the property of taking some route through a brain. Thus we could amend the definition to allow such species to be physical. I shall not attempt this amendment, however. I shall assume here that if a physical process were to occur in a living individual, then it could be brought about when the individual is not living. I assume this, not only because I think it is reasonable, but also to help keep the definition from becoming too complicated. In this case, as in all others in this book, my purpose in defining a term is to enable readers to understand clearly how I am using a term at crucial places throughout the book. Often this requirement of being understandable in important contexts of use conflicts with the requirement that a definition avoid all counterexamples. Where such conflicts arise, my aim is to arrive at an optimum point which strikes a balance between a maximum clarity of use and a minimum of serious counterexamples. Even so, however, I am afraid some definitions will prove to be quite complicated.

PHYSICAL OBJECTS AND PHYSICAL EVENTS

We have been interested here in physical properties, but later we shall also need to consider physical objects and physical events. We can help characterize the latter two using the first. Physical objects are a posteriori individuals with physical properties. They can, however, have some properties that are not physical, such as the property of being believed by someone to be a table, but none have the property of believing something to be a table. The first, then, would be a physical-neutral property but the second would not. Of course, if materialism is true, no object has either property unless all instances of such properties are reducible to instances of physical or physical-neutral properties. It might seem, then, that it is enough to say that something is a physical object just in case it has physical properties and it has a property only if the property is either physical or physical-neutral. Unfortunately, we cannot use this definition and also the one previously given of 'physical-neutral property,' because in accordance with the latter definition, a physical-neutral property of an individual would be defined in terms of physical individuals. We can, however, use our "approximate" definition of 'physical property of individuals' as a guide for a similar definition of 'physical object':

> O is a physical object $=$ df. O has physical properties, and O has no properties that a spatiotemporal individual which is living or is a part of a living individual would have only if it or what it is part of were living.

This definition allows a physical object to have properties that are not a posteriori as well as a posteriori properties which meet the independent definition of 'physical-neutral property.' It eliminates, however, objects that have thoughts and sensations on the assumption that living beings would have thoughts and sensations only when living. Thus a Turing machine that has thoughts, a brain in vitro that has sensations, and a living thing that has a property it would have only when living are not physical objects. Of course, they may be reducible to physical objects.

We can characterize physical events in terms of physical properties and physical objects. Physical events, such as a certain gas having its temperature rise 10°, are events with physical properties, and they are constituted only of physical objects with physical properties, in the sense that the occurrence of a physical event entails that there is an object with a property only if both object and property are physical. Thus because both a gas and the property of having a temperature rise are physical, an event constituted of a gas and a temperature rise is physical. This is also true of an event of a brain's C-fibers firing, but it is not true of an event which is a brain having a sensation. If there is such an event, then neither it nor the brain in question is physical.

FOREWORD TO MATERIALISM AND SENSATIONS

I believe that with the last amended versions of the definition of 'P is a physical property of individuals' we will find that our characterization of materialism is sufficient to distinguish it clearly and distinctly from the many theories opposed to it. Let us, then, return to the problem sensations pose for materialism. The aim of this book is to discover whether or not there is some way a materialist can resolve this problem. For each sensation, his choice is either to reduce it to something physical or to eliminate it completely. It might seem, then, that a materialist has only two basic alternatives given the seeming truth of statements such as 'People sometimes have intense and throbbing pains.' The first is to defend the thesis that, whether such a statement is true or not, there really are no sensations at all. Because this view eliminates all sensations, I shall call it "eliminative materialism." The second, while granting the truth of such statements, is to justify the reduction of all sensations, including pains, afterimages, itches, and tickles, to physical phenomena. I shall call this view "reductive materialism." There is, however, a third alternative, sometimes overlooked, perhaps because 'sensation' is used to refer to two quite different kinds of entities. Both sensory experiences, such as imaging and aching, and certain objects of sensory experience, which I shall call "sensa," such as afterimages and aches, are called "sensations." Consequently, it is possible to eliminate one of these two kinds of entities referred to by 'sensation' and to reduce the other kind. In particular, there is the version of materialism which denies that someone having an ache consists of two individuals, a person and an ache, being in a certain relationship. Rather, on this view there is only the person in a nonrelational state of hurting. Thus, instead of there being a sensum which is a pain with the phenomenal properties of being intense and throbbing, there is only the person aching intensely and throbbingly. Sensory experience consists of nonrelational, objectless events and states of persons which are modified adverbially. And, according to this third version of materialism, which for lack of a better name I shall call "adverbial materialism," each of these objectless sensory experiences, which I shall call "sensings," is reducible to or nothing but some physical event.

Each of these three distinct versions of materialism faces its own unique set of problems. The question before us is whether any of these three positions can successfully resolve the problems sensations pose for it. In this book I shall argue for the thesis that both the reductive and eliminative approaches to sensations fail, but that there is some reason to accept the approach of adverbial materialism. Part I considers reductive materialism and attempts to show why it fails. Essential to reductive materialism is the theory that all sensations are identical with physical phenomena, for to be reduced to something entails being identical with it. The converse entailment, however, does not hold, because the identity theory is compatible with monistic theories that are incompatible with materialism. In much current discussion relevant to reductive materialism, criticism has been directed at the identity theory, although often it has not been clear whether the objections apply to the identity theory itself, or to the theory when conjoined with materialism. An example of the first sort is the objection discussed and rejected in Part I that, because sensations are private and brain phenomena are public, no sensations are identical with brain phenomena and the identity theory is false, whether or not conjoined with materialism. Another objection, also discussed and rejected, is compatible with the identity theory but not with materialism. It argues that persons are ontologically basic and therefore are not reducible to anything more basic, whether it be a mere body or an entity consisting of a body and a mind.

It becomes even clearer how important it is to direct objections at the right point when the property objection to reductive materialism is examined. This crucial objection is often directed against the identity theory alone, and I argue that it fails to refute this theory. But it does succeed when its claim is that, while all sensations may be identical with physical phenomena, at least some of them are not reducible to physical phenomena, because some of their phenomenal properties thwart a reduction. This point, which refutes reductive materialism, is argued by showing that there are defeating differences between the case of sensa with phenomenal properties and plausible examples of ontological reduction, such as the reduction of the temperature of a gas to the mean kinetic energy of the gas molecules, and the reduction of water to conglomerations of H_2O molecules. In short, the central problem is that the instances of observable properties which clearly seem to be properties of temperature or water can be "transferred" to sensations to pave the way for reduction, but the instances of phenomenal properties of sensa can be neither transferred to something else nor reduced to something physical.

While much discussion of reductive materialism has been directed, indeed misdirected, at the identity theory, the work on eliminative materialism has been primarily divided among four of its species: analytical behaviorism, Rylean behaviorism, the postulation elimination theory, and the 'sensation' elimination theory. We can interpret these theories as attempting, each in its own way, to establish that there is no descriptive need for sensation terms, and therefore it is justified to conclude that there are no sensations. Analytical behaviorists attempt to show this by providing behavioral analyses of sentences containing sensation terms; Rylean behaviorists support this conclusion by putting sensation sentences in the logical category of nonreferring and thus nondescriptive inference tickets; postulation elimination theorists argue that there is a descriptive need for sensation terms only if there is an explanatory need, but there is no explanatory need for them because physicalistic terms explain at least as well; and 'sensation' elimination theorists claim that the reporting and descriptive roles of sensation terms can, with time, be assumed by physicalistic terms. These four theories, the extant species of eliminative materialism, are each discussed and rejected in Part II. The basic flaw in each position is that sensation terms have descriptive roles which are independent of any explanatory role they may play, and that these roles can be neither assumed by physicalistic terms, nor eliminated without loss of important descriptive power. Neither the elimination of all sensation terms nor the elimination of all sensations is justified and thus the eliminative approach to the problem of sensations fails.

At the end of Part II only adverbial materialism remains unscathed, because it avoids the objections that refute the other two versions of materialism. It interprets sense experience as consisting of adverbial, objectless sensings, such as red-sensings, so that there are no sensa, such as red sensa, with phenomenal properties. It thereby avoids the problem that phenomenal properties pose for reductive materialism. It goes on to state that these adverbial sensings are reducible to, and therefore identical with, physical processes and thus it avoids the objection to eliminative theories that it is unreasonable to eliminate all sensation terms and all sensations. Nevertheless it does face three crucial objections of its own. One is against interpreting sensory experience as objectless adverbial sensings; another is against reducing such sensing events to physical events; the third is against reducing persons who have the property of sensing to physical individuals. The first objection is the most complex and difficult to refute, because there are at least four quite different ways it might be supported. There are certain empirical facts of perception, such as perceptual relativity, illusions, hallucinations, and the time gap between the transmission of stimulus and the resultant perception, which have been used to justify the existence of some kind of sensum, such as a sense-datum or a percept. However, even if these empirical facts alone do not justify the existence of sensa, it may be that the scientific theories that explain such facts will in some way require the theoretical postulation of sensa. There may also be justified philosophical theories that require some sort of sensa. For example, W. Sellars claims that a thoroughgoing scientific realism entails a unified scientific image or description of the world, which in turn requires the postulation of sensa. Furthermore, it might be argued that the most reasonable philosophical theory of perception and the external world requires sensa rather than objectless sensings. If either some form of indirect realism or ontological phenomenalism should prove more reasonable than any form of direct realism, then there would be reason to reject the adverbial theory of sensory experience.

Part III of this book consists of a detailed examination and ultimate rejection of two of the preceding four attempts to support the objection to the adverbial theory of sensory experience. The other two attempts are merely mentioned and rejected provisionally. Each argument for sensa based on some empirical facts of perception is examined and rejected in Chapter 6, and Sellars' reasons for claiming that a unified scientific image of man and the world requires sensa is rejected in Chapter 7. Whether there are scientific theoretical reasons for sensa is not discussed, because no science dealing with sensory experience is yet developed enough to provide reliable clues about what entities its explanations will require. Nor is any critical comparison of direct realism with its alternatives which require sensa attempted here. Such an examination deserves its own book and is a topic for a future date. Nevertheless, given that neither perceptual facts nor the unification of science requires sensa, it is at least initially plausible that acceptable scientific and philosophical theories of perception and sensation can do without sensa. For this reason, although much work remains to be done, I conclude at the end of Part III that it is

reasonable, yet still provisional, to accept the adverbial interpretation of sensory experience.

The second and third objections to adverbial materialism are
that neither objectless sensing events nor persons who sense
are reducible to physical entities. Like the crucial property objection to reductive materialism, the second objection can be
lodged either against identifying sensing events with physical
events, or, granting the identity, against the claim that the events
in question are nothing but physical events. The crucial question is whether either sensings or the appropriate physical
events have any properties that thwart either the identity claim
or the reduction claim. This question is considered in the concluding chapter after the previous results of the book have been
summarized. Based on these results and an examination of the
properties most likely to prohibit either identity or reduction, I
inductively conclude that reduction of sensing events is reasonable. The same conclusion is reached about the third objection
which rejects the reduction of persons who have the property
of sensing. Although this property is neither physical nor physical-neutral, I argue that it is reasonable to construe each particular instance of the property as nothing but an instance of
some physical or physical-neutral property. Thus the existence of
persons, unlike the existence of sensa, does not refute materialism. Once these conclusions are drawn, we can conjoin them
with the results reached at the end of Part III and conclude that,
based on the total evidence now available, although surely not
all the evidence that will become available, the adverbial form of
materialism avoids the problem raised by sensations. It is the
task of the rest of this book to present the evidence currently
available, and to show that it does indeed support this conclusion.

PART I

Reductive Materialism

1. Reductive Materialism and the Identity Theory

We are here concerned with that version of materialism I have called "reductive" materialism. Essential to this version is that theory known as the mind–body identity theory, that is, the theory that each sensation is strictly identical with, i.e. the same entity as, some physical entity. We can state the theory as follows:

$$(x)(y)[Sxy \supset (\exists z)(Pzy \cdot x = z)], \quad \text{or} \quad (x)(y)[Sxy \supset Pxy],$$

where $Sxy = x$ is a sensation of y, and $Pzy = z$ is a physical phenomenon of y, where 'physical' is defined as was done in the introduction.

TWO VERSIONS OF THE IDENTITY THEORY

I have called the preceding theory "*the* identity theory," but, strictly, there are at least two versions often discussed and often confused, only one of which will concern us here. A version that differs from the first one mentioned above is that all entities that have sensations also have physical properties such as size, shape, and weight.[1] We can state the view as follows:

$$(x)(\exists y)[Sx \supset (Py \cdot x = y)],$$

where $Sx = x$ has sensations, and $Py = y$ has physical properties.

This theory, which I shall call the "weak" identity theory, can be accepted by anyone except those who claim that some entities that have sensations are different from entities that have physical properties. Thus, as Sellars points out, Cartesian dualists would disagree with this version, because although they would agree that some entities with sensations, i.e. persons, also have physical properties, they would claim that some others with sensations, i.e. minds, do not.[2] However, even some dualists could accept the weak theory, namely those who hold that

1. Cf. W. Sellars, "The Identity Approach to the Mind–Body Problem," *Review of Metaphysics* 18 (1965), secs. 28–30; reprinted in Sellars, *Philosophical Perspectives* (Springfield, Ill.: Charles C. Thomas, 1967), Chap. 15.
2. Ibid., sec. 30.

a person consists of a bundle of two radically different kinds of
events, mental events and physical events, but who deny there
are any minds or Cartesian egos. For these dualists, persons
would be the only entities that have sensation. But all dualists
would disagree if we were to revise the statement by classifying
y as a mere body (*By*), or as neither mind nor body (*Ny*). That
is, they would disagree with what some materialists would accept:

$$(x)(\exists y)[Sx \supset (Py \cdot By \cdot x = y)];$$

and with what a neutral theorist, such as Strawson, would accept:[3]

$$(x)(\exists y)[Sx \supset (Ny \cdot Py \cdot x = y)].$$

I have claimed that some mind–body dualists could accept
the weak form of the identity theory. It is, then, not the version
that is essential to the thesis of reductive materialism. The first
version mentioned does not claim that the entities having sensations are the same as those having certain physical properties,
but that the sensations themselves are identical with certain
physical phenomena. This version, which I shall call the
"strong" version, is incompatible with a dualism of sensations
and physical phenomena, and is thus the version that is part of
the thesis of reductive materialism. It is clear that the weak
version does not entail the strong version, but the converse entailment holds. If each sensation is identical with a physical
phenomenon, then it follows that an entity has a sensation only
if it has a physical property, and all entities that have sensations
also have physical properties.

THE EMPIRICAL CONSEQUENCES OF THE
IDENTITY THEORY

We are interested here in the strong version of the identity
theory. Before beginning our examination, it should be noted
that the theory is usually taken to state that sensations are identical with a certain specific kind of physical phenomena, in particular brain processes or states. Let us, then, restate the theory
as follows:

$$(x)(y)[Sxy \supset (\exists z)(Bzy \cdot x = z)],$$

3. See P. F. Strawson, *Individuals* (London: Methuen, 1959), Chap. 3.

where $Bzy = z$ is a brain phenomenon of y. Note that this does not imply that each brain phenomenon is identical with some sensation. No one, I think, has claimed there is such an implication. It has been claimed, however, that the identity theory does imply that there is, using Feigl's terminology, a one-to-one "simultanetity-correspondence" between the mental and the physical.[4] This has been disputed by D. Luce.[5] To see his point, let us first interpret Feigl's claim to be that the identity theory implies a one-to-one correspondence between individual sensations and brain phenomena, but not a correspondence of kinds. We can construe this to state that there are pairs, each consisting of a sensation and a brain process that occur simultaneously, and that each sensation and each brain process is in exactly one pair. This entails that at least one brain phenomenon occurs when a sensation occurs, and at least one sensation occurs when a brain phenomenon occurs. But only the first of these entailed conjuncts is also entailed by the preceding statement of the identity theory, that is:

$$(x)(y)[Sxy \supset (\exists z)(Bzy \cdot Oxz)],$$

where $Oxz = x$ occurs at the same time as z. This is implied because if for some sensation there was no brain phenomenon that occurred at the same time it did, then that sensation would not be identical with any brain phenomenon and the identity theory would be false. But the second conjunct,

$$(x)(y)[Bxy \supset (\exists z)(Szy \cdot Oxz)],$$

is not implied, because the theory is compatible with some brain phenomena occurring when no sensations occur. The most that is implied along this line is that when a brain phenomenon of a certain sort occurs, some sensation also occurs. This implication can be seen by realizing that if for every sensation there is at least one brain phenomenon that occurs at the same time, then there is a set of brain phenomena each of which is accompanied by at least one sensation.

4. See H. Feigl, "The 'Mental' and the 'Physical'," in H. Feigl et al., eds., *Minnesota Studies in the Philosophy of Science*, 3 vols. (Minneapolis: University of Minnesota Press, 1956–62), 2 (1958), p. 376.

5. See D. R. Luce, "Mind–Body Identity and Psycho-Physical Correlation," *Philosophical Studies* 17 (1966): 1–7.

Feigl, however, wants a stronger implication than this, because he thinks that the kind of simultaneity correspondence implied by the identity theory enables us to make inferences about particular mental phenomena "on the basis of intersubjectively accessible" physical data.[6] But unless there is some correspondence of kinds, not merely of individuals, no such inference is possible. Without such a correspondence of kinds, there would be no psychophysical laws relating, for example, all pains to stimulations of C-fibers, and without such laws no purely physical data would enable us to make inferences about which particular mental phenomena occur. Feigl requires at minimum that there occurs at the same time as each brain phenomenon of a certain physiologically identifiable kind (e.g. a stimulation of C-fibers), a sensation of the same phenomenally identifiable kind (e.g. a pain). Then, if we justify that a particular brain phenomenon which is physiologically identifiable as a stimulation of C-fibers is always accompanied by a sensation which is phenomenally identifiable as a pain, we can make the kind of inferences Feigl wishes.

It is clear, however, that the identity theory does not imply the preceding correspondence of kinds, because the theory is consistent with one particular stimulation of C-fibers being identical with a pain, and another being identical with something of some other phenomenally identifiable kind—such as a tickle. Nor is the other "half" of a correspondence of kinds implied: that there occurs, at the same time as each sensation of one phenomenally identifiable kind, a brain phenomenon of the same physiologically identifiable kind. What would be required of an identity theory that implies these last two claims is that it state an identity not merely of individuals but of individuals of certain physiologically and phenomenologically identifiable kinds. This is perhaps the kind of identity theory that Feigl had in mind, but it is not implied by the usual statements of the theory. For our purposes, however, it will not matter which theory is examined. The objections to the theory that we shall consider apply to the first formulation (identity of individuals only), but because the second formulation (identity of kinds) implies the first, the objections will also apply to the second.

6. See Feigl, p. 383.

Furthermore, if the scientific evidence derived by establishing psychophysical correlations supports the second, as some believe, then it also supports the first. We shall, however, continue to use the first formulation because most objections apply more easily and clearly to it.

One consequence of the failure of "the" identity theory to imply a correspondence of kinds is that neither the identity theory, nor any other mind–body theory for that matter, would be refuted if no one-to-one correspondence of kinds is achievable, and no inference from the physical to particular mental phenomena is forthcoming. It is also true that the identity theory is not established if each kind of sensation is found to be in one-to-one simultaneity correspondence with just one kind of brain phenomenon, because all the competing dualistic mind–body theories are also compatible with such a correspondence. This is clearly true of parallelism and epiphenomenalism and, in spite of Feigl's claim to the contrary, also true of interactionism.[7] If there is mental-physical causation and if, as it seems, it is possible that it does not involve temporal succession, then, just as physical causes and mental effects can be simultaneous for epiphenomenalism, so also could mental causes and their physical effects be simultaneous for interactionism. In this way, the temporal succession of physical events would be unbroken. However, although all the competing mind–body theories are compatible with a correspondence of kinds, such a correspondence has played a special role for materialism. As we shall see in Chapter 4, establishing such a correspondence is an essential part of an important attempt to justify the elimination of sensations.

The preceding discussion might seem to lead to the conclusion that, contrary to Feigl and others, nothing empirical is relevant to a decision among these various views. The decision would seem to be, then, purely metaphysical, something no empirically minded philosopher could allow. For those with empiricist scruples, however, the identity of individuals theory is at least in principle empirically falsifiable, because it does imply the one-to-one simultaneity correspondence of individuals which

7. Ibid., p. 381. I have discussed points supporting the position opposed to Feigl's in J. Cornman and K. Lehrer, *Philosophical Problems and Arguments* (New York: Macmillan, 1968), pp. 219–23 and 237–39.

can be empirically falsified. It is at least possible that, for example, some pains can be shown to begin slightly after their
only plausible physical correlates and end slightly after. This
would refute the identity theory. Interestingly, it would not
refute its rivals, because they are all compatible with time lapses
between events in one-to-one correspondence. This might bring
the empiricist to opt for the identity theory because it would
enable him to be consistent in maintaining a mind–body thesis
while eschewing pure metaphysics. Nevertheless, there are arguments for and against the other positions which rely on scientifically testable premises, some of which we shall examine as we
proceed.[8]

THE IDENTITY THEORY AND REDUCTIVE MATERIALISM

We have seen that one essential part of the thesis of reductive
materialism is the identity theory, and we have examined something of what that theory does and does not entail. But clearly
there is more to reductive materialism than the identity theory,
because the theory is consistent with other monistic positions
that are not consistent with materialism. Thus someone might
claim that each sensation is identical with some brain event,
but none are really sensations or brain events, because they are
some tertium quid, some neutral entity. Or it might be claimed
that each such thing is really a sensation and, because everything
else is also mental, an idealistic theory is correct.

The second thesis of reductive materialism is that sensations
are really physical, but making sense of 'really physical' is not
easy. One way that may help is to couple the identity thesis
with what can be called the double language theory. Indeed,
most identity theorists hold both views, including Feigl and another principal defender, J. J. C. Smart. Feigl summarizes his
position as follows:

> Certain neurophysiological terms denote (refer to) the
> very same events that are also denoted (referred to) by
> certain phenomenal terms. The identification of the objects

8. This is especially true of the claim that sensation–brain-process
identity statements are reductive identity statements much like temperature–mean-kinetic-energy identity statements (see Chap. 3), and the
claim that sensation terms are not needed for scientific explanations of
human behavior (see Chap. 4).

of this twofold reference is of course logically contingent, although it constitutes a very fundamental feature of our world as we have come to conceive it in the modern scientific outlook. . . . We may say that neurophysiological terms and the corresponding phenomenal terms, though widely differing in [meaning], and hence in the modes of confirmation of statements containing them, do have identical *referents.* I take these referents to be the immediately experienced qualities, or their configurations in various phenomenal fields.[9]

Smart maintains a thesis much the same as Feigl's but he states it specifically in terms of sensations and brain processes. He says that

in so far as "after-image" or "ache" is a report of a process, it is a report of a process that *happens to be* a brain process. It follows that the thesis does not claim that sensation statements can be *translated* into statements about brain processes. Nor does it claim that the logic of a sensation statement is the same as that of a brain-process statement. All it claims is that in so far as a sensation statement is a report of something, that something is in fact a brain process. Sensations are nothing over and above brain processes.[10]

We should carefully note four important features of the theses of these two men. First, both Feigl and Smart discuss certain expressions of language and what these expressions refer to or are used to talk about. Thus, both men are taking a linguistic approach to the mind–body problem. But this should not be taken to mean that they are concerned only with language, because what these expressions refer to are not other linguistic expressions, but some kinds of nonlinguistic phenomena. Thus, both men are interested in getting from certain facts about language to certain conclusions about nonlinguistic reality.

9. Feigl, "Mind–Body, Not a Pseudoproblem," in S. Hook, ed., *Dimensions of Mind* (New York: Collier Books, 1961), p. 38.

10. J. J. C. Smart, "Sensations and Brain Processes," *Philosophical Review* 68 (1959): 144–45; reprinted in V. C. Chappell, ed., *The Philosophy of Mind* (Englewood Cliffs, N.J.: Prentice-Hall, 1962), pp. 160–72.

Second, both men stress that the psychological expressions and the physiological expressions they are considering differ widely in meaning, so that the psychological sentences are not analyzable or translatable into physiological sentences. They claim only that these two different kinds of terms have the same *referents*, not that they have the same *meanings*. They claim, for example, that the referents of the expression 'brain process' include the referents of the expression 'sensation,' but the two are clearly different in meaning. Consequently, although they are like analytical behaviorists in being linguistic philosophers, they are not analytical behaviorists (see chap. 4), because they deny that psychological sentences are synonymous with behavioral sentences.

Third, although both Feigl and Smart are double language theorists, there is one important point on which they disagree. As the preceding quotations show, they have very different views about the common referents of psychological terms and certain physiological terms. Feigl claims that the common referents are immediately felt qualities, that is, feelings in their uninterpreted or raw state. Smart, on the other hand, claims that sensation terms refer to brain processes, but these surely are not uninterpreted feelings. This is a most important difference for our purposes, because Smart's thesis, if generalized to include all psychological terms, becomes a version of materialism, but Feigl's thesis is inconsistent with materialism. Because we are here interested in materialism, we shall consider Smart's theory. It is an example of a materialistic double language theory, because it consists of two claims: that sensation terms and certain physiological terms have common referents, and that these common referents are in every case something physical, in particular, brain processes. It is this second claim which has been used to construct one plausible version of the statement that sensations are really physical. Just how to go about establishing such a claim will be one of the main problems considered in this book.[11]

Fourth, both Smart and Feigl hold not only the double language theory but also the identity theory. Smart claims not only

11. I have discussed the more general problem of establishing ontological reference claims in *Metaphysics, Reference, and Language* (New Haven: Yale University Press, 1966), esp. part II.

that sensation terms and certain physicalistic terms have common referents, but also that sensations are identical with—are the same things as—certain brain processes. It might seem that there is no need to state the double language theory and the identity theory as separate theses because each entails the other. But neither entails the other. The identity theory does not entail the double language theory, because the former is compatible with there being no language but the latter, as previously stated, is not. And, as we shall see in more detail later, the other entailment fails because the double language theory is compatible with there being no sensations, but the identity theory is not (chap. 5). The consequence of this for our purposes is that we should distinguish carefully between the two theories and the various reasons relevant to each theory. This is important, not only because it has not often been done, but because doing it may show us that one theory is justified when freed from the other. Our immediate task, however, is to examine reductive materialism and the identity theory.

OBJECTIONS TO REDUCTIVE MATERIALISM AND THE IDENTITY THEORY

Many objections have been raised to reductive materialism and to the identity theory, but I do not think it necessary to catalogue them all.[12] Most are easily refuted. There are, however, three we shall consider in some detail because they are more forceful than the rest and not so easily refutable. We can call them: the objection from persons as ontologically basic; the privacy objection; and the property objection. The first is an objection to materialism in general, but the last two apply only to reductive materialism because they are raised against the identity theory.

OBJECTION: PERSONS ARE ONTOLOGICALLY BASIC

P. F. Strawson has discussed the concept of a person, that is, "the concept of a type of entity such that both predicates ascrib-

---

12. For some objections I shall not discuss, see R. Brandt, "Doubts about the Identity Theory," in *Dimensions of Mind*, pp. 62–70; J. Kim, "On the Psycho-Physical Identity Theory," *American Philosophical Quarterly* 3 (1966): 227–35; N. Malcolm, "Scientific Materialism and the Identity Theory," *Dialogue* 3 (1964–65): 115–25.

ing states of consciousness *and* predicates ascribing corporeal characteristics, a physical situation etc. are applicable to a single individual of that single type." [13] It is Strawson's contention that persons are an ontologically basic kind of entity. That is, persons are a kind of entity, *B,* for which there is no other kind, *K,* at the same level of generality as *B,* such that the entities referred to when persons are referred to are also entities referred to when *K*'s are referred to.[14] For the materialist, idealist, and Cartesian, persons are ontologically derivative because, for each of them, in referring to persons we are always also referring to some entities of another kind, that is, bodies, minds, or embodied minds. But, according to Strawson, persons are not in any way reducible to more basic kinds of entities. What a person is identical with is, in the last analysis, neither a body, nor a mind, nor an embodied mind. Thus, if Strawson is right, materialists, idealists, and Cartesians are wrong in their claims about the kinds of entities that are ontologically basic.

Strawson's argument

Strawson's argument to establish his thesis can be construed as having two parts. First, he attempts to show that it is correct to ascribe states of consciousness to something in such a way that the relationship between the entity and states of consciousness is not a contingent one of causal dependence, but is rather some kind of "nontransferable ownership." That is, the entity that has or owns a certain state of consciousness, has it in some kind of noncontingent way. Here Strawson tries to destroy what he calls "the no-ownership theory," i.e. the theory that the only kind of ownership of states of consciousness or experiences is the contingent ownership expressed by the causal dependence of such states upon certain bodies. Second, having established some kind of necessary owners of experiences, he tries to prove that these owners are persons by eliminating the only other possibilities: bodies, and Cartesian egos or pure subjects of experience. Having established both these points, Strawson can then conclude that it is wrong to claim that either bodies or minds are ontologically more basic than persons because such claims

13. Strawson, pp. 101–02.
14. This is not exactly how Strawson would construe 'ontologically basic.' For his discussion of ontological priority, see Strawson, pp. 15–17.

imply that the ownership of experiences is, contrary to what Strawson has shown, transferable from persons to either bodies or minds.

I think that Strawson has established neither part of his argument, indeed that none of his arguments against bodies and Cartesian egos as the owners of experiences succeeds. I shall here, however, consider only his argument to establish that there are noncontingent owners of experiences, and since bodies have only a contingent relationship to experiences, there must be something that is not a mere body, and materialism is false.[15] Let us state this argument as follows:

(1) Any body's ownership of experiences is contingent; for example, the relationship between bodies and certain experiences is causal.

(2) There are noncontingent owners of experiences.

(3) If bodies are merely contingent owners of experiences and there are noncontingent owners, then materialism is false.

Therefore

(4) Materialism is false.

Although it is not clear what a noncontingent or necessary owner of experiences is, I think we can safely concede to Strawson that no body, no physical object, is a necessary owner of experiences.[16] The second premise, however, is more debatable, and we must carefully examine Strawson's attempt to establish it.

Strawson's attempt to disprove the no-ownership theory and thereby prove there is a necessary owner of experiences goes as follows.[17] The no-ownership theorist, like anyone else, must use noncontingent ownership words in some of his sentences if he wishes to assert true sentences. Such words can be neither omitted nor eliminated by rephrasing the sentences; they are

15. See my "Strawson's 'Person'," *Theoria* 30 (1964): 145–56, for a discussion of Strawson's argument against Cartesian egos.

16. This claim is true only if analytical behaviorism is false, because if each psychological sentence is analyzable into a behavioral sentence, then there is a clear sense in which experiences are necessarily related to bodies. But there is reason to reject analytical behaviorism, discussed in Chapter 4.

17. See Strawson, pp. 94f.

essential to the sentence. For example, it is often true to say
something of the following form: "All experiences of person *P*
are contingently dependent upon a certain body *B*." In this sentence some expression that functions like 'of person *P*' is necessary, because if we eliminate it altogether, the sentence is false.
Furthermore, the no-ownership theorist cannot claim that 'experiences of person *P*' can be replaced in the sentence by 'experiences contingently dependent upon body *B*' on the grounds
that the two expressions have the same meaning. They differ in
meaning because with the former the sentence is synthetic, but
with the latter it is analytic. Thus, infers Strawson, *P*'s ownership of experiences is necessary and cannot be reduced to
contingent ownership by bodies. Therefore, there must be a
noncontingent kind of ownership, and materialism is false.

Objection to Strawson's argument: Does Strawson's refutation
of the no-ownership theory succeed? I shall use a logical analogy
to show that it does not. Strawson's premises have the following
form:

> (1) In sentences of the form 'All *Q*'s of *P* are contingently
> dependent upon *R*,' the phrase 'of *P*' cannot be
> eliminated (is necessary) if the sentence is to be true.
> (2) '*Q*'s of *P*' does not mean and cannot be replaced in the
> sentence by '*Q*'s contingently dependent upon *R*' if
> the sentence is to remain contingent.

The form of the conclusion Strawson draws from these premises
is:

> (3) *P*'s ownership of *Q*'s is a different kind from *R*'s con-
> tingent ownership.

But let us take a sentence of this form: 'All orbits of the Morning Star are contingently dependent upon Venus.' We can now
make the following statements:

> (1) In the sentence 'All orbits of the Morning Star are
> contingently dependent on Venus,' the phrase 'of the
> Morning Star' cannot be eliminated (is necessary) if
> the sentence is to be true.
> (2) 'Orbits of the Morning Star' does not mean and can-
> not be replaced in the sentence by 'orbits contingently

dependent on Venus' if the sentence is to remain contingent.

If Strawson's form of argument is valid, then by logical analogy we can conclude:

> (3) The Morning Star's ownership of its orbit is a different kind from the contingent ownership of that orbit by Venus.

But this conclusion is surely false. The Morning Star's ownership of its orbit is the same kind as Venus' ownership. Both are contingent. What Strawson seems to have overlooked is the possibility that two logically independent expressions can be used to refer to the same thing. Thus Strawson's premises are consistent with the theory he thinks he refutes, that is, the theory that *P*'s ownership of experiences is no different from a body's ownership because 'person *P*' and 'body *B*' both refer to the same thing, a particular body.

Two revisions of Strawson's argument

It might be replied that Strawson's argument can be strengthened by claiming that there is a sense in which 'of person *P*' is necessary and 'of the Morning Star' is not. Thus the preceding analogy and objection to Strawson's argument would fail. It might be claimed not only that 'of person *P*' can neither mean nor be replaced by 'contingently dependent on body *B*' if the sentence is to remain contingent, but also that it cannot be replaced by *any* physicalistic expression if the sentence is to remain both contingent *and* true. Thus person-expressions are necessary in the sense that they are needed to make sentences of the form 'All experiences of *x* are contingently dependent on body *B*' both true and contingent. But, so goes this reply, neither 'the Morning Star' nor any synonymous term is needed to make 'All orbits of *x* are contingently dependent upon Venus' both true and contingent because, for example, 'the entity located at *x, y, z, t*' could be used instead.

The objection to this reply is that 'person *P*' is not necessary in this sense either, because it could be replaced with, for example, 'the entity with fingerprints *F*' and what would result would be contingent and, we can suppose, true if and only if the original statement is true. This reply fails, consequently, and with it this attempt to resuscitate Strawson's argument.

Let us examine one more attempt to prove that there are necessary owners of experiences and that bodies are only contingent owners. There is an interpretation of necessary ownership which makes plausible the claim that persons necessarily own experiences, but bodies do not. Let us say that P's are necessary owners of experiences just in case the sentence 'All P's have experiences' is necessary, and P's are at best contingent owners just in case the sentence is contingent. Using these definitions, it is plausible to say that persons but not bodies are necessary owners of experiences because 'All persons have experiences' is necessary, but 'All bodies have experiences' is contingent. Thus given these interpretations and premise (3) of the previous argument, we can conclude that materialism is false.

The problem now, however, is premise (3). The crux of premise (3) is, in effect, that no persons are identical with bodies if persons necessarily own experiences and bodies do not. But, again by logical analogy, we can see that this is false. The sentence, 'All featherless bipeds have feet' is necessary; the sentence 'All humans have feet' is contingent, but it is false that no featherless bipeds are identical with humans. Thus although on this interpretation of necessary ownership we can show persons have it and bodies do not, we cannot also show that materialism is false, because persons might well be merely bodies nonetheless.

We have found no reason to think that persons are ontologically basic and thus no reason to think they are not identical with bodies. Materialism, therefore, can avoid the first objection. Let us, then, turn to the second, the privacy objection.

THE PRIVACY OBJECTION

Six senses of 'private'

In its simplest, but essential, form, the argument expressing the privacy objection has three premises: all sensations are private; all brain (physical) phenomena are public; and nothing is both private and public. It follows from these premises that no sensations are brain phenomena (or any other physical phenomena). Clearly, to evaluate this argument we must understand how to interpret 'private' and 'public.' In general, because 'public' is taken to be a contrary or the contradictory of 'private,' let us agree and concentrate on 'private.' Unfortunately there are several philosophically relevant senses of 'private' which we must examine.[18] We can list the most relevant as follows:

(a) x's are private $=_{df.}$ At most one person has each x.

(b) x's are private $=_{df.}$ Each x is necessarily owned by one person.

(c) x's are private $=_{df.}$ One and only one person can experience each x.

(d) x's are private $=_{df.}$ All x's are experienced but none are perceivable through the senses.

(e) x's are private $=_{df.}$ At most one person knows whether or not there is a certain x.

(f) x's are private $=_{df.}$ The person having an x is the final epistemological authority about whether the x exists (or whether it is the same as he thinks it is).

I think that (f) is the only sense of 'private' that will make the argument even initially plausible, because for each of the others one of the three premises of the privacy argument can quickly be shown to be dubious. The privacy argument fails if we use sense (a), because there seems to be no less reason to say that at most one person has a brain process than to say that at most one person has a pain. It might be replied that two people *can* have the same brain and, thus, the same brain events, but they cannot have the same pain. But if, as is possible, one

18. For discussions of privacy and other senses of 'private,' see A. J. Ayer, *The Concept of a Person* (New York: St. Martin's Press, 1963), pp. 52–81, esp. pp. 79–80; K. Baier, "Smart on Sensations," *Australasian Journal of Philosophy* 40 (1962): 57–68; R. C. Coburn, "Shaffer on the Identity of Mental States and Brain Processes," *Journal of Philosophy* 60 (1963): 89–92; H. H. Price, "Some Objections to Behaviorism," in *Dimensions of Mind*; R. Routley and V. Macrae, "On the Identity of Sensations and Physiological Occurrences," *American Philosophical Quarterly* 3 (1966): 88–103; and R. Rorty, "Mind–Body Identity, Privacy, and Categories," *Review of Metaphysics* 19 (1965–66), secs. 5 and 6. One sense not listed here concerns privileged access. That is, x's are private just in case the person having an x has a unique way of knowing whether the x exists (or whether it is the same as he thinks it is). However, the same objection that applies to the final epistemological authority interpretation also applies to this one.

and only one pain is correlated with each C-fiber stimulation of one brain, and two people have the same brain, then they can have the same pain. We have already discussed sense (b) when examining Strawson's objection. It is no more forceful if used in the privacy objection. The only sense in which we found it plausible to claim that experiences are necessarily owned by persons is the third sense: they are necessarily owned by persons just in case 'All persons have experiences' is necessary. Brain processes, of course, are not necessarily owned by persons in this sense because 'All persons have brain processes' is contingent. But one thing can be both public and private in this sense, and the third premise is false. For example, 'All persons have experiences occurring when brain processes occur' is contingent, but some experiences (private) are identical with experiences occurring when brain processes occur (public).

If we turn to sense (c), we can see that it begs the question against the identity theory because if each pain is identical with a brain phenomenon that can be experienced, then pains can be experienced by more than one person, and thus it is dubious that all are private in sense (c). The same objection applies to sense (d) because if pains are identical with perceivable phenomena, then they are perceivable through the senses although perhaps not perceivable as pains. Sense (e) of 'private,' the sense relevant to the private language argument (see that section of chap. 2), raises the problem of other minds. Skeptics about our knowledge of other minds claim that no one other than the person who has a pain can know he has it. But although refuting such skeptics is no easy task, there is no reason to accept their skeptical conclusion. Thus there is no reason to think that sensations are private in sense (e).

The privacy argument and final epistemological authority

We are left with sense (f), the sense of 'private' often used in the privacy argument against the identity theory.[19] We can state the argument using this sense of 'private' as follows:

(1) Any sensation is an entity such that the person who has it is the final epistemological authority about whether it exists.

19. See Baier

(2) No brain phenomenon is an entity such that the person who has it is the final epistemological authority about whether it exists.

Therefore

(3) No sensations are brain phenomena.

In this argument premise (2) seems true, and it is hard to find reason to deny that (1) is true, because the person whose pains are in question would seem to know whether he has a pain in a way that cannot be overturned by the evidence of others. The argument then seems sound, but before we conclude that it is, we should examine the concept of final authority.

It is tempting to claim that someone has final authority about something just in case he cannot be mistaken about it, that is, his knowledge of it is incorrigible. These two concepts are different, however, because someone can have final authority about something, but his claim about it be proven wrong. Consider an umpire in a baseball game as a clear case of someone with one kind of final authority. If he states that a batter in the game is out and he does not change his mind within an appropriate amount of time, it follows that the batter is out no matter what evidence to the contrary someone else has. But if, within an appropriate amount of time, he changes his mind, then the batter is not out and his previous statement is overturned. Thus although no one else can overturn an umpire's call, he can himself, and thus he can prove his previous decision wrong. The concept of final authority applied to one's relationship to his own sensations is much like this one applied to an umpire in a baseball game. We might, then, try the following definition:

> *P* has final epistemological authority about whether there are *x*'s = $_{df.}$ If *P* states that there is (is not) an *x* and *P* does not state there is not (is) an *x* within an appropriate length of time, it follows that there is (is not) an *x*.

Although the umpire analogy and much current discussion would lead us to discuss 'final epistemological authority' in terms of statements, it is, I think, easier and less debatable to talk in terms of beliefs instead. For aside from the problems raised by cases of verbal ignorance and slips, there is no reason to think that for sensations, unlike batters, the person must state his change of mind if the original claim is to be overturned. That is, this definition is unsatisfactory because it requires that if *P* fails to make a statement expressing his change of mind within the appropriate time, then his original statement is true regardless of his later beliefs. Let us, then, talk of beliefs rather than statements in the definition. There is still another problem to be avoided: there can be cases of those who do not know what certain sensations are, or who have, temporarily perhaps, forgotten what they are or have mistaken them for others. Thus their beliefs could be mistaken as a result. A satisfactory definition must avoid this problem. I think the following definition succeeds in this:

> *P* has final epistemological authority about whether there are (are not) *x*'s = $_{df.}$ If at any time *t*, *P* believes that there is (is not) an *x* at *t*, *P* does not change this belief within an appropriate interval of time after *t*, and *P* understands what *x*'s are at *t* and during the interval after *t*, it follows that there is (is not) an *x* at *t*.

Objection to the "final authority" argument: We can use the preceding definition to help show where the "final authority" version of the privacy argument fails. Its plausibility rests, I believe, on a confusion between two different interpretations of the premises, on one of which both premises are plausible but the argument is invalid, and on the other, the argument is valid but there is no reason to accept both premises. On the first interpretation the two premises become

> (1a) Any sensation is such that if at a time *t* a person *P* believes that he has (does not have) a sensation at *t*, *P* does not change this belief "soon" after *t*, and *P* understands what sensations are at *t* and during this interval after *t*, it follows that *P* has (does not have) a sensation at *t*.
>
> (2a) No brain phenomenon is such that if at a time *t* a person *P* believes that he has (does not have) a brain phenomenon at *t*, *P* does not change this belief "soon" after *t*, and *P* understands what brain phenomena are at *t* and during this interval after *t*, it

follows that *P* has (does not have) a brain phenomenon at *t*.

The privacy objection is often attacked by attacking premise
(1a) on the grounds that once highly confirmed lawlike relationships are scientifically established between each kind of
sensation and certain kinds of brain phenomena, the person
having a sensation will no longer be the final authority about
it.[20] Thus it is said that the claims of the isolated individual who
reports that he has a pain when the established physical correlate of pain, let us say a firing of C-fibers, is lacking, or who
reports no pain when there is a firing of C-fibers, will be overruled by the superior weight of the scientific evidence. Aside
from the immediate reply that no scientific evidence is sufficient to overrule a man's claim that he has a pain or that he
does not have a pain, the reply has also been made that in the
face of a conflict between the scientific evidence and the person's report, the most reasonable hypothesis is that at the time
of the report, at least, the person was ignorant of what sensations are. Thus neither his final authority nor highly confirmed
scientific laws would have to be overruled.[21]

Fortunately for our purposes we do not have to adjudicate
this debate, because the version of the argument using (1a) is
clearly invalid. The middle term in the first premise mentions
sensations while in the second premise it mentions brain phenomena. This fallacy can be avoided by mentioning neither
sensations nor brain phenomena in the middle term, but using
a variable instead. What results are two premises from which
we can validly deduce the conclusion. Thus:

(1b) Any sensation, *E*, is such that if at a time *t* a person
believes that he has (does not have) *E* at *t*, *P* does
not change this belief "soon" after *t*, and *P* understands what *E* is at *t* and during this interval after
t, it follows that *P* has (does not have) *E* at *t*.

(2b) No brain phenomenon, *E*, is such that if at a time
t a person *P* believes that he has (does not have) *E*

20. See Smart, "Brain Processes and Incorrigibility," *Australasian
Journal of Philosophy* 40 (1962): 68–70; Rorty; and Routley and Macrae, p. 100.
21. See Rorty.

at t, P does not change this belief "soon" after t, and P understands what E is at t and during this interval after t, it follows that P has (does not have) E at t.

We can see the problem for this version of the privacy argument by taking as a substituend for 'E' in (1b) the description 'the 10,000*th* red sensation that occurred between t_1 and t_2 in Paris.' What results can be written as

the 10,000*th* red sensation that occurred between t_1 and t_2 in Paris is an entity such that if at time t a person P believes that he has (does not have) at t the 10,000*th* red sensation that occurred between t_1 and t_2 in Paris, P does not change this belief "soon" after t, and P understands what such a sensation is at t and during this interval following t, it follows that he has (does not have) at t the 10,000*th* red sensation that occurred between t_1 and t_2 in Paris.

This substitution instance of (1b) is clearly false because no one person has final authority either about whether one of his own sensations is the 10,000*th* red sensation had by various people somewhere, or about when such a sensation occurs. Thus (1b) is false, and the second version of the argument fails. Its problem basically is that the phrase 'final epistemological authority' is intensional and thus which description is substituted affects the truth value of the sentences using it. We can conclude, then, that the privacy objection fails, because we have examined both versions of the most plausible interpretation and found they both fail.

Incidentally, it might be noted that although (1b) has been shown false, (1a) has not been affected. The belief mentioned in (1a) is specified merely as a person's belief that he has (does not have) a *sensation*. It is not a belief that he has E. Premise (1b), unlike (1a), by having 'E' occur within a belief context, opens the way to objections via exotic descriptions of sensations. Furthermore, if (1a) and the identity theory are true, then (2b) is also false for we could then substitute 'the pain P reports having at t' for 'E' in (2b) and prove that substitution instance false.

THE PROPERTY OBJECTION TO THE IDENTITY THEORY

Neither the argument from the ontological priority of persons nor the privacy objection succeeds in refuting reductive materialism. This leaves only one more objection to consider, the property objection, the most serious of all. It is usually aimed at the identity theory, and arises from the fact that mental phenomena seem to have properties inappropriate to physical phenomena, and physical phenomena have properties inappropriate to mental phenomena. The particular way the problem arises for an identity theorist, however, depends not merely on his holding that theory, but also on whether in addition he is a materialist, idealist, or neutral theorist. As we have seen, Smart is a materialist, and he has considered the objection as it applies to that position. As Smart puts it, the objection grants that "it may be possible to get out of asserting the existence of irreducibly psychic processes, but not out of asserting the existence of irreducibly psychic *properties*." [22] Thus, the objection goes, although sensations may be identical with brain processes and thus there would be no irreducibly psychic process, nevertheless these brain processes would have two quite different sorts of properties, physical and psychic. Thus even assuming, for example, that the sentence 'I see a yellowish-orange afterimage' is a report about some brain process, that brain process would have the property of "being a yellowish-orange afterimage." If this is a property, it is certainly a psychic property, that is, a property that lies outside a materialistic framework. Thus, if there are entities with such properties, materialism is refuted.

Smart's reply

Smart thinks that he has a way of eliminating psychic properties. What he proposes is that, although a sentence such as 'I see a yellowish-orange afterimage' is a report about some brain process, it does not, as some others think, attribute some psychic property to the brain process. To show that it does not, Smart provides what I take to be a rough translation of the sentence. Thus the adequacy of Smart's claim rests upon the adequacy of translations such as the one he provides. He claims that when "a person says, 'I see a yellowish-orange after-image,' he is say-

22. Smart, "Sensations and Brain Processes," p. 148.

ing something like this: '*There is something going on which is like what is going on when* I have my eyes open, am awake, and there is an orange illuminated in good light in front of me, that is, when I really see an orange.' " [23]

Will this translation solve the problem? To see that it does not, let us examine Smart's translation of 'I see a yellowish-orange afterimage.' Whereas the original sentence, call it P_1, seems to specify in some respect what is going on, the translation, call it M, does not. The consequence of this is that, although P_1 is a sufficient condition of M, it is not a necessary condition, because there is a sentence that implies M, but does not imply P_1. Such a sentence is P_2: 'I see a roughly spherical shape.' Thus M and P_1 differ in meaning. To avoid this problem we might try to translate P_1 into M_1, which would refer not merely to an orange but to some n number of things that have only one thing in common, their yellowish-orange color. Thus, since not all of the n things would be spherical or any other one specific shape, P_2 would be eliminated. However, we would have a related problem because there is a sentence such as 'I see a colored afterimage' which implies M_1 but does not imply P_1. Thus M_1 and P_1 also differ in meaning. I believe that any other emendations of M would fail in a similar manner because the crucial part of M—'there is something going on'—is just too general. Psychic properties cannot be eliminated by this kind of translation, nor, I believe, by any other.[24] Consequently their elimination or the reduction of their instances requires a different approach.

The property objection and identity

As stated thus far, the property objection to materialism is that there seem to be nonphysical properties of sensations, and thus, even if sensations are identical with brain phenomena, materialism would be false because there would be entities with nonmaterial properties. But this is not an objection to the identity theory. Someone who holds that theory and in addition is a neutral theorist, could avoid this objection by admitting that the

23. Ibid., p. 149.
24. I have discussed this and other objections to Smart's position in *Metaphysics, Reference, and Language,* pp. 41–49.

entities in question are neither physical nor mental because they have both psychological and physical properties.

The objection, however, can be brought to bear on the identity theory. As so directed, it uses the principle of the identity of indiscernibles or at least that part of it we can call "the principle of the nonidentity of discernibles." The full principle can be stated as follows:

$$(x)(y)[(x = y) \equiv (F)(Fx = Fy)].$$

The part that concerns us is:

A. $(x)(y)\{(\exists F)[Fx \cdot \sim Fy) \lor (\sim Fx \cdot Fy)] \supset x \neq y\}$,

that is, if there is some property of x but not of y, or conversely, then x and y are not identical.

As has been pointed out, however, principle A is too strong a requirement for contingent identity, which is the kind which interests us, because some properties are not shared by entities clearly contingently identical.[25] In particular, those that are *intensional* or nonextensional properties, and those that are *intentional* properties are often not shared. A property, P, is intensional just in case some instantiation of 'Px' using a singular term for 'x' is intensional, and it is intentional just in case some such instantiation of 'Px' is intentional. As I have pointed out elsewhere, not all intensional sentences are intentional and not all intentional sentences are intensional.[26] For this reason, let us keep these two kinds of properties distinct. For example, the sentence 'Lee has the property of being such that if he had won the battle of Gettysburg, then he would have won the Civil War' is intensional but not intentional. And because any sentence with a singular term substituted for 'Lee' is also intensional but not intentional, we can conclude that the above complex property is intensional but not intentional. On the other hand, the sentence 'Alaska has the property of being thought of by John' is intentional but not intensional. It might be thought that the intentional property expressed in this sentence is not intensional. This is mistaken, because there are terms such as

25. See Routley and Macrae, pp. 90–98.

26. See Cornman, "Intentionality and Intensionality," *Philosophical Quarterly* 12 (1962): 44–52. Much of the same discussion reappears in *Metaphysics, Reference, and Language,* pp. 25–32.

'Pegasus' which when substituted for 'Alaska' result in an intensional sentence. Thus the property is both intentional and intensional. I think that all intentional properties are intensional, but because the converse is false, let us coin the term *'extensional'* to mean 'neither intensional nor intentional.' We can now modify the principle of the nonidentity of discernibles as follows:

$$B.\ (x)(y)\{(\exists F)\{\mathcal{E}F\cdot[(Fx\cdot\sim Fy)\ \mathbf{v}\ (\sim Fx\cdot Fy)]\} \supset x \neq y\}$$

Here $\mathcal{E}F = F$ is extentional.

Using this modified principle, we need find either one extentional property of a sensation that is not a property of the physical phenomenon supposedly identical with the sensation, or the converse. This, incidentally, shows another way to rule out the two objections already considered. Both 'necessarily owned by P' and 'private' in the sense of final epistemological authority, and in several other senses, are nonextentional properties. But sensations such as afterimages do have extentional properties such as being homogeneously yellow, dim, fading, and circular that none of the one-to-one simultaneity correlates of afterimages seem to have. Furthermore, the chief candidates for such physical correlates, brain processes, have properties that afterimages seem not to have, such as being irreversible, following nerve paths, moving through a brain, and being located in physical space. Thus, according to the property objection, there are some extentional properties not jointly shared or lacked by sensations and their physical correlates, and so sensations are not identical with their physical correlates. From this we can conclude that the identity theory and, therefore, reductive materialism, is false.

Sensations and the problem of a spatial location

One species of the property objection most often discussed centers on the property of having a spatial location. In short, sensations such as afterimages have no location in physical space, while brain processes do; therefore sensations and brain processes are not identical. Some philosophers have argued not only that this species of the argument can be rebutted, but also that it can be surmounted in such a way that, at most, empirical, scientific problems stand in the way of a justification of the identity theory. J. Shaffer, who has argued this way, admits that the present fact that

> it makes no sense to speak of [mental states] occurring in a volume occupied by a brain means that the Identity theory cannot be correct. For it is a necessary condition for saying that something is identical with some particular physical object, state, or process that the thing be located in the place where the particular physical object, state, or process is. If it is not there, it cannot be identical with what is there.[27]

But Shaffer argues that although there is no language rule requiring mental states to be spatially located, neither is there any rule requiring them not to be spatially located. Consequently we are free to adopt a new rule of language, one which prescribes that a mental state is "located in that place where its corresponding [brain] process is located." [28] If this one new rule were adopted, Shaffer believes that the identity of mental states and brain processes could then be empirically established, because the criterion of identity, he claims, is that brain processes and mental states be identical if and only if they exist at the same time and at the same place, and each is an empirically necessary condition for the presence of the other. Given the new rule, and since the other two conditions of identity can be empirically tested, the identity theory can be either verified or falsified empirically. Thus the only problems facing the identity theory are empirical.

There are, I think, several objections to this way out of the spatial location problem and into a justification of the identity theory. N. Malcolm has raised several, none of which, however, are damaging. In stating one of his objections, Malcolm argues as follows:

> Suppose we had determined, by means of some instrument, that a certain process occurred inside my skull at the exact moment I had the sudden thought about the milk bottles. How do we make the further test of whether my

---

27. J. Shaffer, "Could Mental Events Be Brain Processes?" *Journal of Philosophy* 58 (1961): 815–16.
28. Ibid., p. 816.

thought occurred inside my skull? For it would have to be a *further* test: it would have to be logically independent of the test for the presence of the brain process, because Smart's thesis is that the identity is *contingent*. But no one has any notion of what it would mean to test for the occurrence of the thought inside my skull *independently* of testing for a brain process.[29]

Malcolm seems to think that if the relationship between thoughts and brain processes is contingent, as Smart, Shaffer, and most others think, then the test for the spatial location of mental phenomena must be logically independent of the tests for the location of the corresponding brain phenomena. There are two mistakes here. First, the most that might follow from the claim that the identity of thoughts and brain processes is contingent is that the total test for the occurrence of a mental phenomenon (not merely the test for its spatial location) is logically independent of the test for the occurrence of the corresponding brain phenomenon. But, clearly, part of the total test includes finding out that a mental phenomenon occurred at some time, and the test for this is logically independent of a test to discover that a brain phenomenon occurred at some time. But, second, not even this much follows, for it is surely logically possible that perceiving certain behavior of another is, for example, the total test or criterion for his being in pain, that perceiving this same behavior is also at least part of the test for his behaving that way, and that the relationship between this behavior and his being in pain is contingent. And this is true even if perceiving his behavior were to entail both his behaving that way and his being in pain.

Malcolm's second objection is quite different. He argues that talking about future conventions as Shaffer does is irrelevant to the spatial location problem because "our philosophical problem *is* about how things are. It is a question about our *present* concepts of thinking and thought, not about some conjectured future concepts."[30] But clearly the problem is not about concepts, either present or future; it is about mental and physical phenomena. It is true that concepts are in some way relevant, but their relevance is not so simplistically described in terms of

29. Malcolm, pp. 119–20.
30. Ibid., p. 119.

the concepts being the subject matter of the problem. We might get at their relevance and to a more plausible objection to Shaffer's handling of the spatial location objection if we conjoin Shaffer's claim that at present "it makes no sense to speak of" mental states having spatial locations, with his claim that spatially locating mental states violates no present rule of language. Although I am not sure what Shaffer means by 'makes no sense to speak of x,' I should think it means either that sentences such as 'John's yellow afterimage is three inches behind his eyes' are obviously (conceptually?) false, or that they are meaningless. If they are false, then it would seem illegitimate to adopt Shaffer's new rule for the location of mental states merely for the reason that it would make the sentences true. If they are meaningless, then there is some rule of language violated and, again, we are not free to adopt Shaffer's rule. Thus, according to this objection, the nature of our present concepts is relevant in this case, not because the problem is about them, but because there are attempts to solve the problem, such as Shaffer's attempt, that depend on changing rules governing the concepts in an unjustified way.

There is some weight to this objection. Shaffer's way out of the spatial location problem is something like trying to get out of a chess problem by stipulating that kings can move five spaces to avoid checkmate. In both cases, rules would be violated in unjustified ways. Nevertheless, I think that if the location problem were the *only* one confronting the identity theory, then it would be unreasonable to claim that the problem is sufficient to refute the theory. If, for example, the case of pains and stimulations of C-fibers parallels exactly, except for spatial location, an acceptable example of identity—such as one often cited, the case of the temperature of a gas and the mean kinetic energy of its molecules—then a change of rules might indeed be justified. But this kind of a change of rules, as the last step in identifying mental and physical phenomena, is quite different from what Shaffer tries to do.

Shaffer, in effect, is claiming that a sufficient condition for a sensation being identical with a brain process is a conjunction of two statements: that the two entities are in one-to-one simultaneity correspondence, from which it follows by his convention that they are in the same place; and that the two entities are empirically necessary conditions of each other. Thus not only is the spatial location problem avoided but we have an empirically testable way to establish the identity theory. The problem with this is that we can apply the principle of the nonidentity of discernibles to properties other than spatial location to conclude that afterimages and brain processes are not identical even if they are in one-to-one simultaneity correspondence and are empirically necessary conditions of each other. But we cannot maintain they both are and are not identical, so either Shaffer's new rule or his sufficient condition of identity must be rejected, unless we can find some way to show that the principle of the nonidentity of discernibles does not apply to mind–body identities. Because, as we shall see next, this last move is the crucial one, let us not further debate the spatial location objection. It is but one species of the property objection that, in spite of Shaffer's attempt to the contrary, is of no more relevance to the identity theory than other species. All extentional properties not shared or lacked in common by sensations and brain phenomena must be handled somehow, and we have found no reason to think concentrating on spatial location is uniquely fruitful.

An attempt to avoid the property objection
to the identity theory

The most promising attempt to avoid the property objection to the identity theory can be construed as claiming that the principle of the nonidentity of discernibles in the forms previously stated should not be used to evaluate mind–body identity claims. This is what is essential to H. Putnam's view that mind–body identity claims are theoretical identity claims. And, as he says,

> Accepting a theoretical identification, e.g., "Pain *is* stimulation of C-fibers," does not commit one to *interchanging* the terms "pain" and "stimulation of C-fibers" in idiomatic talk. . . . For instance, the identification of "water" with "H_2O" is by now a very well-known one, but no one says "Bring me a glass of H_2O," except as a joke.[31]

For our purposes we can take Putnam's claim to be that certain kinds of identity claims, in particular theoretical identity

31. H. Putnam, "Minds and Machines," in *Dimensions of Mind,* p. 158.

claims, can be justified, even though predicates expressing extentional properties are true of one member of the identity, but form what Putnam calls "deviant" sentences when predicated of the other.[32] Indeed, not only is this true, but Putnam also claims that 'Pain is stimulation of C-fibers' can itself be deviant, and also true.

There are two claims here, one clearly true but irrelevant to the property objection, and one very relevant but, although plausible, not clearly true. To see both claims, let us distinguish two kinds of deviant sentences. First, there is what we can call a "regularity-deviant" sentence, which, according to Putnam, "deviates from a semantic regularity (in the appropriate natural language)." [33] An example Putnam gives of this kind of deviant sentence is the counterpart for the ancient Greeks of 'I am a thousand miles away from you.' [34] According to Putnam, this sentence would have been deviant *then,* because there was *then* no context in which to use the sentence without some change of meaning. But *now* with telephones, contexts of use have developed which do not require any change of meaning. With this example guiding us, we can define 'regularity-deviant' more precisely as follows:

A grammatical sentence S is regularity-deviant at time $t =$ df. At t there is no actual context in which S would acquire a literal regular use without some change of meaning.

There is a difference between regularity-deviant sentences and what we can call "category-deviant" sentences, such as, 'The square root of two drinks conjunctions.' Such sentences are not merely regularity-deviant, because sentences merely regularity-deviant are meaningful, but category-deviant sentences are in an important way meaningless. We can define 'category-deviant' as follows:

A grammatical sentence S is category-deviant = df. S contains terms from different logical categories in such a way that S is meaningless, i.e. S is category-meaningless.

32. See Putnam, pp. 153ff.
33. Ibid., p. 161*n.*
34. See Putnam, p. 154.

It follows from this definition that if a sentence is category-deviant then there never would be a context in which it would acquire a literal regular use without some change of meaning.[35]

The principle of the nonidentity of discernibles and category deviancy: It is clear that the kind of deviance Putnam considers, regularity-deviance, will not help avoid the property objection by forcing a revision of the principle of the nonidentity of discernibles. A regularity-deviant sentence can be either true or false. Thus if '*Fa*' is true and '*Fb*' is regularity-deviant, version *B* of the principle will apply unamended if '*Fb*' is false, as it might be, and it will follow that *a* is not identical with *b*. But it is impossible that a sentence is meaningless and has a truth value. Thus if pains and stimulations of C-fibers are in different categories, then at least some of the predicates meaningfully ascribable to one would not be meaningfully ascribable to the other. Version *B* of the principle of the nonidentity of discernibles gives us no way to handle such purported cases of "cross-category" identity, because it is not applicable to cases where a predicate expressing a property is true or false of one member of the identity claim but neither true nor false of the other. We can correct this deficiency in either of two ways. Both take the "semantic ascent." The first states that if some predicate is true of one member, but not true of the other, then they are not identical. We can express this as follows:

C. $(x)(y)\{(\exists F)\{\mathcal{E}F\cdot[(F$ is true of $x\cdot F$ is not true of $y)$
$\qquad\qquad\qquad$ v $(F$ is true of $y\cdot F$ is not true of $x)]\} \supset x \neq y\}$

The second way of revising *B* states that if some predicate is true of one member but false of the other, then they are not identical. This becomes:

D. $(x)(y)\{(\exists F)\{\mathcal{E}F\cdot[(F$ is true of $x\cdot F$ is false of $y)$
$\qquad\qquad\qquad$ v $(F$ is true of $y\cdot F$ is false of $x)]\} \supset x \neq y\}$

These two statements of sufficient conditions of nonidentity are importantly different. Principle *C* entails that if a predicate is true of one member of a purported identity but is meaningless when applied to the other, then the two are not identical. But principle *D* requires a case where a predicate is true of one and

35. See Appendix for a discussion of logical categories and meaninglessness.

false of the other. Thus if we use *D*, then no predicate which results in a meaningless sentence when predicated of one member of a purported identity can be used to disprove the identity. This is surely relevant to the spatial location objection if, as Shaffer claims, it is senseless, or meaningless, to locate sensations such as afterimages spatially. And, if all other extentional properties neither shared nor lacked in common by sensations and brain processes could be treated similarly, then the property objection would be avoided. It is important for our purposes, consequently, to decide two issues. The first is whether we should accept principle *C* or principle *D*, because one gives us the beginning of the way out of the property objection but the other does not. The second is whether all predicates expressing extentional properties that are not jointly true or jointly false of sensations and brain processes are meaningless when predicated of at least one of them.

Putnam's second point about theoretical identities applies to the first issue, because if Putnam is correct, then it is irrelevant whether interchange of the terms of a theoretical identity statement in extentional sentences preserves truth value. Thus if mind–body identity statements are theoretical identity statements, then predicates meaningless with sensation terms and true with brain-process terms, or conversely, are irrelevant for a test of nonidentity, and principle *C* should be rejected. But although Putnam's claim is clearly relevant, it is not clearly true. Indeed it seems false if taken to imply that identity can be maintained even if interchange of terms leads from true to false sentences. It is generally agreed that 'A volume of water is identical with a conglomeration of NaCl molecules' is a *false* theoretical identity sentence. But not only does it seem that this sentence and many other theoretical identity sentences (especially those including observation terms such as 'water') would be true only if at least some extentional predicates are true with one of its terms just in case they are true with the other, it also seems we would test the claims by interchanging the terms in at least some linguistic contexts.[36] The water–NaCl identity claim is refuted by interchanging the terms in linguistic contexts such as '*x* is wet' and '*x* dissolves in conglomerations of H_2O mole-

---

36. The expression 'theoretical sentence' is defined on p. 79, and observation term' is defined on p. 69.

cules.' Let us, however, construe Putnam's claim differently so that it implies that there is a species of theoretical identity statements which is justified but where interchange of terms in some linguistic contexts leads from true to meaningless, rather than false, sentences. If we can find an example of such a species, then we will be justified in rejecting C and accepting D.

A reason to accept principle D: One example of a theoretical identity statement often cited in discussions of the mind–body identity theory is 'The temperature of a gas is identical with the mean kinetic energy of the gas molecules.' It is claimed not only that this is a justified theoretical identity statement, but also that it is a clear case of one phenomenon, temperature, being reduced to another. Although it is certainly worth debating whether temperature is indeed identical with and, in addition, reducible to mean kinetic energy, I shall not debate these issues here, but will assume that the identity and reduction are at least plausible enough to warrant the use to which they are put where discussed throughout the book. What is of special interest to us in our present discussion is that there are certain linguistic contexts in which interchange of the terms of this identity statement seems to lead from true to meaningless sentences. For example, the linguistic context 'x is 80° centigrade' is often made true when 'the temperature of a gas G' is substituted for 'x.' But what results is clearly not true and indeed seems meaningless when 'the mean kinetic energy of the molecules of gas G' is substituted for 'x.' If we were to apply principle C to the temperature–mean-kinetic-energy identity statement, it would quickly be proven false, but it is at least initially plausible.[37] In order not to settle such cases prematurely, we should reject C. We can accept D instead, for D does not require us to reject this identity statement nor does it have other harmful consequences.

We have completed the first step in our attempt to discover whether the property objection to the identity theory is avoidable. The next step is to see whether we can justify the claim that all those predicates not jointly true or jointly false of sen-

37. There are other examples, such as Russell's claim that 2 is identical with the class of all classes of pairs, that provide additional reason to reject C. For more examples, see Routley and Macrae, pp. 94–95.

sations and brain processes result in meaningless sentences when predicated of either sensation terms or brain-process terms. If we can do this, then the property objection to the identity theory is refuted.

'Sensation,' 'brain process,' and meaningful predication: It would be at best a most tedious task to list and test all the predicates that express properties of sensations and of brain processes. Indeed it would be most difficult merely to list all the kinds of sensations whose properties would have to be considered. We would have to catalogue not only pains and afterimages, but also sensory sensations such as sounds, tastes, smells; bodily sensations such as itches, tickles, hunger pangs; and others such as various kinds of twinges, qualms, and what G. Ryle calls "thrills." [38] There is, however, a way to short-circuit this task. It has often been claimed that the terms 'sensation' and 'brain process' belong in different logical categories. If this is true then, by assuming the category principle that no predicates are meaningfully predicable of terms in two different logical categories, we can conclude that no predicates are meaningfully ascribable to both sensations and brain processes and thus principle *D* will not disprove the identity theory.

There are two problems with this quick move. The first is to find an adequate criterion of category difference and to apply it to 'sensation' and 'brain process.' The second is that the assumed category principle that no predicates are meaningfully predicable of terms in different categories is false. There are predicates such as 'interesting,' 'contemplated,' 'denoted,' 'discussed,' 'of some category,' and 'entity,' which are meaningfully predicable of terms in any category. These "high" predicates are, then, significantly predicable across all categories. There are also other "relatively high" predicates, such as 'object' and 'event,' which are significantly predicable within several but not all categories.[39] Thus not only is the above principle false, but the identity theory is refuted using principle *D* if some high or relatively high predicate is extentional and true of either sensations

38. For a fuller listing and discussion of kinds of feelings, see G. Ryle, *The Concept of Mind* (New York: Barnes and Noble, 1949), Chap. 4.

39. High and relatively high predicates are discussed in the Appendix, p. 305 and p. 309.

or brain processes, but not true of the other. We must, consequently, both amend the category principle and give reason to think all high and relatively high extentional predicates are jointly true or false of sensations and brain processes. We can accomplish the first task easily by amending the category principle to read:

> For any predicate, P, if A and B are of different categories and P is not either a high or relatively high predicate, then P is not meaningfully predicable of both A and B.

Although this point will arise again later, I shall here assume that there is reason to think that all high or relatively high extentional predicates are jointly true or false of both sensations and brain processes.[40] Many, such as 'interesting,' 'contemplated,' and 'discussed' are not extentional, and many others, such as 'entity,' 'denoted,' and 'of some category' are true of both sensations and brain processes. Consequently, if we can show that 'sensation' and 'brain process' are of different logical categories, then we can conclude, tentatively at least, that all extentional predicates meaningfully ascribable to both sensations and brain processes are jointly true or false of them, and that the property objection to the identity theory fails.

A criterion of category difference: There have been several attempts to give an adequate criterion of category difference. G. Ryle, who originated much of the discussion about categories, states a criterion which can be put as follows:

$$\{(\exists X)[U(AX)\cdot N(BX)] \lor (\exists Y)[U(BY)\cdot N(AY)]\} \supset D(AB).[41]$$

This criterion states that if there is one term, X, that goes meaningfully with A, $U(AX)$, but not with B, $N(BX)$, or one that goes meaningfully with B, $U(BY)$, but not with A, $N(AY)$, then A and B are in different categories, $D(AB)$. There are, however, counterexamples to this criterion. If we let A be the high predicate 'interesting,' $B =$ 'person,' and $X =$ 'irrational number,' we get $U(AX)$ and $N(BX)$. From this with Ryle's criterion we get the false result: $D(AB)$. There is a modified

40. This assumption is challenged in Chapter 3.
41. See Appendix.

version of this criterion that escapes this problem and, I think, all others, and so we shall use it. It is:

$$\{(\exists X)[U(AX)\cdot N(BX)]\cdot(\exists Y)[U(BY)\cdot N(AY)]\} \supset D(AB).^{42}$$

We want to let A = 'sensation' and B = 'brain process,' and want to find an appropriate X and Y. Because some sensations are tastes that are bitter and some brain processes move through brains, we can let X = 'bitter' and Y = 'move through brains.' The result is $U(AX)$, $N(BX)$, $U(BY)$, and $N(AY)$, from which we can conclude that 'sensation' and 'brain process' belong in different categories.

*Conclusion about the property objection
to the identity theory*

We have now all the information needed to refute the property objection to the identity theory. In the previous discussion we have concluded:

(1) 'Sensation' and 'brain process' are in different logical categories.

From this, with the previously amended category principle, we can infer:

(2) No extensional predicates that are neither high nor relatively high are meaningfully ascribable to both sensations and brain processes.

Then, using a claim we have tentatively assumed,

(3) Each high or relatively high extensional predicate is jointly true or jointly false of sensations and brain processes,

and conjoining it with (2), we can conclude:

(4) No extensional predicates are true of sensations and false of brain processes, or false of sensations and true of brain processes.

With (4) we can show that principle D cannot be used to refute the identity theory, because (4) is the denial of the state-

42. This principle is justified in the Appendix.

ment required by *D* as sufficient condition for the nonidentity of sensations and brain processes. And, because we found it reasonable to accept *D* as the correct principle for evaluating the property objection to the identity theory, we have found reason to reject the objection.

THE PROPERTY OBJECTION TO REDUCTIVE MATERIALISM

The reductive materialist has a plausible way to avoid that version of the property objection which is directed at the identity theory. There still remains, however, the crucial version that grants that sensations and brain processes might be identical, but claims that if they are identical then each has the extentional properties of the other. Consequently what we call "brain processes" would have phenomenal properties of sensations, and because they are properties no physical phenomenon has, materialism would be false. Furthermore, according to this objection, it is irrelevant whether it is a category mistake to ascribe these phenomenal sensation predicates to brain processes, because we can still state the objection without category mistakes by using the double language theory. By assuming that 'brain process' refers to the same entities as 'sensation,' and that the identity theory is true, then, according to this objection, it follows that whatever predicate results in a true sentence when substituted for '*P*' in 'Some sensations have phenomenal property *P*' is true of entities referred to by 'brain process,' whether or not the predicate is meaningfully predicable of 'brain process.' Consequently, because there are entities referred to by 'brain process,' there are entities with extentional properties that are neither physical nor physical-neutral, and materialism is false.

This is by far the most difficult objection facing reductive materialism. Its independence of whether or not there are categories and category differences adds to its effectiveness. Unlike the version of the property objection directed against the identity theory, it is not refuted by invoking categories. Thus an antimaterialist, unlike someone who opposes the identity theory, need not take a stand on the issue of categories.

But how is this objection, raised against combining the identity theory with the further claim that sensations are nothing but brain processes, to be refuted? It is not enough to show that sensations are identical with brain processes; they must also be reduced to brain processes. Consequently, if a reductive materialist is to refute the preceding objection, he must show not only that statements identifying sensations and brain processes are plausible, but also that statements asserting that sensations are reduced to or nothing but brain processes are plausible. I find only one way for a reductive materialist to establish the second plausibility. The only cases I know in which a reduction of individuals has involved contingent identity statements, is when the statements have been theoretical identity statements, that is, statements expressing that certain entities are identical with theoretical entities postulated by some scientific theory. All such "theoretical" reductions, then, would be reductions of the entities by means of their identification with theoretical entities whose behavior is explained by the theoretical terms of some science. Many of these reductions would involve the reduction of the theoretical entities of one science to theoretical entities of another science. An example of this would be the reduction of a gene in biology to a DNA sequence which is a theoretical entity of chemistry. Presumably such chemical entities could then be reduced to theoretical entities of physics. The reductions that would be most relevant to our interests, however, would be those in which some entity which is experienced, perhaps through observation, is reduced to a theoretical entity. This would be the case if water is theoretically reduced to conglomerations of H_2O molecules and the temperature of a gas to the mean kinetic energy of the gas molecules. The reductive materialist, in his reply to the property objection to the reduction of sensations, must make a similar claim about sensations. He must give reason to believe that each sensation is theoretically reducible to a physical entity and so each is not only identical with but is also nothing but something physical.

We have seen that a theoretically reduced entity must be identical with a theoretical entity which is explained by some scientific theory. This is clearly not sufficient for the reduction of one entity to another because it is compatible with the reducing entity having properties that are not expressed by the theoretical terms of the science, such as biological properties of genes and observable properties of water. If genes and water have such properties, then, unless their instances of those prop-

erties are not reduced to instances of theoretical properties of
the relevant sciences, mere identity would be established. There
would be no reduction. Consequently, if reduction is to be established, more than identity and scientific explanation are
needed, and, consequently, more than the results of science are
required. What else we need can be seen by remembering that
if one entity is theoretically reduced to another, then the first
is *nothing but* the second, which is a theoretical entity. Following our discussion of this in the introduction (p. 9), we can
adopt the following definition:

> An entity, *e*, is theoretically reduced to an entity, *r*, which
> is Φ = $_{df.}$
> (1) *e* is identical with *r*;
> (2) some acceptable scientific theory, *s*, which is Φ, ex-
>   plains *r* in terms of *s*-properties of *r* (properties as-
>   cribed to *r* by theoretical terms of *s*), and not in terms
>   of properties ascribed to *e*;
> (3) *r* has the *s*-properties ascribed to it in *s*;
> (4) *e* has an extentional property, *P*, only if
>   (a) *P* is an *s*-property, or
>   (b) *P* is Φ-neutral, or
>   (c) *e*'s instance of *P* is nothing but an instance of
>   some property that is an *s*-property or is Φ-
>   neutral.[43]

In this definition, conditions (1) and (4) entail that *e* is
nothing but *r*. It is basically conditions (2) and (3) that distinguish a reduction as theoretical. It is here that theoretical
reduction goes beyond reductive materialism. Condition (2)
requires there be explanations in terms of theoretical terms of
some science and (3) requires that we give these terms a realistic rather than an instrumental interpretation. Reductive materialism, however, requires only that sensations be reduced to
something physical. It does not require that the reducing entity
be a theoretical entity of some science. Furthermore, reductive
materialism is compatible with instrumentalism; but if instrumentalism is true, there is no theoretical reduction.

43. Of the technical terms in this definition, 'Φ-neutral' is defined on
p. 8 and 'theoretical term' on p. 77. Scientific explanation is discussed on
pp. 76–77.

For ease of discussion, I shall abbreviate the preceding complex characterization of theoretical reduction by saying that *e* is theoretically reduced to *r* just in case all extentional properties of *e* either are what we can call "reductive" properties of *r*, or they (more accurately, their instances) are reduced to reductive properties of *r*.[44] If we instantiate the definition so it specifically applies to the theoretical reduction of sensations to physical entities, then we can call the relevant reductive properties "materialistic" properties. This helps point out an important similarity between this definition and the one given of 'materialism' in the Introduction. Both rely crucially on the concept of an instance of one property being nothing but an instance of another property. The previous characterization needed one amendment which we can now make using the notion of an extentional property. We can now say that an instance *i* of a property, *P*, is nothing but an instance *j* of another property which is Φ or Φ-neutral, just in case *i* is identical with *j* and all *extentional* properties of *i* are Φ or Φ-neutral.

The reductive materialist's reply to the previous objection, in short, is that because all extentional properties of sensations either are *materialistic* properties of brain processes or are reducible to such properties, the problem that the phenomenal properties of sensations raise for reductive materialism is solved. Because this solution depends on the theoretical reduction of sensations, someone might question whether there are any cases of plausible theoretical reduction of experienced entities. The examples usually cited in reply as the most plausible candidates are the reduction of water to conglomerations of H_2O molecules and, more often, the reduction of gas temperatures to the mean kinetic energy of gas molecules.[45] In both cases it is claimed that certain observable entities are reduced to theoretical entities of science. In the case of temperature we can un-

44. Although in this abbreviation I speak for the sake of ease of the reduction of properties, strictly speaking, as in the parentheses, it is the reduction of *instances of* properties that is relevant. The difference between these two kinds of reduction is discussed on p. 116.

45. See E. Nagel, "The Meaning of Reduction in the Natural Sciences," in A. Danto and S. Morgenbesser, eds., *Philosophy of Science* (New York: Meridian Books, 1961), pp. 288–312, on reducing the temperature of a gas to the mean kinetic energy of the gas molecules.

pack this claim using the preceding definition, by instantiating
e to temperatures of gases and r to the mean kinetic energy of
the molecules of gases, and by letting $s =$ the atomic theory of
gases, and $\Phi =$ micro-theoretical. What results is a statement
of the theoretical reduction of gas temperatures, a statement
which is, I believe, quite plausible. For water we would instantiate e to volumes of water, and r to conglomerations of H_2O
molecules, and would let $s =$ micro-physical, and $\Phi =$ micro-
theoretical. Similarly we can construct the reductive materialist's claim that sensations of pain are theoretically reduced to
firings of C-fibers, by instantiating e to sensations of pain and r
to firings of C-fibers and by letting $s =$ the (yet to be developed)
neurophysiological theory of brains, and $\Phi =$ physical. The task
confronting us is to evaluate this last claim.

CONCLUSION: ON THE THEORETICAL REDUCTION OF SENSATIONS

Is a theoretical reduction of sensations plausible? This is a difficult question even to begin to answer, in part because there is at
present no scientific theory of brains and sensations sufficient to
meet condition (2) of the definition. The only way I can find to
proceed is to compare the case of sensations and brain phenomena with the most plausible examples of the theoretical reduction of experienced entities. In doing this I shall concentrate
primarily on two central comparisons. The first will be a comparison of the claim that sensations are identical with some
brain phenomena with the corresponding claims for the most
plausible examples of theoretical identity. I shall do this by discovering whether sensation–brain-phenomenon identity statements are not only theoretical identity statements, but are the
kind of theoretical identity statements we find in the most
plausible examples of theoretical reduction. This will be the
first task of the next two chapters. To complete it, we must
carefully classify sensation–brain-phenomenon identity statements. I shall do this by first classifying the terms in the statement as either theoretical terms, observation terms, or phenomenal terms. This requires one more preliminary task: to define
'observation term,' 'theoretical term,' and 'phenomenal term.'
This will be done in Chapter 2, where I shall also use the definitions to classify sensation terms. Then, in Chapter 3, the re-

sults obtained in Chapter 2 will be used to complete the task. If this comparison of the two sorts of identity statements is favorable, then, although the relevant sciences are not yet developed, I shall conclude that it is reasonable to expect their future development and to accept the theoretical identity of sensations with some brain phenomena. We are now in the position of having rejected the strongest philosophical objections to the identity claim. With the addition of a favorable comparison we would be in a position to accept the theoretical identity claim if no scientific problems arise for it. I shall assume we are justified in thinking none will arise. This would leave only conditions (3) and (4) of the characterization of theoretical reduction to be satisfied. Although I shall not debate it here, let us assume that some form of scientific realism is at least acceptable, and thus we can agree to condition (3) here.

Thus far, we have not considered the point crucial to the property objection, for that objection can grant all of the first three conditions. Its claim is that the fourth is not met. Consequently, the second central comparison facing us is one between the ways, in the cases of the most plausible candidates for theoretical reduction, that those properties which seem to thwart theoretical reduction are or most reasonably can be handled, and the ways that are available to handle them in the case of sensations. If both of these crucial comparisons show important similarities, then it will be reasonable to claim that reductive materialism has resolved its problem with sensations. If, however, there are important disanalogies in either case, then the claim that sensations are theoretically reducible is unreasonable, and the preceding reply to the property objection fails. If that occurs, then, because I can find no other plausible reply, we should finally reject reductive materialism. As I have previously done, I shall assume that the reduction of temperature to mean kinetic energy is one of the most plausible examples of theoretical reduction. Thus a major part of the last task in Chapter 3 will be to make the relevant comparisons between reducing sensations to brain phenomena and reducing temperature to mean kinetic energy. Where helpful I shall also consider other plausible candidates for theoretical reduction, such as the reduction of water to conglomerations of H_2O molecules, to elucidate relevant features of theoretical reduction.

2. Sensation Terms

The task before us in Chapter 2 is to classify sensation terms to prepare for comparing sensation–brain-phenomenon identity statements with an example of a reductive theoretical identity statement, i.e. a temperature–mean-kinetic-energy statement. It might seem that all we need to do is characterize theoretical sentences and test whether sensation–brain-phenomenon identity statements fit the description. But because theoretical sentences are usually classified according to whether they contain theoretical terms, we shall instead attempt to reach a satisfactory definition of 'theoretical term' to discover whether the terms of sensation–brain-phenomenon identity statements are theoretical. However, we are not merely interested in the general category of theoretical identity statements, but in that species to which temperature–mean-kinetic-energy statements belong. Because 'temperature' is often classified as an observation term, we should also define 'observation term.' The relevance of this task is further emphasized by the fact that observation terms and theoretical terms are often considered mutually exclusive. If so, coming to understand one more clearly may well help us understand the other. I shall begin with 'observation term' because, as we shall see, it can be defined without using the concept of theoretical, but the definition of 'theoretical term' depends on 'observation term.'

OBSERVATION TERMS

Although 'observation term' has been frequently used and discussed, surprisingly few attempts have been made to provide an adequate characterization of it. It is clear, however, that observation terms are generally understood to apply to perceivable states of affairs. That is, observation terms are used to describe and report physical objects that are seen, heard, touched, tasted, and smelled, rather than unobservable theoretical entities or the phenomenal data of experience. They are, then, taken to be applicable only to publicly or intersubjectively observable objects and their properties. We might, then, begin a definition by saying that an observation term is a term used to refer to physical objects or to those properties of physical objects that can be perceived. Thus I can perceive people and stars but not numbers. However, this will not do because theoretical terms such as 'molecule,' 'atom,' and 'ion' are not supposed to be observation terms, but if any volume of water is identical with some conglomeration of H_2O molecules, then in seeing, tasting, and feeling water, we are seeing, tasting, and feeling a conglomeration of H_2O molecules. Thus we can use 'conglomeration of H_2O molecules' to refer to perceivable objects. Furthermore, because molecules are made up of ions which consist of neutrons, protons, and electrons, we must admit that we can also use terms like 'ion' and 'neutron' to refer to perceivable objects. All these terms would, on this first attempt, be observation terms.

It surely could be objected that we are not able to see molecules, ions, and electrons, but only infer that there are such things by means of a complicated theory, so that these terms are really theoretical rather than observation terms. This does not, however, show that we do not see electrons, but at most that we do not know that we see them, because when we see illumination in a cathode ray tube we see streams of electrons. And we also sometimes ask for a glass of H_2O or for the NaCl. The point is that there is nothing at all odd about the claim that Jones saw, for example, a glass of water, but he did not know that what he saw was a glass of water. Thus scientifically ignorant people can see a conglomeration of H_2O molecules or a stream of electrons and not know that they have seen them. Consequently, although we want to say that 'electron' and the like are not observation terms, there is a sense in which we can be said to see electrons. Thus we cannot use this sense of 'see' to distinguish observation terms from nonobservational theoretical terms. Since this problem seems to arise, however, because we can see something and not know that we see it, we might try to avoid the problem by using 'see that something is x,' which entails 'know that something is x,' instead of 'see x.' Thus although it is possible for someone to see water, for example, and not know that what he is seeing is water, it is not possible for someone to see that something is water and not know that what he is seeing is water. Thus, the present claim would go, 'water' is an observation term, but 'H_2O' is not because although we can see that something is a volume of water, we cannot see that something is a conglomeration of H_2O molecules.

I think that this will not help, however, because certain

problems will drive us back to using 'see *x*.' One problem is that we can correctly say "I see that tomorrow is your birthday" or "I see that the stock market is rising" without looking at anything, even if we were blind. This is because 'see that' often functions like 'understand that' or 'realize that.' We can correct this defect by using:

'see, by looking, that something is *x*,'

but this is not sufficient. Neither 'birthday' nor 'stock market' is an observation term, but we can see by looking, at a newspaper for example, when your birthday is and how the stocks are doing. To avoid this problem we must talk of looking at the thing in question. So we should use:

'see, by looking at something, that it is *x*.'

Thus I do not look at your birthday to find when it is, nor do I look at the stock market to find out what it is doing. Another example, however, still causes trouble. A doctor, for example, can say as he looks at a patient, "I see by looking at you that you have the measles." Here he is looking at the patient and sees that he has the measles. But surely 'measles' is not an observation term for measles are not observable unless cases of measles are to be identified with their symptoms. Then we could claim that the doctor would see my measles by looking at my symptoms. However, doctors do not, and there seems no reason to, identify a case of measles with its symptoms, so that this seems to be a most dubious way out of the difficulty. Or consider a physicist who is looking at two objects in a balance scale. He might claim to see that the two objects have a mass difference between them.[1] In this case he is seeing the objects and the scale, but seeing neither a mass difference nor, unlike the measles example, something observable that we might try to identify with a mass difference.

There is only one way I find to avoid this last problem. It is to specify a sense of 'perceive' relevant to the fact that we see neither measles nor mass differences by looking at *them*. That is, although we can see, by looking at someone, that he has the measles, and by looking at two objects, that they have a mass

1. This example comes from F. Dretske, "Observation Terms," *Philosophical Review* 73 (1964): 37–38.

difference between them, there is a sense in which someone's case of measles and some mass difference are not things we perceive. We must, consequently, return to 'perceive x' in place of 'perceive that something is x' to avoid this objection.

The sense of 'perceive x' relevant to observation is one for which we can be said to perceive something only if it is what I shall call "a proper stimulus." [2] That is, we should say that someone, S, perceives something, O, if and only if O appears in some way to S as a result of O's being a proper stimulus of S. There are two terms in this statement that may need some explanation. The first is 'proper stimulus.' Whereas anything that results in the external sense receptors of someone being stimulated might be called a stimulus, something is a *proper* stimulus if and only if either it transmits whatever directly stimulates a receptor—as a table transmits light waves—or nothing is transmitted and it directly stimulates a receptor as in taste and touch. This eliminates light waves and sound waves as things we perceive in this sense. Furthermore, let us call something a proper *observation* stimulus just in case it is a proper stimulus and nothing affects any stimulus energy transmitted from it before the stimulus affects the receptors, except any medium that is normal for transmission of that particular kind of stimulus energy. In this way we can eliminate as proper observation stimuli those objects seen by means of mirror reflections or by amplification or distortion of the transmitted stimulus before it reaches a sense receptor, as in microscopes. It is clear, I think, that no cases of measles and mass differences are proper stimuli. However, while some individual electrons may be proper stimuli, none are proper observation stimuli. Thus we have isolated one sense in which we do not perceive measles, mass differences, and single electrons. From here on, let us use 'observe' to express a restricted sense of 'perceive' for which something is perceivable only if there are conditions in which it would be a proper observation stimulus.

The other term to explicate is 'appear to S.' I take this term to be a generic way of saying what can more specifically be said by specifying which of S's senses is affected by the stimulus object. Thus for visual stimulation we would replace 'appears

2. See R. Chisholm, *Perceiving* (Ithaca, N.Y.: Cornell University Press, 1957), pp. 142ff., for a discussion of 'proper stimulus.'

to *S*' with 'is visible to *S*'; for auditory stimulation we would use 'is heard by *S*'; for olfactory stimulation, 'is smelled by *S*,' etc.

We are now ready to use the sense of 'perceive' characterized above to avoid the problems facing 'perceive that something is *x*.' There are several things to be noted first. We are interested not merely in what is, as a matter of fact, observed, but also in what is observable; and we are interested only in what is observable by any standard observer under standard observation conditions. Abnormal powers of perception, unique characteristics such as a powerful imagination, and unusual observation conditions may result in things appearing to some observers in ways they would not normally appear. Furthermore, for certain quantitative terms, such as 'length,' 'volume,' and 'weight,' it is not necessary that all entities to which they apply be normally observable, but only that some are. To incorporate this point into the definition, we must explicitly distinguish among what I shall call a quantitative term (a general noun or predicate that takes numerical modifiers), a specifying term (numerically modified quantitative term, such as 'volume of 1 cubic micro-millimeter'), and a qualitative term (a general noun or predicate that is neither a quantitative term nor a specifying term, such as 'red'). Then, let us say that an observation term is either an observation qualitative term, an observation quantitative term, or an observation specifying term. And, because we can say that a specifying term is an observation term just in case its quantitative term is, we need not define these specifying terms separately. Let us, then, take as at least one defining condition of a term 'O' being an observation (qualitative, quantitative) term:

> The following is true: 'Some (*O*, instance of *O*) is observable by any standard perceiver under standard conditions.'

And following the above discussion we can interpret this as:

> The following is true: 'Under standard conditions, some (*O*, entity having *O*) would be a proper observation stimulus of any standard observer, *S*, such that, as a result, the (*O*, instance of *O*) would appear in some way to *S*.'

We have, I think, avoided the problem facing 'perceive that' but the original problem for 'perceive *x*' has returned. We must, therefore, add some additional condition to the definition if we are to avoid it. The problem arose because certain theoretical terms can be used to refer to observable objects. It is surely true to say that we can observe H_2O in beakers, NaCl in shakers, and, perhaps, even streams of electrons flowing in cathode ray tubes. Such things are proper observation stimuli which affect us so that as a result, they appear in some way to us. It is not enough, then, that a term meets the above conditions, because as we become more and more at home with the theoretical terms of science we can quite easily come to use them in place of non-theoretical observation terms. We must, consequently, distinguish between "pure" observation terms and theoretical terms which we may come to use in place of the "pure" terms.

The terms giving rise to the problem are "theory laden" in the sense that for any such term 'T', the sentence 'There is a T' entails that there is something which is unobservable. For example, although we can use 'conglomeration of H_2O molecules' to refer to observable objects, the sentence, 'Something is a conglomeration of H_2O molecules' entails that there is one H_2O molecule. This gives us a way to rule out such theory-laden terms. We should add the requirement that the existence of the observable entity does not entail that there is something unobservable. However, while we can rule out theoretical terms this way, we will still be faced with classifying sensation-terms as observation terms, if a version of the identity theory that identifies sensations with something observable is correct. We can avoid this problem by requiring that what is observable be physical.[3] The result is the following definition:

'O' is an observation (qualitative, quantitative) term $=$ df.

(1) the following is true: 'Some (O, instance of O) is observable by any standard observer under standard conditions,' *and*

(2) for any nonlogical (qualitative, quantitative) term 'P', if 'Something (is an O, has O)' entails 'Something (is a P, has P),' then 'P' meets condition (1) and '(Any P, the property P)is physical' is true.

---

3. Here physical properties, objects, and events are to be characterized following the discussion in the Introduction.

We have found a way to distinguish observation terms from nonobservation terms that at least avoids the objections mentioned above. In the above example, it is false that one H_2O molecule is observable by any standard observer under standard conditions. The second condition has the added advantage of avoiding a problem we have not yet considered, the problem raised by nonobservation terms such as 'queen of trump,' 'chess king,' 'United States senator,' and 'good man.' Such terms whether "game laden" or conceptually burdened in some other way, all meet condition (1), but they fail to meet condition (2) because in each case there is some 'P' such as 'permitted to take non-trump,' 'permitted to be castled,' 'being elected,' and 'being good' which fails to meet condition (1). There may be problems the above definition does not avoid, but I have found none, and I think it is sufficient for our purpose of contrasting observation terms with theoretical terms.[4]

Before moving on, it might be interesting to note that given the above definition of 'observation term' there is nothing which guarantees that such terms remain inviolate because they refer to the observation base upon which all knowledge is erected, while the theoretical terms used to erect the theoretical superstructure change as theories come and go. Observation terms, as here defined, have no special status. Consider a possible situation some years in the future where science has become such a dominating influence that all "nonscientific" terms, such as 'water' and 'salt' have dropped out of the language because people have come to use only the corresponding theoretical terms to refer to what they perceive. In such a world there would be no "pure" observation terms because no terms would meet the second defining condition of 'observation term.' I see nothing wrong with this, because it seems to me that in such a case a theoretical term has taken on an added dimension of meaning, a new role, namely, that of the observation term whose place it

4. My first attempt at this definition in "Mental Terms, Theoretical Terms, and Materialism," *Philosophy of Science* 35 (1968): 48–52, faced problems. See P. Machamer, "A Recent Theory/Observation Drawing," and my reply "Observing and What It Entails," forthcoming in *Philosophy of Science*. The amended version stated in the preceding article is the same as the version stated here.

has taken.[5] The only implication this has for what we are considering is that we should not define 'theoretical term' in such a way that no theoretical term can be used to refer to what is observable, unless we decide to stop calling a term theoretical if it takes on such an observational role. But I think it is important on independent grounds to distinguish those terms that meet both defining conditions of 'observation term' from the "theory laden" observation terms we have contrasted with them. We should, therefore, keep this future science-dominated world in mind when defining 'theoretical term.'

EMPIRICAL TERMS

It is clear that what is called the observation vocabulary of a science includes observation terms, but it is not clear that the only nonlogical (and nonmathematical) terms which belong to this vocabulary are observation terms. It is usually granted that there are at least two other kinds of terms that belong to the observation vocabulary, in both cases terms defined using only observation (and logical) terms. There are those explicitly defined by observation terms such as Hempel's example:[6]

The cephalic index of a person $x =$ df.
$$100\ \frac{\text{maximum skull breadth of } x}{\text{maximum skull width of } x}$$

We can call these *observationally defined terms*. There are also those terms given a fixed, but incomplete, meaning by using a set of reduction sentences containing only observation terms, such as another Hempel example:[7]

If a small iron object is close to x at t, then x is magnetic at t if and only if that object moves toward x at t.

5. See W. Sellars, "Scientific Realism or Irenic Instrumentalism," in R. Cohen and M. Wartofsky, eds., *Boston Studies in the Philosophy of Science* (New York: Humanities Press, 1965), pp. 186–93, for a discussion of this point; reprinted in W. Sellars, *Philosophical Perspectives*, pp. 337–69.
6. C. Hempel, *Fundamentals of Concept Formation in Empirical Science* (Chicago: University of Chicago Press, 1952), p. 10.
7. Hempel, p. 26.

Following Carnap, we can call these *pure disposition terms.* In both of these examples, although the terms are defined by observation terms, neither fits the above definition of 'observation term' because neither a cephalic index nor the magnetic characteristic of objects appears in some way to us. Yet both terms, as defined above, seem to fit more appropriately in the observation vocabulary than in the theoretical vocabulary. Furthermore it is possible that some terms defined in these two ways are or can become observation terms. Let us, therefore, use 'empirical term' to mean any term which is either an observation term, or explicitly defined by observation terms, or partially defined, as in reduction sentences, by observation terms. Then we can say that the observation vocabulary is that set of terms which includes only logical terms and empirical terms.

THEORETICAL TERMS

The literature about 'theoretical term' is at best only a little more helpful than the literature on 'observation term.' [8] Generally theoretical terms have been regarded as nonobservation terms with the results that people have been unable to decide whether certain terms are observational or theoretical because there seem to be reasons for calling them both, and reasons for calling them neither.[9] However, some philosophers have made helpful suggestions. Hempel says that theoretical terms "usually purport to refer to not directly observable entities and their characteristics; they function in a manner soon to be examined more closely, in scientific theories intended to explain empirical generalizations." [10] Carnap claims that they are terms introduced by means of postulates in a theoretical language,[11] and Sellars says that theories "not only explain why observational constructs obey inductive generalizations, they explain what, as far as the observational framework is concerned, is a random component

8. Some of the problems facing attempts to define 'observation term' have been discussed in Dretske.

9. See P. Achinstein, "The Problem of Theoretical Terms," *American Philosophical Quarterly* 2 (1965): 193–203.

10. Hempel, "The Theoretician's Dilemma," in H. Feigl et al., eds., *Minnesota Studies* 2 (1958): 42.

11. R. Carnap, *Meaning and Necessity* (Chicago: University of Chicago Press, 1958), p. 40.

in their behavior." [12] From these quotations we can put together a first approximation of a definition of 'theoretical term':

'*T*' is a theoretical term = $_{df.}$

(1) '*T*' is a nonlogical constant introduced by means of postulates in theories that explain generalizations about observable objects and their properties whether

(a) the generalizations are empirical, i.e. can be formulated using only empirical (and logical) terms, *or*

(b) they can be formulated only if theoretical terms are also used, *and*

(2) '*T*' is one of a group of terms that do not usually refer to directly observable entities and their properties.

There are several problems with this definition. First, strictly speaking, for most scientific theories, even those which have been subsequently axiomatized such as classical mechanics, no terms were introduced by means of postulates because the theories were not introduced as postulate systems. Putting Carnap's point this way, we can see that what is essential for theoretical terms is that they be introduced into language as part of the explanatory vocabulary of a scientific theory, whether or not the theory is axiomatized. There are two things to notice here. The first is that by 'explanatory vocabulary' I mean that vocabulary used to formulate and explain generalizations about what is observed. The second is that the term 'introduced' is important. Terms which are part of the vocabulary of a theory could be terms which were in the language before the theory was formulated. Most of these terms, which include many observation terms, are not theoretical terms. However, any term which, although taken from a preexisting vocabulary, has been explicated to become part of the scientific vocabulary (e.g. 'atom') should be considered a term introduced as part of the scientific vocabulary because it is essentially a new term. Any terms so introduced would, by the present definition, be theoretical if they meet the rest of condition (1) and condition (2). We

12. Sellars, *Science, Perception and Reality* (London: Routledge and Kegan Paul, 1963), p. 122.

could, incidentally, add to the definition of 'observation term' that it is not a term introduced in this way, and so make the two classes of terms exclusive. Nothing, however, seems to be gained by this, and the fact that terms can acquire and lose certain roles may, as a consequence, be overlooked.

The second problem with the initial definition concerns condition (2). It surely seems true that most theoretical terms are not observation terms, but it does not follow that most of them do not refer to directly observable entities or characteristics. Theoretical terms such as 'H_2O' and 'NaCl' are often used to refer to observable entities, although they are surely not observation terms. Indeed we use many and may well come to use many more such nonobservation terms to refer to what we observe. I think, therefore, that the most we should say in (2) is that most theoretical terms are not observation terms. However, this majority does not seem to be something essential, so we can omit (2) altogether in the final definition. Nevertheless there is another relationship between theoretical terms and observation terms which should be included in any definition of 'theoretical term.' This is brought out in a quotation from Carnap:

> It seems best to reconstruct the language of science in such a way that terms like 'temperature' in physics or 'anger' or 'belief' in psychology are introduced as theoretical constructs rather than as intervening variables of the observation language. This means that a sentence containing a term of this kind can neither be translated into a sentence of the language of observables nor deduced from such sentences, but at best inferred with high probability.[13]

The relevant point here is that if in the language of science a contingent sentence containing just one nonlogical term cannot be deduced from observation sentences, then the term is neither an observation term, nor an observationally defined term, nor a pure disposition term, and it must be a theoretical term of some sort. However, this is not a necessary condition because it may be that some theoretical terms are or will become observation terms or translatable into the language of observables. Consequently, although we should use this condition in the definition

13. Carnap, p. 230. See also Carnap, "The Methodological Character of Theoretical Concepts," in *Minnesota Studies* 1 (1956): 69.

of 'theoretical term,' we should not use it alone nor conjoin it with another. We should use it in disjunction with the other condition we have been considering.

The third problem facing this first approximation is that it cannot be used as the final definition, because 'theoretical term' is used in the definiens in (1b) and thus the definition is circular. The easiest way to avoid this problem would be to omit (1b), but this would be to ignore the important point it stresses.[14] There are two kinds of empirical generalizations explained by scientific theories: universal and statistical generalizations. The first is of the form:

$$(x)[O_1x \supset O_2x],$$

so that we can infer one observation sentence, O_2a, given merely another, O_1a. If all generalizations explained by scientific theories were of this kind, then it is surely reasonable to hold that the theoretical terms used in the explanation are in principle eliminable insofar as their explanatory function is to establish inferential relations among empirical statements. Statistical generalizations, however, are of the form:

$$\frac{n}{m} \; O_1\text{'s are } O_2\text{'s},$$

so that given O_1a and $\frac{n}{m} > 1/2$ we can infer that it is probable that O_2a. For this kind of empirical generalization we can arrive at a universal generalization only if some further condition is added to the antecedent, so that we might get for example:

$$(x)[(O_1x \cdot Px) \supset O_2x]$$

and

$$(x)[(O_1x \cdot {\sim}Px) \supset {\sim}O_2x],$$

which taken with

$$\frac{n}{m} \; O_1\text{'s are } P\text{'s}$$

would imply the original statistical generalization and thus explain it. For many statistical generalizations, 'P' would be an observation term. Where this is true, theoretical terms are again

14. See Sellars, pp. 120–23, for this point.

in principle eliminable. In some cases, however, as Sellars points out, microconditions and thus microvariables are required to arrive at a universal generalization so that '*P*' would be a theoretical term. But even in such cases, theoretical terms are in principle eliminable when $\dfrac{n}{m} > 1/2$, if, as it seems, probabilistic inferences among empirical statements are adequate for the purposes of scientific explanation. The case is different, however, where the behavior of some observable entities is random on the macro level but not on the micro level, so that the relevant empirical generalization would have $\dfrac{n}{m} < 1/2$ but the generalization formulated using theoretical terms would have $\dfrac{n}{m} > 1/2$. In such a case we cannot rely on the empirical generalization because no scientific explanation is adequate if it cannot provide generalizations at least sufficient for making probabilistic inferences among empirical statements. In such a case, Sellars' point is that we must use a generalization that contains theoretical terms.

It is because (1b) stresses an area in which theoretical terms may well be essential that we should try to incorporate it into a final definition while avoiding the circularity. We can do this by mentioning nonempirical terms, rather than theoretical terms, in a way that can accommodate any need for generalizations that warrant inferences only if they contain nonempirical terms.

There is one last point we should consider before we give a final statement of the definition of 'theoretical term.' I have talked of scientific theories explaining empirical generalizations about observable entities and their characteristics. I should, then, give some indication of how I am using the term 'explain.' I shall adopt what is the standard view in many quarters, namely that empirical generalizations, and consequently those singular empirical statements which are instances of the generalizations, are explained by being deducible from the theoretical explanatory statements in conjunction with certain rules relating certain theoretical terms with certain observation terms. To take an example relevant to our interest in theoretical terms, let us consider Boyle's Law as an empirical generalization. We can formulate it: $PV = kT$. From such a generalization we can deduce that a certain volume of gas under certain pressure has a certain temperature, but the law in turn can be deduced from two other premises. The first is a theoretical statement relating the mean kinetic energy of the molecules of a volume of a gas to the pressure exerted on a container of the gas by means of impacts of molecules per second. The second is a bridge statement or correspondence law which relates the mean kinetic energy of the gas molecules to the temperature of the gas. In this case we have an identity statement of the form: $E = kT$. Thus Boyle's Law is explained by the kinetic theory of gases because the law is deducible from a statement of the theory when the statement is conjoined with the appropriate correspondence rule.[15] I shall, for the sake of brevity, continue to use the term 'explain' in the final definition, but shall construe it in terms of what is required by the deductive theory of explanation.

We can now define 'theoretical term' as follows:

'T' is a (scientific) theoretical term = df.

(1) 'T' is a nonlogical constant in a (scientific) explanatory vocabulary which is not an empirical term, i.e. neither an observation term nor an observationally defined term nor a pure disposition term, *or*

(2) 'T' is a nonlogical constant introduced into a language as part of the vocabulary of a (scientific) theory in order to explain the behavior of observable entities by generalizations, whether empirical or requiring nonempirical terms, sufficient to establish inferential relationships among empirical statements.

Although this definition, as desired, leaves open the possibility of observational theoretical terms, we shall also be centrally interested in nonobservational theoretical terms, that is, terms which meet the definition of 'theoretical term' but fail to meet the first defining condition of 'observation term.' Thus theoretical terms such as 'atom' and 'electron' are not observation terms, but terms such as 'temperature' and 'pressure' would seem to

15. For a discussion of Boyle's Law, explanation, and reduction, see E. Nagel, "The Meaning of Reduction in the Natural Sciences," in A. Danto and S. Morgenbesser, eds., *Philosophy of Science,* pp. 288–312.

qualify both as theoretical and observation terms. They are theoretical by the second condition because they are quantitative terms introduced to help formulate the kind of mathematical generalizations required for the mathematical deductions used in the explanations of physics.[16] 'Pressure,' for example, is an observation term because some pressures, e.g. at the bottom of a swimming pool, are observable, by feeling them, by a standard observer under standard conditions. These two classes of terms, then, are neither mutually exclusive nor exhaustive. We have already seen that there are certain empirical terms which seem to be neither theoretical nor observational. We have seen that observationally defined terms such as 'cephalic index' and many candidates for pure dispositional terms such as 'magnetic,' 'malleable,' and 'soluble' violate the definition of 'observation term.'

CLASSIFICATION OF SENSATION SENTENCES

We are now ready to determine whether the term 'sensation' is a theoretical term. Instead of working with the word 'sensation' in isolation, however, I shall first examine it in the context of a sentence such as:

I feel (he feels) a sensation of pain,

because much of the work done previously on this topic has been centered on sensation sentences. We have three classifications available from our previous discussion:

Observation sentence = df. Sentence containing either some observation terms or some variables which take only observation terms as true substituends, and containing no other variables or nonlogical constants.

Empirical sentence = df. Sentence containing either some empirical terms or some variables which take only empirical terms as true substituends, and containing no other variables or nonlogical constants.

16. It might be noted here that 'temperature' has been called by some a theoretical term, see Achinstein, p. 193, and Carnap as quoted above (note 13); and by others an empirical term, see Sellars "Theoretical Explanation," in B. Baumrin, ed., *Philosophy of Science: The Delaware Seminar,* 2 vols. (New York: John Wiley, 1963), 2: 71–72.

Theoretical sentence = df. Sentence containing either some theoretical terms or some variables which take only theoretical terms as true substituends.

It is obvious by now that these three classes are neither exhaustive nor exclusive. We need to consider, however, only three additional classes of sentences, which we can call "phenomenal sentences," "reports," and "expressive sentences."

As I shall use the term, a report is always an assertion used to refer to something someone is or very recently was aware of. More specifically, a report is an assertion used to make an identifying reference to something someone is or recently was aware of. A report, then, is not primarily a sentence used to describe something we are aware of or experience in some way. Indeed, although all reports are descriptive statements if we construe a descriptive sentence broadly as any sentence that classifies something in some way, not all sentences that achieve identifying reference are true descriptions, nor are all accurate reports accurate descriptions. Thus 'I see Smith's killer' may well achieve identifying reference, but falsely describe the man picked out.[17] And 'The object I see is between 20 feet and 200 feet tall' may accurately pick out one object in some context, but it does not provide an accurate description. Furthermore, not all true descriptive statements are successful reports, for while 'The object I see is yellow' may be a true description of an object seen, it would fail to pick it out from a group of yellow objects.

Generally we divide reports into two classes: observation reports, such as 'I see a red object,' and phenomenal reports, such as 'I have a sharp pain.' That is, a report is not any statement used to make identifying reference to something someone is aware of. If it were, then 'What I see is the conglomeration of H_2O molecules over there' would be a perceptual report, and 'What I feel is in one-to-one simultaneity correspondence with a firing of C-fibers of my brain' would be a psychological report. We should, consequently, limit reports to statements containing only observation terms or phenomenal terms as nonlogical constants. But we have not defined 'phenomenal term.'

17. For a similar distinction, see K. Donnellan's discussion of the referential and attributive use of referring terms in "Reference and Definite Descriptions," *Philosophical Review* 75 (1966): 281–304.

For our purposes, we can give a two condition definition of 'phenomenal term,' similar to that of 'observation term.' The first condition will take it as true that phenomenal objects and properties exist when and only when sensed. But because if one version of the identity theory is true, firings of C-fibers occur when and only when they are sensed, the second condition is added to avoid classifying 'firings of C-fibers' as a phenomenal term. We must eliminate physical entities. Let us begin with the following definition:

'S' is a phenomenal term = df.
 (1) The following is true: 'There is an (S, instance of S) when and only when it is experienced by someone, whether or not it is also perceived,' *and*
 (2) For any nonlogical term, 'P', if 'There is an (S, S entity)' entails 'There is a (P, P entity)' then 'P' meets condition (1) and '(Some P, the property P) is physical' is false.

On this definition, all sensation terms are phenomenal terms but not all psychological terms are, because one often has beliefs when not experiencing them. Furthermore, words such as 'red,' 'loud,' and 'sweet,' are phenomenal terms if applied to sense-data, but they are not, by the first condition, if they are applied to physical objects. And, expressions such as 'sensation in a one-to-one simultaneity correspondence with a firing of C-fibers' are ruled out by the second condition, because if there are such sensations then it follows that there are firing C-fibers, firing C-fibers are physical, and 'firing C-fibers' does not meet condition (2).

There are, however, two counterexamples to the preceding definition. First, on some interpretations of 'sense-datum,' sentences such as, 'There is a red sense-datum now' would entail 'There is a subject experiencing a red sense-datum now.' But it is plausible to argue, as did Hume, that no subjects of experiences are experienced at all. Consequently, on the preceding definition, this Humean view would be forced to claim that 'sense-datum' is not a phenomenal term. We must, then, amend the consequent of the second condition to correct this defect.

The second problem arises for one who accepts the adverbial sensing theory of sense experience instead of a theory that sense experience consists of relationships between subjects of experiences and phenomenal objects, such as sense-data or percepts. Because a case of someone sensing red-ly might sometimes occur when no one is experiencing this experience of sensing red-ly, the verb 'to sense red-ly' would violate the first condition of the definition and would fail to be a phenomenal term. We must amend the definition to avoid this consequence, especially since the adverbial theory will play a central role in some of our later discussions (see Chapters 6 and 7). I believe this can be accomplished by adding a disjunct to the first condition based on the fact that these events of sensing or experiencing, while often involved in perception, are not themselves identical with any events of persons perceiving objects. Our final definition, then, will be:

'*S*' is a phenomenal term = df.

(1) The following is true: 'There is an (*S*, instance of *S*) when and only when it is experienced by someone, whether or not it is also perceived, *or* each *S* is an event of a person experiencing in some way but it is not an event of the person perceiving some object,' *and*

(2) For any nonlogical term, '*P*', if 'There is an (*S*, *S* entity)' entails 'There is a (*P*, *P* entity)' then

(a) either '*P*' meets condition (1) or '(Each *P*, *P* entity) is a subject of experiences' is true, *and*

(b) '(Some *P*, the property *P*) is physical' is false.

We can define 'report' using 'observation sentence,' and 'phenomenal sentence.' First, however, we must define 'phenomenal sentence':

Phenomenal sentence = df. Sentence containing either some phenomenal terms, or some variables which take as true substituends only phenomenal terms, and containing no other variables or nonlogical constants.

For 'report' we have:

Report = df. Either an observation sentence or a phenomenal sentence that is an assertion used to make identifying reference to something someone is (or recently was) aware of.

It might be thought that because sensation terms are phenomenal terms it is quite obvious that many sensation sentences are reports. However, although it is generally agreed that observation sentences are reports, not everyone agrees this is true of phenomenal sentences. Some think they are expressive sentences, which, unlike reports, are not used to make assertions or statements about something, because they have no truth value. They are used merely to express feelings and emotions. Thus, unlike many sentences with truth value that can be used to express one's feelings, these have only that one use. And, because one cannot express another's feelings or emotions, they can only express those of the speaker using them. The definition of 'expressive sentence' we shall use is:

> Expressive sentence = df. Sentence used merely to express some feeling or emotion of the speaker rather than to make assertions that refer to something.

It will be noted that the last two definitions of kinds of sentences are quite different from the first three definitions which are stated solely in terms of the kinds of linguistic expressions contained in the sentences. In the first definitions nothing is stated about whether the sentences can be used to make assertions or whether they are referential, and nothing is stated about what they refer to. However, in the last two there are claims made about the reference or nonreference of the sentences, and about whether they are used to make assertions or not. Although many observation sentences and some empirical sentences are thought to be reports, many philosophers, especially empiricists, do not consider theoretical sentences to be reports. However, nothing in the definition of 'theoretical sentence' prohibits such a sentence from being a report. Incidentally those who claim theoretical sentences are not reports do not claim that they are expressive sentences, but rather that they are merely computational devices or inference tickets which help us move inferentially from one observation sentence to another (see the discussion of Rylean behaviorism in Chap. 4).

I know of no one who claims that the sentence 'I feel (he

feels) a pain' is an observation sentence. Even if each pain were identical with some observable physical event, as an identity theorist might claim, 'pain' would not be an observation term. Although there would be a sense in which pains would be perceivable because 'pain' would meet condition (1) of the definition of 'observation term,' 'pain' does not meet the second condition because pains are not physical. They are individuals with extentional properties that are neither physical nor physical-neutral. On the other hand, there have been many who would claim that all psychological terms are empirical terms because all are explicitly definable by observation terms. This is the program of logical or analytical behaviorism associated primarily with the early work of Carnap and Hempel, but both of these men and most others have since given up the program because no adequate analyses of psychological expressions in terms of physicalistic expressions have been produced. I shall not here go into the various well-known problems which have justified the rejection of this program.[18] I shall merely accept the rejection as justified and turn to a different classification of psychological terms. Carnap later attempted to give partial definitions of psychological terms by reduction sentences, but also gave up this attempt.[19] Here also the rejection seems justified so that we can dismiss classifying psychological terms as empirical.

Of the three classifications we have left, the most likely one is reports. It surely seems to most of us that when we say 'I have a pain' or 'He has a pain' we are using the phenomenal term 'pain' to refer to and identify what I am or he is aware of. Many of us consider these two sentences relevantly like 'I see a red object' and 'He sees a red object.' In both cases we seem to be reporting something someone is aware of, the main important difference being that in the latter, unlike the former, he and I are *observationally* aware of something.

18. See the discussion of analytical behaviorism in Chapter 4. I have discussed some of the problems confronting analytical behaviorism in my *Metaphysics, Reference, and Language*, pp. 17–34, and, at a less difficult level, in Cornman and Lehrer, *Philosophical Problems and Arguments*, pp. 242–53.
19. See Carnap, "The Methodological Character of Theoretical Concepts," pp. 69–75.

Objection to Construing Sensation
Sentences as Reports

It seems plausible to construe sensation sentences as reports. Most philosophers who debate the mind–body problem, whether dualist or monist, construe them this way. This is the view taken by Smart in his attempt to justify the identity theory. He says,

> it seems to me as though, when a person says 'I have an after-image,' he *is* making a genuine report, and that when he says 'I have a pain,' he *is* doing more than 'replace pain-behavior,' and that 'this more' is not just to say that he is in distress. I am not so sure, however, that to admit this is to admit that there are nonphysical correlates of brain processes. Why should not sensations just be brain processes of a certain sort? [20]

The most forceful objection to claiming that sensation sentences are reports, whether of nonphysical phenomena or of brain processes, is based on the private language argument which has been used to defend the claim that no psychological sentences are reports. This is, then, an important objection not only for Smart's version of the identity theory, but also for our investigation of sensation terms. And although, as I have shown elsewhere, Smart has failed to answer the objection, we shall find that it can be refuted.[21]

Generally those philosophers who deny that sensation sentences are reports construe self-ascriptive and other-ascriptive sensation sentences quite differently. It is, for example, often claimed that 'I am in pain' is not a report but rather a verbal expression of pain something like 'Ouch!' Wittgenstein, who instigated the private language argument, has been interpreted as holding such a view of sensation sentences. Smart interprets him this way on the basis of Wittgenstein's claim that one way we might learn the use of words like 'pain' is that such words

are connected with the primitive, the natural, expressions

20. J. J. C. Smart, "Sensations and Brain Processes," *Philosophical Review* 68 (1959): 144.
21. See *Metaphysics, Reference, and Language,* pp. 46–48, for a criticism of Smart.

of the sensation and used in their place. A child has hurt himself and he cries; and then adults talk to him and teach him exclamations and, later, sentences. They teach the child new pain-behavior.

"So you are saying that the word 'pain' really means crying?"—On the contrary: the verbal expression of pain replaces crying and does not describe it.[22]

This passage suggests that Wittgenstein held that when 'pain' and other sensation terms are used self-ascriptively, what results is neither a theoretical sentence nor a report, but instead, merely a verbal expression of pain. That is, sensation sentences in their self-ascriptive use are expressive sentences. This view of Wittgenstein is often supported by arguing that he accepted the private language argument. Nevertheless in spite of the preceding quotation, and although he originated the private language argument, I believe Wittgenstein accepted the view that sensation sentences, whether self-ascriptive or other-ascriptive, are often reports. I shall try to show this in my examination of the private language argument.

THE PRIVATE LANGUAGE ARGUMENT

I wish to consider the form of the private language argument which stems from Wittgenstein,[23] but my primary aim is not to reconstruct his views faithfully. I wish to consider the strongest version of the argument I can construct. That version has two parts: one attempts to show that there are no private languages, and the other that there are no reports of private psychological entities because such a report would have to be a sentence of a private language.

To begin the first part of the argument, let us assume that '*E*' is an expression of a private language of one person, *A*. That is, at most *A* can know the rules for the correct use of '*E*.' But if at most one person can know such rules, then no one, including *A*, can distinguish the difference between obeying the rules and

22. L. Wittgenstein, *Philosophical Investigations,* 2d ed. (Oxford: Basil Blackwell, 1958), §244. All references in this chapter which are not footnoted are to numbered paragraphs of Part I of that book.

23. See especially §§243–74. See also N. Malcolm, "Wittgenstein's *Philosophical Investigations*" in Chappell, *The Philosophy of Mind,* pp. 74–81.

merely thinking that he is obeying the rules. Furthermore, if no one can make this distinction, then no one can know whether he is obeying the rules. And because someone can know how to apply an expression correctly only if he can obey the rules for its correct use, it follows that there are no meaningful expressions of a private language, that is, there are no private languages. We can lay out the crux of this argument as follows:

(1) If at most one person, *A*, can know any rules for the use of '*E*,' then no one can distinguish the difference between someone obeying and merely thinking that he is obeying the rules.

(2) If no one can distinguish the difference between someone obeying and merely thinking that he is obeying a rule, then no one can know whether someone is obeying the rule.

(3) If no one can know whether someone is obeying a rule, then no one can obey the rule.

(4) If no one can obey any rules for the use of an expression, then no one can know how to use the expression correctly.

(5) If no one can know how to use an expression correctly, then the expression is meaningless.

Therefore

(6) If at most one person, *A*, can know the rules for the use of '*E*,' then '*E*' is meaningless.

The second half of the argument concerns entities that are private in the sense that for any one of them, *E*, only one person, *A*, can know when it exists or occurs.[24] But if only *A* can know this, then only *A* can know whether an expression, '*E*,' which is used to denote *E*, actually does denote *E*, and if only *A* can know whether '*E*' denotes *E*, then only *A* can know the rules for the correct use of '*E*.' If we take these premises with the con-

24. This is not the only sense of 'private' that is philosophically interesting. Six others have been delineated in Chapter 1 in the discussion of the privacy objection to the identity theory. However, the sense used here seems to be the one with which Wittgenstein is concerned (see §243, §272, §273), and it is the sense for which the private language argument is most plausible.

clusion (6) of the first argument, we can conclude that if *E* is a private entity then '*E*' is meaningless. Consequently because terms like 'sensation,' 'pain,' and 'afterimage' are not meaningless, we can conclude that they do not denote private entities and thus sentences using such terms are not reports of private entities. This argument can be reconstructed as follows:

(7) If *E* is a private entity of *A*, then at most *A* can know whether it exists or occurs.

(8) If at most *A* can know whether *E* exists or occurs and '*E*' is used to denote *E*, then at most *A* can know whether '*E*' actually does denote *E*.

(9) If at most *A* can know whether '*E*' denotes *E*, then at most *A* can know the rules for the use of '*E*.'

(6) If at most one person, *A*, can know the rules for the use of '*E*,' then '*E*' is meaningless.

Therefore

(10) If *E* is a private entity of *A* and '*E*' is used to denote *E*, then '*E*' is meaningless.

(11) No psychological expressions such as 'sensation,' 'pain,' and 'afterimage,' are meaningless.

Therefore

(12) No psychological expressions are used to denote private psychological entities.

And because if (12) is true then no psychological sentences are used to make identifying reference to private psychological entities, we can conclude:

(13) No psychological sentences are reports of private psychological entities.

According to the objection we are considering, (13) yields:

(14) No psychological sentences are reports.

Examination of the premises

Each of the two preceding arguments contains at least one dubious premise. We can, I think, grant that all the premises except (1) and (9) are plausible, but these two are surely open to serious criticism. Someone, however, might think that (3) is dubious, because we can be following a rule and not know it. However 'follow' in the sense of 'obey' seems to imply an understanding by someone of what he is following. On this interpretation we can obey a rule only if we can understand the rule and what it would be like to follow or not follow it. The important distinction here is between 'follow' in the sense of 'obey' and 'follow' in the sense of 'act in accordance with.' For the latter, premise (3) would surely be false, but for 'obey' it seems reasonable to grant it.

Objection to premise (1): Rules and memory: Premise (1) is not so easily defended. It surely seems that at least *A* could distinguish between obeying and merely thinking that he is obeying the rules for the use of '*E.*' This is the beginning of a good objection, but in order to develop it fully we must first decide how to interpret the consequent of premise (1), namely,

>   (a) No one can distinguish the difference between someone's obeying and merely thinking that he is obeying the rules for the use of '*E.*'

I propose to construe this sentence as follows:

>   (a1) There is a difference between someone's obeying and his merely thinking that he is obeying the rules for the use of '*E,*' and
>   (a2) It is not possible that someone distinguish this difference, i.e. it is not possible that anyone have grounds for determining whether someone correctly or incorrectly thinks that he is obeying these rules.

I admit that this is not the only way to reconstruct what Wittgenstein intimates, but there are two reasons why I think it is as plausible a reconstruction as any. First, as we shall see when we examine Wittgenstein's reply to an objection to (1), he defends something like premise (1) by considering the justification of—and thus the grounds for—this kind of distinguishing. Second, because (a2) entails that no one can know whether someone correctly or incorrectly thinks he is obeying these rules, it guarantees the truth of (2). This is an important point, because if one other plausible interpretation of (a) were used, then (2) would seem to be false. Indeed, as interpreted by

J. J. Thomson, premise (2) is false.[25] This is because she seems to interpret (a) as:

> (a3) It is not possible that there be a difference between someone's obeying and merely thinking that he is obeying a rule.

On this interpretation, (a) is true of many rules such as Thomson's example, "Whenever you feel the least bit gloomy, think of your Mummy." But because for such rules, you actually are obeying them whenever you think that you are, you cannot infer from (a3) that no one can know whether or not he is obeying the rules. Someone can know he is obeying such rules whenever he knows that he thinks that he is obeying the rules. However, because (a1) rather than (a3) seems to be true of linguistic rules, we can avoid Thomson's objection by interpreting (a) as the conjunction of (a1) and (a2).

A reply to the objection: No private justification: The objection to premise (1) as we are now interpreting it, is that even if at most *A* can know the rules of use for '*E*,' it still seems that at least *A* could find grounds for determining whether he correctly or incorrectly thinks that he is obeying the rules. The usual reply, which stems from Wittgenstein, is that *A* could justify that he had so determined only by reliance upon his memory of the rules for '*E*' or at least of how he used '*E*' in the past. Consequently there would be no grounds independent of his own memory which he could use to justify that he was correct or incorrect in thinking that he was obeying the rules. But, according to Wittgenstein, "justification consists in appealing to something independent" (§265). Furthermore, justifying one memory report by basing it on another will not do either because, according to Wittgenstein, "If the mental image of the time-table could not itself be *tested* for correctness, how could it confirm the correctness of the first memory? (As if someone were to buy several copies of the morning paper to assure himself that what it said was true.)" (§265). Wittgenstein seems to assert here that if there is no way independent of other memory reports to test a particular memory report, then that report cannot be used to justify something else.

25. J. J. Thomson, "Private Languages," *American Philosophical Quarterly* 1 (1964): 24.

Problems for the reply: Three kinds of justification: There are at least three reasons to reject this reply. First, the general claim of which this is an instance is dubious. This claim, that if something, *p*, is not independently testable, then *p* cannot be used to justify something else, is equivalent to the claim that if anything can be used to justify something else, then it is itself justifiable by another. This rules out the case of one thing which is used to justify another, being itself justified not because it is evident in relation to something else, but because it is self-evident or initially credible. Many, including most empiricists, would reject this general claim because they hold that empirical knowledge is founded on incorrigible reports which, while they are used to verify and falsify certain claims, are not themselves verifiable or falsifiable by anything else. This is surely not an unreasonable position. It seems, then, that if someone wishes to maintain Wittgenstein's restricted claim that there are no self-evident or initially credible *memory* reports which can be used to justify claims, then he must provide some reason to think that such a position is wrong, if not in general, then at least in the case of memory reports.

The second problem is that there is at least a coherence kind of justification applicable to memory reports which are not independently testable. As A. J. Ayer has pointed out, this kind of justification is overlooked by Wittgenstein by his misuse of the newspaper analogy.[26] It is true that if one copy of one edition of a newspaper reports something, then we do nothing to justify the report by examining other copies of the same edition of the newspaper. But this is not the correct analogy for memory. If we take a news report about something from one specific edition of one newspaper to be analogous to a memory report about something (e.g. one past use of a rule) from one specific "remembrance" of one person, then just as there can be other news reports in other editions of that same newspaper, so, it would seem, there could be other memory reports from other "remembrances" of that one person. And just as a coherence of the different newspaper reports would justify them all to some degree, so, it would seem, would a coherence of the different memory reports justify them all to some degree. Such a justification

26. A. J. Ayer, "Can There Be a Private Language?" *Supplementary Proceedings of the Aristotelian Society* 28 (1954): 63–76.

may be enough to make it reasonable to rely on certain memory reports even when they are not testable independently of memory.

The third problem stems from the fact that the argument is not used to disprove the thesis that there can be only private languages, but rather to prove that there can be no private languages. Consequently, the proof must hold true of private languages even under those conditions in which there are public languages. Under these conditions, we can surely check many of our memory reports and if we find reason to trust them in the independently testable cases, then we have some grounds for trusting them in the cases which are not independently testable. For all three of these reasons, we can conclude that it is not implausible to hold that memory reports which individually are not independently testable may, nevertheless, be justifiable in ways which would give us grounds for relying on them. If so, it may well be that some of us can rely on them to help justify that we are obeying rather than merely thinking that we are obeying rules of a private language. Consequently, we have found reason to doubt premise (1) and thus the argument used to establish (6), an essential premise in the main argument to show that psychological terms do not denote private entities.

Objection to premise (9): *Meaning and reference:* The most crucial problem for the main argument, however, lies in the objection to premise (9). It can be generated from something Wittgenstein said in §274, although just before this in §273 we find what sounds something like a remnant of the picture theory of meaning which, ironically, seems to be behind an acceptance of (9). In §273, Wittgenstein asks the rhetorical question, "Or is it like this: the word 'red' means something known to everyone; and in addition, for each person, it means something known only to him? (Or perhaps rather: it *refers* to something known only to him.)" Here Wittgenstein's implied answer is that it is not like this at all. In §274 he says, "Of course, saying that the word 'red' 'refers to' instead of 'means' something private does not help us in the least to grasp its function; but it is the more psychologically apt expression for a particular experience in doing philosophy." In §273 Wittgenstein could be taken to equate reference with at least some part of meaning much as in the *Tractatus*. However, this seems contrary to what is intimated in §274 where he claims that saying 'red' refers to something private does not help us understand the function or use of 'red.' If we take the doctrine that the meaning of an expression is its use, or more accurately, I think, that we can find out its meaning by examining its use, and accept what I have extracted from §274, namely, that talking about the private reference of a term will not help us understand its function or use, then we can see a problem for (9). Premise (9) implies that a necessary condition of being able to grasp the rules for the correct use of an expression is being able to know the reference of the expression. But if we can come to understand the use of some particular expression independently of knowing its reference, as §274 intimates, then (9) is surely false. It is, perhaps, because Wittgenstein in some way still equated reference with meaning at the same time he equated meaning with use that (9) seemed true.

We can even use the beetle in the box example to help support this independence of use and private reference, although—still partly held captive by the picture theory—Wittgenstein was not clear about this. The beetle which only I can see has no place in the language game (§293) (or, as a philosopher of a different sort might say, within the linguistic framework).[27] That is, this sense of 'beetle' would have a use in language, even if what was in each person's private box differed radically even to the extent that some of them were empty. In this case, the use and, therefore, the meaning of 'beetle' does not depend on what is in the box. For the purposes of understanding and using language (and perhaps also for science), what is in the box is irrelevant; "it cancels out, whatever it is" (§293). But—here Wittgenstein would seem to disagree—it does not follow that it cancels out for all purposes, nor that it does not deserve all the philosophical attention it has received.

This objection to premise (9) can be made in a different way. It is surely possible for many people to come to know the rules of correct use for many expressions because these rules include grammatical rules, logical rules, and rules of appropriate and inappropriate public contexts of use which we can discover by examining the expressions as they are commonly used. Such

27. I have discussed linguistic frameworks in "Linguistic Frameworks and Metaphysical Questions," *Inquiry* 7 (1964): 129–44, and in *Metaphysics, Reference, and Language,* pp. 162ff.

rules can be learned by observing others and trying oneself to use the terms in public situations and public discourse.[28] We can, then, come to know these rules in publicly observable linguistic contexts. In this regard a psychological expression is no different from other expressions. Consequently for psychological expressions, as for many others, being able to know what it denotes is not a necessary condition of being able to know the rules of its correct use. Consequently, premise (9) is false.

The only way I can find to avoid this objection is to consider in (9) rules for the *true* application of '*E*' rather than rules for its *correct* use, because if we cannot know whether '*E*' denotes *E* then we cannot know whether '*E*' truly applies to *E*. However, to get from this to a true interpretation of (9) requires that there be rules of truth. It is not clear that there are such rules, but if there are they would seem to be rules for verifying that expressions truly apply to things. However, let us grant here that (9) is acceptable on this interpretation because the problem transfers to (6) which, if the argument is to remain valid, must be reformulated in a way which makes it quite dubious. We must interpret (6) as:

> (6a) If at most one person, *A*, can know the rules for verifying that '*E*' is truly applied, then '*E*' is meaningless,

which entails that if '*E*' is meaningful then it is possible that more than one person knows the rules for verifying that '*E*' truly applies to something. But this is highly dubious, especially when we realize that it is one version of the verifiability criterion of meaning which has been shown to be dubious.[29] There seem to be many meaningful expressions which are used in such ways

28. For a more detailed discussion of this point, see *Metaphysics, Reference, and Language,* pp. 161–66.

29. Thomson claims (p. 29) that one premise of the private language argument is the principle of verification, but as I have interpreted the argument this would be true only if we change premise (9) from what I take to be its intended meaning to a version which considers rules of truth. Objections aimed at the general concept of a verifiability criterion of meaning are discussed briefly in Chapter 4 and in *Metaphysics, Reference, and Language,* pp. 181f.; and objections to specific formulations of the criterion, in "Indirectly Verifiable: Everything or Nothing," *Philosophical Studies* 18 (1967): 49–56.

that we cannot verify them to be truly applied. Consequently, although we can perhaps salvage (9) by talking of rules of truth, this results in (6) becoming dubious instead of merely lacking justification as it does on the previous interpretation. Thus because either premise (9) or (6) is dubious, we can reject the private language argument to prove that no psychological terms denote private psychological entities.

REJECTION OF THE OBJECTION TO SENSATION SENTENCES
AS REPORTS

Because we can reject the private language argument, we can also reject the objection based on the argument that sensation sentences are not reports. However, there is reason to reject the objection even if the argument were sound. The conclusion of the argument is:

(12) No psychological expressions denote private psychological entities,

from which we can conclude:

(13) No psychological sentences are reports of private psychological entities.

However, the objection we have been discussing goes on to conclude:

(14) No psychological sentences are reports,

but this is highly dubious and does not follow from (13). To infer (14) using (13), something like the following two premises is needed:

(15) If psychological sentences are reports, then they report psychological entities.
(16) All psychological entities are private entities.

However (16) is dubious because it is not clear that psychological entities are private in the relevant sense that at most one person can know that one exists. Indeed this is exactly what Wittgenstein seems to deny because he seems to accept, as I think Malcolm shows, a quite reasonable premise, namely,

(17) Psychological sentences are very often reports.

From this, with (13) and (15) we can conclude the denial of (16):

> (18) Not all psychological entities, e.g. pains, are private entities.[30]

Once we see that the conclusion is that at least some psychological entities are not private, we can see how Wittgenstein's concept of outward criterion becomes relevant. We can also see a possible explanation of why Wittgenstein thinks that 'pain' and 'red' can both be names, yet function very differently. Both words can be used to make reports, but while we can observe whether 'red' is truly applied by observing what it denotes, we cannot do this with 'pain' in the case of other people. Thus while we can find grounds sufficient to justify the ascription of 'red' to something by observing what it denotes, we cannot do this for other-ascriptive uses of 'pain.' But because if (18) is true, then we can know there are sufficient grounds available for justifying other-ascriptive pain reports, we can conclude that there must be something observable that provides these grounds. Furthermore, because what 'pain' denotes is not observable, what provides these grounds in the case of 'pain' must, unlike the case of 'red,' be different from what 'pain' denotes. Whatever this turns out to be is the outward criterion for a person's (inner, but not private) pain.

However, the version of the private language argument I have presented seems to be unsound, and because it is as plausible a version as I can find, we should conclude that (12), and thus (13) and (18), remain unjustified. Consequently, however much we would like to avoid scepticism with regard to other minds by the guarantee of public criteria for psychological phenomena, no one, at least so far, has provided reason to think that there is such a guarantee. We shall see below, however, that a suggestion by W. Sellars about sensation terms may provide the beginnings of

---

30. See Malcolm, pp. 93–100. See also J. W. Cook, "Wittgenstein on Privacy," *Philosophical Review* 74 (1965): 312, where he points out that for Wittgenstein "we must, if we are to give an account of that language game, reject the view that sensations are private." As Cook points out, this has often been misunderstood, for example by G. Pitcher, *The Philosophy of Wittgenstein* (Englewood Cliffs, N.J.: Prentice-Hall, 1964), p. 297. As mentioned above, Smart also misconstrues him in this way. See Smart, pp. 141 f.

a different way to justify the claim that there are publicly observable phenomena which function as criteriological grounds to justify beliefs about the mental phenomena of others.

SENSATION SENTENCES AS THEORETICAL SENTENCES

We have found no reason to reject the claim that sensation sentences are reports. But perhaps there is an overriding reason to classify them in some other way. In his later writings, as we have already seen (note 13), Carnap came to the position that many psychological terms are theoretical terms rather than defined empirical terms, so that a sentence containing one of them is a theoretical sentence. In this passage Carnap singles out 'anger' and 'belief' as theoretical terms, but I should think that 'sensation' and 'pain' would do equally well. None of these terms is an observation term, because no one observes anger, beliefs, sensations, and pain. None is explicitly definable or partially definable by observation terms. Given the definition of 'theoretical term' and that these terms are part of an explanatory vocabulary, it follows at once that these psychological terms are theoretical terms. Many people would object to this conclusion because they are convinced that when someone says something like 'I think the pain has lessened,' what he says does not belong in the same class with 'I think an electron has passed through the cloud chamber.' In the electron case he is making an assertion about something he is not aware of, although, perhaps, basing his assertion on what he is aware of. But in the pain case he surely is aware of his own pain, so that 'pain' is not a theoretical term like 'electron.' This objection emphasizes a difference between self-ascriptive and other-ascriptive uses of psychological terms. While it may be plausible to consider pains of others to be like electrons because we are not aware of them, but rather base our claims about them on what we are aware of, this is not the case with our own pains. We report our own pains.

SELF-ASCRIPTIVE AND OTHER-ASCRIPTIVE SENSATION SENTENCES

The preceding discussion suggests that perhaps we should grant that other-person sensation sentences are theoretical, but should conclude that first-person sensation sentences are not. If we proceed in this way, however, we are faced with a problem, because sensation terms taken in isolation seem to meet the first defining condition of 'theoretical term' from which it follows by the definition of 'theoretical sentence' that all sentences containing a sensation term are theoretical sentences. We could avoid the problem by reformulating the first defining condition but we need not do this. Another way to avoid it is to take the view, suggested by a preceding quotation from Wittgenstein, that when 'pain' and other sensation terms are used self-ascriptively, they are neither theoretical terms nor reporting terms because they merely function as verbal expressions of feelings in the way that 'Ouch!' does. That is, in their self-ascriptive use they are expressive terms, and are, therefore, not part of any theoretical vocabulary. Thus, even without reformulating the definition of 'theoretical term,' first-person sensation sentences would not be theoretical.

It is true that many times when someone says of himself, for example, 'That hurts!' he is doing no more than giving a verbal expression of pain. But one problem with this view is that there are many other times when it seems to be a report, for example when we reply to the probing of a doctor with a calm, relaxed, 'That hurts.' Another problem is this. When a doctor repeats to a nurse what I said, he is not expressing pain, but telling her where I hurt. But if the first-person expressive view is correct, then 'That hurts' when said by me is quite different when said by the doctor because it has a truth value in the latter but not in the former case. Consequently 'hurt' would be an ambiguous term functioning differently in the two cases. The doctor and I would not be making assertions about the same thing, because I would not be making an assertion about anything. If a different view avoids these problems and has no others, it will be preferable.

Perhaps we should return to the view that while first-person sensation sentences are reports about sensations, other-person sensation sentences are nonreporting or pure theoretical sentences. If we do this, however, we also must do one of two additional things. If we assume that no theoretical sentences are reports, then we must reformulate the first condition for 'theoretical term' to avoid a contradiction. If we do not reformulate this condition, then we must admit that some theoretical sentences are reports, and, more specifically, that all first-person sensation sentences are both theoretical sentences and reports.

Should we pick one of these two alternatives? Both face a problem similar to the one we found confronting what I shall call the "nonreporting or pure theoretical (others) and expressive (self)" view. Both the "pure theoretical (others) and report (self)" view and the "pure theoretical (others) and theoretical-report (self)" view imply that when I say 'That hurts' I am doing something different from what the doctor does when he says it of me. He is merely explaining, without reporting, presumably some of my behavior. Consequently, a doctor could be right in denying that something hurts me in giving his explanation, and I could at the same time be right in reporting 'That hurts.' It is possible that 'pain' as a pure theoretical term should not be part of the correct explanation of my behavior (if, for example, epiphenomenalism is true) and that, nevertheless, there is pain for me to report. This is a strange consequence of a view and should be avoided if we can do so with no additional complications.

SENSATION SENTENCES AS THEORETICO-REPORTS

The most plausible view left is that sensation sentences are theoretico-reports in both their self-ascriptive and other-ascriptive uses. That is, as suggested by W. Sellars, both the doctor and I are using explanatory language to refer to something that someone, namely myself, is aware of.[31] There are several reasons to prefer this view to the others we have examined. First, it accords with what seems to be true, that both the doctor and I report my pain. Second, it enables us to classify sensation terms as belonging to the theoretical vocabulary without having to reformulate the first defining condition of 'theoretical term' which in all other cases appears satisfactory. Third, it allows us to call sensation terms univocal in both first-person and other-person uses. This does not mean, however, that in all their uses sensation sentences must be used both as parts of explanations and as reports, because as with many other theoretical sentences, e.g., 'That H_2O is cold!' they can be used merely as reports. However, when they are used to explain they are also often re-

31. See Sellars, *Science, Perception and Reality*, p. 195, and "The Identity Approach to the Mind–Body Problem," *Review of Metaphysics* 18 (1965): 446; reprinted in Sellars, *Philosophical Perspectives*, pp. 370–88.

ports, because they explain by making an identifying reference to something someone is aware of. Thus if someone partially explains my behavior by saying that I have a backache, then on this view he is asserting that part of what explains my behavior is something that I am aware of. Incidentally, on this view sensation sentences can also be used to express feelings, but this is nothing unusual because it is true of many sentences with truth values, e.g. 'He is the dirtiest person I have ever seen!'

This view may have other advantages as well. Sellars suggests that it may provide a basis for the solution of the problem of other minds. On this view, mental episodes such as sensations are not absolutely private because

> the fact that overt behaviour is evidence for these episodes is built into the very logic of these concepts as the fact that the observable behaviour of gases is evidence for molecular episodes is built into the very logic of molecular talk.[32]

If Sellars' suggestion can be developed, it may help us find a clearer interpretation of Wittgenstein's concept of outward criterion by construing it as an epistemological rather than a logical concept. We might then better understand his previously mentioned claim that 'red' (which occurs in pure reports) and 'pain' (which occurs in theoretico-reports) can both be names yet function (epistemologically) in importantly different ways.

Sellars' suggestion likens sensation terms which are theoretico-reporting terms, such as 'pain,' to pure theoretical terms such as 'electron.' What seems to lie behind this analogy is the view that theoretical terms receive whatever intersubjective or public empirical significance they have through their ties with observation terms. Because these ties are logically contingent and are expressed by correspondence rules, no set of observation sentences entails any contingent sentence with only theoretical terms. But, although this relationship is contingent, given that observation sentences are the source of the public empirical significance of a theoretical sentence, the statements that justify it and are its epistemological criteria are the observation sentences that express the observations predictable and explainable by the theo-

32. Sellars, *Science, Perception and Reality*, p. 195.

retical sentence and relevant correspondence rules. The analogy, then, is that sensation terms also receive whatever public empirical significance they have through their logically contingent ties to observable behavior predictable and explainable by the sensation sentences and the sentences that express the contingent ties between sensations and behavior.

CONCLUSION

We have found reasons which weigh against all construals of sensation sentences except the one that construes them as theoretico-reports, and we have found reasons for construing them as theoretico-reports. We shall, consequently, classify sensation terms as theoretico-reporting terms, that is, as theoretical terms used to make identifying reference to entities we are, or recently were, aware of.

We have finished the task of this chapter which was to classify sensation terms. This was the first step required for the comparison of sensation–brain-phenomenon identity statements with an example of a reductive theoretical identity statement, the temperature–mean-kinetic-energy identity statement. In the next chapter, using the results reached in this chapter, I shall first characterize various kinds of theoretical identity statements, then show to which kinds the two identity statements which concern us belong, and finally compare the two identity statements to discover if the analogy is close enough to justify claiming that sensation–brain-phenomenon identity statements are reductive theoretical identity statements. If the analogy is close enough, then there is reason to think that sensations are reducible to brain phenomena, and the enduring problem that sensations cause materialists may at last be laid to rest.

3. Sensation-Brain-Phenomenon Identity Statements

In this chapter we are to make two comparisons between the reduction of sensations to brain phenomena and the reduction of temperature to the mean kinetic energy of molecules to discover whether the analogy is close enough to make the reduction of sensations to brain phenomena plausible. The first comparison is between sensation–brain-phenomenon identity statements and statements that identify gas temperature with mean kinetic energy of gas molecules. The second is between ways available for handling properties of sensations and properties of temperatures that seem to thwart reduction. Our first task, then, is to compare a sentence such as:

(1) Each sensation is identical with a brain process of kind B,

with:

(2) The temperature of a gas is identical with the mean kinetic energy of the molecules of the gas.

It will be noted that in (1) sensations are being identified only with certain brain processes. This is because not all brain processes occur when someone is having a sensation. As we have seen, a necessary condition of specifying which brain process is identical with a sensation is discovering a brain process that occurs at the same time as that sensation, and this is an empirical and therefore scientific problem. The philosophical task at this point is to classify statement (1) by classifying its two key terms, 'sensation' and 'brain process of kind B.' However, in order to classify 'brain process of kind B' we must have some additional information, because some brain processes are observable but others are not. Therefore we must speculate a bit about which kind of brain process is appropriate for identification with sensations. If we talk of sensations of pain, then following the most usual claims we can say that:

(3) A sensation of pain is identical with a firing of C-fibers of the nerve cells of a (human-like) brain.[1]

1. See H. Putnam, "Minds and Machines," in S. Hook, ed., *Dimensions of Mind*, p. 153.

We shall, from here on, deal specifically with (2) and (3) in classifying and comparing the two kinds of identity statements.

KINDS OF THEORETICAL IDENTITY STATEMENTS

There are many kinds of theoretical identity statements, as can be seen by recalling that any identity statement containing just one theoretical term is a theoretical identity statement. Thus if we substitute a theoretical expression for 'x' in 'Each x is identical with a y,' then the resulting statement will be a theoretical identity statement whether we substitute for 'y' an observation term, a nonobservational empirical term, or a theoretical term. We can make finer distinctions than this, because using the terminology we have already developed, we can define two additional kinds of observation terms and four species of theoretical terms:

A. 'T' is a pure observation term $=$ df. 'T' meets both defining conditions of 'observation term' and does not meet either sufficient condition of 'theoretical term,' e.g. 'water.'

B. 'T' is a theory laden observation term $=$ df. 'T' meets the first but not the second defining condition of 'observation term,' and there is a nonempirical theoretical term 'P' such that 'There is a T (T thing)' entails 'There is a P (P thing),' e.g. 'conglomeration of H_2O molecules.'

C. 'T' is an observational theoretical term $=$ df. 'T' is a theoretical term that meets the first defining condition of 'observation term,' e.g. 'conglomeration of H_2O molecules' and 'pressure.'

D. 'T' is a nonobservational theoretical term $=$ df. 'T' is a theoretical term that does not meet the first defining condition of 'observation term,' e.g. 'neutrino' and 'pain.'

E. 'T' is a pure theoretical term $=$ df. 'T' is a theoretical term which fails to meet the first defining condition of 'observation term' and of 'phenomenal term,' and which is not definable by observation terms or phenomenal terms, e.g. 'neutrino' and 'proton.'

We can illustrate some of the more usual kinds of theoretical identity statements. Examples of pure observation term–observational theoretical term identity statements are:

> Each body of water is identical with a conglomeration of H_2O molecules.

and:

> Each amount of the lightest gas is identical with a volume of the element an ion of which is present in all acids.

Both statements are also examples of pure observation term–theory laden observation term statements. There are also identity statements with two observational theoretical terms, with two nonobservational (but not pure) theoretical terms, and with two pure theoretical terms. An example of the first is:

> Each volume of the element an ion of which is present in all acids is identical with a volume of atoms each consisting of one proton and one electron.

An example of the second kind requires theoretico-reporting terms that are not observation terms. We can use sensation terms as an example:

> Each sensation of pain is identical with a sensation in a one-to-one simultaneity correspondence with a firing of C-fibers.

We can illustrate an identity statement with two pure theoretical terms by:

> Each atom of the element an ion of which is present in all acids is identical with an atom that consists of one proton and one electron.

The Classification of Temperature–Mean-Kinetic-Energy Identity Statements

The task confronting us now is to classify theoretical identity statement (2) as precisely as possible. To do so, we must classify individually the two expressions flanking 'is identical with.' Let us first consider 'the temperature of a gas.' The crucial word here is 'temperature,' because the only other nonlogical term, 'gas,' is, as it is used here, a pure observation term. We should classify 'temperature' the same as we previously classified 'pressure,'

that is, as an observational theoretical term. We can be more
precise than this, however, and call both of them observation
terms and also theoretical terms, because they meet *both* defining conditions of 'observation term' and the second sufficient
condition of 'theoretical term.' Both terms are often classed as
theoretical terms because they occur in quantitative formulas
such as $PV = kT$, and because they are measured by means of
instruments.[2] We previously used similar reasoning to classify
them as theoretical (see the discussion of theoretical terms in
Chap. 2). As we have seen, physical science explains generalizations by means of mathematical deductions from theoretical
statements, and explains particular observable phenomena by
mathematical deductions from the explained generalizations.
Physical science, then, explains a particular phenomenon by
using terms to describe the phenomenon and to formulate
generalizations that are quantitative. The term 'temperature' is
introduced to formulate generalizations such as $PV = kT$ which
are an integral part of the scientific explanation of some of the
observable behavior of gases. Thus 'temperature,' like other
quantitative terms, is introduced into the scientific vocabulary to
explain the behavior of observable phenomena by generalizations. Because of this, 'temperature' meets the second sufficient
condition for being a theoretical term.

   For many, once a term is classified as theoretical it cannot also
be called an observation term, but we have decided against such
a dichotomy. The term 'temperature' (and 'pressure' also) is an
observation term. It is, of course, true that standard observers
do not see the temperature of something, but we do not observe
only with our eyes. Temperature is the degree of heat of something and this we can feel. Someone might object that we cannot
feel that the temperature of a room is 72° because we must use
a thermometer to decide this. We can grant this. Yet we can feel
that the temperature has dropped or risen, or that it is relatively
high or low. And we can feel the temperature or degree of heat
of a room even if we cannot feel that it is some specific degree.
We can conclude, then, that some temperatures of gases such as
air are observable, by feeling them, by any standard observer
when he is in conditions standard for feeling temperatures of

   2. Cf. P. Achinstein, "The Problem of Theoretical Terms," *American
Philosophical Quarterly* 2 (1965): 195–203.

such a gas. Thus 'temperature' meets the first defining condition of 'observation term,' which is enough to conclude it is an observational theoretical term. But 'temperature' also meets the second defining condition. For any contingent sentence of the form 'Something (is a *P*, has *P*)' entailed by 'Something has temperature,' it is true that under standard conditions some physical (*P*, instance of *P*) would appear in some way to any standard observer (see p. 69).

Let us turn to classifying the phrase 'the mean kinetic energy of the molecules of a gas.' In this case, the crucial expression for deciding whether this phrase meets the first condition of 'observation term' and thus whether it is an observational theoretical term is 'mean kinetic energy.' Whether or not someone perceives the average kinetic energy of a group of entities depends on whether it is identical with something perceivable, such as a gas temperature. If it is not identical with something such as a temperature, then it is not perceivable, because no group of things with a certain average kinetic energy of the group results in the average kinetic energy of the group appearing in some way to a standard observer under standard conditions. Thus whether the phrase 'the average kinetic energy of the molecules of a gas' meets the first defining condition of 'observation term' depends on whether temperatures are identical with mean kinetic energies. If they should be identical, as we have assumed, then the phrase would meet the first condition of 'observation term.' It fails to meet the second condition, however, because 'There is a molecule' fails to meet condition (1). Because 'molecules' and 'kinetic energy' are theoretical terms by the second sufficient condition, 'the average kinetic energy of the molecules of a gas' is theoretical. Assuming the identities, the phrase is, then, an observational theoretical term, and is therefore not a pure theoretical term. Furthermore, it does not meet the first condition of 'phenomenal term,' because 'All mean kinetic energies of gases exist when and only when sensed' is false. With this information we are ready to classify temperature–mean-kinetic-energy identity statements, such as statement (2). They are theoretical identity statements that have flanking the identity sign one term that is both an observation term and a theoretical term, and another that is an observational theoretical term, but is neither an observation term nor a phenomenal term. We need now only classify the sensation–brain-process identity statement (3) before comparing (2) and (3).

THE CLASSIFICATION OF SENSATION–BRAIN-PROCESS IDENTITY STATEMENTS

The job of classifying the sensation–brain-process identity statement (3) is partly done, for we have already classified sensation terms and, a fortiori, 'sensation of pain' as theoretico-reporting terms. It is also clearly a phenomenal term for it meets both defining conditions of 'phenomenal term' (see p. 81). Furthermore, as we have seen, 'sensation of pain' is not an observation term, because it fails to meet the second defining condition stated for 'observation term.' It would, however, meet the first condition if it proved to be identical with some observable physical process. Thus, on the assumption that (3) states the correct identity relationship for sensations of pain, whether or not 'sensation of pain' is an observational theoretical term depends on whether or not 'firing of C-fibers of the nerve cells of a brain' meets the first defining condition of 'observation term.'

It is clear that 'firing of C-fibers of the nerve cells of a brain' is a theoretical term. It is an explanatory term of the science of physiology and is introduced into the scientific vocabulary to help explain the transmission of nerve impulses in the brain, which in turn helps explain observable human behavior. It is clearly not a phenomenal term. Even if such firings are identical with sensations of pain and consequently exist when and only when sensed, they are physical, and thus 'firing of C-fibers' fails to meet condition (2). It would, however, meet condition (1) if there are the appropriate identities. The only questions remaining are whether this is an observation term, or, if not, whether it at least meets the first defining condition of 'observation term.' It fails to meet the first condition. Although some brain processes are observable, and although firings of C-fibers might be proper stimuli of standard perceivers if they can be recorded on instruments attached to the skull, no such firings would be proper *observation* stimuli that appear in some way to standard observers. An instrument would be needed to transmit something that directly stimulates the sense organ if something is to appear as a result. Thus 'firing of C-fibers of the nerve cells of a brain' is a nonobservational theoretical term, and it would also be a pure theoretical term if such firings should be found not to be identical with any sensations.

We can now conclude that sensation–brain-process identity statements, such as (3), are theoretical identity statements with one term that is a phenomenal term and a theoretico-reporting term, and with another term that is a nonobservational theoretical term and would be a pure theoretical term if no brain processes should be identical with sensations. With this settled we can pass on to a comparison of the two kinds of identity statements.

SIMILARITIES BETWEEN THE TWO KINDS
OF IDENTITY STATEMENTS

Let us first concentrate on the similarities. Both kinds of statements are theoretical identity statements with one term that is a pure theoretical term unless certain identities obtain, and one nonpure theoretical term. And, in both cases, it is the entities referred to by the nonpure theoretical term that are to be reduced to the entities referred to by the "pure" theoretical term. One difference, which we will consider later, is that 'temperature' is an observation term, but 'sensation' is a phenomenal term and also a theoretico-reporting term. This difference uncovers another similarity, because it is surely reasonable to construe all observation terms as reporting terms, that is, as terms used to make identifying reference to entities we are, or recently were, aware of. Thus we can classify both 'sensation' and 'temperature' as theoretico-reporting terms.

There is another relevant similarity. In Chapter 1, we concluded that sensation–brain-process identity statements are cross-category statements. Although we discussed the meaningless sentences that result from interchanging 'temperature of a gas *G*' with 'mean kinetic energy of the molecules of gas *G*' in Chapter 1, we did not show that temperature–mean-kinetic-energy identity statements are cross-category statements. We can do this by again using the principle:

$$\{(\exists X)[U(AX)\cdot N(BX)]\cdot(\exists Y)[U(BY)\cdot N(AY)]\} \supset D(AB)$$

and letting A = temperature of a gas, B = mean kinetic energy of the molecules of a gas, $X = 27°$ centigrade, and Y = an average number of ergs. This satisfies the sufficient condition of the preceding principle from which we can infer that 'temperature of a gas' and 'mean kinetic energy of the molecules of a gas' are in different logical categories. Thus temperature–mean-kinetic-energy identity statements are cross-category identity statements.

There is another important likeness that philosophers do not establish but which is essential. For each instance of a specific gas temperature, there is at the same time one specific mean kinetic energy of the gas molecules. That is, there is not only a one-to-one simultaneity correspondence between each particular instance of temperature and some mean kinetic energy, but there is also such a correspondence between certain kinds (amounts) of temperature and certain kinds (amounts) of mean kinetic energy. Although, as we saw in Chapter 1, a correspondence of kinds is not entailed by the mind–body identity theory we are considering, it is essential for scientific reduction, because without such a correspondence there are no laws, without laws there are no theoretical explanations of observable phenomena, and without theoretical explanations there are no theoretical reductions. Because only scientists establish whether such a correspondence of kinds obtains between sensations and certain brain processes but have not done so yet, we can only assume, in line with advances in science, that there is this similarity. This is what we shall do.

DIFFERENCES BETWEEN THE TWO KINDS OF IDENTITY STATEMENTS

The preceding are important similarities between the two kinds of identity statements we are considering. They give us initial reason to conclude that they are further alike in that if one is a plausible theoretical identity statement, then the other is also. We have not shown these grounds to be sufficient, however, because we have not examined whether there are important differences which would provide overbalancing counterreasons. We have already noted one difference: 'temperature' is an observation term, but 'sensation' is a phenomenal term. But this difference, rather than hindering the reduction of sensations to brain processes, would seem to help it. If the temperature of a certain gas, a phenomenon that can be experienced by many through observation, can be reduced to something that is a pure theoretical entity, then, ceteris paribus, reduction of a sensation,

experienced by only one and theoretical for all others, to something that is a pure theoretical entity should be at least as
reasonable.

There is another difference, related to the preceding difference, that is also helpful. The role of 'temperature' in scientific
explanations differs from the role of 'sensation.' The term 'temperature of a gas' is used both to explain and to describe observable behavior of gases. That is, 'temperature of a gas' is
used to describe certain observable phenomena and to explain
these phenomena through its link to the mean kinetic energy of
gas molecules. But 'sensation of pain' is not used to describe
observable behavior that is to be explained, because it is a nonobservational theoretical term. Its function in explanation is
more like that of 'mean kinetic energy of gas molecules' which
is used to explain but not to describe observable phenomena.
Consequently, if, as many people think will happen, physiology
develops to such a point that sensation terms are not needed to
explain observable behavior, which is the subject matter of science, then the reduction of sensations of pain to what takes over
their explanatory role, perhaps the firing of C-fibers, is more
plausible than if sensation terms also had the role of describing
observable phenomena.[3]

So far we have found several similarities and two differences
between sensations and temperatures, all of which provide reason to think that the first analogy that we are examining between
the two is a close one. There are, however, differences which
count against the analogy and, consequently, against the theoretical reduction of sensations. One difference is that the kinds
of entities involved in the sensation–brain-process reductions are
different from those in the temperature–mean-kinetic-energy reduction. While in the latter case certain instances of properties
of gases are being reduced to instances of other properties, in the
former certain objects are being reduced to certain events or
processes. One question this raises is whether differences between
objects and properties make the analogy too weak to support the
conclusion that sensations are theoretically reducible. This
would occur if it destroyed either of the two analogies we are
considering, but I do not find that it does. As discussed in Chap-

3. See the discussion of the postulation elimination theory, Chapter 4,
for an argument very similar to this.

ter 1, theoretical identity claims about two entities are justified by showing they have all the same properties, especially the same theoretical properties. This is true of gas temperatures as well as gases. In addition, the theoretical reduction of temperatures of gases to mean kinetic energies of gas molecules is justified by showing that the extentional properties of whatever the temperature of a gas really is either are or are reducible to those reductive properties ascribable to it within the kinetic theory of gases. Thus the crucial points in both of our analogies concern the properties of whatever is being reduced, whether or not what is being reduced is itself a property or something else. Therefore, for our purposes I see no damage to either analogy.

A DAMAGING DIFFERENCE: REDUCING OBJECTS TO EVENTS

There is an importantly damaging difference related to the preceding one. In the temperature reduction case, the reduced and reducing items are the same kind of entity, instances of properties, but in the sensation case they are not. In the latter case, objects or individuals are being reduced to processes or events. One problem that arises is whether there has been a scientifically justified case of reducing an object to an event or process. If there has been no such reduction, then there is reason to reject the sensation-reduction claim. A more serious problem, however, is that the property objection to the identity theory rearises. It will be remembered that in Chapter 1 the property objection to the identity theory was avoided by using a category principle implying that only high and relatively high predicates are meaningfully ascribable to both sensations and brain processes, and by assuming that each high or relatively high extentional predicate is jointly true or jointly false of sensations and brain processes. But we have just found two relatively high predicates, 'event' and 'object,' each true of one but false of the other. Thus, using version D of the principle of the nonidentity of discernibles (p. 52), it would seem we can conclude that no sensations and brain processes are identical, and so sensations are not reducible to firings of C-fibers.

It might be replied at this point that we cannot use principle D because both being an event and being an object are intentional and therefore are not extentional properties. For example, 'The Holy Grail is an object' is true but neither it nor its denial entails that there is such an object. We can sidestep the problems for formal logic this reply raises by using the predicates 'occurring event' and 'existing object' instead, because they clearly are extentional. I do not know how to avoid this problem without changing the category principle so that no predicate except high predicates are meaningfully ascribable to entities of different categories. But this would make the category principle clearly false because 'object' is not a high predicate, yet it is meaningfully ascribable to both stones and numbers, which are entities of different categories. And, of course, it will not help to save this revised category principle by construing 'event' and 'object' as high predicates, because then the property objection arises using high predicates and the revised category principle.

One way someone might try to avoid both of the preceding problems is to point out that physics may ultimately become a pure process science in which all physical objects are reduced to certain locations in the ongoing spatiotemporal continuous process which makes up the physical universe. It would turn out that a chair is really a spatiotemporal set of events, events that are not happenings to objects, but are merely certain parts of one continuous process. If, then, an object such as a chair turns out to be a bundle of events or processes, might not an object such as a sensation of pain also turn out to be a bundle of events such as firings of C-fibers?

One difficulty with this reply is that it requires objectless events, and firings of C-fibers require C-fibers which are objects or individuals. This problem can be overcome by claiming that pains are identical with those objectless events to which firings of C-fibers are reducible. A more serious problem is that, although all objects would turn out to be merely certain locations in a spatiotemporal continuum, the reduction of an observable object, such as a chair, to such a theoretical location is through the intermediate identification of the chair with a collection of "provisionally basic" particles, each one an object. Then each particle would be reduced, perhaps to a particular quantum of energy, and spatiotemporal changings of energy would be taken as constituting the continuous spatiotemporal process that makes up the physical universe. The relevant point here is that for an object to be reduced to processes and events in this way, and I know of no other, it seems it must be first reduced to, or at least be identifiable with, a group of "basic" particles. But although C-fibers may be identifiable with a group of particles, neither a firing of C-fibers, nor any other event that is a happening to an object, is so identifiable. Thus, although all may be process, only certain parts of such a process would be identifiable with objects, and none of these parts are identical with processes that are events happening to objects such as brains.

A way to avoid the two problems:
Reducing sensations to parts of brains

There is a way to avoid both problems generated by trying to reduce objects to events that the preceding discussion of C-fibers, particles, and process suggests. Why not identify each sensation of pain, not with the firing of C-fibers, but with firing C-fibers just as a gas is identified with rapidly moving molecules instead of the rapid movement of molecules? Each sensation, such as a pain or an afterimage, would be identical with some part of the brain, such as certain nerve fibers, when that part is in some state. On this view, both reduced and reducing entities are objects, and the preceding problems are avoided. Also the similarities and helpful differences between the temperature case and the sensation case remain. Consequently, unless some additional problem arises, the comparison of the two cases seems to support the claim that the theoretical identity of pains and firing C-fibers and, similarly, the theoretical identity of other sensations and parts of brains when in certain states are the right sort for the theoretical reduction of sensations to physical phenomena.

One problem that might confront this object–object identity view is a reborn property objection, because although mental *objects* and physical *events* might well be in different logical categories, mental objects and physical objects might be in the same category. If they are in the same category then the identity claim, and consequently the reduction claim, seem quite dubious. Some afterimages are yellowish-orange, fading, dim, circular, and homogeneous, but no brain parts such as nerve fibers seem to have these phenomenal properties. Furthermore, the spatial location problem might be raised again. A toothache is in a tooth and it cannot also be in the brain where C-fibers are located. The latter problem, however, might be solved even without relying on putting mental and physical objects in different categories. It is plausible to argue that whereas the 'in' of the sentence 'C-fibers are *in* the brain' is to be unpacked as 'located spatially within the volume of,' the 'in' of 'A toothache is *in* a tooth' is rather 'experienced as located spatially within the volume of.' Thus a toothache could both be in (experienced as in) a tooth and in (spatially) a brain. The problem with the phenomenal properties of sensations, however, is not to be handled so easily.

A problem for reducing sensations to parts of brains: Homogeneous red sensa: Phenomenal properties play a central role in an argument by W. Sellars against identifying sensa with theoretical entities. For example, a red sense impression has the property of being "ultimately homogeneous," but brain parts, being conglomerations of scientifically basic theoretical particles, lack that property, and, therefore, according to Sellars, no sensations are brain parts and the identity theory is false. As a result the theoretical reduction of sensation also fails. He says that the "feature which we referred to as 'ultimate homogeneity' and which characterizes the perceptible qualities of things, e.g., their colour, seems to be essentially lacking in the domain of the definable states of nerves and their interactions" (*SPR,* p. 35).[4] This way of putting his objection makes it seem to depend on the argument that because each macro part of a brain is composed of discrete particles and is thus discontinuous, no macro part of the brain has any homogeneous property. This is a weak argument, because if each of a group of discrete particles were the same color, then it would certainly seem the macro entity they constitute would have the property of appearing homogeneously colored to normal perceivers under normal conditions. And this, it is plausible to argue, is one clear meaning of the claim that a physical object *is* homogeneously colored. What is important, however, is not that homogeneity is lacking if brain parts are composed of discrete particles, but that none of the discrete constituent particles is colored. Indeed, Sellars says that "it doesn't make sense to say of the particles of physical theory that they are coloured" (*SPR,* p. 35). Consequently, argues Sellars, because if none of the particles are colored then no group of

4. All references to Sellars in this discussion which are to *Science, Perception and Reality,* I shall abbreviate as *SPR.*

them is colored, no expanse consisting of such particles is a homogeneous or even a heterogeneous colored expanse. Thus no red sense impressions are identical with a section of a brain.

An immediate objection to this argument can be raised against the premise that if none of the constituent particles of something is colored, then the thing itself is not colored. But why could not some group have a property none of its constituents have, especially if, as seems reasonable, we construe being colored as appearing colored to a normal perceiver under normal conditions? Sellars is aware of this objection to which he replies,

> It does not seem plausible to say that for a system of particles to be a pink ice cube is for them to have such and such imperceptible qualities, and to be so related to one another as to make up an approximate cube. *Pink* does not seem to be made up of imperceptible qualities in the way in which being a ladder is made up of being cylindrical (the rungs), rectangular (the frame), wooden, etc. The manifest ice cube presents itself to us as something which is pink through and through, as a pink continuum, all the regions of which, however small, are pink (*SPR,* p. 26).

But this answer will not do, because the only reason Sellars gives for denying that a thing can be actually colored when its imperceptible constituents are not is that the relationship between pink expanses and imperceptible particles seems different from the relationship between ladders and their parts. Furthermore, if to be homogeneously colored is to appear so to a normal perceiver under normal conditions, then whatever "presents itself to us as *ultimately homogeneous*" in color (*SPR,* p. 26) is indeed both homogeneous and colored, whether or not physical objects consist of discrete colorless particles.

A defense of Sellars' argument: A principle of reducibility: To defend his claim, Sellars adopts a principle of reducibility that seems to achieve his aim, but, as he says later, he accepts it without argument (*SPR,* p. 35). The principle is:

> R1. If an object is *in a strict sense* a system of objects, then every property of the object must consist in the fact that its constituents have such and such qualities and stand in such and such relations or, roughly, every

property of a system of objects consists of properties of, and relations between, its constituents (*SPR*, p. 27).

Sellars goes on to conclude, "With something like this principle in mind, it was argued that if a physical object is *in a strict sense* a system of imperceptible particles, then it cannot as a whole have the perceptible qualities characteristic of physical objects in the manifest image" (*SPR*, p. 27). To get to this conclusion and the refutation of the identity theory based on it, Sellars seems to interpret the principle as:

R2. For any object, *O,* that is a system of objects, if *O* has a kind of property, *K,* then *K* is a kind of property the individual constituents of *O* have.

This interpretation of the principle is too strong, however, because it is falsified by, among others, the property of having such and such a temperature. Groups of molecules of a gas have a property of this kind, but none of the individual basic scientific particles that constitute a gas have such a property.

In order to accommodate cases like the temperature example, which surely should be done, a different version of the principle of reducibility is required. Sellars has very recently pointed out that he rejects R2 because of its reference to any kind of property, but he seems to accept it when amended to refer only to those kinds of properties that are expressed by primitive, or undefined, predicates.[5] We can express such a principle by talking of predicates instead of properties as follows:

R2a. For any object, *O,* that is a system of objects, if a primitive predicate of kind *K* is true of *O,* then some predicate of kind *K* is true of the individual constituents of *O.*

The point of this change seems to be that while 'is homogeneously colored' is primitive but 'has a rising temperature' is not primitive, the preceding objection fails. Thus something can have a rising temperature without its constituents having a rising temperature, but nothing can be homogeneously colored with-

5. See Sellars, "Science, Sense Impressions and Sensa: A Reply to Common," *Review of Metaphysics* 24 (1971): 423.

out its parts also being colored. However, there seems to be no reason to require this of colors but not of temperatures. These observable properties seem equally reducible or irreducible. Part of the reason for this may be that the observation term 'temperature' seems no more or less definable than the observation term 'color'. Thus R2a, as much as R2, seems to founder because of its inability to construe rising temperatures but not homogeneous colors as reducible.

Following my previous discussion of reduction, I would suggest an interpretation of R1 which can accommodate the reducibility of temperature and seems quite close to the sense of R1:

> R3. For any object, O, that is nothing but a system of objects, if O has a property, P, of kind K, than either K is a kind of property the individual constituents of O have, or O's instance of P is nothing but an instance of a property of or relation among at least some of the individual constituents of O.

There is one difference between R3 and R1, which is not relevant to our present purpose, but which should be noted because it reflects a point crucial to several arguments throughout the book. R3 does not state that property P is reducible to or nothing but some other property or relation, but that O's instance of P is so reducible. To reduce a gas to a certain group of molecules certainly requires that each particular instance of temperature of the gas be reduced to some particular instance of mean kinetic energy of gas molecules. If R3 is correct, however, this reduction of a gas does not require that the property of having a certain temperature be reduced to the property of having a certain mean kinetic energy unless identity of instances entails identity of properties. But I think this entailment does not hold. For example, there are cases where one instance of someone's being killed is identical with an instance of being shot, but, clearly, the property of being killed is not identical with the property of being shot. It might be that each instance of being killed turns to be an instance of being shot, but still the two properties would be distinct.

Because R3 accommodates the temperature example, but neither R2 nor R2a does, Sellars should construe R1 as R3.

But if he does that, then his preceding argument that sensations are not identical with any physical objects fails, because R3, unlike R2 and R2a, is compatible with something appearing homogeneously red being reducible to some brain phenomenon consisting of certain scientifically basic physical particles having some quite different kind of property.

Another problem for reducing sensations to brain parts: The colors of brains and of some sensations differ: Although we have found reason to reject Sellars' argument that phenomenal properties refute the theoretical *identity* of sensa and brain parts, it should be noted that we have still to examine whether phenomenal properties refute theoretical *reduction* of sensations. Before we turn to this, however, let us consider one more objection that might seem to refute the theoretical identity of sensations and brain parts. If a sensation is identical with a brain part, both have all the same extentional properties. But some sensa, such as afterimages, are yellow, and no brain part is yellow. Therefore at least some sensations are not identical with brain phenomena. This argument, suitably supplemented, appears decisive for a naïve realist who rejects category distinctions and thus agrees that the same color terms are applicable to both physical objects and sensations. It does not, however, affect a scientific realist such as Sellars. For such a naïve realist, each brain part has one occurrent sensuous color which is a nonrelational property, and which, while it is the color that appears to a normal perceiver in normal observation conditions, is not to be analyzed as so appearing. But the brain parts which are candidates for identity with yellow afterimages are not yellow because that color does not normally appear to those who observe brains. And nothing both is and is not occurrently yellow in this sense. The scientific realist, however, can claim that brain parts are physically colored in the sense that is to be analyzed as appearing a certain color to normal observers in normal conditions. But a sensation is not yellow in this sense, because if it appears at all, it appears as a brain phenomenon and thus does not appear yellow to normal observers in normal conditions. Thus on this view it is possible that one entity is "sensation-yellow," that is, yellow in a naïve realistic sense, and is not "physical-yellow" at the same time. Consequently this second objection to identifying sensations with brain parts has no force for a scientific realist such as Sellars. However, as we have seen, a naïve realist can avoid it only by employing category distinctions.

Fortunately for the naïve realist it seems meaningless to talk of rapidly firing sensations and aching or fading brain parts, and thus we can again use the criterion of category difference (p. 57) to conclude that sensation terms and brain-part terms are in different logical categories. This might be used to justify the ambiguity of 'in' because its function in pain sentences differs from its function in physicalistic sentences. This reinforces the preceding attempt to refute the spatial location objection as applied to pains and firing C-fibers. It also has the consequence that 'yellow,' 'sweet,' 'loud,' 'smooth,' and the like are different when used with sensation terms from when used with physicalistic terms.[6] Of course there are important similarities especially for a naïve realist. Indeed, the similarities may be so great on his view that even with the category distinction, it is false that one entity is "sensation-yellow" but not "physical-yellow." Rather than resolve this problem, however, let us accept a conception of physical color like that of a scientific realist. This guarantees the compatibility. We are interested here in theoretical reduction and that entails at least a minimal form of scientific realism (defined in Chap. 7). For such a view the physical color of brain parts poses no problem for identifying the parts with sensa.

CONCLUSION ABOUT THE THEORETICAL IDENTITY
OF SENSATIONS AND BRAIN PARTS

We have reached the point where we can draw a conclusion about the strength of the first analogy between sensations and temperatures. Once we adjusted the identity claim to one identifying pains with brain parts, we found no damaging differences between sensation–brain-part identity statements and temperature–mean-kinetic-energy theoretical identity statements. Consequently, because the latter are the kind we find in one of the most plausible examples of theoretical identity, we can conclude, by an analogical argument, that the former are the right kind for a plausible theoretical identification of sensations and brain phenomena—if, as we have been assuming, there are no

6. For two who agree with this consequence see R. Chisholm, *Perceiving*, pp. 126–37; and Sellars, pp. 47–49.

scientific objections to a correspondence of kinds which is essential for theoretical identity. On this assumption, theoretical identity seems acceptable. The question remaining is whether the additional claim of theoretical reduction can be accepted. This takes us to the second crucial comparison between sensations and temperature. Are the ways available to handle the observable properties of temperature that initially seem to thwart reduction also available for the phenomenal properties of sensations? I shall argue that neither they nor any other ways are available. There is an irreparable disanalogy between sensations and temperatures, indeed, between sensations and any of the most plausible candidates for reduction.

A CRUCIAL DIFFERENCE BETWEEN OBSERVABLE PROPERTIES
AND PHENOMENAL PROPERTIES

We are interested in the way that the fourth condition of theoretical reduction (p. 60) would be met in the reduction of temperatures of gases to the mean kinetic energy of gas molecules. That is, we are interested in the means available to accommodate extentional properties which initially seem to be properties of the reduced entities, temperatures, but which are not what I have called "reductive" properties of the reducing entities. In the case of gas temperatures, initially there clearly seem to be certain extentional properties of air temperatures which we feel, but which are neither what I have called s-properties (theoretical properties ascribed to the mean kinetic energy of air molecules within the kinetic theory of gases), nor micro-theoretical-neutral properties (see Intro.). The observable properties of being uncomfortably hot or cold are examples of extentional properties that seem to be true of air temperatures, but they are not reductive properties of the mean kinetic energy of air molecules. What can be done in this case is the same as what can be done by someone who wishes to establish the reduction of observable physical objects, such as water, to a conglomeration of theoretical entities, such as H_2O molecules. In both cases, the observable properties that we take to be properties of the air temperature or of water are no longer to be construed as properties of the physical entities. Rather they are construed as phenomenal properties of sensa caused in perceivers by that to which the temperature and water are said to be reduced. The claim would be that air temperatures really do not have those "observable" properties we seem to feel them to have. Thus, it is not that temperatures with felt properties would be reduced, but rather that they would be reduced only when stripped of these qualities. What we would feel would be sensations with certain properties caused in us by the kinetic energy of the air molecules. Similarly, water would not have the properties we directly experience. We would directly experience, as in tasting, certain sensa with certain phenomenal properties. Thus, by adopting something like a Lockean indirect realism, these phenomenal properties that are neither s-properties nor micro-neutral properties are stripped from temperature and water, and the fourth condition for theoretical reduction is met.

It is clear we cannot use the same treatment of those extentional phenomenal properties that seem to be properties of sensations but which are not materialistic properties of brain entities. No phenomenal properties of sensa, such as being aching, yellowish-orange, bitter, and loud, are materialistic properties of brain entities. But—here the analogy breaks down—these phenomenal properties experienced as properties of sensations cannot be "transferred" to sensations in order to eliminate the nonmaterialistic properties of sensations. This is a crucial disanalogy, because it is by "transferring" from air temperature and water the felt properties we attribute to them, that the reduction of the temperatures and water to theoretical entities is made acceptable. The analogy with temperature and water will not justify the theoretical reduction of sensations.

Are we now in a position to reject the claim that sensations are theoretically reducible to brain entities? As concluded at the end of Chapter 1, there seemed to be just one way to settle this issue and that is by comparing the theoretical reduction of sensations with a plausible case of theoretical reduction. But our comparison has led us to a vitally damaging disanalogy. We also concluded at the end of Chapter 1 that the only way that seems available to refute the property objection to combining the identity theory with materialism is by showing the plausibility of the theoretical reduction of sensations to brain phenomena. Consequently, it seems that we should reject reductive materialism.

I find only two ways that these conclusions might be avoided.

First, perhaps the phenomenal properties that sensations initially seem to have can be eliminated in some way which differs from the disposal of felt qualities in the temperature and water cases, and thus in spite of the crucial disanalogy with temperature and water, the case of sensation meets the fourth condition for theoretical reduction. Second, although we have taken the temperature and water cases as our models of theoretical reduction, it may be that there are different examples which are equally good models, and which provide some way to meet the fourth condition without transferring phenomenal properties from sensations. At least the possibility of such a reduction is countenanced in condition (4c) which allows for the reduction of instances of nonreductive properties. Our last task, then, in examining reductive materialism, will be to see whether either of these last two attempts to save reductive materialism succeeds.

Rejection of the three ways to dispose
of phenomenal properties

There are only three ways to dispose of the phenomenal properties that sensations seem to have: (1) transfer the phenomenal properties to something other than sensations, (2) show that neither sensations nor anything else have phenomenal properties, and (3) show that there really are no sensations and thus there is nothing to have phenomenal properties. Alternative (1) can quickly be rejected, and (3) is not available for a reductive materialist. Not only can I find nothing to which the phenomenal properties of sensations can be transferred, but even if there were something, it would as a result have nonmaterialistic properties and materialism would be false. A reductive materialist must either eliminate or reduce phenomenal properties. It may be that they can be eliminated by eliminating what has them, sensations, as in (3), but although in Parts II and III we shall examine in detail attempts to do this, this move is not available to a reductive materialist. To eliminate sensations is not to identify and reduce them to something physical as is required by reductive materialism.

Alternative (2) is no more promising. It requires that no matter what nonphenomenal properties sensations might have, e.g. those properties discoverable only by the detailed investigations of neurophysiologists, no sensations have any of the phenomenal properties they are experienced to have by the person who has the sensation. Whatever pains turn out to be, none are aching or throbbing; no sounds are loud; no tastes are bitter; no afterimages are yellow. I know of no way to establish, or even make plausible, such an initially implausible thesis. It could be made plausible if sensation terms were pure theoretical terms which express either functional states or causes which intervene between stimulus and resulting behavior, but whose intrinsic properties will come to be uncovered only as the scientific theories using the terms in explanations develop. Thus on this view all sensations might turn out to be nothing but states of central nervous systems, because those states have those functions or are, in fact, those causes. Both the central state and functional state theories are implausible, however, if there are sensa as number (2) requires.[7] Some sensation terms would be reporting terms that we would use to report sensa and their phenomenal properties we experience. At least those properties would not await the development of theory.

Notice that this view differs from the thesis mentioned in Chapter 1 that when science has reached a certain point, a person will no longer be the final authority about whether or not he has a certain sensation, such as a yellow afterimage. The present thesis requires that no afterimage a person has is ever yellow, no matter what he believes or science establishes about the correlates of brain entities, because nothing has such a phenomenal property. Unlike the previous claim, the present one is not at all supported by the scientific ideal of a complete catalogue of lawful relationships between sensations and brain entities. Indeed, the claim in Chapter 1 is established only if it is shown that there are yellow afterimages, throbbing pains, loud sounds when and only when physical correlates exist. But the present claim must reject that there are such correlations, just the correlations science seems to be discovering. We should, therefore, reject (2), the last alternative, as a viable way to dispose of phenomenal properties. Consequently we can conclude that there is no way to dispose of the phenomenal properties that

7. For examples of central state theories, see D. Armstrong, *A Materialist Theory of Mind* (London: Routledge and Kegan Paul, 1968); and D. Lewis, "An Argument for the Identity Theory," *Journal of Philosophy* LXII (1966): 17–25.

sensations seem to have, and that the analogy with the theoretical reductions of temperature and water is irreparably damaged. If we are to show that the theoretical reduction of sensations to brain parts is plausible, it will have to be by analogy with a different example.

Rejection of the reduction of sensations with phenomenal properties

Although we are not justified in admitting that there are sensations while eliminating phenomenal properties, it may be that we can find an example of theoretical reduction where instances of troublesome properties are theoretically reduced to instances of acceptable properties. This is one possible kind of theoretical reduction taken into account in the fourth condition of the definition of theoretical reduction (p. 60). As previously argued, this kind of reduction does not entail a reduction of the properties involved. Thus an argument to show that two properties are not identical and, consequently, that one is not reducible to the other, would not disprove such a theoretical reduction.

The question before us is whether the reduction of a sensation having a phenomenal property to some brain part having a materialistic property can be made plausible by comparison with some plausible theoretical reduction. Once again a helpful example is one involving temperatures of gases, but this time we shall be interested in the reduction of a gas having a certain temperature to the molecules of the gas having a certain mean kinetic energy. This is a case in which an entity is theoretically reduced *with* a property rather than a case in which the property is transferred from the entity to something else. Thus it is importantly different from the reductions of gas temperatures and water. If the sensation case can be shown to be analogous to the gas case, the theoretical reduction of sensations may be made plausible and the objection to reductive materialism refuted.

At first glance the analogy seems quite close, because in addition to all the previously shown similarities between the sensation case and the temperature case, there is also the fact that both sensations and gases are objects and that in both cases the properties which raise problems are properties we report. Nevertheless, once again there are crucial disanalogies which derive in part from the one we have previously noted. In the case of the theoretical reduction of gases with their temperatures we find, first, that each instance of gas temperature is reduced as well, and, second, that this is justified by claiming that the felt qualities which seem to be properties of the gas temperatures are really properties of sensations. But neither move is at all plausible for sensations with phenomenal properties. The first is implausible because it entails that each instance of a phenomenal property of a sensation is identical with some instance of a physical or physical-neutral property of a brain part. But it is initially evident that instances of bitterness of taste, loudness of sound, phenomenal color of afterimages, and the throbbing of pains are not identical with instances of physical properties or of physical-neutral properties, and I find no way to overturn this weight of evidence. Furthermore, we have seen that Smart's attempt to reduce the property of being a yellowish-orange afterimage to a physical-neutral property fails (see the discussion of the property objection in Chap. 1), and I can find no other way to accomplish such a task.

Part of the implausibility of the first move derives from the second disanalogy. Those purported felt qualities of temperatures that would thwart the reduction of gas temperatures to the mean kinetic energy of molecules and the reduction of gases with temperatures to groups of molecules with only reductive properties, can be transferred to sensations. But there is no way to transfer the nonmaterialistic properties of phenomenal properties, such as the shimmering quality of the redness of a sensation. Consequently just as we saw no way to eliminate the phenomenal properties of sensations so that sensations could be reduced to brain parts, so also we find no way to eliminate properties of the phenomenal properties of sensations so that the phenomenal properties of sensations would be reduced. And, just as the analogy of sensations with temperature fails, so also does the analogy of sensations with gases fail.

Conclusion about Reductive Materialism and Foreword to Eliminative Materialism

We have rejected all the ways a reductive materialist might try to rid himself of the problem posed by phenomenal properties of sensations. Each one is either unjustified or leads to results a reductive materialist cannot accept. But we found that some way to dispose of this problem is required if the reduction of sensations to brain parts is to be plausible. The conclusion we have reached, consequently, is that, whether or not sensations are identical with brain parts, they are not reducible to brain parts, because sensations carry with them nonreducible phenomenal properties. Thus reductive materialism, which requires such a reduction, is itself unjustified and should be rejected. We have found, however, no reason to reject the identity theory, and, thus far, no reason to reject eliminative materialism. Indeed we have concluded that there seem to be no philosophical objections to the identity theory once it is amended to state that sensations such as afterimages and pains are identical with brain parts rather than brain processes. What we have found reason to reject is combining the identity theory with materialism. It also seems plausible to conclude, by like reasoning, that we should reject combining the identity theory with idealism or phenomenalism. Thus not only are reductive materialists mistaken, but so also is someone like Feigl who conjoins the identity theory with the claim that the common referent of sensation terms and certain physiological terms are "raw feels." That is, Feigl is mistaken if, as it seems, he construes raw feels as uninterpreted, unconceptualized entities with only phenomenal properties.[8] Perhaps only a double aspect or neutral theory that ascribes both phenomenal properties and physiological properties to whatever it is that 'sensation' and 'brain part' jointly denote escapes unscathed.

To reject "reductive idealism" in this way is not, of course, to reject "eliminative idealism." But I am not sure how one might justify it, because those ways available for justifying eliminative materialism, which in Part II we shall find to be most plausible, depend on the replacement of sensations in explanations by brain entities that explain in the physical sciences the same observable behavior that sensations explain. But there is

---

8. Someone might try to support Feigl, however, by adopting scientific instrumentalism (see Chap. 7) and pointing out that the most plausible candidates for identity with sensations are theoretical brain parts. Consequently the theoretical terms used to explain the behavior of these entities do not express their properties, and the entities have only phenomenal properties.

reason to deny that brain entities will be eliminated in favor of
sensations in a similar way, because, although in science explanatory physical entities often replace discarded nonphysical
explanatory entities, the converse is false. However, neither the
demise of reductive idealism nor the implausibility of eliminative
idealism are sufficient to justify the rejection of idealism, because
there remains a version unaffected by the preceding remarks.
The most plausible version of idealism I can find, and what I
believe is a fruitful reconstruction of Berkeley's ontological phenomenalism, is that each physical object is a conglomeration of
sense-data, not in the sense that the physical objects are logical
constructions out of sense-data, but rather that they are theoretical constructions out of sense-data.[9] That is, the relationship
between physical object sentences and sense-data sentences is
not analytic, as is claimed by the analytic phenomenalist, but
rather the contingent relationship that holds between theoretical
sentences and the relevant observation sentences. But discussing
this is a matter for another time. The point relevant to our present purposes is that a materialist must reject the reductive version of his thesis if he is to resist refutation.

Eliminative materialism and adverbial materialism remain to
be examined. We shall consider the former next. Although it
has not received as much attention as reductive materialism,
because the center of discussions has been the identity theory
which an eliminative theorist would deny, there have been recent
claims relevant to the elimination of sensations in the works of
Hempel, Ryle, Quine, and Rorty. Each of these men can be
taken to represent a distinct version of eliminative materialism.
What these views have in common, which makes them versions
of eliminative materialism, is the claim that there is no descriptive need for any sensation terms and so we are justified in concluding that there are no sensations. While phenomenal properties of sensations and thus sensations are not reducible to brain
phenomena, this is no problem for these views, because for them
there are no sensations and thus no phenomenal properties of

9. This is basically the position A. J. Ayer adopted after rejecting his
previous view that physical objects are logical constructions. See Ayer,
The Problem of Knowledge (Baltimore: Penguin Books, 1956), pp.
130–33. See also Cornman, "A Reconstruction of Berkeley: Minds and
Physical Objects as Theoretical Entities" (forthcoming *Ratio*).

sensations. What distinguishes each view from the other three is its reasons for claiming that there is no descriptive need for sensation terms. It will be our task in Part II to examine the different reasons these men supply for eliminating rather than reducing all sensations. We shall do this by stating and explicating the views of the first three men in Chapter 4. The versions of eliminative materialism which result will be quickly rejected. Rorty's version, however, requires a more detailed examination. This will constitute Chapter 5.

PART II

Eliminative Materialism

4. Three Versions of Eliminative Materialism

We have found reason to reject the attempt to identify sensations with and also reduce them to physical phenomena, but this does not cast doubt on the quite different approach to materialism which attempts to show that there really are no sensations. The quick objection to this claim is that we are obviously aware of phenomena such as pains, afterimages, and the data of our senses, which if not reduced to physical phenomena both exist and are mental. If there were only one version of eliminative materialism which flatly denied the truth of any sensation sentences that entail that there are sensations, then the theory could be quickly rejected. But, as we shall see, there are at least four others, none committed to such an implausible flat denial of sentences that seem to be true. Each differs importantly from this naïve version of eliminative materialism which we can characterize in the following way. Naïve eliminative materialism construes sensation terms on the model of pure observation terms. They are neither theoretical nor expressive terms. They are pure reporting terms, where reporting terms are those used to make identifying reference to what we are aware of. Consequently if certain sentences using sensation terms, such as 'ache,' are true, then there are pains and naïve eliminative materialism is refuted. It is because of this that the naïve view must claim that reports such as 'I have a toothache' are always false in spite of all our experiential evidence to the contrary. But this proves fatal to the naïve theory, because if sensation sentences are pure reports about what we are aware of, then there is nothing, including proof that sensation terms are not needed for explanation, to override the strong experiential evidence that there are toothaches. We can, therefore, quickly reject the theory.

None of the three versions of eliminative materialism that we shall examine in this chapter is open to such a quick refutation. All three sharply distinguish between pure observation terms and sensation terms, likening the latter more to theoretical terms, much as we have previously done. Two of the theories argue for the claim that sensation terms are not referring terms but have a different linguistic function. Thus we would not need to claim that 'I have a toothache' is always false to avoid being committed to the existence of pains. One of these theories is based on a behavioral analysis of sensation sentences, while the other is based on construing their function to be warranting inferences among observation sentences. The third theory agrees with the naïve theory that sensation terms are referring terms, but it construes them as a kind of theoretical term so different from pure reporting terms that the relevant kind of argument for eliminative materialism is not based on the evidence of experience which appears to falsify the theory, but is based instead upon reasons derived from the theoretical needs of science. Each of these theories, which I shall call respectively "analytical behaviorism," "Rylean behaviorism," and "the postulation elimination theory," has its own separate problems. We shall, then, examine each one separately.

ANALYTICAL BEHAVIORISM

Analytical behaviorism is the theory that all sentences using psychological or mentalistic terms are transformable by analysis of what they mean into sentences using no psychological terms, but containing only terms used to describe bodily behavior and bodily dispositions to behave. This theory, then, claims that although there are many true sentences using psychological terms, we do not have to infer from this that these terms refer to mental objects, events, and states, because we can reformulate every one of these sentences in such a way that we use only physicalistic terms. Consequently, the analytical behaviorist admits that sentences such as 'I like you,' 'Smith believes that it is raining,' and 'Jones suffers from inferiority feelings' are in many cases true, and therefore he is not committed to defending the implausible sentence 'There are no mental phenomena such as beliefs and feelings.' But having made this admission, he claims that he can still consistently be a materialist because to admit that a sentence is true is not to commit oneself to what it refers to. The analytical behaviorist who is a materialist says psychological sentences really refer to human bodily behavior, and he attempts to show this by the way he analyzes them. It may be, then, that by considering language, by "operating on a semantical plane," the eliminative materialist can avoid the predicament we saw facing the naïve eliminative materialist.

In discussing analytical behaviorism we are interested in the analysis of what certain linguistic expressions mean, and therefore we are interested in meaning analysis. This can be defined as the linguistic method that analyzes the meaning of a linguistic expression (the analysandum) in either of two ways. The first is by providing another linguistic expression (the analysans) synonymous with the analysandum. The second way is by providing expressions such that each is synonymous with certain key expressions containing the analysandum, and none contains any expression synonymous with the analysandum. The first kind of meaning analysis is explicit definition and the second is contextual definition. The distinction between these two is important because only the latter is relevant to analytical behaviorism, as some examples will show. We can give an explicit definition of 'human' by saying that 'human' equals by definition 'rational animal.' Examples of more complicated explicit definitions can be derived from the definitions in Chapter 2 of 'observation term' and 'theoretical term.' We have also seen an example of a contextual definition. In Chapter 1 the definition of 'final epistemological authority' is in the context of the sentence '*P* has final epistemological authority about *Q*' and no set of terms in the analysans is synonymous with 'final epistemological authority.'

It is easy to see why only contextual definitions are relevant to analytical behaviorism. Consider the following sentence:

The average American family has 2.4 children.

Let us assume that it is true, but, of course, in using the sentence we are not talking about—referring to—an existing family. Although the sentence is true, there really is no such family. This would puzzle someone who thinks that if the sentence is true then there is such a family. To correct this mistake we should find some way to show him that the sentence, even if true, does not refer to this strange family. We cannot accomplish this by reducing the average family to ordinary families, because that would require that we identify the average family with some ordinary family which must exist if the sentence is to be true. But there is no such family with 2.4 children. We must instead eliminate this average family in some way. One obvious way is to restate the whole sentence containing 'average American family' so that no expression in it even appears to refer to any average family. For this purpose an explicit definition will not help, because the analysans of 'the average American family' would be synonymous with it and thus would seem to refer to that same strange family. What will succeed, however, is a contextual definition, such as the following:

> The number of children in United States families divided by the number of American families equals 2.4.

Here there is neither 'the average American family' nor any expression synonymous with it. Here the only families and children referred to are the ordinary ones, and no one need wonder about the strange family with its fractional child. It would seem we have "analyzed away" a very strange kind of entity by a contextual definition because we have shown that no expression which seems to refer to such an entity needs to be used. We need only use expressions which refer to ordinary entities. Thus, if we are to analyze away certain entities, we should use contextual definitions. Let us see if using them will help the materialistic analytical behaviorist.

AN ATTEMPT TO JUSTIFY ANALYTICAL BEHAVIORISM:
VERIFIABILITY CRITERION OF MEANING

Many people would doubt that sentences involving sensation terms could be contextually defined in terms of sentences containing only behavioral terms. There are others, however, who say that no matter how difficult it may be to find adequate contextual definitions of this kind, it can nevertheless be done. This confidence in analytical behaviorism was expressed by C. Hempel who at one time claimed

> All psychological statements which are meaningful, that is to say, which are in principle verifiable, are translatable into propositions which do not involve psychological concepts, but only the concepts of physics. The propositions of psychology are consequently physicalistic propositions. Psychology is an integral part of physics.[1]

1. C. Hempel, "The Logical Analysis of Psychology," in H. Feigl and W. Sellars, eds., *Readings in Philosophical Analysis* (New York: Appleton-Century-Crofts, 1949), p. 378.

An example of a sensation sentence which Hempel claims to be verifiable, thus meaningful and translatable into a physicalistic sentence, is a statement "that Mr. Jones suffers from intense inferiority feelings of such and such kinds. . . ." [2] Because this sentence can only be confirmed or falsified by observing Jones' behavior, the sentence "means only this: such and such happenings take place in Mr. Jones' body in such and such circumstances." [3] This sentence about Jones that Hempel uses as an example is not relevantly different from other sensation sentences. Consequently his argument can be generalized to conclude that the meaning of any sensation sentence, indeed any psychological sentence, is the behavior of some person or persons under certain conditions. If this is correct, we can find a physicalistic sentence that has the same meaning as each sensation sentence. And, because the relevant physicalistic sentences are about certain bodily events and states, we can conclude that all sensation sentences can be analyzed into sentences using only behavioral terms—that is, analytical behaviorism is true. But, of course, the crucial question is whether Hempel's argument is sound.

It is crucial to Hempel's argument that the meanings of sentences are the conditions of their verification. This implies that if there is no way to verify a sentence, then it has no truth value and is cognitively meaningless. Thus his argument implies the verifiability criterion of meaningfulness. Consequently, because there are reasons to reject the verifiability criterion, there are reasons to reject Hempel's argument. There is no need to delve deeply into the two main problems facing the verifiability criterion of meaning, because both have been fully discussed elsewhere. The first problem is that the criterion is supposed to provide a way to decide whether or not any particular sentence is verifiable and thus empirically meaningful, but none of the many attempts has succeeded. Each attempt has resulted in a criterion either so broad that it allows obvious cases of nonsense to count as cognitively meaningful, or so narrow that it requires that many theoretical sentences of science are meaningless. This has been the history of attempts to formulate the criterion from

2. Ibid.
3. Ibid.

A. J. Ayer's first attempt to the most recent.[4] On the basis of this history of failures, it seems reasonable to conclude that no such attempt will succeed, and, therefore, that the verifiability criterion of meaning should be rejected.

It might be replied that the failure of any attempt to define 'empirical verifiability' is not sufficient to cast doubt on a verifiability theory of meaningfulness, because such a definition, while helpful for utilizing the theory as a criterion for deciding the meaningfulness of specific sentences, is not an essential part of the theory itself. Thus the theory might be plausible, although 'empirical verifiability' is not definable and perhaps even irremediably vague. The second objection to the criterion is compatible with the reply, for it states that the criterion is self-defeating whether or not 'empirical verifiability' is definable. This objection is that if the verifiability criterion of meaningfulness is true, then the only sentences that have truth value are analytic sentences and empirically verifiable sentences. Consequently, the criterion itself, if it is true, must be either analytic or empirically verifiable. But it is not analytic, because there is nothing self-contradictory about the claim that some nonanalytic, nonverifiable sentences are true. Indeed it would seem that most people untutored in theories of meaning would reject the criterion as false because they think many religious and ethical utterances, among others, are true. Consequently, it does not seem to be a true generalization based upon empirical observation of the actual ways in which people use and respond to sentences. It seems that it is not analytic, and if it is empirically verifiable, then it seems to be false.

Some defenders of the criterion recognizing this problem have claimed that the criterion is a rule of language. It is, then, neither an analytic nor a verifiable statement. But it surely does not seem to be a rule that can be derived from the actual use of language, because 'true' and 'false' are, as a matter of fact, applied to many sentences which would have no truth value according to the

4. For this series of attempts, see A. J. Ayer, *Language, Truth, and Logic* (New York: Dover Publications, n.d.), pp. 5–16; I. Scheffler, *The Anatomy of Inquiry* (New York: Knopf, 1963), pp. 150–54; D. Makinson, "Nidditch's Definition of Verifiability," *Mind* 74 (1965): 240–47; and J. Cornman, "Indirectly Verifiable: Everything or Nothing," *Philosophical Studies* 18 (1967): 49–56.

criterion. Other defenders have claimed that the criterion is not a rule governing the way language is ordinarily used, but rather a proposed rule for how language should ideally be used. Some of these defenders have justified adopting such a proposed rule by claiming that it is surely a necessary rule for a meaningful language of empirical science. But although it may well be that the language of science should meet an adequate verifiability criterion, this provides no reason to think that any other meaningful area of language must meet similar requirements.

In short, there is good reason to reject the verifiability criterion. It is acceptable only if there is reason to think that it is true of the way things are or that it is a justified proposed rule about the way things should be. But we have found no reason to accept it as a proposal and good reason to reject its truth, because if it is either analytic or empirically verifiable, as the criterion itself requires of all true sentences, then it is false. Consequently, because Hempel's argument implies the verifiability criterion, we should reject both the criterion and the argument.

Analytical behaviorism is not so easily justified as positivists once thought. If it is to be justified, this must be done by trying to provide some specific contextual definitions of particular psychological sentences. If there are some examples of successful definitions, then there is at least some reason to accept analytical behaviorism; if there are none, then, because of the number of unsuccessful attempts already made, there is good inductive evidence for rejecting it.

EXAMINATION OF A PARTICULAR BEHAVIORAL ANALYSIS

Most attempts to analyze particular psychological sentences have concentrated on sentences of two kinds. The first are sentences expressing dispositions or capacities and lacking any clearly phenomenal elements, such as sentences containing 'believe,' 'think,' 'know,' and 'doubt.' The second, while they express states involving phenomenal components, express these states with words, such as 'anger' and 'pain,' that have obvious relationships to bodily behavior and tendencies. I know of few attempts, such as Smart's unsuccessful analysis of 'I have a yellowish-orange afterimage,' to analyze sentences containing phenomenal terms that have no obvious relationship to bodily behavior or bodily dispositions. These last sentences seem clearly

to be the most difficult to analyze in behavioral terms. Consequently, because there is reason to doubt behavioral analyses of
easier examples, such as belief sentences, there is reason to
reject the more difficult cases.[5] Nevertheless, to see the sort of
problem that arises, let us consider a proposed analysis of a
sentence which, while it expresses a disposition, seems to involve also some element of feeling or sensation. It, then, should
not be the kind of sentence involving a phenomenal element that
is the hardest to analyze.

C. A. Mace claims "that the analysis of '*A* likes *B*' is of the
form '*A* is disposed to seek *B*'s company, to perform acts con-
ducive to *B*'s welfare, and to exhibit distress when harm befalls
B.' " [6] Before examining this analysis, it should be noted that
Mace restricts "behavioristic analysis to the analysis of so-called
'mental acts' as distinct from the so-called 'objects' or 'contents'
of those acts." [7] Although he is an analytical behaviorist who
wishes to eliminate sensa, such as mental images and sense-data,
he does not do so by analysis. Unfortunately, like many others,
Mace does not provide a way to justify their elimination. Let
us assume here, however, that if Mace's analyses of mental-
act sentences succeed then analytical behaviorism can somehow
accommodate mental objects. This generosity need not worry
the opponents of analytical behaviorism, because we shall find
reason enough to reject a behavioral analysis of '*A* likes *B*'
where there is no question of what is to be done with a phenomenal object. We can, then, ignore Mace's problem with
sensa without incurring unjustified consequences.

The first task that confronts us in evaluating Mace's analysis
is how to interpret 'is disposed to.' Some dispositions are mental
and someone might claim that '*A* likes *B*' means the same as '*A*
is favorably disposed towards *B*' where the disposition is mental.
What Mace wants, of course, are bodily dispositions, that is,
bodily states of readiness, or tendencies, to behave in certain
ways. Another problem is that 'seek *B*'s company' appears to be
a psychological term, because it seems equivalent to something

5. For an attack on different kinds of behavioral analysis of belief
sentences, see R. M. Chisholm, *Perceiving*, Chap. 11.
6. C. A. Mace, "Some Implications of Analytical Behavorism,"
Aristotelian Society Proceedings 49 (1948–49): 4.
7. Ibid., p. 5.

like 'try to find and be with *B*.' It surely is psychological if Chisholm is correct, because it is intentional by his criterion of intentionality, and that, he claims, is sufficient for its being psychological.[8] Let us replace it with something clearly behavioristic: 'move towards and stay with *B*.' A third problem arises because 'perform acts' also seems to be nonbehavioral, especially if we interpret acts as involving some kind of agency. We can remove this problem by using 'behave in ways' instead. Incorporating the above changes, let us construe Mace's analysis as follows:

> *A* likes *B* = df. *A* (*A*'s body) has a tendency to move towards and stay with *B*, to behave in ways conducive to *B*'s health, and to behave in distressed ways when harm befalls *B*.

Two objections to this reconstruction of Mace's analysis immediately arise. First, it is possible that one person likes another but his body does not have all three tendencies stated in the analysans. This would be the case if he were completely paralyzed so that his body had no tendency to behave in any of the three ways specified. It would also be the case if his one relevant tendency were to stay away from the person he liked because of an uncontrollable fear of angering him by blundering in some of his many ways. Second, it is possible that someone's body has all three behavioral tendencies towards someone, but does not like him. He may, for example, be a bodyguard dedicated to his job but disliking the person, or an underling who cannot help but be a sycophant although he hates his superior.

We can avoid the objection raised by the paralysis case that '*A* likes *B*' does not entail Mace's analysans, by transforming the analysans into the consequent of a subjunctive conditional which begins: 'If *A*'s body should be normal, then . . .' But this would not avoid the objection derived from the man fearful of blundering. It might be avoided, however, by claiming that the man surely has all three tendencies to some degree, but the contrary tendencies caused by his fear are so much stronger that the three tendencies are never exhibited, not even momentarily. Perhaps, then, we can grant Mace the entailment from analysan-

8. See Chisholm, pp. 168–73; and Cornman, "Intentionality and Intensionality," *Philosophical Quarterly* 12 (1962): 44–52.

dum to analysans, but I see no way to save the converse entailment. It is surely possible that the sycophant and the bodyguard have normal bodies, have all three tendencies, but do not like the person in question.

There is, in general, another way to raise counterexamples to the latter entailment. Let $Lxy = x$ likes y, $Nx = x$'s body is normal, use $x \dashrightarrow y$ to express subjunctive conditionals and use $\Diamond$ and $\Box$ to express the logical modalities of possibility and necessity. Also let Tx be filled in by "body-tendency" analyses of the kind we have derived from Mace. We then have the following schema for a modal argument to disprove any such analysis:

$$(1) \Diamond [(Nx \dashrightarrow Tx) \cdot (\sim Nx \cdot Tx \cdot \sim Lxy)]$$

Therefore

$$(2) \Diamond [(Nx \dashrightarrow Tx) \cdot \sim Lxy]$$

Therefore

$$(3) \sim \Box [(Nx \dashrightarrow Tx) \supset Lxy]$$

Therefore

$$(4) \sim [Lxy =_{df} (Nx \dashrightarrow Tx)].$$

Actually Tx can be dropped from both premises, because as long as $\sim Nx$ is true then $\sim Lxy$ is compatible with many kinds of tendencies x would have if his body should be normal. Thus $\Diamond [(Nx \dashrightarrow Tx) \cdot (\sim Nx \cdot \sim Lxy)]$ and this entails (2). The same kind of argument can also be devised against analyses like Mace's nonsubjunctive attempt which requires $\Box [Tx \supset Lxy]$. But this is falsified not only by the bodyguard and sycophant counterexamples, but also more generally, because $\Diamond [Tx \cdot \sim Nx \cdot \sim Lxy]$ and thus $\sim \Box [Tx \supset Lxy]$.

An objection to basing eliminative materialism on analytical behaviorism

We have found no way to construct a body–tendency analysis of 'A likes B,' and I can think of no other kind of behavioral analysis that is any better. Certainly one in terms of occurrent behavior will fail. But even if some behavioral analysis were to succeed, there is still a problem remaining for an eliminative materialist who tries to justify his position by means of analytical behaviorism. His problem, at base, is how to justify the inference from the behavioral analysis of sensation terms to the elimination of sensations. Because I have elsewhere discussed this specific problem and the more general problem of inferences from premises about language to ontological conclusions, I shall merely briefly sketch the problem here.[9] The eliminative materialist who wishes to use analytical behaviorism to support his position must grant that many sentences such as '*A* likes *B*,' '*A* has a toothache,' and '*A* has a yellowish-orange afterimage,' are true, but he must also claim that there are no mental states, events, or objects. As an eliminative materialist he can claim either that sensation terms really refer to behavioral phenomena, or that none of them are referring terms. The first alternative is plausible only if sensation terms refer to the same entities that certain behavioral terms refer to. But if analytical behaviorism is correct, then there is good reason to think that no behavioral terms have the same referents as sensation terms, because generally the most plausible candidates, the terms in the behavioral sentences used to contextually define the sensation terms, do not have the same referents as the sensation terms they help define. Although whatever is referred to by the behavioral sentences is also referred to by the sensation sentences synonymous with them, it is easily seen in most cases that none of the terms in the behavioral sentences are extentionally equivalent to, and thus none have the same referents as, the sensation terms in the analyzed sensation sentences. Thus the most hopeful way to justify the inference from analytical behaviorism to eliminative materialism involves showing that no sensation terms refer. This would parallel the move made in the average American family example from the contextual definition of 'average American family' to the elimination of the average American family.

The preceding remarks give us a hint of the kind of argument an eliminative materialist might use:

> (1) Each sensation term *s* in a sentence S_s is contextually definable by (and thus S_s is synonymous with) some behavioral sentence.

9. See Cornman, *Metaphysics, Reference, and Language,* esp. Chap. 3, for a discussion of inferences from language to ontology.

(2) If (1), then no behavioral terms in sentences that contextually define *s* refer to the same entities as *s*.

(3) If no behavioral terms in sentences that contextually define *s* refer to the same entities as *s*, then no behavioral terms refer to the same entities as *s*.

(4) If no behavioral terms refer to the same entities as *s*, then either *s* refers to something nonbehavioral or *s* is not a referring term.

(5) If two sentences are synonymous, then they refer to exactly the same entities.

(6) No behavioral sentences refer to nonbehavioral entities.

Therefore

(7) No sensation sentence refers to nonbehavioral entities.

Therefore

(8) No sensation term refers to nonbehavioral entities.

Therefore

(9) No sensation term is a referring term.

Although only premise (5) is clearly acceptable, the crucial premise here is (6). It is the one that makes the essential move from a purely linguistic fact about certain sentences to a claim about what kind of entity is not referred to by those sentences. A nonmaterialist who accepted analytical behaviorism, and thus premise (1), could counter (6) with the claim that sensation terms are clearly reporting terms and thus clearly referring terms. Consequently, some behavioral sentences do refer to nonbehavioral entities, namely, those sentences synonymous with sensation sentences, and premise (6) is false. The chief problem for the eliminative materialist who depends on analytical behaviorism is to overcome this objection to (6) or similar objections to similar arguments that move from language to ontology.

CONCLUSION ABOUT ANALYTICAL BEHAVIORISM

We have found two objections to the adoption of analytical behaviorism by an eliminative materialist. First, there is reason to think the program of analytical behaviorism will not succeed because no behavioral analyses of sensation sentences, such as '*A* likes *B*,' seem to be forthcoming. Second, even if this program were to succeed it is far from clear how to use the results of the program to justify eliminative materialism. The eliminative materialist, consequently, should look elsewhere to find support for his thesis. Historically many of those who embraced analytical behaviorism turned, at its demise, to the identity theory as a means of supporting materialism. This is because those who stressed meaning analysis also tended to distinguish sharply between the concepts of meaning and reference, and to utilize them for different purposes. Thus when behavioral analysis failed, it was natural to turn to a theory that seemed to achieve the same results by considering the reference of sensation terms in a way that avoids the problems that arise for meaning analysis.[10] But although, as we shall see, one who adopts an identity of reference theory can also be an eliminative materialist, we have already seen that this is not possible for an identity theorist. He must turn to reductive materialism. What would serve the needs of an eliminative materialist would be a theory which shows that no sensation terms are referring terms, but which does not depend on behavioral analyses of sensation terms. The only candidate for this task I can find is what I have called "Rylean behaviorism."

RYLEAN BEHAVIORISM

I call the view we shall now discuss "Rylean behaviorism" because it stems from the work of Gilbert Ryle. But, although I shall take my discussion of it from Ryle's work, I do not wish to say that it is Ryle's behaviorism because I am not sure that it is his view.[11]

For purposes of discussing Rylean behaviorism, I shall interpret Ryle's position as follows. Essential to his view is the theory of logical categories. He thinks that philosophical problems such

10. For such a change, compare Herbert Feigl's views in "Logical Analysis of the Psychophysical Problem," *Philosophy of Science* 1 (1934): 420–45; and in "The 'Mental' and the 'Physical'" in H. Feigl et al., eds., *Minnesota Studies* 2 (1958): 370–497.

11. I have discussed Ryle's views in *Metaphysics, Reference, and Language,* pp. 38–45, 63–70, 244ff.

as the mind-body problem arise because philosophers have mis-construed the logical categories of the key phrases the philoso-phers use to formulate the problems. A very common mistake is to construe sentences as belonging to the category of reports and descriptive sentences when they do not. Only sentences with certain logical features belong to this logical category. Other categories delineated in a like manner would be those of ex-clamations, laws, mathematical sentences, and poetic sentences. The sentences of each of these categories have certain logical features in common which the sentences of no other category have. It is at least one important task of a philosopher to show this.[12]

According to Ryle, it is mistaken to think that when we use psychological expressions we are talking in the same category as when we use physical expressions, but are referring to a radically different kind of substance, state of affairs, or process, as a dualist would claim; nor are we talking in the same category about the same kind of thing, as identity theorists such as Feigl and Smart claim. Rather we are talking in two different logical categories and talking about one kind of thing—a person. As Ryle says:

> When we speak of a person's mind, we are not speaking of a second theatre of special-status incidents, but of certain ways in which some of the incidents of his one life are ordered. His life is not a double series of events taking place in two different kinds of stuff; it is one concatenation of events, the difference between some and other classes of which largely consist in the applicability or inapplicability to them of logically different types of law-propositions and law-like propositions. Assertions about a person's mind are therefore assertions of special sorts about that person. So questions about the relations between a person and his mind, like those about the relations between a person's body and his mind are improper questions.[13]

An example of the technique Ryle uses to establish his thesis that

12. This philosophical task, which I have called "use analysis" is discussed in *Metaphysics, Reference, and Language*, pp. 227–57.

13. G. Ryle, *The Concept of Mind* (New York: Barnes and Noble, 1949), pp. 167–68.

psychological sentences belong to a logical category different from the category of physical sentences is the way he handles the sentence, 'Jones boasted from vanity,' or, in other words, 'Jones boasted because he is vain.' According to Ryle this sentence explains why Jones boasted by stating that in boasting he satisfied "the law-like proposition that whenever he finds a chance of securing the admiration and envy of others, he does whatever he thinks will produce this admiration and envy." [14] For Ryle, then, the sentence 'Jones is vain' comes to something like a general sentence about Jones which can be used to explain and predict some of Jones' behavior. This Rylean interpretation of 'Jones is vain' is not a behavioral analysis because the analysans contains such nonbehavioral terms as 'think,' 'find,' 'admiration,' and 'envy.' Nor is Ryle identifying vanity with any physiological or psychological process, event, state, or individual, because no term in the analysans refers to anything suitable as a referent for 'vanity.'

Ryle, then, is neither analytical behaviorist, identity theorist, nor dualist. He seems, however, to agree with the analytical behaviorist on one important point. Psychological terms, such as 'vanity,' are not referring terms. To boast from vanity is not to be caused to boast by whatever 'vanity' refers to. This is an essential tenet of Rylean behaviorism. What makes it Rylean is the way this tenet is justified. On Ryle's interpretation of 'Jones is vain' it turns out to function as what he calls "a partly open hypothetical." This makes it, as he calls it, law-like because a law is "an open hypothetical," that is a hypothetical the antecedent of which "can embody at least one expression like 'any' or 'whenever'," [15] but which mentions no particular things or persons. But a law does not belong in the category of reports and descriptions; it belongs in the category of inference tickets. Its function is solely to license or warrant inferences among observation statements. It is, then, like a formal rule of inference such as modus ponens which does not refer to some special logical realm. The main difference here is that laws are nonformal or logically contingent rules of inference. Thus laws are neither reports nor descriptive sentences and, concludes Ryle, the same is true of law-like sentences. They refer at most to those entities

14. Ibid., p. 89.
15. Ibid., p. 120, and see also p. 123.

which are referred to in the observation sentences they are used to explain and predict. As Ryle says,

> But to speak as if the discovery of a law were the finding of [some] unobservable existence is simply to fall back into the old habit of construing open hypothetical statements as singular categorical statements. . . . It is to fall back into the old habit of assuming that all sorts of sentences do the same sort of job, the job, namely, of ascribing a predicate to a mentioned object.[16]

This Rylean approach to a person's vanity, when generalized, leads to the conclusion:[17]

> To talk of a person's mind is not to talk of a repository which is permitted to house objects that something called 'the physical world' is forbidden to house; it is to talk of the person's abilities, liabilities and inclinations to do and undergo certain sorts of things, and of the doing and undergoing of these things in the ordinary world.[18]

But to talk about abilities, liabilities, and inclinations, i.e. dispositions, is to use open and partly open hypotheticals which are merely inference tickets and thus do not refer to some unobservable realm of entities. And to talk about doing and undergoing things in the ordinary world is to use sentences that refer only to observable behavior. Thus all talk "about" a person's mind is really about a person's actual and possible overt behavior, even though it uses nonbehavioral terms. There are, then, no nonbodily events, processes, states, or objects belonging to persons. Persons are merely bodies, albeit unique bodies because of the unique laws and law-like statements that apply to them. This is the thesis of Rylean behaviorism, although perhaps not Ryle's behaviorism.[19]

16. Ibid., p. 122.
17. I have ignored here what Ryle says about achievement words, because sensation terms are not achievement words. This comes out in premise (2) below. Achievement words such as 'win,' unlike sensation terms, refer to occurrent behavior, because, depending on context, they refer to what behavioral terms such as 'run' refer to.
18. Ryle, p. 199.
19. For Ryle's remarks on behaviorism, see *Concept of Mind*, pp. 327–30.

AN ARGUMENT FOR RYLEAN BEHAVIORISM

Let me put the crux of this Rylean argument to substantiate Rylean behaviorism in a more perspicuous form:

(1) All psychological sentences (including sensation sentences) either (a) refer to observable behavior, or (b) function as open or partly open hypotheticals.

(2) No purely psychological sentences refer to observable behavior.

Therefore

(3) All purely psychological sentences, e.g. 'Jones is vain,' either are, or function as, open or partly open hypotheticals.

(4) All statements that are or that function as open or partly open hypotheticals are law statements or law-like statements.

(5) All law statements are in the category of inference tickets.

(6) No inference tickets refer to unobservable phenomena.

(7) All law-like statements are in the same category as laws.

Therefore

(8) No purely psychological sentences refer to unobservable phenomena.

(9) If (2) and (8), then no psychological term is a referring term.

Therefore

(10) No psychological term is a referring term.

There is much to debate in this argument. Indeed no premise is clearly true. Premise (1) might be doubted on the grounds that Rylean attempts to analyze psychological sentences in terms of explicit open or partly open hypotheticals face some counterexamples similar to those facing Mace's behavioral analyses. The Rylean analysans of 'Jones is vain,' that is, 'Whenever Jones finds a chance of securing the admiration and envy of others, he does whatever he thinks will produce this admiration and envy,' fails because 'whenever' and 'whatever' are surely too strong. Jones might not "act out of vanity" every time he thinks he has an opportunity to impress others, and there may be many things he would not do to achieve admiration and envy. He might, for example, find that the actions most likely to produce the admiration and envy of some of his cohorts are morally repugnant to him. He might try other things instead. Furthermore, he may not care about the envy of others or their admiration, or even both. He might be so self-centered that he acts completely for his own delight.

All these points are true, but the objection based on them misconstrues this "Rylean analysis." It is not an attempt to produce an open or partly open hypothetical synonymous with 'Jones is vain'; it is to show that the function of 'Jones is vain' is the same as that of a partly open hypothetical, whether or not it is analyzable into one. This raises a new objection. How is this claim about the function of 'Jones is vain' to be established if it cannot be shown by analysis? One way is to try to exhibit that it has this function in several contexts of its use. This can be bolstered by using the claim made in Chapter 2 that such sentences are theoretical, and adopting a plausible empiricist doctrine that the function of theoretical sentences is to warrant inferences among observation sentences. These tactics would put us well on the way to justifying not only premise (1), but also the statement, essential to the argument, that all sensation sentences are inference tickets. There surely is some plausibility to this move, because, from a scientific, and thereby third person point of view, sensation terms such as 'pain' function like 'electron.' Both are theoretical terms that function to explain, but not describe, observable behavior.

Let us, for our purposes here, grant premise (1). Let us also grant premise (4) on the somewhat shaky grounds that laws are statable as one kind of open hypothetical sentence, and that partly open hypotheticals, being like open hypotheticals, are also like laws and thus law-like. And, although this way of justifying (4) certainly raises questions about (7), even granting the debatable view that all law-like sentences have one category in common, I do not wish to debate (7) here. Nor do I wish to debate (2) as some identity theorists might who claim that sensations are identical with observable brain phenomena. We have found the most plausible candidates for the identity claims to be unobservable brain phenomena. I wish to concentrate on premises (5) and (6), because I think that no matter how the Rylean argument is varied to avoid objections to the other premises, the argument will always depend upon premises that function very much like (5) and (6) and will be open to the same objections.

The conjunction of (5) and (6) is dubious. We can grant either premise, depending on how we define 'inference ticket,' but then not the other. We can grant (5) if we limit the laws it refers to as laws used to explain what is observable, and define an inference ticket as a general hypothetical statement which can function to warrant the derivation of a singular observation statement from another singular observation statement and certain correspondence rules. But using such a definition renders (6) at least dubious, because if (6) is true then not only no psychological terms but also no pure theoretical terms of physics are referring terms. That is, (6) is true only if scientific instrumentalism is true, i.e. only if the pure theoretical terms of science are merely nonreferring "auxiliary marks, which serve as convenient symbolic devices in the transition from one set of experiential statements to another." [20] This seems to be Ryle's position, for, as we have seen, he denies that to discover a law, as in the physical sciences, is to uncover unobservable entities that "intervene" between observations. But the issue between scientific instrumentalists and realists is far from settled (this is discussed in Chap. 7). Furthermore in Chapter 2 we found reason to conclude not only that sensation terms are theoretical terms, but also that they are reporting terms, and thereby referring terms. Thus no matter whether it is reasonable to adopt scientific instrumentalism regarding pure theoretical terms, there is still the objection that it is unreasonable to adopt it about sensation terms, and nothing in the Rylean approach to behaviorism provides reasons sufficient to override this conclusion. We have, once again, in the conjunction of (5) and (6) a move from language to ontology, a move there is no more reason to accept

20. Hempel, "Theoretician's Dilemma," in *Minnesota Studies* 2 (1958), p. 86

in this case than in any of the other cases we have already examined.[21]

The situation is no better if we define 'inference ticket' in a way to insure the truth of (6). This would require what I think is the more usual conception of inference tickets, namely, that inference tickets are merely nonformal rules of inference that contain referring terms only if they are observation terms. Whereas the dubious move from language to ontology for the first definition of 'inference ticket' would be in premise (6), for the second definition it would be in premise (5) which would entail that no law statements refer to anything unobservable.

CONCLUSION ABOUT RYLEAN BEHAVIORISM

A Rylean approach to materialism depends on a Rylean argument to establish that sensation terms are not referring terms, and such a Rylean argument depends on an instrumental construal not only of the pure theoretical terms of the physical sciences, but also of those theoretical terms that seem to be reporting terms as well. Both of these construals are open to debate, and the second seems to be implausible, especially after the discussion of sensation terms in Chapter 2. Rylean behaviorism, then, like analytical behaviorism, fails. Although each fails in a different way, both fail because they do not provide reason to override the plausible position that sensation terms are referring terms. Both attempt to supply such reasons by eliciting certain features of language: one involves claims about synonymy and the other claims about linguistic function or use. Neither attempt succeeds, but both kinds of behaviorism would fail even if their claims about synonymy and function were correct. We have seen that the move from the synonymy of contextual definitions to nonreference, and the move from the function of warranting inferences to nonreference are both dubious.

It might be noted, however, that the move from inference-function to nonreference could be made somewhat plausible if an additional premise were to be established. This premise, perhaps held by Ryleans, states that no sentence has more than one linguistic function. If this were true, then no sentence that functions to warrant inferences would also function to describe, re-

---

21. I have also discussed this kind of inference by Ryle in *Metaphysics, Reference, and Language,* pp. 63–70.

port, or refer to any phenomena whether observable or not. But there is good reason to deny this univocality of linguistic function. Many sentences have several functions, such as the observation sentence 'He has a broken leg,' which can function both to explain and to describe observable phenomena.

We have examined the only two positions I have found that attempt to justify eliminative materialism by denying that sensation terms, and many other psychological terms, are referring terms. Because both these attempts fail, we should turn to some other kind of approach to eliminative materialism. We want, then, a theory that grants that sensation terms are referring terms, but denies that there are any sensations. One way to reach this conclusion is to claim that sensation terms are referring terms that do not denote. That is, they are referring terms much like the pure observation terms 'horse' and 'unicorn,' but like 'unicorn' and unlike 'horse,' there is nothing to which they refer. This is the position stated by naïve eliminative materialists who flatly deny that any sentence implying that there are sensations is true. We have already rejected this view however. Another, much more sophisticated theory states a very similar position, but avoids both the implausible claim that there is nothing at all that sensation terms ever denote and also the naïve construal of sensation terms as pure reporting terms. I have called this "the postulation elimination theory."

THE POSTULATION ELIMINATION THEORY

The postulation elimination theory is premised on construing mental phenomena as postulated theoretical entities and pointing out that there is a way to justify the elimination of theoretical entities that is not available for eliminating observable entities. It is by stressing the elimination of mental entities in this way which is unique to theoretical entities that the postulation theory differs markedly from naïve eliminative materialism. The latter, but not the former, depends on the same unsophisticated kind of empirical evidence to justify the nonexistence of sensations that justifies the nonexistence of unicorns and other observable entities.

A quick and clear statement of the argument which is the core of the postulation elimination theory is found in the work of

Quine, who claims mental entities are "creatures of darkness"
because not available to the precise intersubjective scrutiny of
science. He wishes to eliminate them and other unsavory charac-
ters such as meanings and universals. His argument for their
elimination is:

> If there is a case for mental events and mental states, it must
> be just that the positing of them, like the positing of mole-
> cules, has some indirect systematic efficacy in the develop-
> ment of theory. But if a certain organization of theory is
> achieved by thus positing distinctive mental states and
> events behind physical behavior, surely as much organiza-
> tion could be achieved by positing merely certain correla-
> tive physiological states and events instead. . . . The bod-
> ily states exist anyway; why add the others? [22]

Having established this much it is an easy step to the rejection
of mental states over and above physical states and the justification of materialism. The crucial claim in this argument is that
we are justified in believing there are mental states only if postulating them is in some way required within the context of a
scientific explanatory theory. According to Quine, then, mental
phenomena, like electrons, are postulated theoretical entities.

In order to see how construing sensations as postulated theoretical entities enables Quine to provide a quick justification of
materialism, let us consider a different example, the bright
flashes of light in the sky we call "lightning." How might we
explain this observed phenomenon? One way, which we now
call primitive, is to say that the lightning is caused by the god
Zeus who throws thunderbolts across the heavens. Here Zeus is
a theoretical entity postulated to explain occurrences of lightning. Another, more scientific way, is to claim the flashes are the
result of discharges of atmospheric electricity. How we interpret
the flashes depends on how we explain them. Given the one
theory we call them "Zeus' thunderbolts," but given the other we
say "electrical flashes." Here, then, we have one and the same

22. W. V. Quine, *Word and Object* (Cambridge, Mass.: Massachusetts
Institute of Technology Press, 1960), p. 264. See also Quine, *The Ways
of Paradox* (New York: Random House, 1966), pp. 208–14.

phenomenon referred to in two radically different ways, but the phenomenon does not have both the property of being thrown by Zeus and the property of being the result of an electrical discharge.

Consider what someone I shall call a "physicalist" would say about Zeus' thunderbolts. He would *not* claim that they are identical with electrical flashes. He could, then, avoid the property objection to "reductive physicalism." He would say instead that there really are no thunderbolts thrown by Zeus although what people have called "Zeus' thunderbolts" certainly exist. In this way he could eliminate Zeus' thunderbolts but rebut the objection that there really are thunderbolts thrown by Zeus because we can all see them. This physicalist would not deny the phenomena exist, but claim only that they should not be called "Zeus' thunderbolts." And he is surely justified because once there is no need to postulate a thrower of lightning to explain the observed phenomenon, there is no reason to think there is such an entity, and therefore, no reason to regard the observed phenomenon as something thrown by this individual. Our physicalist would conclude by saying that what some people have called "Zeus' thunderbolts" should more accurately be called "electrical flashes."

Our physicalist would treat Zeus, the thrower of thunderbolts, somewhat differently. He would surely deny that Zeus is identical with discharges of atmospheric electricity, and thus would not be claiming Zeus can be reduced to electrical discharges. He would deny that Zeus exists. But granting that there is a postulated cause of lightning flashes he would agree that there is something people have mistakenly referred to using 'Zeus, the thrower of thunderbolts,' namely, that postulated, unobservable cause. It is much more accurate to call the postulated cause "discharge of static electricity." He would, then, eliminate Zeus because what he is postulated to explain is more accurately and effectively explained by another postulated theoretical entity. Although at one time we might have been justified in calling this cause "Zeus," that time is long past. We can get from science a much clearer understanding of unobservable causes, and scientific results lead to the conclusion that the cause of lightning is not Zeus but electrical discharges.

SENSATIONS AS POSTULATED THEORETICAL ENTITIES

How could a materialist apply the thunderbolt example to mental phenomena such as sensations of pain? Because sensations are not observed phenomena and because it seems reasonable to interpret them as causes of certain observable human behavior, it would seem he should interpret sensations of pain as theoretical entities postulated as the unobserved causes of what is observed. He would then agree with Quine. Furthermore, as a materialist, he would have to claim that they are theoretical entities with a status, in principle at least, much like that of Zeus as the thrower of thunderbolts. That is, he must claim that sensations of pain are entities postulated as part of a somewhat primitive theory used to explain observable human behavior, behavior we sometimes call "pain behavior." He, then, would liken pain behavior to Zeus' thunderbolts. It is important to notice that if this interpretation of sensations and other mental entities is correct, then sensations instead of being identical with brain processes should be candidates for delivery to the pile of discarded and thereby nonexistent postulated entities where we find Zeus, demons, witches, gremlins, the ether, and others. Because, it would seem, purely physiological explanations of observable human behavior are, in principle at least, completely adequate, there is, in principle, no need to postulate nonphysiological causes. And where there is no need for a postulated entity we should discard it. This is the thesis of the postulation elimination theorist.[23]

The postulation elimination theorist construes sensation terms differently from either analytical behaviorists or Rylean behaviorists. He differs from both these theorists by construing sensation terms as referring terms. He would agree that if sensation terms were needed for some purpose in science, then they would denote and what they would denote would be sensations. His thesis differs from analytical behaviorism, in addition, in not entailing any claim either about synonymy of expressions or about the relationship of synonymy of expressions to reference.

23. Many of the points in the preceding discussion grew out of my reading of R. Rorty, "Mind–Body Identity, Privacy, and Categories," *Review of Metaphysics* 19 (1965): 24–54. However, Rorty is not, as I interpret him, a postulation elimination theorist. His view is discussed in detail in Chap. 5.

It also differs from Rylean behaviorism because its claim that necessary theoretical terms of science denote is incompatible with the scientific instrumentalism on which Rylean behaviorism is based. All these are differences that enable the postulation elimination theory to avoid the objections to these two other versions of eliminative behaviorism. Furthermore, because the postulation elimination theory does not state that any physical phenomena are identical with sensations, it avoids the objections to reductive materialism. Unfortunately, however, the theory faces damaging objections of its own.

EXAMINATION OF THE POSTULATION ELIMINATION THEORY

One immediate objection to this kind of justification of materialism is that sensations should not be relegated to the limbo of discarded theoretical entities. According to many dualists they are not theoretical entities at all, because the term 'sensation' is not a theoretical term. It functions quite differently from theoretical terms such as 'electron'; it is not a term introduced as part of an explanatory theory. Thus sensations are not postulated theoretical entities. How a materialist might reply to this has already been indicated. The term 'sensation' is surely a term in the science of psychology used in explanations of human behavior. It is clearly not an observation term. Therefore, it is a theoretical term and sensations are postulated theoretical entities as Quine's argument and the postulation elimination theory require.

Who is right here, the materialist or dualist? To find out and to examine the complete thesis of the postulation elimination theorist more thoroughly, let me display the argument essential to his position as follows:

(1) Postulating a theoretical entity is justified only if postulating it is required to explain, predict, or organize some part of the subject matter of empirical science, i.e., only if it is required for scientific purposes.

(2) No postulation of mental entities is required for scientific purposes.

(3) All mental entities are postulated theoretical entities.

Therefore

> (4) Postulating mental entities is not justified.
> (5) If postulating a postulated theoretical entity is not justified, then the claim that it does not exist is justified.

Therefore

> (6) The claim that mental entities do not exist is justified.

We can grant premises (1) and (5). Together they entail Occam's razor as applied to postulated theoretical entities. That is, they entail that we are not to multiply entities beyond necessity in the sense that, if it is not necessary to postulate a theoretical entity for the purposes of science, then we should not assume it. On this interpretation, Occam's razor is restricted to postulated entities.[24] That is, it is restricted to entities, such as neutrinos and the ether, that can be justified to exist and justified not to exist only if there are sound reasons derived from the theoretical requirements of science. Not only is this application of Occam's razor justified, but premises (1) and (5) are also acceptable, because the entities to which the razor applies should not be assumed to exist and, furthermore, should be assumed not to exist unless required by science.

An objection can surely be raised to premise (2). At its present stage of development science requires psychological terms to formulate the laws and theories that apply to human beings. The science of psychology is not now replaceable by or reducible to physiology or any other physical science; physiology is not capable of explaining all the human behavior explained using psychological terms. This is particularly true of much abnormal behavior explained by depth psychology using terms such as 'unconscious desire,' 'repression,' and 'superego.' It may be that these theoretical terms and the corresponding theoretical entities are headed for the limbo where we find Zeus and the ether, because what they are used to refer to, the causes of certain observable behavior, will be more accurately and effectively referred to by physiological terms. But this has not happened yet and so

24. For more on Occam's razor, see *Metaphysics, Reference, and Language*, pp. 209–10.

premise (2) is false. And it cannot be "made to come true" as easily as Quine suggests, by simply positing physiological phenomena as these causes instead. There must be a theory ready to accept and utilize these alternative phenomena, and there is none at this point.

It might be replied that (2) can be amended to avoid this objection by having it state that no mental entities are required for scientific purposes when science is completed, whether or not they are in fact needed at this time. I think we can grant this version of (2) because there is some reason to think that physiology is developing toward the point when it will suffice to explain all that psychology explains. But to keep the argument valid and premises (1) and (5) true, both premises would have to be revised so that the entailed conclusion would be: the claim that mental entities do not exist is justified when science is completed. But this revised conclusion does not entail the original one which is what is required for the postulation elimination theory to be justified now. Many scientific postulations are justified at a certain stage of science, although they may not be justified later as scientific theories change. The justification of such postulations at one time depends on their being required by the scientific theory that best explains a certain subject matter at that time.

I think that the most we can do with this problem is to leave premise (2) unamended and to claim that although it is not justified now there is reason to think it will be justified some day. Thus although the argument is not acceptable now, it will be acceptable some day if all the other premises are justified. And since there is nothing a philosophical investigation can do to hurry the day when (2) will be justified, a philosopher's job is to concentrate on the rest of the argument to see whether it is only our present limited state of knowledge that keeps eliminative materialism from being justified. Since we have already granted that premises (1) and (5) are acceptable, the one remaining task is to examine (3).

Examination of premise 3:
Theoretico-reporting terms and postulated theoretical entities

Our task is to decide whether or not sensations are, like electrons, postulated theoretical entities as required by Quine's argu-

ment and the postulation elimination theory. We left this issue at
the point where a dualist argued that sensations are not postulated theoretical entities because the term 'sensation' is not a
theoretical term, and the materialist replied that they are postulated theoretical entities because 'sensation' is a nonobservation
term used in scientific explanations. Both of these arguments are
unsound, although the dualist's conclusion is correct. Once again
we can turn to the classification of sensation terms in Chapter 2
to show why this is true. Just as we found that neither the analytical behaviorist nor the Rylean behaviorist gave us reason to
override the conclusion in Chapter 2 that sensation terms are
theoretico-reporting terms, so also the postulation elimination
theorist has produced no argument to counter that conclusion.
We shall use it, then, to evaluate premise (3).

Because we have reason to classify sensation terms as theoretico-reporting terms, we can agree, contrary to our dualist, that
sensation terms are like 'the ether' and 'electron' because they
are theoretical terms. Furthermore, they are all nonobservational
theoretical terms (p. 102) because none of them meet the first
defining condition of 'observation term' (p. 69). But sensation
terms are also unlike 'the ether' and 'electron' in an important
way. Both 'the ether' and 'electron' are pure theoretical terms
and, therefore, unlike sensation terms, are not theoretico-reporting terms. This difference is crucial for it shows why, although
both sensations and electrons are theoretical entities, only electrons are *postulated* theoretical entities. If a pure theoretical
term were to denote something, we could justify that it did only
if it played some role in theoretical explanations of what is observed. Thus once the pure theoretical term 'the ether' lost its explanatory role, there was no reason to think it denoted anything
even if there is reason to claim it is a referring term. The case
is different for reporting terms, whether pure or theoretical.
Clearly a term that is theoretical because it is a nonempirical
term with an explanatory role does not denote postulated entities if it also is a reporting term. What we are aware of is not
postulated. Furthermore, if a term has a reporting use, then
whether it denotes anything does not depend on its being required for the explanation of some observable phenomena. If it
became unnecessary for this explanatory purpose, as might happen to sensation terms with the advance of physiology, it would

still have its reporting use, and the entities it denoted, if any, could not be discarded merely because they were no longer needed for explanation.

CONCLUSION ABOUT THE POSTULATION THEORY

We can conclude that our dualist is right, although for the wrong reasons. Sensations cannot be done away with in the way we have dispensed with Zeus, demons, gremlins, and the ether in the past. Quine's quick argument, consequently, fails. He has misconstrued sensations. They are not postulated theoretical entities because 'sensation' is a reporting term, and thus whether or not it denotes sensations does not depend solely on its explanatory role.

Must eliminative materialism fail also? It has seemed that for a version of eliminative materialism to succeed, the term 'sensation' must be construed as a referring term, but not as an observation term. It might seem, then, that it must be a pure theoretical term like 'Zeus,' if eliminative materialism is to resist refutation, because it does not denote something observable and so is not an observational theoretical term like 'Zeus' thunderbolt.' But this fact does not force us to that conclusion, because 'sensation' is, like 'Zeus' thunderbolt,' a term used to report things we are aware of, albeit nonobservationally. Thus, contrary to first appearances, it might seem that the most fruitful approach for eliminative materialists might be to use an analogy with these discarded thunderbolts to eliminate sensations. There is, however, another difference between these two terms that destroys this kind of elimination of sensations. The term 'Zeus' thunderbolt' is a theory laden reporting term in the sense that to report something observed using it is to imply that the postulated theoretical entity, Zeus, exists. The term 'sensation' is not theory laden in this way, and, therefore, although the thunderbolts are eliminated by eliminating Zeus, there is no unnecessary postulated theoretical entity the demise of which entails the elimination of sensations.

PRELIMINARY CONCLUSION
ABOUT ELIMINATIVE MATERIALISM

It seems that eliminative materialists cannot merely await the arrival of a completely physiological psychology to see their position "come true," that is, not unless they can replace Quine's argument based on the postulated status of sensations with one better justified. There seem to be two facts about sensation terms that have blocked the three preceding attempts to justify eliminative materialism. The first is that sensation terms seem to be referring terms and we have found no reason to think they are not. This fact led to the demise of analytical behaviorism and Rylean behaviorism. The second is that it is not enough to agree that sensation terms are referring terms, perhaps on the grounds that scientific realism is true and sensation terms are theoretical terms. We have reason to think that sensation terms are reporting terms, and thus are terms that denote phenomena people are aware of. This led to the rejection of the postulation elimination theory. It seems, then, that an eliminative materialist, if he is to avoid the objections to the three preceding theories, must somehow accommodate two statements: (1) there are entities we are aware of that sensation terms refer to, and (2) there really are no sensations. And, although it may seem that these two statements are irreconcilable, a theory has been proposed which claims to reconcile them. We shall examine it next in Chapter 5.

5. The 'Sensation' Elimination Theory

Of the four theories we have examined, only two agree with one statement we have found reason to accept, that sensation terms are referring terms. But both of these theories, reductive materialism and the postulation elimination theory, face obvious objections we have found no way to counter. It seems that sensations are not identical with and also reducible to brain entities because they have phenomenal properties we have found no way either to eliminate or to reduce to physical properties. And it seems that sensations cannot be eliminated by construing them as unnecessary postulated theoretical entities, because we directly experience them, and so they are not postulated. Recently, however, R. Rorty has made a new attempt to solve the materialist's problem with sensations in a way that avoids both of these objections.[1] Although Rorty claims his theory is a version of the identity theory, he does not construe the relation between brain processes and sensations to be "strict identity, but rather the sort of relation which obtains between, to put it crudely, existent entities and non-existent entities."[2] Such a theory can, I think, best be explicated as a subtle kind of eliminative materialism that does not construe sensations as postulated. Thus it avoids the objection to the postulation elimination theory. And, not claiming that sensations are strictly identical with brain processes, it avoids the property objection to reductive materialism. It is, consequently, a position deserving close scrutiny.

A Fourth Kind of Eliminative Materialism

To characterize the theory, which I call the 'sensation' elimination theory, let me contrast it with reductive materialism and the postulation elimination theory. This can best be done, as previously, by construing all three theories to be about the reference of sensation terms. All three theories agree that sensation terms are referring terms. In this regard all three differ from the other two versions of eliminative materialism we have examined and rejected. We have seen that according to the latter

1. R. Rorty, "Mind–Body Identity, Privacy, and Categories," *Review of Metaphysics* 19 (1965–66): 24–54.
2. Ibid., p. 26.

theories, psychological terms are not referring terms. Analytical behaviorism states that psychological terms are incomplete symbols and therefore are not referring terms. Rylean behaviorism takes an instrumentalist or inference ticket view of psychological terms, that is, the view that they are merely nondenoting symbolic inference devices, and thus function solely to warrant inferences among observation claims.

The postulation elimination theory differs from reductive materialism and the 'sensation' elimination theory in two ways. First, it construes sensation terms as pure, and therefore nonreporting, theoretical terms. Although both of the other theories agree that sensation terms are referring terms, they construe them, as we have, to be reporting terms, and thus terms used to refer to entities we are aware of. Second, whereas it is possible that the postulation theory is true but there is no sense in which there are entities denoted by any sensation terms, this is not possible for reductive materialism and the 'sensation' elimination theory. For the postulation elimination theory, sensation terms are like 'Zeus, the thrower of thunderbolts.' The latter, because it has been used to refer to the unobserved and postulated cause of lightning flashes, can be said to denote something only if there is a cause of lightning flashes to be called, mistakenly or not, "Zeus." Similarly, for the postulation elimination theory, sensation terms denote only if there are postulated causes of observable behavior. But because the postulation elimination theory does not entail that there are causes of observable behavior (whether or not postulated), it is compatible with sensation terms not denoting at all. If this were true, sensation terms would be like 'the ether' which does not denote at all, but which would denote only if there were some medium to transmit light in vacuums to be called, mistakenly perhaps, "the ether."

But it is not possible that the other two theories are true and no sensation terms denote anything. Both classify sensation terms as reporting terms and claim that often what sensation terms such as 'pain' report is exactly what is denoted by certain physicalistic expressions such as 'stimulation of C-fibers.' Thus, for both, some sensation terms denote something. But they disagree about whether sensations are to be considered identical with anything physical. Both theories agree that what we denote when using sensation terms are nothing but certain brain entities, and thus that these brain entities exist. But while the identity theory agrees that there are sensations because they are identical with such brain entities, the 'sensation' elimination theory denies there are sensations and thereby denies the identity claim.

OBJECTION TO THE 'SENSATION' ELIMINATION THEORY:
IT IS INCONSISTENT

At this point an objection might be raised against the 'sensation' elimination theory. Surely, according to this objection, for any term '*p*,' if what is denoted by '*p*' is nothing but what is denoted by '*q*,' and what '*q*' denotes, namely *q*, exists, then *p* exists, for it follows that *p* is identical with *q*. For example, if what is denoted by 'LBJ' is what 'the president of the U.S.A. in 1968' denotes, and the president exists in 1968, then it follows that LBJ is identical with the president in 1968, and LBJ exists in 1968. Another way to put this objection is that if it is granted, as is done by a 'sensation' elimination theorist, that the referents of sensation terms and certain physicalistic terms are identical, and that these physicalistic terms denote brain processes, then the identity claim of the identity theory and with it the existence of sensations are entailed. The 'sensation' elimination theory, according to this objection, is inconsistent.

This objection can be refuted. Two of the claims of the 'sensation' elimination theory are:

(a) What is denoted by 'sensation' is nothing but what is denoted by 'brain process,'

and:

(b) Brain processes are denoted by 'brain process.'

The objection states that (a) and (b) together entail:

(c) Sensations are identical with brain processes.

But because the 'sensation' elimination theory denies (c), it is inconsistent. It is true that (a) and (b) entail:

(d) There are brain processes

and also

(e) What is denoted by 'sensation' exists.

But (a), (b), (d), and (e) do not entail (c). To show that they do not, I shall list seven cases in which statements of the same form as (a) and (b) are true and then point out that in some of the cases the corresponding claim of the same form as (c) is false. From this we can conclude that sentences of the same form as (a) and (b) do not entail (c). Thus (a) and (b) do not entail (c) and the objection fails. The seven statements are:

(1) What is denoted by 'the Morning Star' is nothing but what is denoted by 'Venus,' and Venus is denoted by 'Venus.'

(2) What is denoted by 'unicorn horn' is nothing but what is denoted by 'narwhal horn,' and narwhal horns are denoted by 'narwhal horn.'

(3) What is denoted by 'water' is nothing but what is denoted by 'conglomeration of H_2O molecules,' and conglomerations of H_2O molecules are denoted by 'conglomeration of H_2O molecules.'

(4) What is denoted by 'lightning flash' is nothing but what is denoted by 'electrical flash,' and electrical flashes are denoted by 'electrical flash.'

(5) What is denoted by 'Zeus' thunderbolt' is nothing but what is denoted by 'flash of electrical charges,' and flashes of electrical charges are denoted by 'flash of electrical charges.'

(6) What is denoted by 'Zeus, the thrower of thunderbolts' is nothing but what is denoted by 'discharge of static electricity,' and discharges of static electricity are denoted by 'discharge of static electricity.'

(7) What is denoted by 'pink rat' is nothing but what is denoted by 'pink-rat appearance,' and pink-rat appearances are denoted by 'pink-rat appearance.' [3]

The examples relevant to rebutting the objection mentioned above are (2), (5), (6), and (7). In each of the other three cases it is generally agreed that claims of the form of (a) and (b) are true and that the corresponding identity claims of the form of (c) are also true, whether or not the first two entail the third. The Morning Star is identical with Venus, water is

3. Several of these examples and the following discussion of them are derived from Rorty, pp. 27–35.

identical with certain conglomerations of H_2O molecules, and flashes of lightning with electrical flashes. And, of course, in each case we would agree that these entities so "reduced" exist. But we would think differently in the other four examples. Surely there are narwhal horns, electrical flashes, discharges of static electricity, and pink-rat hallucinations, but although people have mistakenly referred to these entities as unicorn horns, Zeus' thunderbolts, Zeus, and pink rats, it does not follow that they are unicorn horns, Zeus' thunderbolts, Zeus, and pink rats. In each of these cases, then, we should reject the identity claim, but at the same time accept the corresponding denotation claims. We can conclude from this that a conjunction of statements of the form of (a) and (b) does not entail identity claims of the form of (c), and therefore this objection to the 'sensation' elimination theory fails. There is no reason to doubt that the theory is consistent. But is it plausible?

AN ATTEMPT TO JUSTIFY THE THEORY BY ANALOGY

An obvious way to try to justify the 'sensation' elimination theory is to show that its claim that what is denoted by sensation terms is nothing but what is denoted by 'brain process,' is relevantly analogous to one of the above mentioned examples where we are justified in making the two claims about denotation, and also justified in denying the corresponding identity claim. Let us, therefore, compare it with each example.

Consider the second example about 'unicorn horn.' Here we have a claim about the common referents of two different pure or nontheoretical observation terms when, for example, people have pointed to a narwhal horn and called it a unicorn horn. Such people have made a straightforward empirical mistake. This can be shown by gathering evidence to justify that there are no unicorns and thus no unicorn horns, or by tracing the history of the particular horn in question. But in many cases of using sensation terms to talk about something, no mistake can be shown by piling up this kind of nontheoretical, empirical evidence in these ways. In such cases a claim that someone is having a sensation does not entail any nontheoretical, empirical falsehood. We cannot, therefore, justify the claim of the 'sensation' elimination theory by likening sensation terms to 'unicorn horn.'

The fifth example about 'Zeus' thunderbolt' concerns two terms that, although they are observation terms, are not pure observation terms. That is, both terms in the fifth example, unlike those in the second example, are theory laden observation terms, because although they are used to report what is observed, a statement that entails there are thunderbolts of Zeus or flashes of electrical charges also entails that there is some postulated theoretical entity, i.e. Zeus or an electrical charge. Here again we would agree that there are phenomena denoted by 'Zeus' thunderbolt,' namely lightning flashes, but deny the corresponding identity claim that these phenomena are identical with thunderbolts thrown by Zeus, because there is no being named 'Zeus.' In this case we deny that Zeus' thunderbolts exist because their existence entails that Zeus exists and we reject the latter claim for reasons quite different from the nontheoretical empirical grounds used in example (2). The statement 'Zeus exists' is not a false observation statement nor does it entail one. It is, let us say for our purposes here, a pure theoretical statement about the unobserved cause of lightning flashes. It, then, competes with the "more scientific" theoretical explanations of the occurrences of lightning flashes and is rejected because, roughly, some scientific theory that competes with it has more explanatory and predictive power. It might be noted in passing, however, that one could consistently, if not plausibly, maintain that lightning is caused by Zeus, while accepting all available empirical evidence and also the justification of a competing scientific explanation of lightning, if he were to subscribe to an instrumentalist view of scientific theoretical terms.[4]

Can we liken sensation terms to 'Zeus' thunderbolt'? One difference is that 'Zeus' thunderbolt' is used to report something perceivable, but sensation terms are not. This does not seem to be a crucial difference, however, because both terms are used to refer to phenomena that we experience, in the one case via perception, in the other not. But there is an important difference.

4. This, in effect, is what Berkeley does in combining his instrumentalist view of scientific theoretical terms with his claim that God is the cause of the sensory ideas that make up the world. I have discussed this in "Theoretical Terms, Berkeleian Notions, and Minds," in C. M. Turbayne, ed., *Berkeley: Principles of Human Knowledge; Text and Critical Essays* (Indianapolis: Bobbs-Merrill, 1970), pp. 161–81.

The term 'Zeus' thunderbolt' is theory laden because its use to report some observable phenomena entails that there is a postulated theoretical entity, Zeus. But many sensation terms are not theory laden in this way, unless the entities they are used to refer to are themselves postulated theoretical entities, because a claim that there are sensations does not entail that there is any other postulated theoretical entity.

The question at this point is whether what sensation terms are used to refer to are postulated theoretical entities. Because something is such an entity only if we do not experience it, we can conclude that what sensation terms refer to are postulated theoretical entities only if we do not experience the entities referred to. Consequently we can use the fifth example to justify the elimination of sensations only if sensation terms are nonreporting, or pure, theoretical terms. But the 'sensation' elimination theory cannot take this tack, because it construes sensation terms as reporting terms. Furthermore, the theory is certainly correct in this; as we have already seen (in chap. 2), sensation terms are theoretico-reporting terms. Consequently the fifth example cannot help the justification of the elimination of sensation terms and sensations.

The sixth example differs from the two previously discussed because it concerns two terms neither of which, for our purposes, are observation terms, either pure or theory laden. It is like the fifth example, however, in that we justify the denial of the existence of Zeus, and thereby the denial of the corresponding identity claim about Zeus and electrical discharges, on theoretical grounds. Indeed both terms of the sixth example are pure theoretical terms, because they neither meet the first defining condition of 'observation term' or of 'phenomenal term,' nor are they definable by observation terms or phenomenal terms (see p. 81). It is examples such as this that the postulation elimination theory uses to justify its position. It is claimed that sensation terms are, in principle, like 'Zeus' in that their scientific explanatory roles can be taken over by physiological terms, and thus sensation terms are unnecessary for explanation and prediction. But we have already rejected this construal of sensation terms. Sensation terms are used to report phenomena we experience whether or not they have any explanatory function, and therefore we cannot justify their elimination merely by eliminating their explanatory function, as long as they have a reporting function. Example (6) fails to help justify the elimination of sensations.

It is clear that example (7) will not help, because the elimination of pink rats results from construing the referents of 'pink rat' to be sensations rather than physical objects. As Rorty notes, we cannot eliminate sensations by construing them as the referents of sensation terms.[5] This leads us to the conclusion that none of the four examples of justified elimination of entities can be used to provide justification for eliminating sensations. If an eliminative materialist is to justify his position he must take a different line altogether.

ANOTHER ATTEMPTED JUSTIFICATION:
NO NEED FOR SENSATION TERMS

Rorty's approach to the justification of what I have explicated as the 'sensation' elimination theory is such a new line. Although he begins by likening the case of sensations to an hallucination example about demons, he ends by likening it to a physical object example about tables. What he does is liken claims such as: "What is denoted by 'sensation' is nothing but what is denoted by 'brain process,'" to a claim such as: "What is denoted by 'table' is nothing but what is denoted by 'conglomeration of molecules.'" At first glance this move seems self-defeating, because the table case is like example (4) with 'water,' where we do not conclude there is no water. But while admitting this, Rorty seeks to explain this conclusion about tables in such a way that it will aid the 'sensation' elimination theory. He says,

> If there is any point to saying that tables are nothing but clouds of molecules it is presumably to say that, in principle, we could stop making a referring use of "table," and of any extensionally equivalent term, and still leave our ability to describe and predict undiminished. But this would seem just the point of (and the justification for) saying that there are no demons. Why does the realization that nothing would be lost by the dropping of "table" from our vocabulary still leave us with the conviction that there are tables, whereas the same realization about demons leaves

5. See Rorty, pp. 37–38.

us with the conviction that there are no demons? I suggest that the only answer to this question which will stand examination is that although we could *in principle* drop "table," it would be monstrously inconvenient to do so, whereas it is both possible in principle and convenient in practice to drop "demon." [6]

If Rorty is right, then the only relevant difference between hallucination examples such as cases of demons and pink rats, and physical object examples such as cases of tables and water, is that it is very inconvenient to give up table-talk for molecule-talk but quite convenient to give up demon-talk for hallucination-talk. And if this is so, then, although as in example (4) we do not in practice say that there are no tables, we are nevertheless justified in concluding that there are none. This is because if the only thing that keeps us from drawing this conclusion is linguistic convenience, something of no ontological relevance, then the conclusion is justified for purposes of ontology. Rorty's point, then, is that for the purpose of justifying an ontological position, the 'sensation' case is relevantly like the 'table' case which is relevantly like the hallucination case after all. Our task in evaluating Rorty's claim, therefore, is to see whether there are any differences among these three cases sufficient to destroy his justification of the elimination of sensations.

Let us grant that if sensation terms are not needed for correctly explaining, predicting, reporting, and describing, then Rorty has made his point that we are justified in eliminating sensations, while at the same time we are justified in using the terms to avoid inconvenience. Let us also grant what is surely more debatable, that neither terms such as 'table' and 'water' nor sensation terms are needed for either explanation or prediction. The question, then, is whether our ability to report and describe would remain undiminished if these terms were eliminated from language.

The crux of Rorty's case that sensation terms are unnecessary for the purpose of correctly reporting and describing lies in the following passage:

6. Ibid., p. 34.

And why should it not be the case that the circumstances in which we make non-inferential reports about brain-processes are just those circumstances in which we make non-inferential reports about sensations? For this will in fact be the case if, when we were trained to say, e.g., "I'm in pain" we were in fact being trained to respond to the occurrence within ourselves of a stimulation of C-fibers. If this is the case, the situation will be perfectly parallel to the case of demons and hallucinations. We *will,* indeed, have been making non-inferential reports about brain-processes all our lives *sans le savoir.*[7]

Rorty is claiming here that there is no reason why we should deny an exact parallel between demon reports, or pink-rat reports, and pain reports. And he might add that the parallel should extend to water reports. There certainly is at least one parallel here. We can use 'There's H_2O here' instead of 'There's water here,' and it would seem we would be making more accurate reports in so doing. If we can also use some physicalistic expression such as, 'My C-fibers are stimulated' to report the occurrence of what we usually report by 'I'm in pain,' and if, in so doing, we would be making more accurate reports, then both cases would be perfectly parallel to the case of pink-rat reports in the relevant respects, because using 'I see a pink-rat appearance' is more accurate than using 'I see a pink rat.' Rorty thinks this parallel is enough to make his case: just as we do not need 'pink rat,' we need neither 'pain' nor 'water' nor any other sensation terms and observation terms to report and describe what occurs.

First objection: Sensation terms needed for reporting

We can grant that if 'stimulation of C-fibers' and 'pain' refer to the same things, then there is a clear sense in which we would lose no ability to make identifying reference to things, and consequently, a clear sense in which we would lose no ability to report something if we dropped 'pain' and all other psychological terms that refer to what 'pain' refers to. That is, although our ability to refer to things would be diminished in the sense that we would have fewer nonsynonymous terms to use to refer to

7. Ibid., p. 40.

things, our ability to identify *in some way* each thing there is would not be diminished. And, it is clear that it is the latter ability that is relevant to Rorty's claim about our reporting ability.

The problem is, however, whether 'stimulation of C-fibers,' or some other physicalistic term, and 'pain' do refer to the same things. If they do not, then our ability to identify in some way each thing there is would be diminished if we were to drop 'pain' and all other psychological terms that refer to what 'pain' refers to. Rorty, then, can establish his claim about our undiminished reporting ability, only if he has reason to think that some physicalistic terms refer to what sensation terms refer to. But this identity of reference is just what he is trying to establish. Thus he cannot use his claim about our reporting ability remaining undiminished to help justify his identity of reference claim as he tries to do.

Two replies might be made at this point. First, someone might claim that although J. J. C. Smart was wrong to think that topic-neutral language could be used to give the meaning of sensation sentences (see Chap. 1), his mistake can be converted into a sound point. Namely, topic-neutral expressions, although not synonymous with sensation expressions, can be used to identify in some way each thing we now use sensation terms to identify. Thus, contrary to the previous objection to Rorty, we can drop sensation terms without diminishing our ability to identify each thing in some way.

The problem for this reply is whether there is reason to think topic-neutral terms will do the job of replacing the reporting function of sensation terms. Consider first an attempt derived from Smart's suggested translation of 'I have a pain,' a suggestion he later claims is merely an attempt to give "the general purport of sensation reports." [8] Thus we might try to replace 'pain' by:

> Something that happens to someone like what happens when he is stuck with a pin.

This is neutral because there is no implication about whether this something is physical or not. But the problem is that this

8. Smart, "Brain Processes and Incorrigibility," *Australasian Journal of Philosophy* 40 (1962): 69.

reporting expression is not specific enough to pick out from
several things that happen in such situations just what we identify using 'pain.' A more specific phrase might be used, such as:

> An entity of the kind for which it is contingently true that
> things of that kind happen to someone when and only
> when his C-fibers are stimulated.

This description would identify one kind of thing which might
well be what we identify using 'pain,' if there is exactly one kind
of thing that meets the description. But the problem is whether
there is exactly one such kind of thing. There might be none, if
the only kind of thing that happens to someone exactly when
his C-fibers are stimulated is that his C-fibers are stimulated.
This might be the case if there were no one-to-one psycho-
physical simultaneity correspondence of kinds (Chap. 1). It is
also possible that there are several kinds of things, including
pains, that meet this description. If so, then we would sacrifice
univocality of reference by dropping 'pain,' and that seems unjustified. Furthermore we are in no position to decide this issue,
because it cannot be decided without scientific investigation. We
cannot, then, rely on this first reply to the previous objection.

If the second reply is sound, however, we need not worry
about finding suitable topic-neutral expressions to take over the
reporting functions of sensation terms. There is reason enough
to think that pains occur when and only when C-fibers are
stimulated, and so, according to this reply, we can use 'stimulation of C-fibers' to report what we now use 'pain' to report.
Thus 'My C-fibers are stimulated!' could be used to report
what 'I have a pain!' reports. The immediate objection to this
is that nothing can be solved this way, for there is no more reason to think 'stimulation of C-fibers' with this new reporting role
has univocal reference than that it has ambiguous reference,
referring to certain brain states and, in addition, pains. But, in
the spirit of Rorty's argument, a materialist might well reply
that if the *only* thing that *might* be lost is univocal reference,
and there is no reason to conclude it would be lost, then we
are justified in assuming that the reference is univocal. And,
consequently, we can also assume that our ability to identify in
some way each thing there is would remain undiminished if
sensation terms were dropped from language. This brings us

finally to the central question of whether the only thing that might be lost is an unverifiable ambiguity of reference. To see that there is reason to think more would be lost than that, we can turn to the second objection to Rorty's claim.

Second objection: Sensation terms needed for true descriptions

For the purposes of considering the present objection, let us grant Rorty one more point, that not only can we explain and predict everything that occurs without sensation terms and pure observation terms, but also we can report, in the sense of identify, everything there is without such terms. Although Rorty may think we have granted him all he needs to make his point, we shall find that we have not. We have not settled the question of whether or not our ability to describe what there is would be diminished if we dropped these terms from our language. In order to answer this question, we must again be clear about what kind of ability is relevant to Rorty's claim. We can distinguish at least three different kinds of descriptive ability:

(1) The ability to make many different sorts of descriptions of what there is.

(2) The ability to make accurate descriptions of what there is.

(3) The ability to make true descriptions, i.e. use true sentences to describe what there is.

It is clear that the first kind of ability would be diminished if we dropped sensation terms and pure observation terms, but it is also clear that having only this ability diminished would not affect Rorty's point. If the second and third kinds of abilities remain undiminished, his point is sound. If, however, either of these two kinds of abilities are diminished by dropping these terms, then Rorty's argument fails, because more than convenience would be lost.

Consider the second kind of ability. If we would lose accuracy in our descriptions by dropping certain terms, then we could not justify the claim that they are needed only for convenience. This may be the kind of ability Rorty considers, and, if so, we might well agree with him that descriptions without sensation terms and pure observation terms would be no less accurate and precise, no more vague and unclear, than if we used such terms. Indeed using only mathematically formulated descriptions would seem to result in more accuracy rather than less. This is the case when we describe physical objects using scientific theoretical terms rather than pure observation terms. Let us assume, then, that Rorty is right concerning the second kind of descriptive ability.

Descriptions of what there is might well be no less accurate if we dropped sensation terms and observation terms. But would they be complete? Would there be any true descriptive sentences we would be unable to formulate? If there were some, then one kind of descriptive ability relevant to what there is would be lost and Rorty's argument would fail. We could not justify eliminating terms needed for making true descriptions. It seems clear that concerning this kind of descriptive ability a parallel holds between sensation terms and observation terms, but this is the wrong parallel for Rorty's argument. One sentence will provide the same description as another only if the two statements are synonymous. Thus the observation description of a conglomeration of H_2O molecules by the sentence, 'The fluid in the glass is clear and wet' can be made only by a sentence synonymous with that sentence, but there is reason to think that no sentence using only theoretical terms is synonymous with this sentence with its pure observation terms. Generally the attempt to define, either explicitly or partially, theoretical terms by observation terms has been rejected.[9] The view now adopted is that the relationship between theoretical expressions and these pure observation descriptions is logically contingent. I know of no reason to doubt the present view. This justifies the conclusion that no theoretical sentences are synonymous with pure observation sentences that describe observable entities. Consequently, to eliminate all pure observation terms would result in our being unable to provide observation descriptions of what

9. For the opposite view, see D. Lewis, "How to Define Theoretical Terms," *Journal of Philosophy* 67 (1970): 427–46. Lewis' proposal construes each theoretical term of a theory T as a definite description that names a component in the unique realization of T. It does not seem, however, that such a definition would provide a way to produce a theoretical sentence that is synonymous with 'The fluid in the glass is clear and wet.'

is denoted by 'water' that surely seem to be true, and our ability to make true descriptions of what is denoted by 'water' would surely seem to be considerably diminished.

The same conclusion applies to sensation terms. Even if we grant that what is denoted by 'pain' is identical with a stimulation of C-fibers, it would seem we shall still need sensation terms to make the true descriptions of certain stimulations of C-fibers, as, for example, intense, sharp, and throbbing. No neurophysiological sentence is synonymous with 'What I feel is intense, sharp, and throbbing,' and thus no neurophysiological sentence can be used to make the same description. But it seems clear that some such sentences are sometimes true, and thus to eliminate the sensation terms that we apply to what we experience would seem to diminish considerably our ability to describe truly. Rorty, although he may be correct about explaining and predicting, and even if we grant he is right about reporting, seems to be wrong about describing. There is reason to think that more than convenience would be lost if we were to eliminate sensation terms and pure observation terms, and Rorty has given us no reason to think otherwise. The eliminative materialist cannot justify the elimination of sensations in the way Rorty claims he can.

First reply: Non-synonymy of expressions is merely contingent: It might be replied to the previous objection that it is based on a contingent fact dependent on the present state of language. There is no reason why, in the future, theoretical terms could not take on the descriptive roles of both pure observation terms and sensation terms. When that time comes, according to this reply, the last obstacle to the acceptance of the 'sensation' elimination theory will disappear and the theory will be acceptable. And, it might be added, because there is nothing, except perhaps ingrained usage and convenience, to stop theoretical terms from acquiring these roles, it does not matter whether they actually ever do acquire them. If pure observation terms and sensation terms are in principle eliminable, then the 'sensation' elimination theory is justified.

This reply does point to one clear way terms can be eliminated, but, unfortunately, it is not a kind of elimination that will help an eliminative materialist. Let us assume that 'Jones' C-fibers are firing rapidly' has acquired the descriptive role of

'Jones' pain is intense,' that it also retains its theoretical role, and that it does not become ambiguous but rather richer in meaning. Let us also grant that if this role change occurs, then 'Jones' pain is intense' is no longer needed to make a true description of Jones, because 'Jones' C-fibers are firing rapidly' gives us this description of Jones and more. The objection to such a reply is not, as Malcolm might claim, that "conjectured future concepts" are irrelevant to the question of materialism because the question is about our present concepts.[10] The question is about what there is. Questions about concepts whether past, present, or future, are relevant only insofar as they help answer the question of what there is. The objection is, rather, that the reason we would no longer need 'Jones' pain is intense' is that what it states would be entailed by 'Jones' C-fibers are firing rapidly.' Consequently, we could no longer even make certain physiological claims about the brain without implying that there are sensations. This is surely a move in the wrong direction for a materialist.

The failure of the previous kind of linguistic elimination to help the eliminative materialist points to the kind of elimination of terms he requires. The elimination must accomplish at least two things. First, as we have already seen, it must show that the terms eliminated are not needed for any true description. Second, as the present discussion emphasizes, it must also show that all of the descriptive roles played by the eliminated terms in true statements can be played by purely physical or physical-neutral terms, that is, terms that can be used to ascribe physical or physical-neutral properties to entities without implying the existence of anything mental. It is not important, then, which words we use now or ever. What matters is which descriptive roles they play. Merely to eliminate or change terms, and thus to leave untouched the descriptive roles they play, has no ontological significance. Thus because 'stimulation of C-fibers' taking on the descriptive role of 'pain' would accomplish only the elimination of 'pain' and not its role in true descriptions, such an elimination of sensation terms would fail to help the

10. See N. Malcolm, "Scientific Materialism and the Identity Theory," *Dialogue* 3 (1964–65): 119. Malcolm's point has been discussed in the context of the spatial location objection to the identity theory in Chapter 1.

eliminative materialist. Indeed, if this is the only way sensation terms can be eliminated, we should reject the 'sensation' elimination theory, because we must either keep sensation terms to make true descriptions or change other terms in such a way that using them descriptively implies that there are sensations or, at least, entities with phenomenal properties.

Second reply: H_2O without water and sensing without sensations: The previous discussion leads to the conclusion that, contrary to Rorty, the case of water and pain are not "perfectly parallel to the case of demons and hallucinations." There is, however, a new move that would make the cases of water and pink rats perfectly parallel. This is a move that one kind of scientific realist might make, that is, to claim that, although we commonly suppose the referents of pure observation terms to be physical objects and their sensible qualities, what they actually refer to are sensations caused in us by physical objects. It is the theoretical terms of science that refer to physical objects and their properties; they provide the most accurate and comprehensive description of physical objects that is available.[11] If we were to adopt this position, then we could agree that although our ability to describe would be diminished in one way by eliminating pure observation terms, it would not be the relevant way. Nothing would be lost for the purposes of making accurate and complete descriptions. We would still have available all the terms needed to make accurate and true descriptions: theoretical terms to describe physical objects and their properties, and nonobservation terms of a sensation vocabulary, such as 'clear, wet appearance' to describe the sensations and their phenomenal qualities we experience.

This move by a scientific realist makes the cases of water and pink rats parallel because in both cases when we ascribe sensible qualities to what we experience, we are in fact, perhaps unknowingly, describing sensations rather than physical objects. But this move destroys the parallel between the cases of water and sensations. If we make this move, then, although the only thing lost by eliminating pure observation terms is convenience, it seems clear that our ability to describe truly would be vastly

11. See W. Sellars, *Science, Preception, and Reality,* esp. Chapters 1 and 3, for a position much like this one. His and other versions of scientific realism are discussed in Chapter 7.

diminished if all sensation words were also eliminated. We
would then be unable to make descriptions of what we "observe." Indeed, we would be unable to describe sensations in
the ways we ordinarily and "mistakenly" describe physical objects when we use pure observation terms.

A 'sensation' elimination theorist is not defeated yet however.
He might claim that, contrary to what is said above, we do not
need sensation terms such as 'pink-rat appearance' to describe
our sensory experiences. He could defend this claim by denying
any descriptive need for the appearance terminology, and thus
any need for sensation terms to attribute properties to sense
impressions, or appearances. This defense requires that he replace the appearance terminology with another equally adequate
to describe sensory experience. If R. M. Chisholm is right, this
can be done. We can use an adverbial sensing terminology instead. Chisholm says,

> When we say "The appearance of the thing is white," our
> language suggests that we are attributing a certain property
> to a substance. But we could just as well have said "The
> thing appears white," using the verb "appears" instead of
> the substantive "appearance." And in "The thing appears
> white," as already noted, the word "white" functions as an
> adverb. . . . We might say, then, that the word "white,"
> in what we have called its sensible use, tells us something
> about . . . the *way* in which the object appears, just as
> "slowly" may tell us something about the way in which an
> object moves.[12]

And where we do not wish to imply there is an object appearing to someone we can say "He senses whitely" instead of "He
senses a white appearance." In saying the former,

> we are not committed to saying that there *is* a thing—an
> appearance—of which the word "white," in its sensible
> use, designates a property. We are saying, rather, that
> there is a certain state or process—that of being appeared
> to, or sensing, or experiencing—and we are using . . .

the adverb "whitely," to describe more specifically the way in which that process occurs.[13]

If Chisholm is right, then no descriptive ability would be lost by eliminating the appearance terminology, or as I shall call it, "the sensa terminology," if we adopted, instead, the adverbial sensing terminology. That is, in our vocabulary there are two kinds of sensation terms, namely, sensa terms such as 'pain' and 'afterimage' that are used to refer to phenomenal individuals, and sensing terms such as 'hurting' and 'imaging' that are used to refer to phenomenal events and states. However, if Chisholm is correct, only the second kind is needed for descriptive purposes. We might in this way, then, be able to eliminate sensa terms as required by the 'sensation' elimination theory. But even this last elimination is not sufficient to justify some form of eliminative materialism. It surely seems we cannot also eliminate sensing terms without considerably diminishing our descriptive ability, because we often truly describe someone in saying that he is sensing whitely and no purely physicalistic statement makes the same description.

ONE MORE ATTEMPTED JUSTIFICATION:
WHAT EXPLAINS BEST DESCRIBES BEST

The conclusion we have now reached is that, although it may be that neither pure observation terms nor sensa terms are needed for accurate and true descriptions of what there is—because the function of the former can be taken over by the joint use of theoretical terms and sensation terms, and the function of the latter taken over by sensing terms alone—the elimination seems unable to go further. We seem to be left with a residue of sensing terms, and, it surely seems, entities that cannot be eliminated. There is, however, one last move an eliminative materialist might try. He might adopt an extreme version of scientific realism, one which holds that for all persons as well as all physical objects, those pure theoretical terms of science that provide the best available explanations of their observable behavior also provide the best available descriptions of the entities whose behavior they explain. That is, not only is each theoretical sentence at least as accurate a means of description

13. Ibid., p. 96.

as any other sentence available for describing the same thing, but all theoretical sentences that best explain the behavior of a particular entity, when taken together, provide a true description of that entity which is more accurate and more comprehensive than any other description of the same entity. If also, as this kind of scientific realist believes, the theoretical terms of neurophysiology provide the best available explanation of the behavior that sensation terms are used to explain, then some set of neurophysiological sentences would provide a true description of someone that is more accurate and comprehensive than any set that includes sentences such as 'He sensed a white appearance' or 'He sensed white-ly.' On this view, sensa and sensings are to be eliminated, but not because sensation terms do not denote, and not because sensations are useless postulated entities. It is rather because, with the increase in understanding science will bring, the entities we now report, in our state of relative ignorance, using sensation terms will be revealed more clearly to us. We will discover that they are something material, perhaps brain processes, and, when speaking with the learned, will refer to them using only the relevant physicalistic terms.[14]

Once again, we can best understand the argument by putting it in a more perspicuous form:

(1) An object has and only has those properties referred to by the terms used in the best explanations of all its observable behavior.

(2) All the behavior of human beings is best explained by the theoretical statements of neurophysiology.

(3) All properties referred to by the terms in the theoretical statements of neurophysiology are physical properties.

Therefore

(4) A human has and only has physical properties.

The premise easiest to accept is (3), because if theoretical terms of a physical science are referring terms, then it is reasonable to assume that any properties referred to are physical. This is

14. Although Sellars is a scientific realist whose position is very similar to the one described here, there is an important difference. See Chapter 7.

reasonable, even if a phenomenalist were to object that it is false. An analytic phenomenalist might claim that all physical-object statements are analyzable into sensation statements and thus if any physical-object terms refer to properties, then they refer to properties of sensations. But because there is ample reason to think that such analyses fail, there is no force to this objection.[15] An objection, not so easily disposed of, could be raised by an ontological phenomenalist such as Berkeley who might claim that physical objects are really only bundles of sense-data, thus all the properties of physical objects are phenomenal and if any physical-object terms refer to any properties they refer to phenomenal properties. But although this kind of phenomenalism has not been shown to be implausible, neither is there reason to accept it without a careful investigation of its relative merits when compared with its alternatives, a task beyond the scope of this book. Let us, provisionally at least, accept premise (3).

Premise (2) is not as easy to accept. It is first open to the objection raised against premise (2) of the argument for the postulation elimination theory (see that section of Chap. 4), namely, that physiology is now in a stage of development that falsifies (2). The best reply to this point is the one made previously, that is, if this is the only objection to the argument, then, although the argument is not now acceptable, there is reason to think that it will be in the future. There are, however, other objections to this argument, indeed, to premise (2). One is that if physiology is reducible to physics then it may be that physics best explains human behavior. We need not debate this objection, however, because we can amend (2) to conclude "by the theoretical statements of neurophysiology or some other physical science." This requires we also amend (3) in a harmless way.

Another objection to premise (2) necessitates still another amendment. As stated, premise (2) is elliptical. A set of statements best explains something *for some purpose,* and what explains best for one purpose may not explain best for another. Describing human behavior in terms of events and explaining these events using the resources of physiology is not the kind of

15. See A. J. Ayer, *The Problem of Knowledge* pp. 118–29; and R. M. Chisholm, *Perceiving,* Appendix.

procedure best suited for ascriptions of legal and moral respon-
sibility to persons for their behavior. Such ascriptions require
behavior to be construed as actions rather than events, and, although each action has an event component, no one has shown
how to reduce actions to events. Nor has anyone shown how to
relate actions to physiologically explained events by "correspondence rules" or "bridge principles" so that physiological
explanations of event behavior are made relevant to explanations of action behavior. Neither is there any reason to think
that physiological explanations are best for the kind of com-
munication required to conduct the practical affairs of everyday
life. Such explanations are, to say the least, so very cumbersome
and complicated that they would make everyday communica-
tion practically impossible. We must amend premise (2) again.
This time let us replace 'best explained' by 'best explained for
the purposes of science.' These two amendments put premise
(2) in the position of lacking justification only because the
physical sciences are not sufficiently developed yet. There is,
then, nothing more to say now for or against (2).

The central problem lies with premise (1), however. Not only
are there objections to it as stated, but the second amendment
to premise (2) requires an amendment to (1) that sharpens
two objections to the extreme kind of scientific realism the argument requires. The first objection concerns the fact that the
amended version of (1) states, in essence, that those terms that
explain observable behavior best for scientific purposes—certain
of the theoretical terms of science—also describe best what they
explain. But why should there be this correspondence between
scientific explanation and description? It seems no less reasonable to claim that observation terms, perhaps when taken with
certain action terms, are best for description, while scientific
theoretical terms are best for certain explanatory purposes.
There seems to be no reason to reject our ordinary descriptions and those of consummate novelists as inaccurate or misleading, because they and we use observation terms.

The second objection is more serious, because, when (1) is
conjoined with (2) it entails an implausible extreme version of
scientific realism. It has already been mentioned that the debate
about the claim that the pure theoretical terms of science are
referring terms is not resolved. This "minimal" scientific realism

must be justified if amended premise (1) is to be justified, because premise (1) implies that scientific theoretical terms are
referring terms. But what is entailed by (1) conjoined with (2)
goes well beyond this minimal claim. It even requires more
than a position I call "moderate scientific realism": that all
physical objects, but perhaps not persons, have *only* the properties referred to by the theoretical scientific terms that best explain their observable behavior. We have seen that this is one
way to make the case of the table parallel to that of pink rats.
But although the minimal view is plausible, because it is implied by the plausible claim that physical objects have both
pure observation properties and pure theoretical properties, the
statement of moderate scientific realism is neither implied by nor
compatible with this claim. However, although I have found
no one who has yet produced reasons to render moderate
scientific realism plausible, let alone justified, men such as W.
Sellars are attempting to justify it.[16] Consequently I do not wish
to rest the case against the argument on the current lack of
justification for moderate scientific realism.

I shall rest the case rather on the implausibility of the kind
of "extreme" scientific realism which must be justified if the
argument is to be sound. Extreme scientific realism states that
all entities, including persons, have only the theoretical scientific properties referred to by the theoretical terms that best
explain their behavior.[17] But the conjunction of (1) and (2)
entails a kind of extreme scientific realism that states that persons have only the theoretical properties attributed to them in
certain physicalistic theories. That is, no person has any pure
observation properties such as having brown eyes or a perfumed
smell, and no person has any phenomenal properties such as
feeling an intense pain (or intense-pain sensing). This clearly
goes well beyond moderate scientific realism, which is compatible with pain-sensing by people and with a plausible explanation of why we "mistakenly" think that colors, smells,
tastes we experience are properties of physical objects. That is,
it can transfer experienced properties to our sensory experiences

16. See Sellars; also his *Science and Metaphysics* (New York: Humanities Press, 1968).

17. Minimal, moderate, and extreme scientific realism are discussed
in more detail at the beginning of Chapter 7.

either as properties of sensa or as modes of sensing. But this extreme scientific realism cannot use such an explanation, because it denies that there are sensings and sensa. There is for this extreme view, then, nothing like the color and the aching pain we are often so sure we experience. It is not that they are merely modes of sensing, for there are no sensings. Whatever we are aware of which we think is an aching pain or a red object, is really something with properties drastically unlike the sensuous color of an object or the torturous ache of a pain. Not even in the case of a man's own inner experiences is what he is aware of similar to the way it seems to him. It is not merely that it has properties he is not aware of, as would be the case if the identity theory were true; it has none of those properties he is most sure he is aware of. This consequence of this version of extreme scientific realism, which we discussed in Chapter 3 and found implausible there, remains implausible. We should, therefore, reject it and with it the extreme scientific realism that implies it.

The rejection of this extreme position justifies also rejecting the argument we are examining, because the conjunction of premises (1) and (2) of the argument entails the rejected position. Furthermore, because it is reasonable to think that (2) will become justified while the reason to reject the conjunction remains sound, we can conclude that we should reject premise (1).

CONCLUSION ABOUT THE 'SENSATION' ELIMINATION THEORY

We have examined all the ways I have found to justify the 'sensation' elimination theory and found them all wanting. For this reason I conclude we should abandon the 'sensation' elimination theory as a justifiable version of eliminative materialism. Its problem is that it requires that no sensation terms, that is, neither sensing terms nor sensa terms, are needed for true descriptions and there seems to be no justifiable way to show that. Each of the other three eliminative theories also faces, in its own way, this problem and fails to surmount it. Analytic behaviorism attempts to show there is no descriptive need for sensation terms by providing behavioral analyses of sentences containing the terms, but no analysis seems to be adequate. Rylean behaviorism argues against a descriptive need for sensation terms by putting sentences containing them in the class of nonreferring inference tickets, but this move also remains unjustified. The postulation elimination theory states that there is a descriptive need for sensation terms only if there is an explanatory need, and there is no explanatory need. This position might well be sound if sensation terms were pure theoretical terms, but we have seen reason to think they are not. The 'sensation' elimination theory, therefore, faces no problem not equally damaging to the three other versions of eliminative materialism we have examined. It does not face, however, one problem common to each of the others, because it is the only one that can agree with the classification of sensation terms as theoretico-reporting terms, which we found to be the most reasonable classification. It is, then, the most reasonable of the four versions we have examined. But, still, we have seen that it is not reasonable enough to be acceptable.

REJECTION OF ELIMINATIVE MATERIALISM AND FOREWORD TO ADVERBIAL MATERIALISM

The problem about how to handle what seems to be an irreplaceable descriptive role of sensation terms has played a major part in the refutation of all four examined versions of eliminative materialism. I know of no other extant versions and can think of no way for an eliminative materialist to avoid this problem. The conclusion it certainly seems we should draw from this is that a materialist, if he is finally to solve the problem bequeathed to him by Hobbes, must abandon eliminative materialism. But he cannot return to reductive materialism with its problem raised by the phenomenal properties of the objects of sensing, i.e. sensa. He must abandon both reductive materialism and eliminative materialism.

There is but one way a materialist can proceed at this point. While he cannot justify either eliminating both sensings and sensa, or reducing both sensings and sensa to brain parts, perhaps he can justify what I have called "adverbial materialism." This requires eliminating sensa and reducing objectless sensing events to brain events. He can achieve the former if he can justify adopting the adverbial metaphysical position corresponding to the sensing terminology proposed by Chisholm. This would enable him to avoid Hobbes' phantasms, or sensa, and the problem raised by the phenomenal properties which sensa seem to have but which are neither eliminable nor reducible to materialistic properties of brain entities. In this way he could avoid the problem that defeats reductive materialism. He can achieve the latter if he solves the problem of properties that sensing events might have that are neither eliminable nor reducible to materialistic properties of Hobbes' "internal motions," or brain events. He would solve it if he were to justify that each sensing event is nothing but an event which has an extensional property only if the property is either physical or physical-neutral. Both of these requirements of adverbial materialism will be met if three conditions are satisfied:

(1) There are no phenomenal objects of sensings, i.e. there are no sensa,
(2) Each objectless event of a person sensing in a particular way is identical with some physical event,
(3) Each extentional property of each sensing event either is physical or physical-neutral.

Conjoined, these three conditions entail that each sensing event is nothing but some physical event. That is, each sensing event is identical with a physical event that has an extentional property only if the property is physical or physical-neutral, where a physical event is one the occurrence of which entails that there is an object or a property only if it is physical (see Intro.). Presumably these physical events would be brain events.

It may seem that if we can justify that these conditions are satisfied, then we have shown that adverbial materialism is free of the problem sensations raise for materialism. However, while it is necessary to show this, it is not sufficient. To see this consider the following possibility. Let us assume that there are no sensa and that the event of John hurting intensely is nothing but the event of John's C-fibers firing rapidly. Thus all three conditions are met in this case. However, although pain sensa are eliminated and sensing events are reduced, John has the extentional and a posteriori property of hurting intensely, which is neither physical nor physical-neutral. Furthermore, it is possible, given all this, that the particular instances of this property are something over and above any instance of a physical or physical-neutral property. Consequently, if the three preceding conditions are satisfied, then, although phenomenal properties of individuals which are sensa could not be used to show materialism to be false, it is still possible that sensing properties of individuals which are persons would prove it to be false. We must add a fourth condition. The one needed is:

> (4) Each instance of a person's sensing in some way is nothing but an instance of some physical or physical-neutral property.

During the remainder of this book I shall attempt to discover whether we would be justified to conclude that all four conditions are met. If we are justified then we can accept adverbial materialism, but if we should reject at least one of them, then, because we have reached the last way to make some version of materialism plausible, we should reject materialism. The first task, which comprises Part III, is to see whether it is reasonable to reject sensa and accept the adverbial theory of sensory experience as required by condition (1). There are philosophers who have assumed that there are no sensa, but few have presented reasons for rejecting them. Although we have considered Smart's work in the context of reductive materialism because he says that sensations are identical with brain processes, he might also be considered an adverbial materialist because he also says that "there is, in a sense, no such thing as an after-image or a sense-datum, though there is such a thing as the experience of having an image, and this experience is described indirectly in material object language." [18] Ryle, from whose work I constructed a version of eliminative materialism, states a similar view, for he says that imaging "is a proper and useful concept, but that its use does not entail the existence of pictures which we contemplate or the existence of a gallery in which such pictures are ephemerally suspended. Roughly, imaging occurs, but images are not seen." [19] Both of these men seem to agree that there are sensations which are events, such as experiencing pain, and having an afterimage, but neither seems to think there are sensations which are objects, or individuals, such as pains, afterimages, and other sensa. Unfortunately neither man has provided

18. Smart, "Sensations and Brain Processes," *Philosophical Review* 68 (1959): 151.
19. G. Ryle, *The Concept of Mind*, p. 247.

anything like an adequate reason for his elimination of sensa, and the acceptance of objectless sensings. They should at least show that the strongest arguments for sensa fail.

Chisholm, who, as we have seen, proposes the sensing terminology, offers a reason for accepting it which he may also construe as a reason for the corresponding metaphysical doctrine. His claim about the sensing terminology is that

> if what we want to do is describe perceiving in that way which is least puzzling philosophically, then this strange and artificial terminology would seem to be the least misleading. The alternative terminologies entangle us in philosophical questions we can avoid if we talk in terms of sensing.[20]

It is true that by adopting the sensing terminology we can avoid many problems such as those about whether sensa are two dimensional or three, whether they seem to have properties they do not have, whether they have properties they do not seem to have, and whether at most one person can experience each sensum. Unfortunately for us the question is not how to avoid these problems if we so wish, but whether we are *justified* in avoiding them. If there are reasons for the existence of sensa, then merely devising an artificial terminology in which the problems do not arise neither solves nor dissolves the problems. If, however, there is no reason to accept sensa, then, by Occam's razor and the resultant dissolution of these puzzling problems, we are justified in accepting not only the terminology but the corresponding metaphysical view. In short, because sensa raise problems otherwise avoidable, we can consider them guilty unless proven innocent. Consequently our primary concern in Part III is to discover whether there are any reasons for the existence of sensa.

Our first concern is with the most plausible arguments for sensa which are based on certain facts of perception, namely, perceptual relativity, hallucination, the causal facts of perception, and the time gap between the transmission of stimulus and perception. In Chapter 6, I argue that none of these arguments succeeds and so, given just these facts, it is at least as reason-

20. Chisholm, *Perceiving,* p. 124.

able to accept the adverbial theory as it is to accept a sensa theory. But there are other ways to justify sensa. Even if these empirical facts alone do not justify the existence of sensa, it may be that the scientific theories that explain such facts will in some way require the theoretical postulation of sensa. There may also be justified philosophical theories that require some sort of sensa. It might be argued that the most reasonable philosophical theory of perception and the external world requires sensa rather than objectless sensings. If either some form of indirect realism or ontological phenomenalism should prove more reasonable than any form of direct realism, then there would be reason to reject the adverbial theory of sensory experience. W. Sellars offers a different philosophical reason for sensa. He claims that a thoroughgoing scientific realism entails a unified scientific image or description of the world. According to Sellars, such a description eliminates observable properties, such as colors, sounds, and tastes, from the external world, and requires they be transformed into phenomenal properties of sensa. Thus, if Sellars is right, scientific realism and the unification of science provide reason for sensa.

Of these last three ways in which someone might try to justify the existence of sensa, I examine only the reasons Sellars gives to show that scientific realism requires sensa. These are rejected in Chapter 6. I do not discuss whether there are scientific theoretical reasons for sensa, because no science dealing with sensory experience is yet developed enough to provide reliable clues about what entities its explanations will require. Nor is any critical comparison of direct realism with its alternatives that require sensa attempted here. I plan to consider this separately. Nevertheless, given that neither perceptual facts nor the unification of science requires sensa, it is at least initially plausible that acceptable scientific and philosophical theories of perception and sensation can do without sensa. For this reason, although much work remains to be done, at the end of Part III I conclude that, based on the evidence available at this time, including Chisholm's point that the adverbial theory dissolves puzzling philosophical problems, it is reasonable, although still provisional, to accept the adverbial interpretation of sensory experience.

At the end of Part III, the last three conditions still remain to be examined in the concluding chapter. Much of the preliminary work required has already been done in previous chapters. For this reason the previous results of the book are summarized before the examination. Particularly relevant are the reasons which in Part I led to the conclusion that the theoretical identity of sensa and brain parts is acceptable. These same reasons apply to the theoretical identity of sensings and brain events. Thus there already is some reason to accept condition (2). Nevertheless one last attempt is made to discover whether some property of a sensing event or some property of its correlated brain event prohibits identifying the events. This is done in conjunction with a consideration of condition (3) which requires a search for nonmaterialistic properties of sensing events. Because my search turns up no properties that thwart either the identity or the reduction, I inductively infer that there are no such properties and conclude that we can accept conditions (2) and (3).

The last task of the book is to consider condition (4). This is crucial because, in effect, it is a similar condition, when applied to phenomenal objects, i.e., sensa, rather than to persons, that reductive materialism fails to satisfy. Consequently, in my attempt to show that adverbial materialism is acceptable, I must not only examine properties of instances of sensing properties, but also point out why individuals who are persons with sensing properties can meet condition (4), while sensa with phenomenal properties fail to meet the corresponding condition. Once this is accomplished, we are able to accept, provisionally, at least for the present, adverbial materialism.

PART III

On Sensing and Sensa

6. Four Arguments
for the Existence of Sensa

Those objects construed by some as sense impressions or sense-data and by others as percepts have had a checkered career. There has been constant disagreement about their essential properties, for example, whether they are two dimensional or three, and whether some are identical with surfaces of physical objects or not. We need not enter into these debates: whether, for example, we should construe them as sense-data or as percepts. If either of these is the correct construal of a certain class of existing entities, then there are entities of a kind that have serious consequences not only for materialists and identity theorists, but also for an adequate theory of perception. In order to avoid becoming embroiled in such disagreements, therefore, in this chapter I shall continue to use the term 'sensum' for a kind of object of which both sense-data and percepts are species.

There has also been much disagreement tbout the existence of sensa. At some times it has seemed obvious that they exist, while at others, it has seemed equally obvious there are no such things. There have been numerous attempts to show that they exist or at least that it is plausible to assume they exist; there have been as many attempts to show they do not exist. A. J. Ayer has tried to use what he called the argument from illusion to help make their introduction plausible;[1] J. Austin has tried to refute the argument and with it any reason for introducing sense-data.[2] G. A. Paul and others since have tried to show that the hypostatization of sense-data is a mistake resulting from misconstruing perceptual sensation sentences. They are not sentences referring to peculiar "internal" objects we experience; rather they function to state how external physical objects appear to us.[3] In a similar vein, other philosophers have claimed that the logic of all perceptual sensation talk prohibits using it

1. See A. J. Ayer, *The Foundations of Empirical Knowledge* (New York: St. Martin's Press, 1955), pp. 1–57.
2. See J. L. Austin, *Sense and Sensibilia,* G. J. Warnock, ed. (New York: Oxford University Press, 1964).
3. See G. A. Paul, "Is There a Problem about Sense-Data?" in A. G. N. Flew, ed., *Logic and Language,* 1st series (Oxford: Basil Blackwell, 1955), pp. 101–16.

to describe some purported sensory experiences common to all cases of perception. According to these philosophers, such perceptual claims, whether couched in the appearing terminology or the sensa terminology, always imply some doubt or denial about physical objects on the part of the speaker or someone else. Thus in any situation in which there is no such doubt or denial—the usual perceptual situations—no such statements would be true. Consequently, as H. P. Grice says in his statement of this objection,

> But the sense-datum theorist wants his sense-datum statements to be such that some one or more of them is true whenever a perceptual statement is true; for he wants to go on to give a *general* analysis of perceptual statements in terms of the notion of sense-data. But this goal must be unobtainable if "looks to me" statements (and so sense-datum statements) can be truly made only in the *less* straight forward perceptual situations.[4]

This kind of objection to any theory involving sensa has seemed so forceful to some that Grice spends a considerable time showing that in whatever sense perceptual sensation statements imply doubt or denial, it is not logical implication.[5] One can, by a careful choice of additional statements, cancel out the implication of doubt or denial, but this is impossible for logical implication. I find his argument cogent. Furthermore when his points are coupled with the distinction R. Chisholm makes between the epistemic use of appear words, such as those that imply doubt or denial, and their nonepistemic use, this objection can be seen to be refuted.[6] Consequently I shall not consider it here. Nor have I found any other arguments for the nonexistence of

4. H. P. Grice, "The Causal Theory of Perception," *Proceedings of the Aristotelian Society,* Supplementary Volume, 35 (1961): 125; reprinted in R. J. Swartz, ed., *Perceiving, Sensing, and Knowing: A Book of Readings from Twentieth-Century Sources in the Philosophy of Perception* (Garden City, N.Y.: Doubleday, 1965), p. 442. For views similar to those attacked by Grice, see D. M. Armstrong, *Perception and the Physical World* (London: Routledge and Kegan Paul, 1961), pp. 87–93; and A. M. Quinton, "The Problem of Perception," *Mind* 64 (1955): 22–51; reprinted in Swartz, pp. 497–526.

5. Grice, pp. 440–57.

6. See R. M. Chisholm, *Perceiving,* pp. 43–53.

sensa so strong that there is no need for a careful reconstruction and examination of the most plausible arguments for their existence. My present purpose, consequently, is to examine those arguments. In this chapter I shall consider four arguments based on certain premises concerning empirical facts which, taken with certain other premises, are said to justify the conclusion that there are sensa. In the next chapter, I shall examine in detail the claim made by W. Sellars that scientific realism, a kind of thesis accepted by many materialists, requires the postulation of sensa.

THE ARGUMENT FROM PERCEPTUAL RELATIVITY

The argument I wish to consider first is called the argument from illusion by A. J. Ayer, but as will become evident as we proceed, and as brought out by Austin, it is a mistake to characterize the perceptual facts relevant to at least one of Ayer's versions of the argument as involving either illusion or delusion.[7] But, contrary to Austin, the irrelevance of illusion and delusion to the argument as I shall formulate it affects only the appropriateness of the title Ayer gives to the argument rather than its soundness. I shall begin by quoting certain passages from Ayer:

> All our perceptions, whether veridical or delusive, are to some extent causally dependent both upon external conditions, such as the character of light, and upon our own physiological and psychological states. . . . It is held to be characteristic of material things that their existence and their essential properties are independent of any particular observer. . . . But this, it is argued, has been shown not to be true of the objects we immediately experience. And so the conclusion is reached that what we immediately experience is in no case a material thing. . . . We may be allowed to have indirect knowledge of the properties of material things. But this knowledge, it is held, must be obtained through the medium of sense-data, since they are the only objects of which, in sense-perception, we are immediately aware.[8]

If we are to extract a plausible argument from these passages, we must somehow justify the move from claims about the de-

7. See Austin, esp. pp. 20–32.
8. Ayer, pp. 9–11.

pendence of perceptions on perceivers to claims about the dependence of the objects immediately perceived. The most plausible way I find to do this is to talk not about the relativity of perceptions to perceivers, but rather of the relativity of sensible qualities to perceivers, and to construct the argument so that it proves that objects having such properties are perceiver-dependent. The essential claim here is that there are such objects, because if a quality is directly perceived then there is some kind of object that has it, and if a quality of an object is dependent on something, then so is the object. The argument, then, is this:

(1) There are qualities that are directly perceived by perceivers, e.g. sensible qualities such as colors.
(2) If a quality is directly perceived, then there is an object that has it.
(3) All directly perceived qualities are dependent on (vary with certain changes in) perceivers.
(4) If a quality of an object is dependent on something, then the object is also dependent on it.

Therefore

(5) There are perceiver-dependent objects with directly perceived qualities; i.e. there are sensa.

The argument is not yet in its strongest form, however. There are three ways we can easily strengthen it to avoid three obvious objections. The first objection is that premise (2) is false, because even granting that if a quality is directly perceived there is something that has it, whatever this is need not be an object. It might be a quality or an event. If, for example, we perceive the red quality of something, we often also perceive the brightness and intensity of the red quality of the object. Thus we must specify that in this argument we are concerned only with qualities of objects, if premise (2) is to avoid this objection. Let us call such qualities, "first-level properties." The second objection is that premise (4) is false unless we further specify that the properties considered are all nonrelational. For, although a relational property such as *x* being taller than *y* depends on *x,* it does not follow that *y,* of which this is also a property, is dependent on *x.* Let us then substitute the phrase 'nonrelational first-level property' for 'quality' throughout the argument and accept (4).

The third objection is aimed at the inference implicit in (5). Even if it is proved that there are perceiver-dependent objects with sensible nonrelational properties, this does not warrant us to conclude that there are sensa. It is reasonable to construe perceivers and their parts as perceiver-dependent objects which have sensible nonrelational properties but which are not sensa. We can avoid this problem by recasting premise (1) as:

> (1a) There are nonrelational first-level properties which are directly perceived but which are not properties of perceivers or their parts.

As so stated, (1a) is initially plausible, and if the other premises are also, then so is the inference implicit in

> (5a) There are perceiver-dependent objects which are neither perceivers nor parts of perceivers and which have directly perceived nonrelational properties, i.e. there are sensa.

Assuming that we have found the strongest form of the argument, I shall begin to evaluate it.

EXAMINATION OF THE ARGUMENT: A REASON TO REJECT PREMISE (3)

One plausible way to attack the argument is to argue that (3) is false, because sometimes, at least, we directly perceive properties of physical objects and they are not dependent on perceivers. The facts of perceptual relativity support (3) no more than another claim that makes the argument invalid, namely:

> (3a) Which nonrelational first-level properties are directly perceived depends on (varies with certain changes in) perceivers.

The difference between (3) and (3a) is that the former but not the latter implies that each determinate quality directly perceived can be changed, i.e. made to have different nonrelational properties itself, merely by making certain changes in perceivers. For (3a), however, what depends on perceivers is not the nonrelational properties of things but whether such properties are directly perceived. Thus while it is not possible that (3) is true and some such properties are perceiver–independent, it is possible that (3a) is true and some, indeed all, such properties are perceiver–independent. So far as I know, the facts of perceptual relativity alone provide no reason to choose either (3) or (3a). Given merely those perceptual facts, it is reasonable to argue that when a normal perceiver directly perceives a sensible quality, such as color, under normal conditions, he is directly perceiving a perceiver-independent property of a physical object, but when certain changes in the perceiver or conditions occur, he is no longer perceiving a property of a physical object. Consequently, (3) is dubious, and we should not use it to justify a conclusion.

Actually if we wish to find the minimum claim supported by the facts of perceptual relativity, it would be neither (3) nor (3a). While (3) goes beyond the minimum claim by denying that some directly perceived properties are independent of perceivers, (3a) goes beyond it by implying that there are directly perceived nonrelational first-level properties. On one interpretation of perceptual facts that must be considered, there are nonrelational first-level properties, but none of them are directly perceived and only those that are properties of perceivers or parts of perceivers are perceiver-dependent. This is the view that whenever an object is perceived and appears red, for example, neither the physical object nor anything else is red in this sensuous, occurrent sense. There are no red sensa, but only red-sensings, and physical redness, which can be construed in several ways, is not directly perceivable. Either it is a capacity of an object to reflect "red" light waves or to cause the object to appear red normally, or it is a property, such as having a certain molecular surface structure, which explains such capacities. But we do not directly perceive capacities nor the property of having a certain molecular surface structure. By considering the preceding interpretation of perception, we can see that the minimal claim, that is, the claim with the least theoretical or philosophical interpretation which the facts of perceptual relativity support, would be more like:

> (3b) Which properties an object appears to have to a perceiver depend on (vary with changes in) the perceiver.

This claim is compatible with (3), (3a), and the claim that no nonrelational first-level properties are directly perceived.

It might be objected, however, that (3b) is not compatible

with the last claim, because (3b) entails that objects appear to have some property, and the claim that an object appears to have a property, *P,* is equivalent to the claim that *P* is directly perceived. Furthermore, it is reasonable to assume that some of the properties objects appear to have are sensible colors which are nonrelational first-level properties. In addition, it might be argued that some of these sensible colors that objects appear to have are not properties of physical objects or perceivers or parts of perceivers. Consequently, given this interpretation of direct perception of properties, the following claim is justified, regardless of whether (3) or (3a) is true:

> (6) Some nonrelational properties that someone directly perceives are not properties of physical objects or perceivers or parts of perceivers.

And, if we take (2) with (6) we get the conclusion that there are sensa without needing either (3) or (3a).

I believe that it is initially plausible to construe the direct perception of properties so that someone directly perceives a property, *P,* just in case something appears *P* to him. This indeed justifies (6), because some properties that physical objects appear to have are not properties of physical objects, perceivers, or parts of perceivers. However, while (6) can be justified on this interpretation, premise (2) becomes dubious because it would be equivalent to:

> (2a) For any nonrelational first-level property, *P,* if something appears *P,* then some object is *P.*

This is clearly dubious, because it states that whenever something appears *P,* no matter what *P* is or which conditions and perceivers are involved, something (perhaps something else) really is *P.* But, unless there is some independent justification of sensa, there is good reason to think that many times a physical object appears to have a property, but neither that object nor any other object has it. Thus while (6) can be justified on this interpretation of direct perception of properties, (2) becomes dubious.[9] Furthermore (3) remains dubious on this interpretation because it is equivalent to:

9. Cf. Chisholm, Chap. 8, and *Theory of Knowledge,* pp. 94–95.

(3c) All properties that something appears to have are dependent on perceivers.

It is certainly plausible to claim that some properties that physical objects appear to have are properties they have and, consequently, they are not dependent on perceivers.

Incidentally, although the preceding interpretation of the direct perception of properties is plausible and may be the one which would best help explain why someone might find the argument from perceptual relativity forceful, I do not think it fully captures what it is to perceive a property directly. I should not think that we would want to claim, for example, that whenever someone walked through a graveyard and something appears ghostly to him, he is directly perceiving either the property of ghostliness or an instance of that property. Rather, it is that he believes he is directly perceiving this property of something, but he is mistaken. Something appears to have this property but nothing has it in this case and, furthermore, he is not directly perceiving that property at all. Or, in other words, he thinks he is perceiving an instance of a certain property, but he is mistaken. It is not sufficient for someone to directly perceive a property P that something appear P to him.

CONCLUSION: PERCEPTUAL RELATIVITY DOES NOT JUSTIFY SENSA

We have done enough to cast doubt on premise (3), and also on premise (2) for one interpretation of the direct perception of properties. Thus we can reject the argument from perceptual relativity. We have not, however, considered premise (6) which, with (2), provides a different reason to accept sensa. We found one way to justify (6), but then (2) becomes dubious. We can reinterpret direct perception of properties to guarantee the truth of (2), but then I find no way to justify (6) without relying on an independent justification of sensa. That, of course, would make (6) of no value for our purposes. For example, let us say that someone directly perceives a property P just in case he directly perceives an object to have the property. And let us construe 'directly perceives P' to be extentional, so that if someone directly perceives an object to have P then it follows that some object has P. Thus (2) is true. Premise (6) becomes:

(6a) Some nonrelational property that someone directly perceives an object to have is not a property of a physical object or a perceiver or a part of a perceiver.

But it is surely at least as reasonable to assert the denial of (6a): that all directly perceived nonrelational properties are properties of physical objects, perceivers, or parts of perceivers. It seems that premise (6a) is acceptable if and only if it is reasonable to claim there are sensa, and I find no way to justify (6a) without independently justifying that there are sensa. Without some such reason to accept sensa, perhaps because one of the arguments yet to be examined is sound or because sensa are required by a justified scientific or philosophical theory, we have no reason to accept (6a). We cannot, then, use it to justify the existence of sensa.

As I have construed one version of the argument called by Ayer "the argument from illusion," the fact that there are perceptual illusions plays no part. It may be objected, then, that although we can reject this argument which does not rely on any premises about illusory perceptual experiences, we have failed to use the very kinds of perceptual facts needed for a sound argument from illusion, facts that Ayer considers in other parts of his discussion of "the" argument from illusion. We have overlooked the many examples of illusory experiences, especially hallucinatory experiences in which someone thinks he is perceiving an external physical object, but he is not. An argument based on such facts is different from the one we have examined. Let us turn to it now.

THE ARGUMENT FROM HALLUCINATION

Sir Russell Brain claims that there are sense-data and finds the facts of hallucinatory experiences

> relevant to the sense-datum theory of perception, because if having an hallucination to which no object corresponds is a sensory experience in itself indistinguishable from seeing a real object, this is a strong argument for the view that seeing a real object also involves experiencing a sense-

datum which is generated by the brain and is therefore independent of the object.[10]

The point in Brain's account crucial to the argument from hallucination is the fact that hallucinatory experiences are often indistinguishable from veridical experiences. This is reinforced by the fact that in experiences which are only in part hallucinatory, there is no distinction between the hallucinatory and veridical elements of the experience. Brain quotes from someone who describes his experiences after having taken lysergic acid:

> Then my eyes went to the whitish-gold distempered wall above, where the lamp-light fell. The wall began to be covered with an incredibly beautiful series of patterns— embossed, drawn, painted, but *continuously changing*. More colour. Indescribable colour. And all the colours, all the patterns, *were in the wall* in any case—only we don't usually see them, for we haven't eyes to.[11]

Ayer also stresses this fact of indistinguishability in his discussion:

> In the first place it is pointed out that there is no intrinsic difference in kind between those of our perceptions that are veridical in their presentation of material things and those that are delusive. . . . But, it is argued, if, when our perceptions were delusive, we were always perceiving something of a different kind from what we perceived when they were veridical, we should expect our experience to be qualitatively different in the two cases. We should expect to be able to tell from the intrinsic character of a perception whether it was a perception of a sense-datum or of a material thing. But this is not possible.[12]

In constructing an argument from the preceding quotations we must be careful to emphasize two points. First, as pointed out by Austin, the argument Ayer presents is mistaken if it states, as it seems to do, that there is no intrinsic difference in kind

10. W. R. Brain, *The Nature of Experience* (London: Oxford University Press, 1959), p. 10.
11. Brain, p. 12.
12. Ayer, pp. 5–6.

between *any* veridical perceptual experience and *any* hallucinatory experience.[13] Some hallucinatory experiences are so chaotic and incredible that we can easily discern that they are not veridical. We should say at most, therefore, that *some* hallucinatory experiences are indistinguishable in kind from veridical experiences. Second, as usually made explicit by Ayer, the relevant indistinguishability concerns kinds of experiences and kinds of objects experienced, rather than particular experiences and particular objects experienced. It may well be that each particular experience and experienced object is distinguishable from all others, but this does not imply that they are distinguishable as to kind. It is the latter—especially whether these objects are physical objects or sensa—which is relevant to the argument.

Let us begin the statement of the argument as follows:

(1) Some hallucinatory experiences are indistinguishable in kind from veridical perceptual experiences.

(2) If an experience of one kind is indistinguishable in kind from experiences of another kind, then the kind of object experienced in the one is indistinguishable from the kind of object experienced in the others.

(3) If two entities are indistinguishable in kind, then they are identical in kind.

Therefore

(4) The kind of object experienced in some hallucinatory experiences is the same kind of object experienced in veridical perceptual experiences.

This is as much as can be inferred from the claims about indistinguishability. It is obviously not sufficient to justify that there are sensa. One way to proceed to that conclusion is to point out that while in veridical perception either external physical objects or sensa are experienced, no external objects are experienced in completely hallucinatory experiences. We can then deduce that there are sensa as follows:

(5) In veridical perceptual experiences, either external physical objects or sensa are experienced.

13. See Austin, p. 48.

(6) No external physical objects are experienced in completely hallucinatory experiences.

Therefore

(7) In some hallucinatory experiences and in veridical perceptual experiences sensa are experienced.

(8) If sensa are experienced, then there are sensa.

Therefore

(9) There are sensa.

Of these premises we can grant (5), (6), and (8) for our present purposes. We shall find when we examine the argument from the causal facts of perception later on in this chapter, however, that (5) is a crucial premise in that argument, and needs to be carefully amended before evaluating the argument. The form of this amendment depends in part on how 'x is experienced' is construed, but this is not essential to the present argument, nor to the fact that in premise (8) we are construing 'x is experienced' to entail 'x exists.' That is, objects experienced exist. It might be interesting to note that the preceding argument, in using (5), (6), and (8), differs from one quite usual version of the argument. The version discussed by Austin has two parts: the first to establish that sensa are perceived in *some* abnormal situations, and the second to establish, using the indistinguishability premises, that sensa are *always* perceived.[14] In the preceding argument the conclusion that sensa are experienced in both veridical and hallucinatory experiences is reached in the same step of the argument. An apparent advantage of the present version is that those of its premises that are added to the indistinguishability premises seem quite acceptable, but I have yet to find an additional set sufficient to justify that sensa are experienced in abnormal situations (see the revised version of this argument below).

It might seem that we should also accept premise (3) on the grounds of the identity of indiscernibles. Certainly (3) is acceptable if to be indistinguishable in kind is to be indiscernible with respect to kind, that is, if we construe (3) as

14. Ibid., p. 20.

(3a) If there is no way to discern whether two things differ in kind, then they are identical in kind.

As we shall see, however, it is not clear that we can use 'indistinguishable' in this way throughout the argument if premises (1) and (2) are to be true.

Premise (1) must be paraphrased if it is to be both clear and true. The following will suffice for clarity:

(1a) There is no way to discern that some hallucinatory experiences are not veridical experiences.

This construal of (1) with the above construal of (3a) results in our having to interpret (2) as

(2a) If there is no way to discern that an experience, e, of one kind, k_1, is not an experience of a second kind, k_2, then there is no way to discern that the kind of object experienced in e is not the kind of object experienced in experiences of kind k_2.

Initially at least, (2a) seems acceptable, because if there were a way to discover that an object experienced is not the kind experienced in, for example, veridical experiences, then there would be a way to discover that the experience is not veridical. There are, on the other hand, immediate objections to (1a). One is that (1a) is meaningless because it is clearly unverifiable. If there is no way to discover that an experience is not veridical then there is no way to discover that it is hallucinatory. However, I see no reason to accept such a verifiability criterion of meaningfulness (discussed in Chap. 4). If this objection is transformed into one that claims there is no reason to accept (1a), however, then it is more forceful. If we cannot verify (1a), then there is no reason to think it true and it cannot be used as a premise to justify a conclusion.

There are ways to avoid both objections. One way restricts the kind of indiscernibility referred to in premise (1). That is, we might replace (1a) with

(1b) There is no way to discern from any internal properties of, and relations among, one person's experi-

ences that some of his hallucinatory experiences are
not veridical experiences.

This "first-person experiential" indiscernibility is often what is
meant by those who discuss the argument. This version of (1)
is compatible with there being ways for someone else to discern
that these hallucinatory experiences are not veridical, such as
discovery of certain of the causal factors that result in the experience. Thus it avoids both preceding objections. It also is
compatible with verifying that for some of these experiences
nothing internal to them or in their relations to other experiences
of the same person is sufficient for deciding that they are not
veridical. Furthermore, it seems reasonable to think that there
is at least one such hallucinatory experience.

There is, however, a problem with replacing (1a) with (1b).
We must also amend either (2a) or (3a) in a way that results
in at least one of them being false. If we merely change the
antecedent of (2a) to reflect the limitation on indiscernibility
expressed in (1b), what results is false. It is surely reasonable
to think that, although there are some ways to discover that, for
example, no physical object is experienced in some experience,
there is no way to discover merely from the experiential facts of
the person having that experience that it is an hallucinatory experience. We must, therefore, also amend the consequent of
(2) to give us:

> (2b) If there is no way to discern from any internal proper-
> ties of and relations among one person's experiences
> that some experience, e, of kind k_1 is not an experi-
> ence of kind k_2, then there is no way to discern from
> such experiential facts that the kind of object ex-
> perienced in e is not the kind of object experienced
> in experiences of kind k_2.

Of course, this requires that we replace (3a) with

> (3b) If there is no way to discern from such experiential
> facts whether two things differ in kind, then they are
> identical in kind.

This is clearly false, because there being a difference in kind
among experienced objects is consistent with there being no

way to discover this which is restricted only to experiential facts available to the person who experiences the objects. There often are facts available to someone else that can be used to determine which kind something is.

There is, however, a more plausible way to avoid the preceding problems. It is clear there are ways to verify that something is an experience that are independent of determining whether or not it is veridical. Then, on the assumption that there is a fairly large number, although small percent, of such experiences for which there is no way to determine whether or not they are veridical, it is reasonable that at least one of them is hallucinatory. Thus (1a) seems justified. Of course this justification of (1a) depends on there being reason to think that for many experiences there is no way to determine whether or not they are veridical. This is open to the objection that, in principle at least, there is always some way to decide the issue. Nevertheless the situation is complicated by carefully describing an experience to rule out access to all kinds of distinguishing features, such as causal factors, testimony of other perceivers, and discernible consequences, except those internal to the experience itself. And it seems reasonable to think that some experiences meet such descriptions. Rather than debate this point, however, let us provisionally grant (1a) for our purposes here, because there are problems that arise once premise (2a) is further clarified, and they are sufficient to refute the argument.

EXAMINATION OF PREMISE (2a): IS THERE SOME KIND OF OBJECT IN ALL HALLUCINATIONS?

The problem facing (2a) can be raised by considering its consequent:

> C_1 There is no way to discern that the kind of object experienced in e is not the kind of object experienced in experiences of kind k_2.

The antecedent of (2a) does not entail C_1. The former is consistent with:

> C_2 There is no object experienced in experience e, but there is no way to discern that none is experienced.

But C_1 is not consistent with C_2 because C_1 entails that there is

208 *On Sensing and Sensa*

an object experienced in *e*. Consequently (2a) is not an entailment. Furthermore, there seems to be no more reason to claim that (2a) is contingently true than to claim that the corresponding hypothetical with C_2 is true. We can, however, substitute a quite reasonable premise for (2a) by replacing C_1 with

> C_3 If there is an object experienced in experience *e*, then there is no way to discern that it is a kind of object that differs from the kind of object experienced in experiences of kind k_2.

We can call what results, (2c). However, we cannot infer (4) from (1a), (2c), and (3a), but only

> (4a) For some hallucinatory experiences, if an object is experienced in them, then it is the same kind as the objects experienced in some veridical perceptual experiences.

And (4a), (5), and (6) will not yield (7).

A Revised Version: Hallucinations and Apparitions

As the argument was first stated, it seemed that there was no need to prove independently of the indistinguishability premises that sensa are experienced in *some* hallucinations, but this, in effect, is what we must do once we replace (2a) with (2c). In order to move validly from (4a) to (7), we need to add a premise to the effect that an object of some kind is experienced in the relevant hallucinatory experiences. Of course, this is just what an adverbial theorist would deny. Is this denial unreasonable? The strongest case I know to justify that it is unreasonable is based on certain first-person accounts of hallucinatory experiences. Brain cites cases for which an adverbial interpretation might well seem unreasonable:

> Both the drug-induced illusions and the hallucinatory 'apparitions' show that these abnormal experiences are often associated with a modification of normal perception such that the abnormal appearance is integrated into the subject's perception of his environment. When an apparition hides from view an object in front of which it is standing,

or opens and passes through a door known to be locked, it provides the strongest evidence that the sense-data comprising the apparition and those comprising the environment possess the same perceptual status.[15]

It clearly seems to the perceiver in these experiences that he is directly confronted with several objects, some of which, it turns out, are physical objects while others are apparitions. But there is reason to think these situations are not as they seem to such a person if the argument we are presently examining or either of the two yet to be examined is sound. For if any of these arguments is sound, then we are directly confronted with sensa in veridical perceptual experiences, and thus we would never be directly presented or acquainted with external physical objects. This is also true given certain of the causal facts of perception involving a time gap between the transmission of stimulus and resulting perceptual experience, whether or not any of these arguments is sound (see pp. 224–26). Of course, this counterintuitive consequence of theories that propose sensa as directly perceived objects is counterbalanced by the ease with which such theories can accommodate experiences in which there seems to be an "intermingling" of apparitions and physical objects. These theories construe such experiences to be cases in which the complex of sensa perceived results from the joint effect of different causal chains.

If such explanatory value of a sensa theory can override an appeal to a person's own account of his directly perceiving physical objects, then any similar explanatory advantage of the adverbial theory may override the appeal to a person's own account of his directly perceiving apparitions. And, surely, the adverbial theory can explain these experiences equally as well. The seeming direct perception of an intermingling of physical objects and apparitions consists in an experience where the complex way in which the person senses is the joint effect of different kinds of causal chains. It is true that the theory has the counterintuitive consequences that no apparitions are objects of perception in hallucinations, but this is mitigated because, unlike sensa theories, it does not have the counterintuitive consequence that we never directly perceive external physical objects because we

15. Brain, p. 20.

always directly perceive sensa.[16] For sensa theories we always directly perceive sensa, objects that certainly do not seem to be part of any veridical experience. I conclude, then, that the phenomenological evidence derived from a person's account of his own perceptual experiences, both veridical and illusory, to support the claim there are objects directly perceived in hallucinatory experiences, does not provide reason to accept a sensa theory instead of the adverbial sensing theory.

A DEFENSE OF HALLUCINATORY OBJECTS:
A COMBINED SENSING-SENSA THEORY

There is clearly another move open to a defender of the premise that objects of some kind are experienced in all hallucinatory experiences. He might deny that sensa are experienced in veridical experiences, but hold they are experienced when hallucinating and also, perhaps, when dreaming and afterimaging. He would then propose a "combined" theory instead of the sensa theory or the sensing theory. This, of course, would be incompatible with the conclusions of the arguments we are examining, but it would be sufficient to defeat any attempt by a materialist to identify sensings with brain entities while eliminating sensa. One clear advantage of this combined theory is that it is more intuitive than the other two theories, that is, it is best supported by the phenomenological evidence of sense experience. Furthermore, presumably, it would explain the relevant experiences equally as well as the two competing theories.

The combined theory, however, has one theoretical disadvantage which I think overrides the intuitive, phenomenological evidence in its favor. On both the sensa theory and the sensing theory, all qualitatively identical brain processes of the relevant kinds would either produce or be identical with perceptual experiences that are qualitatively identical. But this would not be true for the combined theory, because, depending only on their causal ancestors, some of these brain processes would result in or be identical with adverbial sensing experiences and others would result in or be identical with experiences of sensa. Clearly some explanation of this difference is required and the only one

16. For the difference between direct perception and acquaintance, see the discussion of the revised time-gap argument below.

I find available seems unsatisfactory, namely, that only in this way is one of our intuitions about our own experiences saved.

Of course, if it is established that for the purposes of scientific explanation there is a need to assume sensa in hallucinatory experiences, but no such need for veridical experiences, then the previous theoretical disadvantage would be counterbalanced. But I do not believe that the relevant sciences are yet developed enough to indicate such a need. Provisionally at least, therefore, depending on developments in the relevant sciences, I conclude that the theoretical disadvantage of the combined theory prohibits it from providing grounds sufficient to support the claim that there are objects experienced when hallucinating, afterimaging, and dreaming.

CONCLUSION: NO FACTS RELEVANT TO ILLUSION JUSTIFY SENSA

The argument from hallucination has proved to be more troublesome for the adverbial sensing theory than the argument from perceptual relativity. The mere fact that it is somewhat counterintuitive to claim that no objects, such as apparitions or afterimages, are experienced makes the adverbial theory seem less than satisfactory. Nevertheless we have been unable to find any more nearly satisfactory. Consequently, we can conclude the second version of the argument from hallucination fails to justify that there are sensa in veridical experiences even if we grant (1a). This premise is at least questionable if the kind of indistinguishability expressed in it is to be sufficient for the truth of (2c) and (3a), and the validity of the inference to (4a). We have also found no reason to accept (2a) on which the first version of the argument rests. Therefore the facts of hallucinatory experiences combined with indistinguishability claims fail to justify that there are sensa. And, because I can find no more plausible version, I conclude that we should reject the argument from hallucination as we have the argument from perceptual relativity. Furthermore, because in one way or another both these arguments use all the facts of perception related to illusion and delusion that seem relevant to sensa, we should turn to a different set of perceptual facts in our search for the justification of sensa. Let us consider those involved in the scientific account of the causation of perceptual experiences.

THE ARGUMENT FROM THE CAUSAL FACTS
OF PERCEPTION

There are certain causal facts in the scientific account of perception that some people believe justify that there are sensa. Their view involves claims about how physical objects cause the stimulation of sense organs and, by means of nerve processes, result in perceptual experiences. One whose interpretation of these causal facts leads him to claim that there are sensa is J. Eccles. He says,

> There is much neurophysiological evidence that a conscious experience arises only when there is some specific cerebral activity. For every experience it is believed that there is a specific spatio-temporal pattern of neuronal activity in the brain. Thus with perception the sequence of events is that some stimulus to a sense organ causes the discharge of impulses along afferent nerve-fibers to the brain, which, after various synaptic relays, eventually evoke specific spatio-temporal patterns of impulses in the neuronal network of the cerebral cortex. The transmission from sense organ to cerebral cortex is by a coded pattern of nerve impulses that is quite unlike the original stimulus to that organ, and the spatio-temporal pattern of neuronal activity that is evoked in the cerebral cortex would be again different. Yet, as a consequence of these cerebral patterns of activity, I experience sensations (more properly the complex constructs called percepts) which in my private perceptual world are 'projected' to somewhere outside the cortex.[17]

The question relevant to our interests raised by Eccles' statement is whether there is sufficient reason to interpret these causal facts of perception in the way Eccles has or whether a different interpretation, which does not imply there are sensa, is at least equally as reasonable.

The strongest argument I can find to support Eccles' interpretation is an attempt to base the existence of sensa on the causal fact that the perceptual experience of an object is the

17. J. Eccles, *The Brain and the Unity of Conscious Experience* (Cambridge: Cambridge University Press, 1965), pp. 17–18.

result of a complicated sequence of events that, for the purposes of explaining perception, can be said to begin with an object stimulating some sense organ of the perceiver. But the consequence of this, according to the argument, is that whatever is experienced in this perceptual experience also is an effect of this same process. Therefore, because no cause is identical with any of its effects, what is experienced is not the physical object that stimulates the sense organ. It is rather a sensum. A similar argument could be devised for the existence of pains, itches, tickles, and the like. More precisely, the argument can be stated as:

> (1) In veridical perceptual experiences, a perceptual experience of an object is the effect of a physical object stimulating a sense organ.
> (2) If the perceptual experience of an object is an effect of a physical object stimulating a sense organ, then what is perceptually experienced in the experience is also an effect of the stimulation of the sense organ.
> (3) No object is identical with one of its effects.

Therefore

> (4) In veridical perceptual experiences, what is experienced is not identical with any physical object.
> (5) In veridical perceptual experiences, either physical objects or sensa are experienced.

Therefore

> (6) In veridical (and then surely all other) perceptual experiences, sensa are experienced.

Two of the premises of this argument seem clearly acceptable, (1) and (3). Premise (1) seems central to any interpretation of the causal facts of perception. Premise (3) merely restates the obvious claim that nothing (except possibly an all-perfect being) is self-caused. We need not reject one of the other two premises to refute the argument, however, because as it stands, it is invalid. The most we can deduce from (1), (2), and (3) is:

> (4a) In veridical perceptual experiences, what is experi-

enced is not identical with a physical object that
stimulates a sense organ.

The result is that (6) is no longer derivable, because (4a) no
longer denies one disjunct of (5). We should replace (5) with:

(5a) In veridical perceptual experiences, either physical
objects that stimulate sense organs or sensa are experienced.

The argument is now valid.

Unfortunately, (5a) is not as plausible as (5), because it is
possible that in perception physical objects other than those
that stimulate sense organs are experienced. At one time Russell
claimed that what we see occurs at the end of the causal process
of perception and that this process culminates in the brain.[18]
Whatever we see, then, is physically in the brain as either a brain
part or a brain state. I find only one way that this view could
be made plausible. Like Russell, again, it is to claim that the
experienced object in a perceptual experience is a sensum—for
Russell a percept—and that it is identical with some brain state
or brain part.[19] We have previously seen that this position is
plausible, but even if it were not we need not be concerned, because we can substitute two reasonable premises for (5a):

(5b) In veridical perceptual experiences, either physical
objects that stimulate sense organs or brain entities
or sensa are experienced.

and:

(7) If, in veridical perceptual experiences, a brain entity
is experienced, then it is identical with a sensum.

We have now a valid argument with premises we have found
reason to believe, except for (2) which is yet to be examined.

ARGUMENTS AGAINST ACCEPTING PREMISE (2)

It may seem that premise (2) can quite easily be shown to
be false because (4a) is obviously false and it follows from
(2) in conjunction with two quite acceptable premises, (1) and

18. See B. Russell, *Philosophy* (New York: W. W. Norton, 1927),
p. 140.
19. Ibid.

(3). According to this objection, (4a) is clearly false, because it entails that we never see any physical objects that stimulate sense organs. Thus I never see tables, trees, or any other quite ordinary physical object, even my own hand. But that I sometimes see my own hand is so close to certainty, that whatever entails its denial is obviously false. Thus it is obvious either that (4a) is false or that my hand never stimulates my sense organs. But the latter is quite unreasonable. Therefore (4a) is clearly false.

Although some philosophers, such as Russell, who would accept the argument from the causal facts of perception and thus (4a), would seem to agree that we only see percepts, never external physical objects, nothing in the argument commits them to that view. In particular, (4a) does not entail that we never perceive the objects that stimulate our sense organs. This can be shown by distinguishing carefully between objects experienced and objects perceived. That is, for anyone who defines 'to perceive *x*' and 'to experience *x*' so that they take different kinds of objects as values, (4a) is consistent with the claim that we see physical objects. For example, it is plausible to argue that if someone sees a chair, then as a result of the chair stimulating his eyes, he has the experience of seeing something. And the latter event consists in experiencing a chair-like sensum. On this view, then, all cases of perceiving involve experiencing sensa, and this is clearly compatible with seeing a chair although not experiencing it in this somewhat technical sense.

In spite of the failure of the preceding objection, premise (2) is clearly the place to attack the argument. It surely seems at least plausible to claim that a perceptual experience of one object is an effect of a stimulation of a sense organ and that the only objects involved in the experience and the preceding causal chain are the perceiver, parts of the perceiver, and the object that stimulates his sense organ. Do the causal facts of perception referred to in setting out the argument provide any reason to deny this? Do they provide any reason to think that the experience of seeing a chair involves experiencing a chair-like sensum, rather than to think it involves a chair-sensing? The adverbial sensing theory seems to be as plausible an interpretation of these physiological and psychological causal facts of perception as the sensa theory. These facts require that what results from the stimulation of sense organs is a perceptual state of the perceiver, but they do not seem to require that this state consists in a relationship between a perceiver and an object that is either generated or caused to appear by the stimulation of the sense organ. Furthermore, it seems implausible to argue that some object is generated along with the perceptual state, especially if one takes the view that it is states and events rather than objects that are caused. Thus, there seems to be no reason to accept (2), at least on the basis of the facts relevant to the causal argument.

A defense of premise (2): Perceiving vs. experiencing

At this point someone might rely on the distinction between perceiving and experiencing discussed previously to help justify a revised version of (2). If we assume that although external physical objects may be perceived, none are perceptually experienced, then the following is true:

> (2a) If the perceptual experience of an object is an effect of some physical object stimulating a sense organ, then something is perceptually *experienced* in the experience only if it results from the stimulation of the sense organ.

The argument remains valid with (2a) instead of (2), but now premise (5b), previously found acceptable, becomes open to doubt. As stated, (5b) is not an exhaustive disjunction. Until this point in the discussion, however, there was no reason to consider the missing disjunct 'or nothing is experienced,' because a case of perception is veridical only if at least one object is perceived, and, therefore, on the previous construal of 'to experience x,' at least one object is perceptually experienced. But if we construe 'to experience x' so that it does not take physical objects as values, then we should replace (5b) with

> (5c) In veridical perceptual experiences, either physical objects that stimulate sense organs or brain entities or sensa are experienced, or no object is experienced.

As it now stands the argument is invalid. We need to add a premise to the effect that in veridical perceptual experiences some object is experienced in this technical sense. But it is plausible to claim that in veridical perception external physical objects are perceived but no object is experienced in this sense, because the perceptual experience that occurs when perceiving consists in sensing in some determinate way rather than sensing some object. And, again, nothing about the causal facts we have considered provides any reason for doubting this claim.

CONCLUSION: CAUSATION OF SENSINGS IS AS REASONABLE
AS CAUSATION OF SENSA

We can conclude that there is no reason to accept at least one of the premises of the causal argument, depending on what we take to be the kinds of objects that can be experienced. If external physical objects can be experienced, then there is no reason to accept premise (2); if no external objects can be experienced, then there is no reason to accept the assumed premise that some object is experienced. Thus on both interpretations of 'to experience *x*,' there is sufficient reason to reject the argument. It would, however, be preferable to find reason for an outright rejection of one of the premises, but I know of no way to do this unless a more specific claim about sensa is made. If, for example, someone claims that sensa are identical with brain phenomena or that all of them are simple rather than complex ideas, then there might be good reason either to reject all the previous versions of premise (5) because of a missing disjunct, or, if the disjunct is added, to reject the missing premise that there are such objects of experience. But, given just the causal facts utilized in the causal argument, we can do no better than reject it on the grounds that there is no reason to accept one of its premises.

We have not, however, utilized all the scientific and causal facts of perception and it might be objected at this point that if we had done so we could have constructed a sound argument for sensa. I certainly agree that we have not considered all the perceptual facts relevant to sensa, nor have we examined whether there are any requirements of scientific explanations which, together with certain facts, necessitate the postulation of sensa. We also have not considered one causal fact that many philosophers have thought provides reason to believe there are sensa, namely, the fact that it takes time for the stimulus transmitted from an external object to affect a sense organ and result in a perceptual experience. Although there seems to be no way that the fact of this time gap between the beginning and end of perceptual causal chains will help bolster the preceding causal argument for sensa, it does provide the basis for a different and, I find, more persuasive argument. We will examine it next.

THE TIME-GAP ARGUMENT

Russell was one of the first philosophers to state the time-gap argument. Basing it on the facts that light travels at a finite rate of speed and that certain objects we claim to see are so far distant that it takes light many years to travel from them to our eyes, Russell concludes that we do not see such objects. As he says,

> Moreover, though you see the sun now, the physical object to be inferred from your seeing existed eight minutes ago; if, in the intervening minutes, the sun had gone out, you would still be seeing exactly what you are seeing. We cannot therefore identify the physical sun with what we see; nevertheless what we see is our chief reason for believing in the physical sun.[20]

The argument expressed here is clearly an enthymeme. One additional premise, adequate for validity, can be derived from Ayer's statement of the argument:

> It may even happen that by the time we see it the star has ceased to exist. But if the star no longer exists, we cannot, so it is argued, now be seeing it; and since in every case in which the light has had an appreciable distance to travel it is possible that the object which we think that we are seeing has gone out of existence in the interval, we cannot ever identify it with what we see: for our present experience will be the same, whether the object still exists or not.[21]

The premise we can extract from this statement to help make Russell's argument valid is, in effect, that if something does not exist at a certain time, then it cannot be perceived at that time. Or, with a more precise placement of the modal term, it is that it is impossible to perceive something at a time it does not exist. Given this premise we can state the argument as follows:

20. Russell, *Human Knowledge: Its Scope and Limits* (New York: Simon and Schuster, 1948), p. 204.
21. Ayer, *The Problem of Knowledge*, p. 94.

(1) If something is perceived, then it is perceived during the time a veridical perceptual experience of it occurs.

(2) Any veridical perceptual experience of an external physical object occurs after the stimulus energy transmitted from the object first affects a sense organ.

Therefore

(3) If an external physical object is perceived, then it is perceived after the stimulus energy from it first affects a sense organ.

(4) If an external physical object is perceived after the stimulus energy from it first affects a sense organ, then it is possible it does not exist at the time it is perceived.

(5) It is impossible that something is perceived at a time it does not exist.

Therefore

(6) No external physical objects are perceived.

(7) If no external physical objects are perceived, then sensa are perceived.

Therefore

(8) Sensa are perceived.

Given (8), it follows that there are sensa assuming that 'perceive' is used extentionally throughout. This may cause someone to doubt premise (7) but it is reasonable to hold that because at least sometimes some objects are perceived, then if no external physical objects are perceived, whenever objects are perceived they are sensa. An adverbial theorist might deny this, but if he were to grant (6) he would have to deny that there is ever an occasion when anyone perceives an object. This is considerably less reasonable than an adverbial theorist who agrees that we sometimes perceive external physical objects. And, surely, it is unreasonable to think that we never perceive them. Surely (6) is false.

THE REJECTION OF PREMISE (5)

If we are to deny (6), as is at least initially reasonable, then we should show that the argument which supposedly establishes it is unsound. There seems to be just one way to do this, by attacking premise (5), the premise we derived from the Ayer quotation. Premise (5) is a strong claim, for it states that certain states of affairs are impossible, indeed, that they are logically impossible. If perceiving something when it does not exist is logically possible, then there seems to be no reason to deny it is both physically and humanly possible. But why should anyone think that it is logically impossible? Whether or not it is reasonable, it is at least logically possible that we see a star at a time it no longer exists. There is no contradiction entailed here. We should reject (5).

It may be suggested that a weaker version of (5) would suffice, one that does not involve a modality. But this requires a change in (4). We cannot merely remove the modality from its consequent, because it would then be clearly false. The most we can include in the consequent is that some external physical objects, such as some stars, do not exist at the time they are perceived. Let us use, then,

> (4a) If some external physical objects are perceived after the stimulus energy from them affects a sense organ, then some external physical objects do not exist at the time they are perceived.

This allows us to replace (5) with

> (5a) All objects exist at the time they are perceived.

This is much like a premise in other versions of the argument, and, as in those versions, it is the place to attack our revised version.[22] Even though (5a) does not state that perceiving some-

22. Cf. R. G. Henson, "Ordinary Language, Common Sense, and the Time-Gap Argument," *Mind* 76 (1967): 21–33; and W. A. Suchting, "Perception and the Time-Gap Argument," *Philosophical Quarterly* 19 (1969): 46–56. Henson discusses seeing events and Suchting considers seeing states of objects. Because of these differences, their versions of the argument are too easily refuted. Henson's version is invalid if 'when an event happens' is construed as 'at some time during the occurrence of an event' and has an obviously false first premise if it is construed as

thing when it does not exist is impossible, (5a) is nevertheless unreasonable, because it is quite reasonable to claim that some stars are perceived when they no longer exist. This claim is bolstered by construing perceiving as was done in Chapter 2; that is, the event of a person perceiving a star is the event of the star appearing in some way to him as a result of the star being a proper stimulus of him. This would allow for people sometimes perceiving stars when the stars do not exist.

A Revised Version: No Direct Perception of Objects That Do Not Exist

Not everyone will agree that perceiving something is to be identified merely with having a perceptual experience of a certain kind. To perceive an object, especially to see it or touch it, is seemingly to be in some kind of contact with it, to have it presented to one. But that kind of relationship to an object requires its existence. On this view, perceiving is more like what has been called "direct perception." And indeed if we substitute 'directly perceived' for 'perceived' in premise (5a) it becomes much more plausible. We get:

> (5b) All objects exist at the time they are *directly* perceived.

It may be that the entire argument would be made more plausible if we replace each occurrence of 'perceived' in it by 'directly perceived.' The reasonableness of premises (1), (2), and (4a) remains unaffected. The conclusion they yield instead of (6) is:

> (6a) No external physical objects are *directly* perceived,

which is much more plausible than (6) because it is compatible with many external physical objects being perceived, perhaps indirectly. Furthermore, we can replace (7) with two initially plausible premises:

'at all times during the occurrence of an event.' Suchting's version is invalid because he infers from the time gap that we do not see at a time *t* the state of an object at *t*. We see an earlier state of the object. But, of course, a state of an object when it transmits light waves often endures until we see it later. Incidentally, their attacks on the argument do not affect the version involving direct perception we shall consider later.

(7a) If no external physical objects are directly perceived, then either no external physical objects are perceived, or some are indirectly perceived and sensa are directly perceived,

and:

(9) Some external physical objects are perceived.

Because (6a), (7a), and (9) entail that sensa are directly perceived, which in turn entails that there are sensa, the argument yields the existence of sensa.

AN EXPLICATION OF 'DIRECTLY PERCEIVE'

The present version of the argument is considerably stronger than the previous one. No premise is clearly dubious. But this improvement depends upon the expression 'directly perceive an object' and, although we have used similar terms in stating previous arguments, this is the first one in which how we interpret the expression is crucial. We should, therefore, explain it somewhat. I find this to be more difficult than it might first appear, because I know of no one who has worked very carefully at the task. Two philosophers whose philosophy depends on a clear understanding of direct perception are Berkeley and Russell. Berkeley, through Philonous, asks Hylas, "Are those things only perceived by the senses which are perceived immediately? Or may those things properly be said to be 'sensible' which are perceived mediately, or not without the intervention of others?" [23] Russell, in speaking of knowledge by acquaintance, says that "we have *acquaintance* with anything of which we are directly aware, without the intermediary of any process of inference or any knowledge of truths. Thus in the presence of my table I am acquainted with the sense-data that make up the appearance of my table." [24] Another quite common interpretation is given by N. Malcolm who states the definition "*A directly* perceives *x* if and only if *A*'s assertion that he perceives *x* could not be mistaken." [25]

23. G. Berkeley, *Principles, Dialogues, and Philosophical Correspondence*, C. M. Turbayne, ed. (New York: Bobbs-Merrill, 1965), p. 111.
24. Russell, *The Problems of Philosophy* (New York: Oxford University Press, 1959), p. 46.
25. N. Malcolm, *Knowledge and Certainty: Essays and Lectures* (Englewood Cliffs, N.J.: Prentice-Hall, 1963), p. 89.

These three statements are interestingly different concerning the degree to which they construe 'directly perceive' as a term describing a factual perceptual relationship between a perceiver and an object, and the degree to which they construe it as an epistemological term. Berkeley considers a thing to be immediately or directly perceived when it is perceived without the perception of some intermediary thing. On this construal, 'directly perceive' has no epistemological component. For Russell, however, not only must the object of which we are directly aware be given or presented to the perceiver without any intervening object, but it also seems that we must have noninferential knowledge about it, knowledge not mediated by any other knowledge or premises. Russell, then, adds an epistemological feature to Berkeley's purely factual interpretation. Malcolm's construal, on the other hand, is almost completely epistemological, for it implies nothing about the factual relationship someone has to an object when he directly perceives it.

We need be interested here only in a purely factual sense of 'directly perceive' unless, of course, all senses of it have epistemological implications. I find, however, no such implications, although many people seem to have thought there are, or at least they have not been careful to separate purely factual perceptual questions from epistemological questions about perception. It has been thought that something is directly perceivable in an epistemological sense if and only if it is directly perceivable in something like Berkeley's factual sense. But both halves of this equivalence are questionable. It has been plausibly claimed that sensa are causal, but not epistemological, intermediaries in perception, and, consequently, that there is direct, noninferential knowledge of physical objects despite the causal intermediary.[26] It has also been plausibly argued that claims about physical objects are to be justified by inference from premises containing statements about adverbial sensings.[27] It follows from this claim that, despite there being no intermediary objects, the perceptual knowledge of physical objects is indirect, inferential, and, it would seem, less than certain. These claims certainly suffice to show that the relationship between the epistemological and factual senses of 'directly perceive' is far from obvious. This point

26. Cf. Quinton.
27. See Chisholm, *Perceiving,* pp. 54–95.

is reinforced by noting that directly perceiving in Malcolm's epistemological sense is clearly compatible with indirectly or mediately perceiving in Berkeley's purely factual sense. The converse is also true.

Previously we have attacked the versions of premise (5), but we can now show (5b) to be true by utilizing the factual part of Russell's statement about acquaintance. Clearly, if to perceive something directly is, as Russell claims, to be acquainted with it, to have it present and presented to the perceiver, then (5b) is not only true but analytic, and even versions of (4) and (5) with modalities are true when amended to contain 'directly perceive.' Consequently (6a) is justified. We are not acquainted with physical objects; in other words, physical objects are not present and presented in perceptual experiences. And, on the grounds that (7a) and (9) are true, the existence of sensa seems justified. If we perceive physical objects but do so only indirectly, then our perception of them involves an intermediary that we directly perceive. It is surely reasonable to claim that such intermediaries are sensa.

REJECTION OF THE REVISED VERSION:
DIRECT PERCEPTION WITHOUT ACQUAINTANCE

The only way I find to avoid this conclusion is to claim that there are cases of perception of physical objects in which there are no objects of acquaintance, because no objects are given or presented in those perceptual experiences. That is, premise (7a) is to be attacked. This may appear to be egregiously implausible, but it may seem less outrageous if it is realized that this is merely a claim about the factual character of perception and is compatible with something always being given in a purely epistemological sense. There remains, however, the problem of how it can be that some things are perceived when nothing is directly perceived. The clue to solving this problem is that the sense of 'directly perceive' which results in (5b) being analytic is the Russellian sense involving acquaintance, while what is essential to the truth of (7a) is something like Berkeley's sense which does not imply acquaintance. That is, if physical objects are perceived but are not directly perceived in this Berkeleian sense, then they are indirectly perceived in the sense that whenever they are perceived, other objects which are intermediaries in the perceptual process are also perceived. But if they are perceived but are not directly perceived in the acquaintance sense, then it only follows either that there are perceived intermediaries *or* that the objects are not presented to and present with the perceiver in the experience. It is this second sense of 'directly perceive' we have used to guarantee the truth of (5b). But a direct perceptual realist who subscribes to the adverbial theory could quite plausibly agree that while some physical objects are directly perceived in the Berkeleian sense, many are not directly perceived in the acquaintance sense, because some physical objects are not present and presented in perceptual experiences. He might even go on to argue that no objects of any kind are perceptually given in this sense. Because perceptual experiences are adverbial and because of the time gap, no external physical objects nor any other objects are presented.

In order not to beg the question against such a claim we should replace (7a) with

> (7b) If no external physical objects are directly perceived, then either no external physical objects are perceived, or some are indirectly perceived and sensa are directly perceived, or no objects are directly perceived.

But, because (6a), (7b), and (9) will not yield (8), we need an additional premise, such as

> (10) If an object is perceived, then some object is directly perceived.

Premise (10), however, is just what our direct realist would attack if 'directly perceive' is given the acquaintance interpretation, because it would then be equivalent to:

> (10a) If an object is perceived, then some object is presented to and present with some perceiver.

On the other hand, if (10) is given a Berkeleian interpretation, that is,

> (10b) If an object is perceived, then some object is perceived without a perceived intermediary object,

then (10) and (7b) would be acceptable, but the attack would be switched to the justification of (6a) by (3), (4a), and (5b).

The point at which to attack the argument depends on which premises involve the acquaintance sense of 'directly perceive.' If the acquaintance sense is maintained in (5b) and if the Berkeleian sense is used in (6a), as it must be if the inference to (8) is to be valid, then the inference to (6a) is invalid. What (3), (4a), and (5b) yield is that no external physical objects are present with and presented to a perceiver. Another additional premise is needed, such as one stating that the Berkeleian sense implies the acquaintance sense, namely:

> (11) If an object is perceived without a perceived intermediary object, then it is present with and presented to a perceiver.

If, instead, a Berkeleian sense is used throughout the argument, then the attack switches to (5b). Premises (5b), (10a), and (11) are all shown to be dubious by the fact that it is surely plausible to claim that certain stars are perceived at times they do not exist, because perceiving them consists in star-sensing as a result of stimulus energy from the stars and some of these stars do not exist when the star-sensings occur. And, with no intermediaries, they are directly perceived in a Berkeleian sense but not in an acquaintance sense. The plausibility of this casts doubt on all three premises. And, our direct realist might plausibly continue, the initial reasonableness of the version of the argument using (7a) results from an equivocation on 'directly perceive' in premises (5b) and (7a). Once the equivocation is eliminated, one of these two premises is no more reasonable than its denial.

Our conclusion, then, is that the causal facts involved in the time gap between the transmission of stimulus from an external object and the resultant perceptual experience, like the previous perceptual facts examined in this chapter, do not provide reason to reject an adverbial theory in favor of some theory involving sensa. Once again, we have failed to find a justification for the existence of sensa.

CONCLUSION ABOUT PERCEPTUAL FACTS AND SENSA

We have examined what I believe are the most plausible versions of four arguments for the existence of sensa that are based on certain empirical facts of perception. In each case we found at least one premise that it would not be unreasonable to deny. Furthermore, although we have by no means considered all facts of perception, I know of none we have not examined that would provide grounds for justification of the existence of sensa. Consequently we have finished the task of this chapter. We have found reason to conclude that it is at least as plausible to talk of adverbial sensings as it is to refer to sensa when describing the facts of perception. We have not, of course, justified rejecting a sensa theory for this purpose, but this was not essential to our purpose. We have been trying to find whether it is plausible for a materialist to adopt the adverbial theory, so that he could reduce sensings to brain events while eliminating sensa. We have, then, completed part of this task, but at least one more part remains. It may be that there is no need to talk about sensa in describing the facts of perception, but it may be necessary to assume them for a fully adequate scientific explanation of these facts. We cannot settle this issue now, because no one is yet in a position to judge what assumptions are required for an adequate scientific theory of perception. W. Sellars, however, claims that if one scientific ideal is to be achieved, that is, a unified scientific explanation and description of the world, then science will have to assume sensa. If Sellars' reasoning is sound, it surely provides some reason for the existence of sensa. Consequently, given that at the present stage of our investigation we have found no reason to prefer either the adverbial theory or a sensa theory, a sound Sellarsian argument would tip the scale of evidence in favor of a sensa theory. Materialists, especially the many who accept the ideal of a unified science, would be unreasonable if they advocated the adverbial theory. We should, then, examine Sellars' arguments.

7. Arguments
for the Postulation of Sensa

One of the earlier conclusions we reached is that sensation terms are theoretico-reporting terms and, consequently, that sensations cannot be eliminated on the grounds that they are postulated entities unnecessary for scientific purposes. In this chapter we are interested in the question of whether it is necessary to postulate sensa for any scientific purposes, although, as we have just concluded, none of the clearly acceptable facts of perception make it unreasonable to deny that there are sensa. It might seem that each of these two previous conclusions is the basis for an objection that it is superfluous to investigate the question presently before us, because one conclusion shows that sensa are not postulated entities and the other shows they are not needed even if they are postulated. Because it is clear that there is no sense in proceeding if either of these objections is sound, we should examine them now. First, although it is true that none of the facts of perception we have examined require us to accept sensa, this does not provide reason to deny that when those facts, and perhaps many others, come to be given a fully adequate scientific explanation, the relevant explanatory theory will require the postulation of sensa. Although some theoretical entities, such as positrons, came to have an explanatory function, they were not originally postulated to explain certain observed phenomena. Rather they were required by the scientific theory designed to explain different observed phenomena.

This, however, raises the other objection, because it treats sensa like positrons and it has been argued that they are quite different. We have indeed concluded that sensations are not to be eliminated in the way postulated theoretical entities are, because they are not postulated entities. This conclusion, which is really about sense experience, implies that we cannot justify this kind of elimination of sensations under every interpretation, including the adverbial sensing interpretation and the sensa interpretation. Thus we must use some interpretation of sensations, but this leaves open the question of whether any particular one will be required. It may be that one particular interpretation that involves sensa will be required by a yet to be developed scientific theory that will provide fully adequate scientific explanation of perceptual and other kinds of experiences. Some theoretical requirements of the theory, or of its integration into or reduction to some other theory, may rule out the sensing theory and force the acceptance of sensa. Thus there may be a postulational justification of sensa, but not a postulational rejection of sensations. However, as I have already claimed, no one yet has the evidence needed to decide whether sensa are necessary for scientific explanations. We shall not, consequently, examine that claim, but will instead consider the different, although related, claim of one scientific realist, W. Sellars, that a *unified* science, adequate for a complete explanation and description of what there is, requires sensa.

Sellarsian Scientific Realism

I have claimed that Sellars subscribes to scientific realism (see *SR,* sec. 49).[1] He attempts to justify this hypothesis the way one justifies a scientific hypothesis, that is, he attempts to

1. Throughout this chapter I shall use abbreviations for Sellars' works as follows:

> *CE*: "The Concept of Emergence," with P. Meehl, in H. Feigl et al., eds., *Minnesota Studies* 1 (1958): 239–52.
>
> *IA*: "The Identity Approach to the Mind–Body Problem," *Review of Metaphysics* 18 (1965); reprinted in *PP*, Chap. 15.
>
> *PP*: *Philosophical Perspectives* (Springfield, Ill.: Charles C. Thomas, 1967).
>
> *RA*: "Rejoinder" (to Aune), in H. Castañeda, ed., *Intentionality, Minds, and Perception* (Detroit: Wayne State University Press, 1967), pp. 286–300.
>
> *SM*: *Science and Metaphysics*
>
> *SPR*: *Science, Perception, and Reality*
>
> *SR*: "Scientific Realism or Irenic Instrumentalism," in R. Cohen and M. Wartofsky, eds., *Boston Studies,* vol. 2; reprinted in *PP*, Chap. 14.
>
> *SSS*: "Science, Sense Impressions and Sensa: A Reply to Cornman," *Review of Metaphysics* 23 (1971): 391–447.
>
> *TE*: "Theoretical Explanation," in B. Baumrin, ed., *Philosophy of Science: The Delaware Seminar* 2: 61–78; reprinted in *PP*, Chap. 13.

This chapter is a considerably revised version of my article, "Sellars, Scientific Realism, and Sensa," *Review of Metaphysics* 23 (1970): 417–51. Many revisions result from Sellars' comments in *SSS* on my article.

show that nothing implied by his hypothesis is dubious, and
that some of what alternative hypotheses imply is dubious. He
is, then, attempting to vindicate a leading hypothesis rather
than to validate a conclusion. We can gather what this hypothesis is when Sellars says "that in the dimension of describing
and explaining the world, science is the measure of all things,
of what is that it is, and of what is not that it is not" (*SPR,* p.
173). This is helpful, but, because we have already seen that
there are different species of scientific realism, we must make
some distinctions to discover which species Sellars espouses.
We can begin by distinguishing three kinds which, following
previous discussion, I shall name as follows:

> (1) *Minimal Scientific Realism:* All pure theoretical terms,
>   such as 'electron' and 'nuclear fission' that are required
>   for the best scientific explanation of the observable
>   behavior of physical objects and persons, refer to
>   (often unobservable) objects or properties. (This is
>   a contrary of scientific instrumentalism, i.e. all pure
>   theoretical terms of science are merely nonreferring
>   symbolic devices that help to warrant inferences from
>   observation premises to observation conclusions.)
> (2) *Moderate Scientific Realism:* All physical objects have
>   as constituents and properties only the objects and
>   properties referred to by certain of the pure theoreti-
>   cal scientific terms that are required for the best sci-
>   entific explanation of the observable behavior of the
>   objects.
> (3) *Extreme Scientific Realism:* All physical objects and
>   all persons have as constituents and properties only
>   the objects and properties referred to by the pure theo-
>   retical scientific terms that are required for the best
>   scientific explanation of the observable behavior of
>   the objects and the persons.

Clearly (3) entails (2), and although (2) does not entail (1),
it is generally agreed that (2) is reasonable only if (1) is. Because of this, much of the debate about scientific realism has
centered on scientific instrumentalism versus minimal scientific
realism. But (1) is not sufficient to explicate Sellars' kind of
scientific realism. Although, on the basis of the preceding quo-

tation we should classify Sellars as an extreme scientific realist (see also *SSS,* pp. 397–99) he differs significantly from other extreme realists. Pointing out just how and why he differs from them will bring us to the point on which I wish to concentrate, because it concerns his view of sense impressions, sensa, and their explanatory roles (*IA,* secs. 45–52).[2]

Many philosophers who accept moderate scientific realism would agree with a postulation elimination theorist such as Quine: sensations are pure theoretical entities and can therefore be eliminated, because all human behavior can be explained, in principle at least, using only the terms of neurophysiology and other physical science, and so there is no explanatory need for sensation terms. Consequently, they would find it unjustified to accept moderate scientific realism and reject extreme scientific realism. Sellars, however, is not a postulation elimination theorist. The reason for this is that he disagrees with Quine about what is required to explain human behavior. He thinks that the explanation of certain sorts of human behavior requires sensation terms.

One sort of human behavior is verbal behavior, and one sort of verbal behavior is that which is said to express propositional attitudes about the world. Often when such overt behavior is in response to perceptual stimulation, as when "There is a red and triangular object here" is uttered, the verbal response is said to express a *perceptual* propositional attitude. Such overt verbal behavior must be explained as well as nonverbal behavior (see *SSS,* p. 400), and, according to Sellars, perceptual propositional attitudes are "elements in a 'theory' designed to explain human behavior" (*SSS,* p. 398). But such explanatory entities must themselves be explained. Consequently the nonbehavioral facts that persons have perceptual propositional attitudes about and conceptual representations of the world around them, must themselves be explained in addition to the facts of observable behavior. According to Sellars, then, a person being "under the visual impression that (visually taking it to be the case that) there is (or of there being) a red and rectangular physical ob-

---

2. What Sellars calls "sensa" are a very unique species of what we have been calling sensa (see *SPR,* pp. 101–04). However nothing in the following discussion rests upon keeping these two different senses of 'sensa' distinct.

ject in front of one" (*SM*, p. 14) is used to explain certain
overt behavior. Consequently such "impressions that" must also
be explained if science is to provide a full and unified explanation, and, for Sellars, description of everything that occurs.
And, he says, although sense impressions are not needed to
explain the "white-rat type discriminative behavior" (*IA*, sec.
49) we have in common with other animals, they, or at least
sensa in a unified scientific theory, are needed to explain such
propositional attitudes.

It seems, then, that Sellars disagrees with a postulation elimination theorist such as Quine about what is required to explain
human behavior, that is, he disagrees with Quine's implication
that "correlative physical states" will be able to take over the
explanatory role of all mental entities. More specifically, he
appears to claim that they will not take over the role of certain
theoretical "inner" particulars, sensa, in the scientific explanation of propositional attitudes which are in turn used to explain
certain verbal behavior.

It is not clear, however, why he should not agree with Quine
that, although states of human beings that are physical in the
sense previously defined (see Intro.) cannot assume the explanatory roles of propositional attitudes in the *present,* intermediary stage of scientific development, they can do so once neurophysiology and other physical sciences develop more fully. If
he did accept this, then he would have become a postulation elimination theorist and his justification of sensa would collapse. He
would slide into the "crude" materialism he wishes to avoid
(see *SM*, p. 22).

The one way I find he can avoid this is to put a restriction on
his view of science as the measure of all things. Although he is
an avowed foe of the given, there are many versions of the
given other than the one version he opposes (see *PP*, p. 353)
which are compatible with taking quite literally his claim that
"we must find a place in the world for color in the aesthetically
interesting sense with its ultimate homogeneity" (*SSS*, p. 408).
How such color is to be construed—whether as surfaces of
physical objects, properties of sensa, modes of sensing, or in
some other way—is to be decided by science. But, on this account science must interpret color and other sensuous features
of the world such as sounds, smells, and tastes; it cannot elimi-

nate them or transform them so much that there remains nothing sufficiently like them. I shall call this view Sellarsian, although it may not be acceptable to Sellars. It is a view that fits
both with my construal of sensation terms as theoretico-reporting terms and with my reasons for rejecting the "last attempt"
to justify the 'sensation' elimination theory (in Chap. 5). For
this reason I shall consider Sellarsian, although perhaps not
Sellars', scientific realism in the rest of this chapter.

We can bring out how the Sellarsian position differs from
extreme scientific realism by means of the following definition:

> (4) *Sellarsian Scientific Realism:* All physical objects and
> all persons have as constituents and properties only
> the objects and properties referred to by the pure
> theoretical scientific terms that are required for the
> scientific theory that best explains the observable be-
> havior of these objects and persons in a way that also
> explains and interprets sensuous features of the world
> and human responses to them.

Our Sellarsian, then, can eliminate sensuous color from the external world of physical objects in a Lockean way, but if he
does this he must locate something much like it in perceivers
which will explain verbal responses of persons, such as "That's
a (sensuously) red physical object." According to this Sellarsian,
this explanation requires sensa, and being a scientific realist, he
holds that there are sensa, and they cannot be eliminated for
the reasons that postulated theoretical entities, such as the
ether, have been eliminated. As a result, he disagrees with a
materialist such as Rorty who argues for the elimination of sensations. He also disagrees with identity theorists such as Feigl
and Smart, because he claims there are sensa and none are
identical with brain entities.[3] Thus although he is a scientific
realist, this Sellarsian is neither an eliminative nor a reductive

---

3. Strictly speaking, Sellars would reject this identity claim only if
the relevant brain entities are what he calls "physical$_2$" entities. He
claims that there is a sense—uninteresting for our purposes—in which
sensa are brain entities (*IA*, secs. 28–32) and a sense in which they
are physical, i.e. what he calls "physical$_1$" (see *IA*, sec. 45). His physical$_1$
and physical$_2$ correspond to my scientific$_1$ and scientific$_2$, discussed later
in this chapter.

materialist. For many, this would appear to be an odd combination of views, but that makes it no less important to examine it.

AN EXAMINATION OF SELLARSIAN SCIENTIFIC REALISM AND REASONS FOR SENSA

To begin the examination of the Sellarsian position, let us agree with Sellars that sense impressions, for example, impressions *of* a red and triangular object, which he calls "raw feels" and "nonconceptual episodes," are in fact used to explain perceptual propositional attitudes, such as being under the impression *that* there is a red and triangular object in front of one (*IA*, secs. 22–23), which, in turn, are needed to explain certain verbal behavior in a way that can account for sensuous color. As Sellars says,

> It is therefore crucial to my thesis to emphasize that sense impressions or raw feels are common sense theoretical constructs introduced to explain the occurrence *not* of white rat type discriminative behavior, *but rather of perceptual propositional attitudes,* and are therefore bound up with the explanations of why human language contains families of predicates having the logical properties of words for perceptible qualities and relations (*IA*, sec. 49).

Our task in evaluating Sellars' claim about sensa is not to question whether "impressions of" are or can be used to help explain "impressions that," because we can grant that point. Our task is rather to find out whether, assuming a Sellarsian scientific realism, scientific explanations of "impressions that" *require* both that there are "impressions of" and that such impressions be construed as particulars.

Sellars seems to have no doubt about the first requirement, that sense impressions are required if there are to be explanations of perceptual propositional attitudes. He claims that having an *impression that* implies having an *impression of*. As he says,

> Thus, the fact that a person is under the visual impression that a certain stick in water is bent is taken to imply that he is having a visual impression of a bent object. I shall assume that this is true (*IA*, sec. 21).

But even granting, as we shall do in this discussion, this first requirement, there seems to be no need to grant also that these *impressions of* must be particulars. Although we can and do explain someone's perceptual propositional attitude, such as being under the impression that an object is white, by using statements, such as "He sensed a white appearance," which imply that there are white individuals, we could equally well explain it by saying, "He sensed white-ly" or "He white-sensed." If the adverbial sensing theory functions to explain perceptual propositional attitudes at least as well as sensa theories, then no "inner" particulars, such as sensa, are needed to explain *impressions that,* and Sellars' justification of the existence of sensa fails. Even if sensations under some interpretation are required for explanatory purposes as we have granted, it does not seem that an interpretation of them involving sensa is required.

Sellars has not overlooked this appeal to the adverbial theory, however. Indeed, he thinks that the adverbial theory is correct for the manifest image, or common sense picture of man, in which persons are construed "as subjects of conceptual episodes proper" (*SM,* p. 166) rather than bundles of particulars as in the scientific image. As he understands the manifest image, *impressions of* are states of perceivers rather than particulars. According to him, for the manifest image,

> the correct view is that to have a sensation of a red rectangle is to sense a-red-rectangle-ly or, strictly speaking, because 'sense' is not a complete verb in itself, such as might take an ordinary adverb of manner, it is to a-red-rectangle-ly-sense, which alone is the complete verb (*SM,* p. 168).

And he goes on to say,

> My point in all this is that the only *ultimate* logical subject involved in a person's having a sense impression of a red rectangle is the person, though, of course, impressions are *derivative* logical subjects, in the sense in which smiles as logical subjects are derivative from people smiling and waltzes from people waltzing (*SM,* p. 169).

But, and here is the crucial point, Sellars thinks that the adver-

bial theory will not do for the scientific image in which persons
are bundles of particulars. That image requires that scientific
realism is correct, and

> if scientific realism is correct, at the end of the road some-
> how the phrase

> a red triangle

> will lose its adverbial status and, by a final transposition,
> will become once again a common noun for particulars,
> though not the particulars with which the story began (*SM,*
> p. 172).

Sellars' point is that, along the path from the Aristotelian conception of a person to the "final" scientific picture, there have
been and will be several conceptual changes. The first change
is from the Aristotelian view of a person as a "single logical
subject" who has relationships to sensibly colored physical particulars, to the conception of a person as a single logical subject
caused by physical particulars that are not sensuously colored
to be in color-sensing *states* which are sense impressions. The
"last" change is to the picture of persons consisting of groups
of basic physical particulars in some kind of relationship to a
quite different kind of basic particular, sensa, which are the
finally derived counterparts in the scientific image of sensuously
colored physical particulars in the manifest image (see also
SPR, pp. 99–100).

The question before us is not whether this story of concept
transformation will prove to be correct, even in part. It is why
Sellars thinks that a stage in which persons as groups of basic
physical particles in certain states, such as sensing white-ly, is
ultimately unsatisfactory for the scientific image, and why he
thinks his scientific realism requires the move from such objectless states to a new kind of inner particular, sensa. In what
follows I shall use Sellars' writings to construct three arguments
to justify the claim that the scientific image requires that sensory
experience consist in part of sensa. Because of the complexity
of the issues and of Sellars' statements about them, I am far
from certain, however, that Sellars would agree with these reasons. Indeed, I am sure he would reject the first. Nevertheless,
whether they are Sellars' arguments, they are the most plausible

attempts I have found to base the justification of sensa on scientific realism. Thus anyone who wishes to claim that it is reasonable to deny the existence of sensa should examine these Sellarsian arguments.

FIRST REASON: SENSE IMPRESSIONS ARE ANALOGOUS
TO PHYSICAL OBJECTS

We have seen that Sellars makes the very reasonable claim that it is necessary to assume sensations to explain certain propositional attitudes. He thus construes them as theoretical entities even though he admits that we can have direct knowledge of them. Sensation terms, then, are both theoretical terms and reporting terms. But being theoretical these terms are like all theoretical terms formed by analogy, in the sense that they are "analogical extensions of concepts pertaining to the public or intersubjective world of things and persons" (*SPR*, p. 48). Sellars' view, then, is that in the order of concept formation it is the language of public, observable objects which is basic, and all other concepts that apply to imperceptible entities, such as electrons and sense impressions, are formed by analogy with the basic ones (see *SR*, secs. 19–37). But, because he also claims that "priority in the order of concept formation must not be confused with ontological priority" (*RA*, p. 296n.), Sellars can consistently maintain his theory of concept formation with his scientific realistic position that those manifest image concepts, basic in the order of concept formation, actually apply to nothing at all (*SPR*, pp. 126, 173). Nothing is literally red in the public, occurrent sense of 'red' that is applied to physical objects, although some things, sensa, are occurrently "red" in a different but analogically derived sense.

One argument for sensa that it might seem Sellars would accept is stated by B. Aune in his "Comments" on Sellars. Aune argues that Sellars' quite plausible view of the analogical nature of the formation of sensation concepts requires that sense impressions be inner particulars rather than states, such as sensing red-ly. He considers Sellars' view that "an impression [of a red triangle] is conceived as analogous in certain respects to objects that are red and triangular on their facing side," [4] and concludes

4. B. Aune, "Comments" (on Sellars), in Castañeda, *Intentionality, Minds and Perception*, p. 275.

that "if anything were to be conceived as analogous to a facing surface, it would presumably be the kind of thing that philosophers have called a 'sense datum' or 'sense content,' something which is, plainly enough, a peculiar kind of particular, not a state of having something." [5]

Must the analogy required for concept derivation be an analogy of objects with objects? Why not one of objects with states of a perceiver? Sellars agrees that it can be the latter (*RA*, p. 289), because, as he says, "the *essential* feature of the analogy is that visual impressions stand to one another in a system of ways of resembling and differing which is structurally similar to the ways in which the colours and shapes of visible objects resemble and differ" (*SPR*, p. 193). And states of color-sensing can vary in ways structurally similar to and functionally dependent on the ways colors of visible objects vary.[6] There seems, therefore, to be nothing wrong with a "trans-category analogy" (*SPR*, p. 93) between objects and states for the purposes of concept derivation, and we can quickly reject the first argument for interpreting sensory experience as consisting in part of inner particulars rather than objectless states of perceivers. Let us, then, turn to another argument derived from Sellars.

SECOND REASON: IN THE SCIENTIFIC IMAGE
PERSONS ARE AGGREGATES

The second reason is considerably more complicated than the first. The essential argument here is that the adverbial interpretation of sense impressions requires persons to be single logical subjects, and while this is compatible with the manifest image, the scientific image requires them to be pluralities of logical subjects. Thus although in the manifest image sensory experiences can be construed as states of perceivers that do not involve any inner phenomenal particulars, i.e. sensa, in the scientific image they must be construed as involving sensa. The most relevant passage from Sellars is:

> By 'identifying' in the above manner a person with a plurality of logical subjects, i.e. the constituent parts of the 'computer,' we have undermined the logic of sense

5. Aune, p. 276.
6. Cf. R. Chisholm, *Perceiving*, pp. 143–49.

impressions. For whether these parts be construed as material particles or as nerve cells, the fact that they are a
plurality precludes them from serving either jointly or separately as the subject of the verb 'to sense red-rectangle-
wise' [for 'to sense redly' is not true of particles or nerve
cells taken severally, and, being a primitive predicate it
can be true collectively of wholes consisting of particles or
nerve cells only if it is true of them severally] we must
therefore either introduce another logical subject (an im-
material subject) to do this work, or introduce a new
category of entity ('phantasms' or 'sensa' we might call
them) with predicates the logical space of which is mod-
elled on that of visual impressions, as the latter was mod-
elled on the logical space of colored and shaped physical
objects. [These new particulars with their new predicates
would be those elements in persons construed as pluralities of logical subjects which preserved the irreducibility
of the logical space of color which is so patent a feature
of the world of common sense experience. The counterpart
in this new framework of a person sensing-a-red-rectan-
gle-ly would be the involvement of a red and rectangular
sensum in the total state of the person as a system of scientific objects] (*SSS*, p. 428).

I shall construe the central part of the argument as follows:

(1) If something is a logical subject of 'to sense red-ly,'
then some logical subject of 'to sense red-ly' is a
single logical subject.

(2) If the scientific image is correct, then all single logical subjects are scientifically basic entities.

(3) No scientifically basic entities are logical subjects
of 'to sense red-ly.'

Therefore

(4) If the scientific image is correct, then nothing and,
a fortiori, no person is a logical subject of 'to sense
red-ly.'

(5) If no person is a logical subject of 'to sense red-ly,'
then some sensory experiences of persons consist
in part of red inner particulars, i.e. red sensa.

Therefore

> (6) If the scientific image is correct, then there are
> sensa.

In order to evaluate these premises, we need to clarify the
phrases containing 'logical subject.' I think the following two
rough definitions will suffice for our purposes:

> *s* is a logical subject $=_{df.}$ *s* is an individual for which there
> is a predicate '*P*' such that *s* is a true value of '*x*' in '*x* is *P*'.

and

> *s* is a single logical subject $=_{df.}$ *s* is a logical subject and
> *s* does not consist of a plurality or aggregate of logical sub-
> jects, i.e. *s* is a simple logical subject.

Using these definitions, we can grant that premise (2) is true.
There is doubt about (3), however, because, as seen from the
preceding quotation, postulating Cartesian-like egos as scientifically basic entities which are simple logical subjects of 'to
sense red-ly' is an alternative to positing sensa. Nevertheless
let us grant premise (3) for our purposes, because if the only
way to avoid sensa requires Cartesian egos, then materialism is
surely false if there are no sensa. As we have previously seen, it
is also false if there are sensa. I wish to concentrate on premise
(1). On the face of it, (1) seems clearly false. Persons are subjects of the verb 'to sense red-ly' whether they are single or
pluralities of logical subjects.

*A defense of premise (1): Primitive predicates
and single logical subjects*

We can begin a discussion of one way to defend (1) by considering Sellars' discussion of color words. It seems to be Sellars' view that if an aggregate constituted of *n* single logical
subjects is the logical subject of a primitive term, then the term
must also apply to each of the *n* simple constituents of the aggregate (*RA,* p. 299). But 'red' is a primitive predicate. Therefore if some aggregate is the subject of 'red', then those single
logical subjects which constitute the aggregate are also logical
subjects of 'red.' The same would be true of 'to sense red-ly'.
Thus we have:

(7) If something, *e* (whether an aggregate or not), is a logical subject of a primitive predicate, *P*, then some logical subject of *P* (either *e* or a constituent of *e*) is a single logical subject.

Then, if we conjoin (7) with:

(8) 'To sense red-ly' is a primitive predicate,

we can derive (1). Although we can accept (8) for our present purposes, there are surely the same doubts about (7) that were raised about Sellars' interpretation of his principle of reducibility—version R2a (p. 115). Again the example of a gas with the property of having a rising temperature seems to justify rejecting (7). It is as plausible to construe the observation term 'temperature' to be primitive as the observation term 'red' and the phenomenal term 'to sense red-ly.' Furthermore it seems that gases are logical subjects of 'temperature' while neither their constituents nor any other scientifically basic entities are. But, then, given at least minimal scientific realism, no single logical subjects would be logical subjects of 'temperature.'

A justification of premise (7): The scientific image and basic level descriptions

In the preceding discussion of Sellars' principle of reducibility, we rejected version R2a for the reason I have just used to argue against (7). We are now, however, in a position to pursue the matter in more detail by considering whether R2a and (7) are required by a Sellarsian version of extreme scientific realism. Thus, although there may be no reason to accept these claims if we do not accept a Sellarsian position, it may be that this position not only requires them, but also overrides the reasons I have used to reject the claims. Sellars argues that if science is to produce not only the best explanation of what there is but also the best description or picture, then what he calls *the* scientific image of the universe must be correct. And this is correct only if science becomes unified in the sense that there be one complete description of the universe at the basic level of science to compete with the manifest or common-sense image. If no such unification occurs, then each unreduced scientific theory will present partial and fragmented pictures, and *the* manifest image will triumph. This unity of science in turn requires that all descriptions of objects of the universe that are true at some nonbasic level of science, must have a corresponding true description at the basic level of science. That is, corresponding to each true nonbasic description there must be a true description using only predicates that have individual scientifically basic entities as subjects. If this requirement is conjoined with two additional claims, then we shall be able to derive that (7) is a consequence of the scientific image. Then this conclusion taken with (8) will yield a variation of (1) we can use to derive (4). The first claim is that the second of the above requirements of the correctness of the scientific image implies that all *primitive* predicates have individual scientifically basic entities as subjects. The second is that according to the scientific image all scientifically basic entities are single logical subjects.

We can lay out this new argument as follows:

(9) If the scientific image is correct, then for every description that uses a predicate with a nonbasic entity as subject and that is true at a scientifically nonbasic level, there is a corresponding description true at the scientifically basic level that uses only predicates with individual scientifically basic entities as subjects.

(10) If the antecedent and the consequent of (9) are true, then any predicate that is true only of a nonbasic entity, *e,* is definable by primitive predicates true of some scientifically basic entities that constitute *e.*

Therefore

(11) If the scientific image is correct, then no predicates true only of scientifically nonbasic entities are primitive predicates, i.e. then an entity which is not scientifically basic is a logical subject of a primitive predicate *P* only if some scientifically basic entity is also a logical subject of *P.*

(12) If the scientific image is correct, then if *s* is a scientifically basic entity, then *s* is a single logical subject.

Therefore

(7a) If the scientific image is correct, then if something (whether scientifically basic or not) is a logical subject of a primitive predicate, *P*, then some logical subject of *P* is a single logical subject.

The conjunction of (7a) and (8) yields:

(1a) If the scientific image is correct, then if something is a logical subject of 'to sense red-ly' then some logical subject of 'to sense red-ly' is a single logical subject.

Then the conjunction of (1a), (2), and (3) yields (4) as desired. In examining this argument we can grant both premises (9) and (12) on the grounds that both unpack part of the concept of the scientific image. Granting premise (10), however, is another matter because doubts similar to those concerning R2a and (7) arise. What reason is there to think that a correspondence between true nonbasic descriptions and true basic descriptions requires that the predicates in the former are definable by basic predicates?

A defense of premise (10): Primitive predicates and a Tractarian language: Sellars accepts (10), (see *SSS*, pp. 425–26), and I think that his reason for this derives from his view that Wittgenstein's conception of language in the *Tractatus* is the model for an ideally perspicuous language, that is, for the kind of language Sellars seems to find required for the best picture or description of what there is (see *SPR*, pp. 207–15; and *SR*, secs. 18, 89–90). In such a Tractarian language each primitive subject term names one ontologically basic entity and each primitive predicate ascribes one property or relation to ontologically basic entities. All other names and predicates are incomplete symbols, that is, symbols defined using logical constants with the primitive names and predicates.[7] Consequently each nonbasic, or nonatomic, sentence is logically equivalent to a molecular sentence consisting of atomic sentences joined by truth-functional logical connectives, and each ontologically non-

---

7. However, see Sellars' comparison of *PM*-ese and his own Jumblese (*SPR*, Chap. 7). In Jumblese there are no predicates, but merely ways of characterizing individual constants and variables.

basic entity is to be understood as a logical construction out of basic entities. Given that this Tractarian kind of language provides the best or most perspicuous picture of what there is, and, as Sellars also seems to believe, that the scientific image requires the theoretical terms of science to provide, in this sense, the best picture of what there is, then (10) is justified. For, given the above, the scientific image is correct only if scientific theoretical terms are imbedded in a Tractarian language. And given this, only the theoretical predicates that apply to individual scientifically basic entities are primitive predicates. All predicates that truly apply only to scientifically nonbasic entities, whether theoretical, observational, or phenomenal, are defined by means of those primitive predicates that truly apply to scientifically basic entities.

This Sellarsian defense of (10) is initially plausible, but I find at least two reasons to think that it fails. First, for the scientific image to triumph over the manifest image, and all others, it is only required that for any language structure with any reasonable degree of perspicuity, the theoretical terms imbedded in that structure provide, with only the addition of the logical constants of that structure, a more accurate and comprehensive picture or description of what there is, than any other set of terms imbedded in the same structure. But just as someone who claims that the terms of a phenomenalistic language or of the observation language provide the best picture need not show he can imbed his terms in a Tractarian language structure, neither is this required of someone who champions the scientific image. That is, the scientific image must be best in the sense of being better than all of its alternatives, but need not be best in the sense of being the ideal picture of what there is. At most it would be necessary to imbed the terms in a Tractarian language if an opponent has succeeded in doing it. But even in that eventuality, I think such a success by one competitor would prove sufficient reason for rejecting another only if all else is equal. This is seldom the case.

Second, past failures give reason to think that no program of logical constructionism, an integral part of imbedding any set of terms in a Tractarian language structure, will succeed. For example, there is reason to think that many sentences using only physical object terms are not logically equivalent to any sentence using only sense-data terms, and thus there is reason to think that some physical objects are not logical constructions out of sense-data. Similarly, there is reason to think that pure observation terms are not definable by pure theoretical terms, and so observable entities are not logical constructions out of theoretical entities. But the preceding reasons to reject both a phenomenalistic program of logical construction and a scientific realistic program of logical construction do not provide reason to reject either of the conflicting claims about which kind of terms provides the best picture of what there is. Thus neither the scientific image being best nor a phenomenalistic image being best entails that the nonbasic terms of the image are definable by its basic terms. But this would be entailed if being the best picture entailed being imbedded in a Tractarian language. Thus the preceding defense of (10) fails.

Another defense of (10): Correspondence rules as definitions: I can find just one more way someone might attempt to justify (10). One thing is clear. The scientific image, by requiring that there be one complete description of the universe at the basic level of science, also requires that all nonbasic terms used in true descriptions be either directly or indirectly related to basic-level theoretical terms by correspondence rules. But, according to the present argument, once all such correspondence rules are established, they will, in effect, provide redefinitions of the nonbasic terms they contain. Consequently the scientific image implies such definitions, and premise (10) is true. This argument depends on construing correspondence rules as definitions or, as Sellars says of certain correspondence rules, at least as "anticipations of definitions . . . the implementation of which in an ideal state of scientific knowledge would be the achieving of a unified vision of the world" (*TE,* pp. 77–78). There are, however, different views about the kind of definitions correspondence rules are or may become. The first view is that of H. Putnam who claims about the correspondence rule 'light is electromagnetic radiation,' that it is a definition but that in calling it a definition he does not "mean that the statement is 'analytic.' But then 'definitions,' *properly so called,* in theoretical science virtually *never* are analytic." [8] If one adopts this

8. H. Putnam, "Minds and Machines," in S. Hook, ed., *Dimensions of Mind,* p. 157.

view of correspondence rules as logically contingent definitions, then although the task of showing observable entities to be logical constructions out of theoretical entities will not be completed in the strict sense which requires logical equivalence, what results would seem to be sufficient for scientific purposes and perhaps also for producing a unified scientific view of what there is.

The second view of correspondence rules as definitions stems from Sellars' claim that a correspondence rule can become at least a part of a redefinition of the *observation* term it contains, once all correspondence rules needed to relate the theoretical with the observational are established. Furthermore, according to Sellars, these would be analytic definitions. As he says, "The force of the 'redefinition' must be such as to demand not only that the observation-sign design correlated with a given theoretical expression [be] syntactically interchangeable with the latter, *but that the latter be given the perceptual or observational role of the former so that the two expressions become synonymous* by mutual readjustment" (*SPR,* p. 125). Thus once the ideal state of scientific knowledge is reached, all that is needed for a Sellarsian program of logical construction would be available. That is, as Sellars says, "correspondence rules would appear in the material mode as statements to the effect that the objects of the observational framework *do not really exist—there really are no such things.* They envisage the *abandonment* of a sense and its denotation" (*SPR,* p. 126, and see *SR,* secs. 59–75). The second view goes beyond Sellars' claim about observation terms, however, because it requires that correspondence rules which relate *sensation* terms to basic theoretical terms, will also become definitions of the nonbasic terms they contain. As we shall see later in this chapter, there is reason to think that Sellars would reject this extension of his claim if all basic-level terms in the correspondence rules are both theoretical and physical in the sense previously defined. Furthermore, this rejection is reasonable because if all observation terms are redefined by such predicates, then sensation terms will be needed to carry all the sensory meaning of words like 'red' and 'warm.' Words with such meaning seem not to be definable by terms which are both physical and theoretical. Nevertheless, this alone does not preclude definitions of sensation terms by basic-level terms which are theoretical if some basic-level terms are not physical.

Although it is worth discussing, we need not decide here about whether in an ideal state of science correspondence rules would or should be considered analytic definitions. But again I think that it is the view that ontological reduction requires logical constructionism which prompts someone to argue for the definitions to be analytic.[9] The relevant point for our purposes is that if we grant that either of these two views of definition by correspondence rules is correct, then we should also grant that once 'to sense red-ly' and other adverbial phenomenal terms are "defined" via correspondence rules relating them to scientific basic entities, they no longer will be primitive, and while premise (10) might be true, (8) would be false. If, however, both views about correspondence rules being definitions are wrong, then, while (8) may be true, the argument that the scientific image requires sensa cannot be used to justify the existence of sensa. If we reject both these views about correspondence rules, then we have rejected the last reason to accept the consequent of (10). Furthermore, since it is surely reasonable to claim that some sensation terms are true of nonbasic entities, then we should reject the consequent of (10). But (9) is true, so we should either reject (10) or the scientific image. While it seems more reasonable to reject (10), this need not be done for our present purposes. If the scientific image should be rejected, then even if it required sensa, that would provide no reason to reject objectless sensings for sensa. Consequently, in either case this justification of sensa fails. Either (1a) remains dubious and the argument using it to justify sensa fails because all plausible ways to justify it fail, or the scientific image should be rejected and no attempts to base the justification of sensa on the requirements of the scientific image succeed. In either case the result is that this Sellarsian attempt to show that the scientific image requires the move from objectless sensings as states of persons to sensa as a special kind of particular, also fails. We have not yet found reason to reject sensings for sensa.

9. I have discussed ontology and analysis in Chapter 4 and in some detail in *Metaphysics, Reference, and Language.*

THIRD REASON: SENSING RED-LY IS AN EMERGENT PROPERTY

There is, I believe, one more argument against sensing red-ly and for red sensa that can be extracted from Sellars' writings. As in the previous argument it centers on two consequences of Sellars' conception of the scientific image we have already discussed. The first is that if the property of sensing red-ly is a property of something, then it is a property of persons and is, consequently, a property of groups of basic entities. The second is the requirement that all properties of groups of basic entities are reducible to properties or relations of individual basic entities. In addition the argument is also based on another premise previously discussed, namely, that no scientifically basic entities sense red-ly. But, so goes the argument, if a group of basic entities has a property but individual basic entities do not, then the property is an emergent group property. And, according to our initial attempt to formulate the argument, if something has an emergent group property, then that property is not reducible to properties or relations of individuals in the group. Consequently, if the scientific image is correct, then, as in the previous argument, no person senses red-ly. And, as in the previous argument we can use the premise: 'If no person senses red-ly, then sense experiences consist in part of inner red particulars,' to conclude again that if the scientific image is correct then there are sensa.

Once again I shall try to put the crux of this argument in a more perspicuous form:

(1) If the scientific image is correct, then sensing red-ly is a property of something only if it is a property of a group of scientifically basic entities.

(2) No scientifically basic entities have the property of sensing red-ly.

(3) If no basic entity has a property of a certain kind, but a group of basic entities does, then the property is an emergent group property.

Therefore

(4) If the scientific image is correct, then sensing red-ly is a property of something only if it is an emergent property of a group of scientifically basic entities.

(5) If something has an emergent group property, then it has a group property that is not reducible to properties or relations of the basic individuals that compose the group.

(6) If the scientific image is correct, then all emergent properties of groups of scientifically basic entities are reducible to properties or relations of individual scientifically basic entities.

Therefore

(7) If the scientific image is correct, then nothing, and a fortiori no person, has the property of sensing red-ly.

We can accept premise (1) because it expresses an obvious consequence of Sellars' scientific image. Premise (2) is acceptable if all basic entities are physical, but, as discussed previously, it ignores the possibility of Cartesian-like egos. However, again let us grant (2) for our purposes here because materialists cannot accept such egos. Premise (3) can be seen to be acceptable once we explicate the concept of emergent property following Sellars who says that 'emergence' connotes two or more levels and implies that emergent properties are nonbasic-level properties (*CE,* pp. 246–47). This seems true, which gives us reason to accept, and assume Sellars accepts (3). We are left, then, with (5) and (6). While we shall see that Sellars rejects (5) and is right to do so, it is clear he accepts (6), as can be seen by reviewing his principle of reducibility, R1 (pp. 114–15). As mentioned previously, however, it is not clear that his scientific realism requires either R1 or (6). We shall consider (5) first, because what I wish to say about (6) depends on how we revise (5) to avoid the initial objections.

Examination of premise (5): Reducible emergent properties

Premise (5) concerns reduction of properties, and although it is far from clear what the requirements are for property identity, let alone property reduction, Sellars thinks that one requirement for both is that the predicate expressing the property must be defined by, or "become" synonymous with the predicate expressing the reducing property (*IA,* secs. 8, 16, 37, 41). This is indeed a sufficient condition for property identity. If, as Sellars thinks, it is also a necessary condition, it would seem to bolster (5) because there seems to be no way to define some emergent properties, such as phenomenal properties, by physical properties. Nevertheless we can use another claim by Sellars to show that a definitional reduction of some emergent properties is plausible and thus (5) would be refuted. To see this, let us consider three different senses of what I shall call "scientific" properties. The first two are derived from definitions of 'physical predicate' given by Sellars (*IA*, sec. 45), and the third is modeled on the second.[10]

> *P is a scientific$_1$ property* = $_{df.}$ *P* is a property belonging to a nomological scientific framework that explains the behavior of spatiotemporal individuals.

> *P is a scientific$_2$ property* = $_{df.}$ *P* is a property that is attributed to entities in minimally adequate scientific explanations of the behavior of nonliving individuals which are not causally related to (or part of) living individuals.

> *P is a scientific$_3$ property* = $_{df.}$ *P* is a scientific$_2$ property that is attributed to individual basic-level individuals of physics.

We can now give a schema for three corresponding definitions of 'emergent property' depending on which subscript is used with 'scientific.'

> *E is an emergent$_n$ property* = $_{df.}$ (1) *E* is a property of an entity which is either simple or composed of entities with scientific$_n$ properties, and (2) *E* is not a scientific$_n$ property.

We can also give a schema for three parallel definitions of 'reducible emergent property':

> *R is a reducible emergent$_n$ property* = $_{df.}$ (1) *R* is an emergent$_n$ property of some entity, and (2) *R* is reducible to scientific$_n$ properties.

---

10. A discussion of Sellars' second definition of 'physical predicate' occurs in the Introduction. The reasons given there for rejecting it suggest the versions of the second and third definitions here.

As usually interpreted, psychological properties of thoughts or sense experience are emergent in the sense using 'scientific$_1$' and thus are also emergent in the other two senses. Certain physiological properties of human brains would be emergent in the sense using 'scientific$_2$,' and many observable properties, such as temperature, would be emergent only in the sense using 'scientific$_3$.' For our purpose of examining premise (5), it does not matter which sense is used, because (5) rules out the reduction of any emergent property, no matter what its level, to scientifically basic properties. But this falsifies (5), because the temperature of a gas is emergent$_3$ and, if another claim by Sellars is correct, it is reducible to the average kinetic energy of the molecules of the gas. As we have seen, Sellars claims that in a completed science the correspondence rules tying temperature to micro particles could become definitions of temperature terms, just as Sellars believes can be done for all empirical terms. He claims that "it make[s] sense to speak of turning empirical predicates—and in particular observation predicates —into definitional abbreviations of complex theoretical locutions," and that being so defined, observation terms could continue "to play their perceptual role as conditioned responses to the environment" (*TE*, p. 77). It follows that temperature, although emergent$_3$, is definitionally reducible$_3$, and premise (5) is false. Furthermore, we have previously seen reasons, independent of Sellars' views about correspondence rules, to think the theoretical reduction$_3$ of gas temperatures is plausible. And, given this conclusion about temperature, it seems initially plausible to claim there are also reducible emergent properties of the other two kinds. Consequently the property of sensing red-ly, while emergent$_2$, might well be reducible to scientific$_2$ or even scientific$_3$ properties.

A restricted version of (5): No reduction of sensings

Sellars would agree with the preceding reason to reject premise (5) on the grounds that empirical properties, such as temperature, are reducibly emergent$_3$ (see *TE*, pp. 71ff. and *SSS*, p. 434). Nevertheless it is open to him to reply that phenomenal properties, such as sensing red-ly, are at least emergent$_2$ but not reducible$_2$ and that premise (5) would be true when restricted to apply only to emergent$_2$ sensation properties. He would, then, disagree with the final inference of the preceding argument which assumes an analogy between the temperature case and the sensing red-ly case. While temperature which is only emergent$_3$ is reducible to basic-level properties and relations, the property of sensing red-ly, which is emergent$_2$, is not so reducible. The point is that correspondence rules relating sensation terms to scientific$_3$ terms would not provide definitions of sensation terms in this "ideal" state of science, for, in that state, all the counterparts of sensuous physical colors, among others, will have been relegated to the realm of sensation. This is necessary if there are to be definitions of empirical terms by scientific$_3$ terms in correspondence rules. All aspects of the meanings of empirical terms involving sensuous qualities, such as felt temperature and seen color, must be expunged if observation terms, such as 'gas' and 'table,' are to be defined by scientific$_3$ theoretical terms. But some terms must involve some kind of counterpart of sensuous physical qualities, according to Sellars, or at least our Sellarsian, because something relevantly analogous to sensible physical qualities is needed to explain, among other things, being under the impression that a table is red. Consequently at this final state of science, although sensation terms may be related to certain scientific$_3$ terms by correspondence rules, they are not definable by those scientific$_3$ terms, because there is no further limbo to which the sensuous quality aspect of their meaning can be relegated. According to this argument, then, if the scientific image is correct, sensing red-ly is an emergent$_3$ property of a group of basic or scientific$_3$ entities and it is not reducible to any scientific$_3$ properties or relations. Taking this conclusion with premise (6), it seems that we can derive (7) and are driven to assume sensa as basic-level theoretical entities that replace sensuous physical qualities and objectless sensings.

The inference to (7) is too quick, however, because the way we must amend premise (5) also requires a change in (6) if (7) is to be validly deduced. The new argument replaces (5) with:

> (5a) If something has the property of sensing red-ly, then it has an emergent$_3$ group property of scientifically basic individuals that is not reducible to scientific$_3$ properties of the individuals that compose the group.

The change in (6) required to yield (7) with (4) and (5a) results in a statement in need of examination:

(6a) If the scientific image is correct, then all emergent properties of groups of scientifically basic entities are reducible to scientific$_3$ properties of individual scientifically basic entities.

Examination of premise (6a): The scientific image and non-materialistic reduction: The crucial difference between (6) and (6a) is that where (6) merely requires of the scientific image the reduction of group properties to properties of *basic*-level individuals, (6a) requires reduction to scientific$_3$ properties. Even granting that the scientific image requires a definitional reduction of properties, which there is reason to doubt (see the next section), nothing in the Sellarsian argument that the emergent$_3$ property of sensing red-ly is not definitionally reducible to scientific$_3$ properties prohibits the definition of sensing terms by theoretical terms that apply to scientifically basic individuals, where there is an adjustment in the meanings of *both* sets of terms (see *SPR*, p. 125). One way for such an adjustment to occur would be for some basic-level terms to acquire some counterpart of the sensuous quality meaning of sensation terms. Thus the property of sensing red-ly might in this way be definitionally reducible to properties of scientifically basic entities. Each sentence ascribing sensing properties to a person might become synonymous with a sentence expressing either a relationship among certain basic entities or some nonrelational property the basic entities have in common. Such a reduction to the basic level, which would no longer be a scientific$_3$ level, is certainly compatible with scientific realism and the scientific image even if both require a definitional reduction of properties. Thus even if (6) is acceptable, (6a) is not, and the revised version of the argument fails as did the original version with premise (5).

One last attempt: No definitional reduction of sense experience

Neither our Sellarsian nor Sellars is finished yet, however. Sellars, in discussing the preceding point, claims that "it is exactly [to definitionally reduce the property of sensing red-ly to properties of scientifically basic entities] that I introduce sensa in the theoretical account of what it is for persons to have sensations" (*SSS*, p. 437). We can construct an argument from this remark as follows. Persons have sense experience and because this is an emergent property the scientific image requires it be reduced. This in turn requires a definitional reduction. But the property of having a sense experience involving redness is definitionally reducible to properties or relations of basic level entities only if there are sensa at the scientifically basic level which are red. Consequently the scientific image requires sensa.

We can unpack and fill in this argument by first replacing 'sensing red-ly' by the noncommital term, 'having a sense experience involving redness' throughout statements (1), (2), and (5a) in the preceding argument. Then we can add a premise that is both justified and accepted by our Sellarsian:

> (8) Some entities have the property of having a sense experience involving redness.

Conjoining (8) with (6) and (4) as revised yields:

> (9) If the scientific image is correct, then the property of having a sense experience involving redness is reducible to properties or relations of entities that are scientifically basic.

Two more premises are needed. Let us take (9) with:

> (10) If a property is reducible, then it is definitionally reducible,

and with:

> (11) If the property of having a sense experience involving redness is definitionally reducible to properties or relations of scientifically basic entities, then some of these properties are properties of sensa which are scientifically basic but at most scientific$_1$.

These premises yield that there are sensa if the scientific image is correct. Incidentally, they also yield (5a).

There are various ways to attack this argument. Premise (11) is far from obvious. Is there no way to define sensation term by terms that apply to scientifically basic entities unless sensa terms are used? Languages, ordinary and technical, continually change. For example, 'John hurts' might become synonymous with 'John's C-fibers are firing,' which may then become synonymous with some statement about scientific basic entities in John's brain. And, although these properties or relations of basic entities to which the property of hurting would be reduced would be neither scientific$_3$ nor even scientific$_2$ because of the changes in meaning of the terms expressing them, they would still be properties of basic entities. Incidentally, this kind of reduction of one property "to" another need not be the one kind of reduction Sellars considers (see *IA,* secs. 8, 16, 37, 41), because it does not require that predicates expressing the two properties be synonymous. It is more like a reduction by contextual definition of the average family to ordinary families.

Sellars' reply to this suggestion is that color terms are primitive in the sense that any one of them is definable only if some transposed form of the term is used in the definition. And since no individual scientific$_3$ entities are red or sense-red-ly, something must be sensuously red at the basic level if reduction is to occur (see *SSS,* pp. 437–38). What else but sensa qualify for this? Of course, we can again reply by mentioning the alternative of postulating Cartesian-like egos sensing red-ly at the basic level. However, although this surely casts doubt on (11) as stated, if we amend it by eliminating the phrase 'of sensa,' and thus the reference to sensa, the premise becomes quite plausible. It seems likely that a definitional reduction of the property of having a sense experience involving redness would require some sort of property that is at most scientific$_1$. Whether sensa or egos or something else will be postulated is left to be decided as the relevant scientific theories develop. However, while this move helps the adverbial sensing theorist, it is of no value to the adverbial materialist who cannot allow properties at the basic level that are at most scientific$_1$. He must, then, attack the argument at some other point.

Does reduction of properties require definitions of predicates, either explicit or contextual, as (10) implies? This is a difficult, and, as far as I know, an unanswered question. There are reasons to deny this requirement. Property identity, which is essential to the reduction of one property to another in a strict sense, can be contingent, and it is not clear why those reductions that entail identity should not also be contingent. While it is possible that the property of being red is not the property of being the color of most fire engines, these properties are in fact identical. This conclusion is justified by discovering that all and only instances of being red are identical with instances of being the color of most fire engines. Furthermore, in this case the property of being the color of most fire engines is nothing but the property of being red, and a contingent reduction also seems justified. Of course, if our Sellarsian's desire to imbed the scientific image in a Tractarian language were justified, then definitional reductions of properties would be required, but we have rejected this move. A better reply, however, is that although not every predicate that refers to a property P that is identical with a property Q must be synonymous with or definable in terms of some predicates that refer to Q, at least one predicate that refers to P must be so definable. I must confess that at present I do not know what to say about this reply because the issues involved are still unresolved. While I think that it will not stand up to outweigh the preceding reason for contingent property reduction, I shall say here only that the denial of (10) is at least as reasonable as (10), and so (10) is hardly adequate to support a conclusion. Nevertheless a stronger reason for rejecting this argument would be helpful.

The one place left to attack is premise (6). There are two objections to this, one already prepared by our previous discussion of Sellars' principle of reducibility and the other by the definition of materialism. Premise (6) states that the scientific image requires Sellars' principle of reducibility, R1, when R1 is interpreted as requiring property reduction. However, it is not clear it implies a principle as strong as R1 even when it is interpreted as R3 (p. 116) which requires only a reduction of instances. The scientific image does not seem to entail R1 or R3, even if we grant that it is correct only if all macro objects are identical with groups of basic particulars and each particular has only the properties ascribed to it in the basic science (cf. *SSS*, pp. 414–15). It does not seem that the scientific image requires the reduction of these group properties to properties that are part of the subject matter of the basic science. Nor does it seem that, even if such a reduction were required, it could not be done by postulating properties in the basic science that apply to groups of basic particulars but not to the individual particulars. If, as it seems, either of these two ways of accommodating non-basic group properties is compatible with Sellars' scientific image, then not only does it not require any principle of reduction like R1, but there would also be additional reason to reject the previously rejected Sellarsian argument against identifying sensa with brain parts (see Chap. 3).

While this first objection shows (6) to be dubious, it will not help the adverbial materialist if he requires a reduction of phenomenal properties. Both the view that there are groups of basic particulars with group properties not expressible at the basic level, and the view that such properties can be accommodated at the basic level by adding theoretical group properties at that level, lead to the conclusion that some groups of particulars have scientifically irreducible phenomenal properties, for example, those phenomenal properties of sensations identical with certain groups of particulars. For such a materialist, these group-objects would be neither purely physical nor purely mental (as are raw feels) but perhaps some "neutral" stuff, because they would have both physical and nonreducible phenomenal properties. But of course a materialist cannot accept this. He requires a reduction such as that expressed in either R1 or R3. Consequently our antimaterialistic Sellarsian can revise (6) by mentioning both scientific realism and materialism in its antecedent. This brings us to the second and crucial objection. While adverbial materialism and the scientific image together require the kind of reduction expressed in R3, namely, the reduction of instances of phenomenal properties, as the definition of 'materialism' indicates (p. 9), a materialistic reduction does not require, in addition, the reduction of the phenomenal properties themselves, unless the contingent reduction of all instances of a property either entails or justifies the reduction of the property itself. But if that should be true, we would then have enough additional reason to reject (10) finally, because property reduction would not have to be definitional. Thus because it is reasonable to claim that a contingent reduction of instances is sufficient for the kind of reduction needed for adverbial materialism, whether with or without the scientific image, either (6) is dubious if property reduction must be definitional, or (10) is dubious if the reduction can be contingent. Con-

sequently, this last Sellarsian argument to justify the existence
of sensa fails. At least one of its premises is unacceptable.

CONCLUSION ABOUT SENSATION WITHOUT SENSA

We have finished our examination of the Sellarsian arguments
to justify the postulation of sensa. Like the previous four attempts based on various facts of perception, we also found reasons sufficient to reject these arguments. This is as much as we
can do here to justify rejecting sensa for objectless sensing
events. However, given that the total relevant evidence available at this time consists in the refutation of the five attempts to
justify sensa which we have examined and the current lack of
reason to think there are other scientific or philosophical grounds
for sensa, it seems reasonable to reject sensa now. It might be
argued that we can draw the stronger conclusion that sensa
should not be postulated, because we have reached a point
where we can justify that conclusion by Occam's razor and a
Chisholm-like dissolution of puzzles engendered by sensa (see
Chap. 5). Such a move, however, would overlook the fact that
new scientific or philosophical grounds for sensa may become
available in the future. Although I see no reason to think that
this will occur, it is premature at present to use Occam's razor
to show that sensa should not be postulated, because work will
be done which will provide more evidence relevant to the issue.
Nevertheless, we have done enough here to conclude, for the
present at least, that we can accept the first of the four conditions jointly sufficient for adverbial materialism: there are no
sensa. Our last task, then, is to consider the three other conditions, namely, whether sensing events are identical with brain
events, whether they have nonmaterialistic properties, and
whether instances of properties of sensing in various ways have
only physical and physical-neutral properties. However, because
much work relevant to this task has already been completed in
previous sections of the book, I shall summarize the previous
results before beginning the remaining task.

Summary and Concluding Remarks

SUMMARY

We have reached the point where there are only three tasks left to perform within the scope of the present work. Before we proceed to these tasks, however, let me review how far we have come. We began with examination of one proximate species of materialism which I called "reductive" materialism. As I interpreted it, in a rather more restrictive sense than usual, it entails the reduction of all sensations, that is, sense experiences including sensa, or phenomenal objects of experience, to physical entities. Thus anyone who wishes to reduce events of sense experiencing while eliminating sensa is not a reductive materialist on this construal. I have called him an "adverbial" materialist. We also saw that reductive materialism entails the identity of sensa with physical entities and that the objection that ultimately defeats reductive materialism is aimed at conjoining materialism with such identity claims.

REDUCTIVE MATERIALISM, IDENTITY, AND PHENOMENAL PROPERTIES

Before examining the defeating objection, we rejected three other attempts to refute reductive materialism. The first, derived from Strawson's conception of a person, is that there are necessary owners of experiences, no mere bodies are necessary owners; therefore persons are not mere bodies and materialism, whether reductive or not, is false. The problem found for this objection is that the senses of 'necessary owner' which make it plausible to claim that persons are necessary owners of experiences but bodies are not, do not warrant the inference to the conclusion that persons are not mere bodies. Such kinds of necessity are compatible with 'person P' and 'body B' having an identical referent which is a mere body.

The privacy objection to the identity claim was next considered, and although it is short, precise, and persuasive, it was also rejected. It states that sensations are private, brain processes are public, nothing is both private and public, therefore no sensations are brain processes. First the sense of 'privacy' that made the argument most plausible was found to be that of the ultimate epistemological authority of the person who has a sensation.

Then the argument was rejected on the grounds that the same thing could be both public and private in this nonextentional sense of 'private,' depending on how the entity is described. Thus one thing described as a nagging pain could be private but the same thing described as firing C-fibers could also be public in this epistemological kind of privacy.

The two previous objections fail because, briefly, they involve misuses of intensional concepts of necessity and knowledge. The third objection to reductive materialism, the property objection to the identity theory, is carefully based only on extentional, that is, nonintensional and nonintentional, properties. The objection is that some sensa have extentional properties no brain entities have, and thus at least some sensa are not identical with brain phenomena. This argument seems to be very strong because the properties given as examples, such as being spatially located, swift, irreversible for brain processes, and being dim, fading, homogeneous for afterimages, can be shown merely on conceptual grounds to be the sorts of properties that either sensa or brain phenomena would lack. Thus the objection does not depend on an empirical investigation of properties lacked by one or the other, but on some kind of conceptual inapplicability of certain predicates. Actually, however, this seemingly strong point hides the flaw in the argument. If there is some reason to think that there are different, conceptually incommensurate ways to refer to the same entity, then the *conceptual* inapplicability of a set of predicates to an entity construed as a sensum, or construed as a brain process, is not sufficient to refute the identity claim. If there are plausible examples of identity across conceptual categories, then the objection is weakened. And, if, in addition, it is plausible to construe sensum–brain-phenomenon identity statements as cross-category identity statements, then the objection is refuted. This is indeed what we found to be the case in examining the objection. Thus the third objection fails as did the first two, and does so for a similar reason. In all three cases conceptual or linguistic facts, whether about necessity, knowledge and description, or category absurdity, are mistakenly thought to refute an ontological thesis.

We found, however, that once the property objection is freed from its reliance on the cross-category absurdities involved in predicating the same properties of both 'sensum' and 'brain process,' and once it is redirected to the conjunction of the identity theory and materialism, it resists refutation and constitutes grounds sufficient to refute reductive materialism. The objection grants the identity theory, but states that even accepting that the identity claims are cross-category and that this avoids the problem of predicating the wrong sorts of properties of 'sensum' and of 'brain process,' it must still be admitted that the entities 'sensum' refers to have phenomenal properties, even if it is absurd to claim that an entity has them when the entity is referred to using 'brain process.' Thus it would seem that something has phenomenal properties. And, if these properties are neither reduced to physical or physical-neutral properties nor eliminated somehow, and if instances of these properties cannot be shown to be nothing but instances of physical properties, then reductive materialism is refuted. But despite attempts to use acceptable examples of theoretical reduction as models for ways of handling nonmaterialistic properties of brain parts, we found in each case a crucial disanalogy that made a reduction of sensa based on that model implausible. Phenomenal properties of sensa cannot be "transferred" to something else for this purpose as can be done in the theoretical reductions of gas temperatures and water; they cannot be eliminated while sensa remain; and, unlike the theoretical reduction of each gas with a particular temperature, it is implausible to claim that each instance of each phenomenal property is identical with, let alone reducible to, some physical or physical-neutral property. We concluded that a theoretical reduction of sensa is unacceptable, and because there is no more plausible way to reduce them, we rejected reductive materialism.

ELIMINATIVE MATERIALISM, SENSATION TERMS, AND DESCRIPTION

In spite of the problem that finally defeated reductive materialism, it had the initial plausibility of allowing a materialist to agree that there are sensations such as afterimages and pains, or at least events of hurting and afterimaging. Eliminative materialism, however, lacks that initial plausibility. If it is to be at all plausible, it must somehow defend the claim that, in some sense relevant to ontology, there really are no pains, no afterimages, no hurtings, and no afterimagings. Thus, initially, it seems this view must defend the grossly unreasonable claim that sentences such as 'I have a pain' are never true. We found, however, two ways to defend eliminative materialism that accept such sentences as true. One way relies on analytical behaviorism which states that sensation terms are contextually definable by sentences using only terms that describe bodily behavior and bodily dispositions. And since the relevant behavioristic sentences are true and refer only to bodies, then, according to this justification of eliminative materialism, sentences such as 'I have a pain' are often true. But this does not refute eliminative materialism because such sentences have the same referents as the behavioral terms in the sentences used to analyze them.

There are, however, two other problems that disable this attempt to render eliminative materialism plausible. Not for lack of trying, no successful behavioral analyses of psychological sentences have been produced, not even those that do not involve phenomenal elements, such as feelings or sensa. Much of the work has been done on belief sentences, but even here there has been no success. However, even granting eventual success with behavioral analyses, there remains the problem of how this counterbalances the strong evidence that many sensation terms are successful reporting terms and, therefore, denoting terms, and that no behavioral terms in the sentences that contextually define them have the same referents.

A similar problem confronts Rylean behaviorism, which is another form of eliminative materialism that is compatible with construing 'I have a pain' to be sometimes true in some sense. On the Rylean view, some psychological sentences are true in an instrumental sense, but none are true in a sense that requires reference. While the problem for approaching eliminative materialism by analytical behaviorism concerns inferences from claims about synonymy of sentences to claims about what the sentences refer to, the problem for Rylean behaviorism is justifying inferences from claims about certain logical features of the use of psychological sentences to the claim that they function as nonreferring inference tickets. Any move from logical features of these terms to their nonreference is dubious, especially given the strong reason we found to claim that sensation terms are reporting terms. Further, given a plausible interpretation of Wittgenstein, we can see his sound point about sensation terms to be that 'red' and 'pain' function logically so differently, for example, concerning the criteria for their application, that we can easily be misled if we merely say both are names. Nevertheless, in spite of such important differences, we found both to be not only referring terms but also reporting terms.

The next two forms of eliminative materialism we examined avoid the problem that the first two forms failed to solve. Both the postulation elimination theory and the 'sensation' elimination theory construe sensation terms to be referring terms. Their problem, however, which they share with naïve eliminative materialism, is that, strictly speaking, no sensation sentences such as 'I have a pain' are true. For the postulation elimination theory, this is because sensation terms are pure theoretical terms that, in principle, are not needed for scientific explanation of human behavior. Thus although they are referring terms they are not reporting terms and if there is something they denote it is only certain postulated causes of certain human behavior that are less misleadingly referred to using physiological terms. On this view, the evidence relevant to deciding whether or not sensation sentences are true is not the purely experiential evidence that overturns the naïve eliminative claims, but rather reasons based on theoretical requirements of scientific explanation. Once again, however, we considered what we had found to be the most plausible construal of sensation terms. They are not only referring terms but are also reporting terms. They denote what we are aware of rather than postulated causes of behavior. Thus they denote whether or not they are needed for scientific explanation of human behavior. This proved reason enough to reject this position.

Is there a justifiable way to eliminate sensations that can accommodate sensation terms denoting entities we experience? The 'sensation' elimination theory purports to provide such a way. The central claim of this theory is that physiological terms can assume not only the explanatory and predictive functions of sensation terms, but also their reporting and descriptive roles. Thus although sensation terms are reporting terms that often can be said to denote, they are not needed for any purpose relevant to ontology, although they may well be needed for convenience. And because of this it is reasonable to assume that there really is nothing which, like a sensation, has phenomenal properties. In a way the 'sensation' elimination theory highlights the problem which, in different ways, defeats all four of the attempts to justify eliminative materialism by a consideration of psychological language. Each attempt fails because it does not sustain the thesis that there is no descriptive need for sensation terms. The particular failure of the 'sensation' elimination theory is that it provides no reason to think that for each sensation sentence that, initially at least, seems to be true, there is some physiological sentence which ascribes only physical properties to things yet plays the same descriptive role. This is not to deny, of course, that physiological sentences may come to assume the descriptive role of sensation sentences if there comes a change in the meaning of the physiological terms to accommodate the sensuous quality aspect of the meanings of sensation terms. But, as pointed out in discussing scientific$_3$ properties and basic level properties in Chapter 7, such a change would build into physiological terms themselves elements of meaning which would preclude them from expressing either physical or physical-neutral properties as required by materialists. Whether or not nonphysical terms are needed for explanation of human behavior, it has not been shown that none are needed for description.

We examined one more move the eliminative materialist might make. It is to adopt the view expressed in the slogan "What explains best describes best." Thus where there is no need for a term in the best explanation of what there is, there is also no need for that term in the best description of what there is. Then, given that there is no need for any psychological terms in the best scientific explanations of human behavior, it is easy to conclude that, in spite of the way it may seem to the scientifically ignorant, what we describe using sensation terms will turn out to be something purely physical. It is not that physiological language should assume the descriptive roles of sensation language; it should completely replace it when both complete and accurate descriptions are required. Where one description is better than another, we need not use the second to achieve completeness and accuracy.

If the eliminative materialist makes this move, however, he also adopts a very extreme form of scientific realism that is not only clearly opposed to the Rylean common sense materialism with its scientific instrumentalism, but also goes well beyond what I have called "minimal" and "moderate" scientific realism.

We found this extreme version implausible because it claims that nothing has observation properties and that nothing has phenomenal properties. Thus while a moderate scientific realist can plausibly claim that no physical objects have observation properties because what seem to be observation properties are really either phenomenal properties of a sensum or modes of a sensing, neither move is available for the extreme theory. No person's experiences, not even his own inner experiences, are similar to the way they seem to him. A view with such a consequence is too implausible to support another.

ADVERBIAL SENSING EVENTS, BRAIN EVENTS, AND REDUCTION

With the failure of the last attempt to justify eliminative materialism, we rejected the theory. Because we had previously found reason to reject reductive materialism, only adverbial materialism remained, because it avoids all the objections to the other two. While either reducing or eliminating both sensings and sensa fails, nothing had been shown sufficient to refute the view that eliminates sensa and reduces objectless sensing events. I claimed that this species of materialism would be shown to avoid the problems that sensations raise for materialism if it is reasonable to accept four claims. The first is that there are no phenomenal objects of sensing, that is, there are no sensa. Assuming that it would be reasonable to accept this claim unless there were grounds for the existence of sensa, we proceeded to examine attempts to justify their existence. In general, these attempts are of three different kinds. First, there are arguments based on certain facts of perception, such as perceptual relativity, hallucinatory experiences, the causal processes in perception, and the time gap between transmission of stimulus from objects and perceptual experiences. We examined various versions of four arguments based on these facts and found in each case that it was at least as reasonable to interpret sense experience as consisting of objectless sensing events as to include sensa. Second, it may be that although perceptual facts alone do not justify the existence of sensa, a fully developed scientific theory, adequate for scientific explanation of perception, will require the postulation of sensa. Perhaps certain theoretical requirements of the theory itself, or of its integration into or reduction to some more inclusive theory will force the acceptance of sensa. That is, although, as we have seen, a postulational rejection of all sensations fails, this does not preclude a postulational justification of sensa. We did not examine this kind of justification, because the relevant theories have not yet been developed to the point where there is enough evidence to decide the issue one way or the other. Nevertheless, with the rejection of the four arguments based on empirical facts of perception, it seemed reasonable at this time to assume no postulational need for sensa.

The third kind of justification is not based on perceptual facts nor on theoretical requirements of science, but rather on the implications of some acceptable philosophical theory that interprets those facts and the implications of the scientific theoretical requirements. Two justifications of this kind were mentioned but only one was examined. The unity of science has been and remains an important goal for many philosophers, and many have tried to state the requirements for such a unity. One commonly accepted requirement is that physicalism be true, that is, that the language of physics be made the universal language of science. One motive of analytical behaviorists in reducing the language of psychology to a physicalistic language has been to achieve a unified physicalistic description or image of man and the world. We have seen not only that this attempted reduction of psychological language to a physicalistic language that expresses only physical or physical-neutral properties has failed, but also that it is not required for the unity of science. While it may be true that the language of physics should provide the unified picture, it may come to do so only by becoming so changed that it expresses properties and refers to objects that are neither physical nor physical-neutral. For example, as we have seen, Sellars contends that such a unified scientific image requires a unique kind of scientifically basic particular which is a unique species of what we have called sensa. If Sellars were right, then there would be some reason to reject objectless sensing events for sensa. Nevertheless, upon examining three arguments for such sensa extrapolated from Sellars' writings, we decided that a unified scientific image can accommodate adverbial sensing events as easily as sensa.

Another attempt to base the justification of sensa on the requirements of an acceptable philosophical theory was mentioned. If it should be established that some philosophical theory of perception and the external world that requires sensa, such as indirect realism or Berkeleian phenomenalism, is more reasonable than any theory that does not require them, such as various versions of direct realism, then, ceteris paribus, it would be unreasonable to reject sensa. We are not now in a position to give a final evaluation of such a justification, but if we are right in concluding that no perceptual facts justify sensa and the unity of science does not require sensa, and if it turns out that no scientific theory requires the postulation of sensa, then it is quite reasonable to think that an acceptable philosophical theory that interprets and integrates these facts and scientific requirements would also not require sensa. Because of this, it is reasonable to think that some version of direct realism will be found acceptable. This is assuming, of course, that no reasons for the existence of feelings, emotions, and bodily sensations survive if reasons for the existence of sensa involved with sense perception fail. This is a justified assumption because there seem to be no scientific or philosophical reasons for such entities that are not also reasons for the sensa of sense experience. Furthermore, two of the strongest arguments for sensa—the argument from hallucination and the time-gap argument—are much less plausible when applied to itches, twinges, pains, and the like.

By the preceding steps we came to the provisional conclusion that it is reasonable to accept the first of the four conditions which, if satisfied, free adverbial materialism of its problem with sensations. That is, given the Chisholm-like reasons for preferring sensings to sensa, the evidence now available as a result of our examination of the relevant empirical facts, and the present state of the relevant scientific and philosophical theories, it is reasonable to accept the adverbial interpretation of sensory experience at this time. Of course, this is not to say that no new evidence will become available. Indeed I hope to make more available by a future examination of direct realism and its alternatives. At any one time, however, we can do no better than base our conclusions on the evidence available at that time. This, and only this, is what I claim to have done here.

Concluding Remarks

SENSING EVENTS AND NONMATERIALISTIC PROPERTIES

We have three of the four claims left to consider in our evaluation of adverbial materialism. The second claim is that each event of a person sensing in some way is identical with some brain event of the person. It might be thought we could support the second claim by showing that sensing–brain-event identity statements are, like sensa–brain-part identity statements, cross-category, and by showing that the revised principle of the non-identity of discernibles does not refute such identity claims. But it is questionable whether there is a way to show that the event-identity statements are cross-category using our criterion for category difference, because there is a question of whether there are two predicates, one of which is meaningless when applied to sensings but not when applied to brain events, and the other of which is meaningless when applied to brain events but not when applied to sensings. Indeed, if the third claim is acceptable, then it seems that the statements are not cross-category statements. This is because if, as the third claim states, all extentional properties of events of people sensing either are, or are reducible to physical or physical-neutral properties, then, unless there are predicates that express reduced properties of sensings which are in a different category from the predicates that express properties of brain events, which seems most unlikely, all extentional properties of a person sensing are ascribable to brain events. Furthermore, it would seem reasonable to ascribe to a brain event any property ascribable to it which is a physical, physical-neutral, or reduced property of the correlated sensing event, and to conclude, as a result, that no sensing event has properties that refute identifying it with its correlated brain event. Because of this, let us first examine the third claim and use our results to aid our examination of the second one. I shall proceed by considering those extentional properties of sensing events that I have found to be most likely to thwart the reduction. If each of these can be shown to be either physical or physical-neutral, then I shall conclude that the third claim is acceptable. Of course, if one of these properties is neither physical nor physical-neutral nor reducible to such a property, then the reduction and adverbial materialism both fail.

The kinds of properties that initially raise the problem for the claim that sensations are nothing but brain entities are phenomenal properties of sensa, such as being yellow, round, homogeneous, fading, loud, bitter, rough, intense, and throbbing. But, as we have seen, on the adverbial sensing theory there are no objects to have such properties. To see whether there are any other properties that are troublesome for the view that reductively identifies each particular objectless sensing event with some brain event, let us again concentrate on a specific example. Because we have a candidate for the temporal correlate of events of having pains, let us consider a particular event of John having an intense pain, or adverbially, the event of John hurting intensely, H, and let us assume its temporal correlate is the event of the C-fibers of John's brain firing rapidly, F. What are the sorts of properties an event such as H might have? H clearly has temporal properties: it occurs at ten o'clock, occurs throughout a period of time, and occurs before, during, and after certain other events. It also would seem to be caused by a physical event, perhaps a rib breaking, and, in turn, would seem to cause other physical events, such as John moaning. All these properties are either physical or physical-neutral and, it is reasonable to suppose, are properties of F.

Objections to reducing sensing events to brain events

Which properties of H might be troublesome? Someone might suggest that event H has three properties that are neither physical nor physical-neutral, namely, the property of being identical with an event of someone hurting, being an instance of someone hurting, and being an example of someone hurting. But this suggestion can be rejected because all these properties can be accommodated, although how the third is accommodated depends on how 'example' is interpreted. On one interpretation something which does not exist or does not occur, such as the Fountain of Youth, can be an example of something, such as an object searched for in vain. On this interpretation the third property is not extentional and thus need not be considered. If we give 'example' an extentional interpretation, then the third property becomes much like the other two and can be handled in the same way. My claim in this case is that, although these properties are extentional and are not physical, they are physical-neutral. Consider the reduction of something observable to something theoretical, such as the reduction of water to conglomerations of H_2O molecules. Given that at any one time each volume of water is identical with some conglomeration of H_2O molecules, and that we are justified in either "transferring" all the observation properties of water to sensa or "transforming" them into modes of sensing, the mere fact that this conglomeration of H_2O molecules is identical with, and is an instance and an example of water would not refute the reduction. If all the other properties of each volume of water were theoretical or theoretical-neutral, as is clearly possible, then having these three properties would not stop the reduction. Thus something theoretical could have these properties, and because water with pure observation properties could also have these properties, they are theoretical-neutral. It is also possible that all the other properties of every event that is identical with, or an instance or example of someone hurting are physical and physical-neutral. Thus, by similar reasoning, we can conclude that all three properties are physical-neutral.

There are properties of a different sort that may seem troublesome because they seem to be psychological properties of events and thus neither physical nor physical-neutral. Some event of John hurting intensely may be frightening, annoying, alarming, or disturbing to John as well as to others close to John. Thus the event of John hurting intensely over a long period can frighten and alarm John himself and others around him. But so also can the event of John shaking uncontrollably and the event of the earth quaking severely, alarm and frighten people. In other words, these properties can be properties of events which are physical and of events which are not, and so they are physical-neutral after all. For each one, however, there is a corresponding property of persons which is not physical-neutral and these may seem to raise a problem. Thus John and the others are annoyed, frightened, disturbed, and the like. Of course, the adverbial materialist would handle these cases as he would John hurting. The event or state of John being annoyed, frightened, or disturbed is to be shown to be nothing but some physical event or state. And since I find no unique problems arising for these examples I shall return to a consideration of John hurting intensely.

I have found just one other way someone might try to show that there are troublesome properties of *H*. I have claimed that *H* is a particular event which is John hurting intensely. Using nonadverbial terminology we could describe this to be the event of John having an intense pain. But it also seems that in the sensing terminology this can be translated into the claim that

John hurts in an intense way and the extentional property of being in an intense way is neither physical nor physical-neutral.
There are two replies. First, just as modifying John's hurting
with 'intensely' merely describes the particular event more precisely, so does 'in an intense way.' John hurting in an intense
way is no more than John hurting intensely, and H does not have
the property of being in an intense way. Second, it is not the
event of John hurting that would have such a property; if anything, it is the hurting or pain which John has that has the
property of being intense. But since on the adverbial interpretation there are no hurtings or pains which are individuals or
events or states to which people have relationships when they
hurt, there is nothing to have the property. Again, 'in an intense
way,' like 'intensely,' does not function to ascribe properties to
an event or to some individual involved in the event. They function to specify more precisely a particular event, such as the one
that happens to John at 10:00.

I have talked of John hurting intensely and sensing red-ly. This
might well lead someone to a different sort of objection. Such
locutions are at best barbarous and, it might be further claimed,
they are meaningless because they violate rules of language. Consequently any identity or reduction claims that include such
locutions are nonsense, and there is no justifiable way for a materialist to use them to avoid the problem raised by the phenomenal properties of sensations. I agree that many of these
adverbial locutions, such as 'John sensed red-table-ly,' are barbarous. They offend my linguistic sensibilities, but little should
be based on anything so shifting and tenuous as that. In the
future it may be that the adverbial terminology will become
common and natural, and this might happen even if such talk
breaks rules now enshrined in language.

It is far from clear what sort of rule would prescribe that the
preceding adverbial utterances are meaningless, but, for the sake
of argument, let us assume that there is such a rule now. Furthermore, let us grant something much more dubious, that this is a
rule that can never be changed if language is to remain meaningful. If this should be the case, is there nothing that someone who
holds a metaphysical adverbial theory can do if he wishes to
follow Berkeley and speak with the vulgar while thinking with
those he takes to be the learned? Luckily for such a person, there

is a terminology available to him. There is a sense of '*S* perceives *P*' and a sense of '*S* experiences *P*' that is intentional, because neither these sentences nor their denials entail that there exists or that there does not exist something perceived or experienced. The statement that the old drunkard is seeing or experiencing pink rats again entails neither that there exists nor that there does not exist something he sees or experiences. For those offended by the adverbial terminology or who believe it is meaningless, this intentional terminology is available. Using it we can say that someone experienced a pink rat running across the floor, instead of saying that he sensed pink-rat-running-across-the-floor-ly, or that he pink-rat-running-across-the-floor-sensed. Although in using the first locution we might seem to be committed to attributing properties to some existing individual we are not so committed. We can, then, speak with the vulgar while thinking adverbially.

It should not be thought, however, that because this intentional vocabulary is available, we could have avoided examination of arguments used to justify the existence of sensa. It is false that if there is a way of describing sense experience without implying that there are sensa, we are justified in rejecting them. While it is true that if we cannot describe sense experience without being committed to the existence of sensa, then we are not justified in rejecting them, the converse of this is false. We can describe someone trying to locate the planets with a telescope without implying that there are planets, but nevertheless there are reasons independent of that fact which justify the existence of planets. Similarly, unless we have discovered whether there are such reasons for sensa, we do not know whether to class sensa with planets or with the Fountain of Youth. The fact that we can avoid commitment to the existence of sensa by using an available intentional vocabulary is of no help in settling that issue.

In the preceding discussion I have tried to uncover some extentional properties of event *H* that are neither physical nor physical-neutral by examining the most likely candidates I could find, but I have failed in this attempt. Consequently I conclude we can accept that *H* has no nonmaterialistic properties, that is, no properties incompatible with materialism. And, because there is nothing unique about *H* in this regard, I also conclude that no adverbial sensing events, such as John red-sensing, have non-materialistic properties. Consequently, I find it is reasonable to accept the third of the four claims we have been examining. It would also seem that we have reason to accept the second claim, because no sensing events have properties that prohibit their being identical with brain events. It might seem, however, that, unlike event *H,* the event of John's C-fibers firing rapidly is not frightening or annoying to John. After all, he probably knows nothing about physiology. However, if 'x is frightening to y' is taken extentionally, as it must be if this objection against identity is to have force, then if an event frightens John and that event is identical with John's C-fibers firing rapidly then that brain event frightens John whether he knows it is that brain event or not. It would, as a matter of fact, be that brain event which resulted in his being frightened unknown to him. There is nothing odd here, either categorially or otherwise. Furthermore, all other properties we have examined can quite plausibly be ascribed to the brain event correlated with each sensing event. I can find no other property that would raise problems. Nevertheless, before drawing a conclusion, I would like to examine one last attempt to show that there is such a property.

There is a form of the spatial location objection that applies to events such as *H* and *F,* but not to sensa and brain parts. Previously this objection was avoided by use of claims about cross-category identity. But given an adverbial event view of sense experience, it is meaningful to ask not only when but also where the event of John hurting intensely occurred. One true reply might be that it occurred at ten o'clock in John's room. And, it is plausible to argue, we can further specify where it occurred to the point where we locate its occurrence at *the* place John occupied at ten o'clock. But we can specify it no further because we can locate it no more precisely than the location of the objects stated as being involved in it. According to this objection, however, event *H* did not occur at *the* place at which *F* occurred, because *F* occurred in John's brain and John's brain did not occupy at ten o'clock *the* place John occupied at ten o'clock. One reply to this was discussed in the examination of the spatial location objection. If this is the only problem facing the claim that *H* and *F* are identical, then it is surely justified to claim that they are identical and that, as a result, *H* can be specified more determinately as occurring at the place John's brain occupied at ten o'clock. A stronger reply, however, is to deny that an event can be located no more precisely than the location of the objects stated as being involved in it. A particular event of John smiling might well be identical with an event of John's mouth turning up at the corners. Here it is false that we can locate the event of John smiling no more precisely than the location of John, because this event is identical with an event that can be located more precisely. The same, it is reasonable to claim, would be true if H should be identical with F.

We now have reason to conclude that sensing events have neither nonmaterialistic properties nor properties that prohibit their being identical with their correlated brain events. There remains the task of finding whether F and other brain events have any properties that prohibit identity with H or other sensing events. Again I shall proceed by examining the most likely candidates I can find. In this case they are properties such as being constituted of molecular events, happening to C-fibers of a brain, and occurring in a brain. However, if it is reasonable to claim that F is identical with H on grounds independent of the fact that F has these properties, then I find no objection to saying that the event of John hurting intensely has these properties because it is identical with F. This is because none of the properties raise special problems. The latter two can be handled once we have seen how to refute the spatial location objection, and the first dissipates once we see that having that property is no more troublesome than having the property of being a firing of C-fibers which H would have if identical with F. I see, then, no properties of F that there is reason to deny are properties of H. Thus the property objection is avoided. And, because we have dispatched all other objections to the identity claims that we have examined and there is no reason to think some unexamined objection succeeds, we can agree that it is reasonable to identify sensing events with those brain events, if any, which are correlated with them. This conclusion is reinforced by the fact that all the reasons that we have seen to favor identifying sensa with brain parts also support the identity of sensing events and brain events. In addition, the counterintuitive consequence of identifying yellow afterimages with brain parts so that some brain parts are phenomenally yellow, is avoided for objectless sensings. This not only frees the identity theorist who is also a naïve realist from a difficult problem (see Chap. 3), but also makes it easier for a scientific realist who is an identity theorist, and, obviously, helps the materialist.

We are now in a position to conclude that it is reasonable to claim that each sensory experience consists in objectless sensing events that are nothing but some physical events. We have rejected all examined attempts to justify sensa, and based on the total evidence now available, have provisionally assumed that no other attempts succeed; we have found no nonmaterialistic properties of sensing events; and we have found it reasonable to claim that all sensing events are identical with brain events. The last finding, incidentally, was done without establishing that the identities are cross-categorial. All extentional predicates expressing properties of sensing events seem not only applicable to brain events, but it is also reasonable to conclude that each predicate truly applies to a sensing event just in case it truly applies to the "correlated" brain event. This last conclusion shows that the criterion of category difference does not apply to sensing events and brain events, and more importantly, that we can easily avoid the objection that adverbial materialism is false because some events have properties not ascribable to physical entities.

We can bolster the claim that objectless sensings are nothing but brain events by looking at the results of the previous discussion about the theoretical reducibility of sensa to brain parts. We can see that all the favorable likenesses and differences found to hold between the reduction of sensa to brain parts and the most plausible examples of theoretical reduction also hold between the reduction of objectless sensings to brain events and the same examples. For both sensa and sensings the identity statements contain one pure theoretical term and one term that is both phenomenal and theoretico-reporting. There is also as much reason to predict a one-to-one correspondence of kinds in the sensing case as in the sensa case. The one difference between the two cases is that we can show statements identifying sensa with brain parts to be cross-categorial, but while this is crucial in keeping sensa–brain-part identity statements from being falsified, we have just seen it is not needed for sensings. We also found, of course, that it did not help avoid the crucial disanalogy which refuted the reduction of sensa to brain parts, namely, that there is no way to dispose of the nonmaterialistic properties of sensa. But we have just seen reason to think there are no such properties of sensings. Thus it is reasonable, based on both the previous and the present results, to conclude that sensing events are theoretically reducible to, and therefore, are nothing but brain events.

INSTANCES OF SENSING PROPERTIES
AND NONMATERIALISTIC PROPERTIES

It may seem that we have now done enough to free adverbial materialism from the problem with sensations. However, I have listed an additional task to be completed because it is possible that all sensing events are nothing but physical events but an instance of one of the properties realized in these events is not an instance of some physical or physical-neutral property. If some individual had such a property, then even if all sensing events were reduced, materialism would be incorrect. Furthermore, this is not a possibility we can ignore on the general grounds that no instances realized in an event have properties quite different from the properties of the event. For example, consider the event of John running at time *t,* and let us assume that John runs awkwardly then. It would be true that this particular instance of running is awkward, but it is either false or meaningless to assert that the event of John running is awkward. John may be awkward, certainly his running at *t* is awkward, but this is not true of the event that occurred at *t.* Of course both events and instances, as well as individuals, often have the same or similar properties. Not only, we can assume, was it distressing to watch John while he was running awkwardly, but the event itself and the instance of running might also be distressing to someone watching John. Nevertheless, because there are cases where instances have properties quite different from those of their events, we should check instances independently of events, even if it seems initially reasonable to claim an instance is nothing but something physical or physical-neutral if the event in which it is realized is nothing but something physical or physical-neutral.

We can, however, say this about the relation of events to instances of properties. If an event *e* is nothing but a physical event, *r*, and it is reasonable to attribute to each instance, *i*, of a property realized in *e*, only materialistic properties all of which it is also reasonable to attribute to *j*, an instance of a physical property realized in *r*, then it is reasonable to conclude that *i* is nothing but *j* which is physical. In particular, if we take *H* and *F* as examples again, then *i* is the instance of hurting intensely realized in *H* and *j* is the instance of having C-fibers firing realized in *F*. We have seen reason to think *H* is nothing but *F*. My claim, then, is that if we find reason to think that the instance of hurting intensely realized in *H* has only materialistic properties all of which it is reasonable to attribute to the instance of having C-fibers firing realized in *F*, then we can conclude that the former instance is nothing but the latter, which is clearly physical.

Again I shall proceed by considering which properties are most likely to be troublesome. If all these can be handled, then we shall have grounds for thinking that *i* and other instances of sensing properties meet condition (4) and our last task will be completed. Actually, however, there is little to do. In the case of *i* and other instances of sensing properties, the candidates for nonmaterialistic properties either are just those we have already considered for *H*, or others which, while they are different from those of *H* because *i* is an instance of a property rather than of an event, can be handled like the corresponding properties of *H*. For example, while *H* is an instance and an example of an event of a person hurting, *i* is an instance of the property of hurting. While *H* occurs at ten o'clock, *i* is an instance of a property realized at ten o'clock. Furthermore, it would seem that *H* and *i* differ in the sense in which they are frightening, alarming, and the like. If we assume that all causes are events, then the property of being frightening must be analyzed differently for *i* than for *H*, but this will not affect how a materialist can handle the property. While *i*, unlike *H*, does not result in someone being frightened, we might say instead that the event in which *i* is a constituent results in someone being frightened. Thus although instances of sensing properties have different properties from instances of sensing events, I can find none that raise special problems. We can conclude, then, that it is reasonable to maintain that both *H* and *i* are nothing but physical entities as required by adverbial materialism.

The last conclusion shows the important difference between reductive materialism with its phenomenal individuals, and adverbial materialism with only physical objects and persons as a posteriori individuals. On both views there are individuals which have nonmaterialistic, nonrelational properties. For adverbial materialism, persons have adverbial sensing properties; for reductive materialism, sensa, such as afterimages, have phenomenal properties. The crucial difference is that there is reason to think that i and other instances of sensing properties do not have any nonmaterialistic properties, but that there are instances of properties that sensa have, i.e. being phenomenally red, that have nonmaterialistic properties, i.e. being shimmering. A materialist must reject sensa, but we have seen he cannot reject sensory experience completely. It now seems, however, that he can accommodate objectless sensings.

CONCLUSION ABOUT MATERIALISM AND SENSATIONS

We have completed the three primary tasks I stated at the beginning of the book: to show that both the reductive and the eliminative approaches to materialism fail to resolve the problem posed by sensations, but that there is reason to believe that the adverbial approach succeeds. Nevertheless for many there may remain an uneasy feeling that something more should be done before accepting the success of adverbial materialism. This feeling may result in part from the fact that there are so many ways the provisional conclusion we have reached might be overturned in the future. Scientific discoveries or theories may give reason to reject the correspondence of kinds needed to justify the claim that sensing events are identical with brain events, or they may lead to the postulation of sensa with phenomenal properties. Perhaps philosophical investigations of science, perception, and persons will lead to an indirect realism or Berkeleyan phenomenalism. If this is the total source of the uneasiness, then it is important to remember that the desire for a justification immune to future refutation is, in this area as well as in most others, a desire for the unattainable which, if it cannot be dispelled, should at least be discounted.

But there may be other sources of this discomfort. It may arise because it seems that if sensing events really were physical as required for materialism, then, as with one extreme version of scientific realism, we would have to adopt the most unreasonable thesis that not even a man's own inner sensory experience is at all similar to the way it seems to him. Sensing events might well be identical with brain events, but if they are, then either something is not really physical or sensing events are transformed so much as to be unrecognizable. The latter is surely untenable. The argument imbedded here is a dilemma. The adverbial materialist is faced with the problem of establishing that sensing events are really physical. If he does not justify that they are really physical, then his position is refuted. If, on the other hand, he is to justify that sensing events are really physical, he must claim that they are better described as physical events with only physical and physical-neutral properties and thus they are not at all similar to the way they seem to him. If he makes this claim, then, he is faced with the objection to that extreme version of scientific realism, and, again, his position is refuted. Thus even if the four conditions are met, adverbial materialism fails if this objection is sound. Some materialists might try to avoid the dilemma by accepting the consequences of that extreme scientific realism, but, as I have argued, such a move is implausible.

A better reply is to consider what it is to be *really* physical and whether adverbial materialism requires that sensing events be really physical. If events being really physical implies they are physical in the sense that their occurrence entails that there is an object with property only if the object and property are physical (see the Intro.), then a sensing event, such as H, is not really physical, because, as we have seen, if H occurs it follows that John has the property of hurting intensely which is not a physical property. If, however, an event is *really* physical if it is *nothing but* a physical event, then, because, as we have seen, H is nothing but F, H is really physical. On the first interpretation, which I take to be the more usual one, the dilemma is avoided by grasping the first horn, because it would be false that adverbial materialism would be refuted if H is not really physical. Adverbial materialism requires at most that H be nothing but an event which is really physical, that is, that H be identical with a physical event which has an extentional property only if it is physical or physical-neutral. And, clearly, H can be nothing but F which is really physical, while H is not really physical in this sense. On the second interpretation, the second horn can be grasped. While H is really physical because it is nothing but F, this does not imply anything about which description of the event is better. Event H is identical with F and both have only physical and physical-neutral properties. That is sufficient for adverbial materialism, no matter how this event is described. Consequently, the objection fails on both interpretations, and I know of no others that will sustain it.

Nevertheless I may not yet have gotten to the source of the disquiet. It may arise because it seems difficult to accept materialism if there are individuals, such as John, that have extentional properties that are not physical, not physical-neutral, and not reducible to physical or physical-neutral properties. A dualist might feel that this is all the evidence he needs to justify his own position, but if it is granted that we have before us enough reasons to conclude that each instance of each such property is nothing but an instance of a physical property and that adverbial materialism requires no more, then this dualist has no way to justify an objection here. He must either reject the definition of 'materialism' we have adopted or show that our reasons do not justify the conclusion about instances. We have found no reason to reject the definition; whether there is one we have missed I shall leave to others, such as our unhappy dualist. I suspect, however, that the real source of uneasiness in this case may well be that the reasons I have adduced to support the reductions of H and i and, more generally, the reduction of all sensing events and sensing properties are not adequate to do what a materialist would like to have done. They do not refute nonmaterialistic theories, such as an adverbial dualism and a nonmaterialistic identity theory.

It is certainly true that I have not provided grounds for a justified elimination of all theories opposed to adverbial materialism, and thus I have not resolved the mind–body problem. My aim, however, has been to discover whether there is a plausible form of materialism that is neither quickly refuted nor easily established. This I claim to have done. But should I have tried to do more? While resolving the problem would be more satisfying, I find such a goal unattainable. As discussed in the Preface, my thesis about metaphysical problems, which I have elaborated and defended in *Metaphysics, Reference, and Lan-*

guage, is that they are external problems. That is, they are problems for which a definitive solution would require an investigation of the referents of different sets of terms in order to determine which set, if any, provides the best, most accurate description of what there is. Such an investigation would be independent of the jurisdiction of the rules of the linguistic frameworks of the various sets of terms, because it would consist of a comparison of the terms of each framework with what there is.

In the previous book I argued that we cannot get outside language in the appropriate way to conduct such an investigation, and so we must work with whatever clues we can gather from within some framework. Thus if my thesis is correct, definitive solutions are unattainable. This would leave us with proposed resolutions of external problems that are no more than plausible. That my thesis is correct is confirmed to some degree by the results of the present book which have been reached independently of the thesis. The reasons I have offered in this book will not support stronger conclusions than those for which I have argued, and I have found no way to supplement them so they will justify one particular resolution of the mind–body problem. New evidence may arise to reinforce or overturn my reasons for adverbial materialism, but I do not see how it would be sufficient to establish adverbial materialism or any of its alternatives. This is what I had suspected from my previous examination of the mind–body problem, and, on the basis of my thesis about metaphysical problems, what I had also expected. However unsatisfactory this might be to someone else, it is pleasing to me at least that what I had suspected and expected proved to be correct.

Appendix: Categories

> All [category] propositions are philosophers'
> propositions (not necessarily, of course, of
> professional or paid philosophers), and the
> converse is also, I think, true.
>
> Gilbert Ryle in "Categories"

In the above quotation Ryle expresses the extreme position that the only propositions which are peculiarly philosophical are category propositions, i.e. propositions which assert "something about the logical type of a factor or set of factors." [1] A less extreme view, also expressed by Ryle, is that many philosophical doctrines involve what he calls category mistakes, i.e. mistakes which result from representing certain facts "as if they belonged to one logical type or category (or range of types or categories), when they actually belong to another." [2] If this second view is correct, then many philosophical doctrines can be refuted by representing the relevant facts in their correct categories. And, if the first position, which implies the second, is correct, then all philosophical problems can be handled by correctly understanding which categories are correct for representing the relevant facts.

It can be seen that the concept of category mistake is of current philosophical interest and importance. Aside from Ryle's own attempt to refute Cartesian dualism by showing that it involves a series of category mistakes, we have seen in Chapter 1 how construing sensations and brain entities to be in different categories helps refute the property objection to the mind–body identity theory.[3] In addition, an investigation of this concept is important to clarify certain commonly accepted statements. For example, it is often claimed that people differ from numbers in such a way that it is absurd or nonsensical to talk of people as square roots and numbers as unhappy. The absurdity in such

1. G. Ryle, "Categories," in A. Flew, ed., *Logic and Language,* 2d series, p. 80.
2. Ryle, *The Concept of Mind,* p. 16.
3. See Chap. 4 for a brief discussion of Rylean behaviorism. I have also discussed Ryle's attack on Cartesianism in *Metaphysics, Reference, and Language,* pp. 38–41, 63–70, and 242ff.

cases seems to derive from category mistakes. But to justify that it does, we must examine category mistakes.

If we are to investigate category mistakes, we must also examine category differences because category mistakes involve terms of different categories. It would furthermore seem that we must talk about categories. However, it may not seem that there is any reason to consider what may appear to be quite different: types. Nevertheless, as we shall see, those who discuss types and those who discuss categories are trying to get at much the same thing. Furthermore we have seen above that Ryle often uses the two terms interchangeably. And, because Bertrand Russell's discussion of types predates Ryle's talk of categories, we shall begin by considering Russell's theory of types.

RUSSELL'S THEORY OF TYPES

What first comes to mind in a discussion of Russell's conception of type are those theories of types, both simple and ramified, which he uses to eliminate logical and semantical paradoxes. As will become clear as we proceed, neither the simple theory of types, which orders in a hierarchy individuals, properties of individuals, properties of properties of individuals, etc., nor the ramified theory, which within each type level orders propositional functions depending on the level of variables over which there is quantification, will provide us with the kind of types which can be identified with Rylean categories. However, what we can call simple types and ramified types have one thing in common with Rylean types which we can call logical types. That is, in all three cases when there is predication across types, the result is a type violation and what results is not a significant or meaningful sentence. The simple theory of types makes sentences about all properties meaningless; the ramified theory makes sentences about all properties of a certain simple type meaningless; and Ryle's theory of logical types or categories makes sentences such as 'Next Saturday is in bed' meaningless. Thus all three theories of types function to rule out certain combinations of terms which otherwise might seem significant but which lead to paradoxical or absurd conclusions. Using Russell's terminology we can say that each type theory requires of certain terms "a limited range of significance." However, as we shall see, the scope of the significance ranges allowed by Ryle's theory is quite different from those allowed by either or both of Russell's theories.

This would be all there is to say about Russellean types for our purposes if Russell had not still another conception of type. Russell may have come to this third kind of type by stressing as he did that types and ranges of significance of terms are intimately related. He claimed that a type is a class of all entities which make up the range of significance of some predicate. That is, each predicate can be significantly predicated of a limited range of entities and the class of which these entities are members is a type. We can define this conception of type as follows:

Type = ₐf. Class of all entities which have some predicate significantly (meaningfully) predicated of them.

It is clear that a type defined in this way need not be either a simple or a ramified type because each of the latter places specific limits on the significance range of predicates, but this third definition of type prescribes no specific restrictions. For example, according to the simple theory, if a predicate significantly applies to individuals then it cannot be significantly applied to properties. According to the ramified theory, if a predicate is defined using quantification over predicate variables which are defined using quantification over individual variables, then the predicate cannot be significantly substituted for predicate variables which are defined using only quantification over individuals. This third definition of type, then, embodies a broader conception of type, one which can accommodate simple and ramified types as well as further restrictions within types and orders not required by the simple and ramified theories. For example, neither theory imposes any significance-restrictions on the predicates predicated of individuals, but such a limitation usually is imposed by this broader theory. We can see this by considering still another of Russell's definitions of type, one which is much closer to Ryle's conception of a category. Because of this we can call this Russell's theory of logical types. At one point he states it as follows:

(1) The definition of a logical type is as follows: *A* and *B* are of the same logical type if, and only if, given any fact of which *A* is a constituent, there is a cor-

responding fact which has B as a constituent, which either results by substituting B for A, or is the negation of what so results.[4]

Although Russell claims this is a definition of 'logical type,' it is strictly speaking a definition of 'A and B are of the same type.' We can, however, arrive at a definition of 'logical type' by using the following definition of 'type':

Type = df. Class of all entities which are of the same type.

Thus we can define 'logical type' as follows:

Logical type = df. Class of all entities which are such that given any fact of which one of these entities, A, is a constituent, there is a corresponding fact which has B as a constituent, which either results by substituting B for A, or is the negation of what so results.

This is like Russell's definition of 'number' in that 'logical type' is defined in terms of "same logical type" so that it is the latter definition which is crucial and which requires our close scrutiny.

BLACK'S FIRST OBJECTION

One objection to the previous definition, voiced by M. Black, is that this definition of 'same logical type' in its present form leads to a contradiction. We can see this objection by considering what surely seem to be two facts:

(a) The fact that Russell and Socrates are of the same type.
(b) The fact that continuity and Socrates are not of the same type.

Here the second fact is the negation of what results from substituting continuity for Russell in the first fact, so that by using Russell's definition we can, according to Black, derive another fact:

(c) The fact that continuity and Socrates are of the same type.

4. B. Russell, *Logic and Knowledge*, R. C. Marsh, ed. (London: George Allen and Unwin, 1956), p. 332.

But (c) contradicts (b) which, according to Black, not only shows that something is wrong with the definition but would also "seem to establish that, if there are at least three entities in the world, it is impossible that they should not all belong to the same type." [5]

Black's objection has two parts, both of which are sound if we agree with Black's existential interpretation of the quantifiers in (1). He claims, first, that if we hold (a) and (b) and Russell's definition (1) then we can deduce (c) which contradicts (b). And because (a) and (b) are true we must give up (1) to avoid the contradiction. However, it seems we need one more premise to arrive at (c). From (a), (b), and (1) we arrive at:

> (d) The fact that Russell and continuity are of the same type.

This contradicts neither (a) nor (b). Thus we need another step to derive (c). The following additional premise will suffice and initially seems quite acceptable:

> (e) If two entities are each of the same type as a third, then they are of the same type.

It might seem, then, that someone could maintain (a), (b), and (1) without contradiction if he gave up (e). And, although it may seem that (e) is necessarily true, so that (a), (b), and (1) entail a contradiction after all, (e) is neither necessary nor even tenable as we shall see later in this discussion. However, Black's objection still stands because we can deduce (c) by applying (1) to (a) and (d). And because we deduced (d) from (1), (a), and (b), then we get the contradiction from just (a), (b), and (1) as Black claims.

The second part of Black's objection is also sound, given his interpretation of the quantifiers in (1). We can easily see why this is so by considering phrases of the form:

> (f) The fact that x belongs to some type or other.

We can substitute any entity for x and thus by (1) we can show that any two entities belong to the same type which is contrary

---

5. M. Black, "Russell's Philosophy of Language," in P. A. Schilpp, ed., *The Philosophy of Bertrand Russell* (New York: Tudor Publishing Company, 1944), p. 235.

to facts such as (b). We must, therefore, also find some way to avoid the second part of Black's objection.

Black proposes that we can avoid this objection by talking of words rather than entities as being of the same or different types. Thus Russell's definition could be rewritten:

> (2) '*A*' and '*B*' are of the same type = $_{df.}$ Given any fact of which *A* is a constituent, there is a corresponding fact which has *B* as a constituent, which either results by substituting *B* for *A*, or is the negation of what so results.

On this version neither part of Black's objection applies even if we accept (e). Because for (2), unlike (1), only linguistic entities can be of the same type, we must change (f) to

> (f1) The fact that the term *x* belongs to some type or other.

Therefore we must substitute linguistic terms such as 'Russell' and 'continuity' into the fact expressed in (f1) so that according to (2) we can infer only that the names of those terms, that is, " 'Russell' " and " 'continuity'," are of the same type. Thus Black's objection is avoided.

Black, therefore, has provided a way to avoid the objection, but it retains one bothersome feature of Russell's definition. There surely seems to be something wrong with talking about substituting entities into facts. We do not substitute continuity for the philosopher Russell nor even some other philosopher for him. What we substitute are terms that refer to philosophers and we substitute them into sentences rather than into facts. Thus if we can reformulate Russell's definition so that it refers to sentences and terms rather than to facts and constituents of facts, and so that it avoids Black's objection, then it will be preferable to either Russell's or Black's. We can state this version of Russell's definition as follows:

> (3) '*A*' and '*B*' are of the same logical type = $_{df.}$ Given any true sentence of which '*A*' is a constituent, there is a corresponding true sentence which either results by substituting '*B*' for '*A*' or is the negation of what so results.

Consider Black's objection as modified for this definition. What is now relevant to the second part of Black's objection would be the sentence

(f2) The term x belongs to some type or other.

In such a sentence we would be talking about terms such as 'Russell' or 'continuity' so that the sentences would contain the names of those terms. Thus the constituents of such sentences are " 'Russell' " and " 'continuity,' " and using (3) we could only prove that " 'continuity' " and " 'Russell' " are of the same type. Thus this formulation, although different from Black's, avoids the contradiction in a similar way. Let us, therefore, continue our discussion of Russell's theory of logical types using version (3).

It is important to notice that in both replies Black's objections have been avoided by a restatement of the definition which requires that it is linguistic expressions rather than nonlinguistic entities which are of the same or different types. This is because both restatements avoid the contradiction by making the inference from the relevant (f) claim and the right-hand side of the definition to the left-hand side (the inference that generates the contradiction) involve a jump of one semantic level. Thus this way out of the contradiction requires that the left-hand side refer to linguistic entities. However, because Russell stated his definition as about nonlinguistic entities we might try to see whether we can state a definition which at least allows for the possibility of talking about types of nonlinguistic entities and which avoids Black's objection. The obvious candidate is

A and B are of the same logical type $=_{df.}$ Given any true sentence of which 'A' is a constituent, there is a corresponding true sentence which either results from substituting 'B' for 'A' or is the negation of what so results.

Although this definition is not limited to linguistic entities because there is no restriction on what A and B are, it does not avoid Black's objection. We can use the sentence

(f3) The entity x belongs to some type or other

to construct the objection because 'Russell' and 'continuity' could be constituents of the sentence (f3), from which it follows that Russell and continuity are of the same type.

It might seem that this objection could be avoided if we talk of meaningful or significant sentences rather than true sentences in the definition. Such a change would at least bring the definition closer to the original general definition of a type as something related to the range of significance of linguistic expressions. This change would give us

> (4) *A* and *B* are of the same logical type $=_{df.}$ Given any meaningful sentence of which '*A*' is a constituent, there is a corresponding meaningful sentence which results from substituting '*B*' for '*A*.'

It can quickly be shown that (f3) raises a problem for (4) because both 'Russell' and 'continuity' result in meaningful sentences when substituted into (f3). Thus (4) does not escape the second part of Black's objection, so that it might seem that we should return to version (3) which avoids the objection. However, as we shall see, (3) is faced with another objection which can be avoided only by measures which when applied to (4) avoid Black's objection to it as well. Thus once it is amended we may be as justified using (4) to express Russell's definition about types of nonlinguistic entities as we are using definition (3) about types of terms. Furthermore, there is some reason to use (4) as expressing Russell's definition of type sameness because the resulting definition of logical type is very similar to Russell's original broad definition of type stated above, especially if we limit the definition of logical type to subject-predicate sentences. What we get is

> Logical type $=_{df.}$ Class of all entities which are such that given any meaningful sentence of which the name for any one of the entities, '*A*,' is a constitutent, there is a corresponding meaningful sentence which results from substituting the name of some other of these entities for '*A*.'

BLACK'S SECOND OBJECTION

The second of Black's objections to Russell's definition, which is echoed by F. Sommers and lies behind a point made by A. Pap, has already been intimated. The second part of Black's first objection, which we saw applies to (1) and (4) but not to (2) and (3), can be shown to be merely one species of a larger problem which applies to all four definitions. We found that by using something like (f) we could show that for (1) and (4) any two entities, or terms, are of the same type and this completely vitiates definitions (1) and (4). But the problem is not merely a problem involving (f) claims. As interpreted by Sommers (see below), it is that certain predicates which he calls high predicates are significantly predicated of *all* entities no matter what their category. Examples of high predicates are 'constituent of a fact,' 'interesting,' 'denoted by a word,' 'entity,' and also 'belonging to some type.' Consequently if, as Russell leads us to believe, a sufficient condition for two entities, *A* and *B*, being of the same type is that one predicate can be significantly predicated of both of them or that '*A*' and '*B*' can be meaningfully substitutible into the same sentence, then this is truly a most serious objection not only to (1) and (4) but also to (2) and (3).

There have been at least two attempts to avoid this objection. One, which stems from Russell, is an attempt to avoid the objection by specifying that high predicates are systematically ambiguous.[6] Thus the sentential contexts '—— is thought of' and '—— is denoted by a word' are ambiguous, having different meanings when 'Russell' is substituted into them from when 'continuity' is substituted. Consequently, according to this way out of the objection, because high predicates are ambiguous, the sentential contexts involving them are ambiguous, and thus 'Russell' cannot be substituted into the same sentential context into which 'continuity' fits and the counterexample to the definition of logical type fails. Let us restate the amended version of (4) required by this reply by reference to mutual substitutibility into unambiguous sentential contexts:

> (5) *A* and *B* are of the same logical type = $_{\text{df.}}$ Given any unambiguous sentential context, '*A*' can be substituted into it meaningfully if and only if '*B*' can be substituted into it meaningfully.

Given this definition and the claim that high predicates including 'belonging to some type' are ambiguous, we can rebut the objection because it requires high predicates. However, this is

6. Russell, p. 691.

a most drastic way out because none of these high predicates seems to be ambiguous by any of the ordinary tests of ambiguity. What requires them to be ambiguous is merely an ad hoc way out of an objection. We should, therefore, look for a more plausible way to avoid the objection.

Black claims that there seems to be no way to avoid this objection "except to interpret the theory of types negatively as essentially an instrument for establishing *differences* of type." [7] We can state his suggestion as follows:

> (6) *A* and *B* are of different types if there is at least one unambiguous sentential context into which '*A*' can be substituted meaningfully but into which '*B*' cannot be substituted meaningfully, or conversely.

This formulation clearly avoids the objection because instead of having a sufficient condition of type sameness we have only a sufficient condition of type difference. With only (6) at our disposal, however, we cannot define either type sameness nor logical type which we have been trying to do. And, although for our original purpose of elucidating the concept of category mistake a sufficient condition of type difference may be adequate, a more satisfactory result would be one that provides a definition of type difference, type sameness, and type. Let us, then, try to find a more fruitful way out of the objection.

ANOTHER INTERPRETATION OF RUSSELL'S DEFINITION

We have been interpreting Russell's definition of type as stating that mutual substitutibility into just one unambiguous sentential context is a necessary and sufficient condition of type sameness and this has led to a serious objection. However, although Russell seems to interpret his definition in this way it seems more plausible to interpret it another way. If we look back at any of the versions (1) through (5) the right-hand side always relates to *any* fact or sentence. Although 'any' can be interpreted as 'there is at least one' as in 'Is any person home?' it usually means 'every' as in 'Any person can play.' Indeed, it seems more plausible to interpret 'any' in all these definitions as the universal rather than the existential quantifier. On this interpretation of (5) we find that the necessary and sufficient

7. Black, p. 238.

condition of the type sameness of *A* and *B* is that '*A*' and '*B*' are meaningfully substitutible in *all* the same sentential contexts. From this it follows that the necessary and sufficient condition of the type difference of *A* and *B* is that there is at least one sentential context in which '*A*' and not '*B*' is meaningfully substitutible, or the converse. This version, then, makes Black's sufficient condition of type difference a necessary condition as well so that we can define logical type. Furthermore, on this interpretation high predicates present no difficulty because it is not sufficient to show that two terms are meaningfully substitutible in at least one sentential context; it must be shown that they are substitutible in *all* contexts. Consequently because on this interpretation there seems to be no multiplying of ambiguous terms beyond necessity, no objection generated by high predicates, and no problem about defining logical type, we should prefer this interpretation to other versions of Russell's definition and to Black's negative reformulation.

Although version (5) of Russell's definition of type is the most preferable of those we have examined so far, it also faces objections. The first is adapted from the objection J. J. C. Smart raises to Ryle's theory of logical type which we shall examine later.[8] Smart claims that although the sentence 'The seat of the chair is hard' is meaningful, it surely seems that 'The seat of the bed is hard' makes no sense at all. Consequently, because 'chair' and 'bed' do not both go significantly into one sentential context, we can conclude using version (5) that chairs and beds are of different logical types. But, paraphrasing Smart, if pieces of furniture are not of the same logical type, then we might well ask what is. In other words, Smart's example seems to show that version (5) prescribes a sufficient condition of type difference which separates into different logical types entities which surely seem to belong to the same type. This, then, is an objection to Black's negative reformulation of Russell's definition. We can, of course, avoid it by considering universal substitutibility to be merely a sufficient condition of type sameness, but we cannot rest content merely with that because we need a sufficient condition of type difference to help us identify category mistakes. We should, then, continue the search for a satisfactory

8. J. J. C. Smart, "A Note on Categories," *British Journal for the Philosophy of Science* 4 (1953–54): 227–28.

statement of a condition which is both necessary and sufficient for type sameness.

Another objection to version (5) is that even if it will do as a definition of type sameness, it will not be a satisfactory criterion of type sameness. That is, although version (5) provides a sufficient condition of type sameness, a criterion of type is not merely a sufficient condition. It should be a sufficient condition which can be used to decide that different entities, whether nonlinguistic or linguistic, are of the same type. However, the sufficient condition of type sameness provided by version (5) cannot be met unless all sentential contexts have been investigated, which is at best too unwieldy to help us decide. What is required for a criterion is something like Black's existential interpretation of the sufficient condition which can avoid the objections to Black's interpretation. We should, therefore, continue our search for a satisfactory criterion of type sameness.

Pap's Definition of Type

A. Pap, who rejects the existential version of Russell's definition of type sameness for several reasons, including one like Black's objection, proposes a definition of type which he thinks avoids the troubles facing a definition in terms of type sameness. He states it as follows:

> *A type is a class such that there are families of predicates which can be significantly,* i.e., *correctly or falsely, ascribed to all and only members of it.* A predicate family is a set of predicates such that one and only one member of it must be true of anything of which some member of the set is true or false.[9]

By incorporating the definition of 'predicate family' into the definition we get the following:

> Type = $_{df.}$ Class of all entities for which there is a set of predicates such that:
> (a) each predicate of the set can be significantly ascribed to all and only members of the class, *and*
> (b) one and only one predicate of the set must be true of any entity to which some predicate of the set can be significantly ascribed.

9. A. Pap, "Types and Meaninglessness," *Mind* 69 (1960): 48.

What we have is rather cumbersome. However, we can simplify it considerably by taking as a predicate family one predicate and its complement so that condition (b) is obviated. For example, if we take P and non-P as the members of a predicate family which are significantly ascribable to certain entities as required by (a), then it follows that one and only one of the two predicates must be true of the entities. Furthermore, because non-P can be significantly ascribed to an entity just in case P can, we need mention only P in the definition. What we have is

> Type = $_{df.}$ Class of all entities for which there is a predicate, P, which can be significantly ascribed to all and only members of the class.

When we look at this simplified version of Pap's definition we can see that it is equivalent to the definition of 'logical type' we would get if we defined it in terms of the existential interpretation of version (4) of Russell's definition of type sameness, and limited the contexts to subject-predicate sentences. It would seem, then, that the problem which we saw generated by high predicates would arise all over again. But this is not so, because, as Pap sees, his definition implies nothing about the relationship between sameness and difference of type. Pap is free to define sameness and difference of type as he wishes. What he does is to admit that types need not be mutually exclusive. Indeed one type can even be a subclass of another. He gives an example of such types when he says,

> Physical objects constitute a type because weight predicates and predicates of location in physical space are restricted to physical objects. But there are also predicate families which are restricted to animals: if it is meaningless to ascribe a weight or a location in physical space to a thought, or to a number, it is equally meaningless to say of a stone that it drinks milk or that it expects food, etc.[10]

According to Pap, therefore, entities "which belong to a common type may also belong to different types." [11] What Pap has done is reject the implication

10. Pap, p. 50.
11. Pap, pp. 42–43.

If entities are of a same type, then they are not of different types.

This allows him to avoid the high predicate objection and also Smart's objection. For example, although on Pap's definition both continuity and Socrates turn out to be of a same type, we cannot infer from this the seemingly false conclusion that they are not of different types. And, although Pap might agree with Smart that his definition requires beds and chairs to be of different types, it does not follow from this that they do not have a type, furniture, in common.

Comparison of Russell's definition and Pap's definition

Pap has found a definition of type which avoids the objection we have discussed. It appears that he thought he had done this by proposing a definition different from the existential version of Russell's definition, but what he actually did was point out that the problems for Russell's definition of type sameness arise only if an inference is made which requires the implication stated above. If we reject that implication, then we can accept the existential version in spite of Black's claim that we can save it only by a negative reformulation. It seems clear that if rejecting the implication has no objectionable consequences, then we should prefer Pap's theory of types to those we have already examined.

We can further emphasize the difference between Russell's theory of types and Pap's reformulation by interpreting the difference as a difference in the definition of type difference. As we have seen, both men can use the same definition of type, and, furthermore, Pap could agree to the existential interpretation of type sameness, namely,

> A is of the same type as $B =$ df. There is an unambiguous sentential context such that both 'A' and 'B' can be substituted into it meaningfully.

Where they differ is that Russell seems to interpret type difference so that A and B are of different types if and only if they are not of the same type, or in other words on the existential interpretation of type sameness,

> A and B are of different types = df. No unambiguous sen-

tential context is such that both '*A*' and '*B*' can be substituted into it meaningfully.

Pap, however, seems to have an existential interpretation of type difference, namely,

A and *B* are of different types = ₔf. There is an unambiguous sentential context such that '*A*' or '*B*' but not both can be substituted into it meaningfully.

It is clear that for Pap, *A* and *B* can be of the same type and also of different types contrary to Russell's theory. The question this brings up is whether this difference about type difference is important.

One consequence of Pap's definition is that there is no guarantee of the type and order strata to which Russell's simple and ramified theories lead. That is, if we assume, as both men would, that each property of an individual is a different simple type from each individual to which it is ascribable, then, for example, each property of an individual is of a different simple type from each individual to which it is ascribable. And if we also make the assumption that each property of an individual is ascribable to each individual, then on Russell's theory we get the beginning of the hierarchy of Russell's simple theory of types. But given these two assumptions, we do not get the hierarchy on Pap's theory because although it follows from the assumptions that each property of an individual and each individual are of different types, it does not also follow, as it does for Russell, that they have no types in common. It might be thought that this is an important difference between the two theories because Pap's theory does not have Russell's guarantee against paradoxes. However, although on Pap's theory a hierarchical guarantee is missing given the addition of only these two assumptions, it does not follow that there is no way Pap's theory can be supplemented to avoid the paradoxes. Indeed the underlying assumption common to both theories, that each property is of a different type from that to which it is ascribable, is all that is needed to avoid the "simple" paradoxes. Thus it is not meaningful to say that the property of being impredicable is impredicable because, according to both theories, if it is meaningful, then the property of being impredicable is ascrib-

able to itself from which it follows that the property is of a
different type from itself, which is false on either interpretation
of type difference.

AN OBJECTION TO PAP'S DEFINITION

We have found no objections to Pap's theory which are the
result of an incapacity to avoid paradoxes. There is, however,
another reason we might prefer a different kind of theory. It
might be claimed that Russell's way of avoiding the paradoxes
seems to be somewhat ad hoc, devised as it is merely to avoid
paradoxes. However, it is not completely ad hoc because there
are consequences of Russell's theory which go well beyond the
mere avoidance of paradoxes. That is, not only does Russell's
theory allow us to avoid paradoxes, it also has consequences for
significance and ambiguity which are independent of the paradoxes. Although some of these consequences are undesirable,
taken all together they do provide us with a way to test the theory and perhaps to discover certain nonsignificant sentences
which will have important philosophical as well as nonphilo-
sophical consequences. This is not so for Pap's theory. For example, we cannot define a type or category mistake as the use of
a sentence which predicates a predicate, appropriate to one
logical type, of an entity that belongs to a different logical type,
and then go on to infer, as we might want, that the sentence
involves a conceptual or semantical mistake and is therefore
meaningless. This is because given Pap's definition of type difference we can infer at most that there is one predicate which
results in a meaningless sentence. Many predicates would be
appropriate to many different types such as the predicates appropriate to stones and also to animals, two entities of different
types. Here, then, is an important point at which Pap diverges
from Russell and, as we shall see, from Ryle as well. But this
is not the only important inference we cannot draw given Pap's
definition of type difference. There really is nothing we can
infer from a case of type difference except what we use to establish that type difference: that there is at least one predicate
which is not predicable of the entities in question. Pap's theory,
then, is completely ad hoc for it functions only to avoid paradoxes, but cannot be justified or rejected on any independent
grounds. Indeed, his version of the simple theory of types comes

down to the statement that no property is ascribable to itself. This avoids the paradox but does so by fiat instead of by a conceptually testable theory.

THE PROBLEM OF HIGH PREDICATES AGAIN

Although this objection to Pap's theory by no means demolishes it, it is sufficient, I think, to set us looking for a theory which has more semantical explanatory and predictive power than Pap's, but which can avoid the objection to Russell's theory. However, in moving away from the discussion of Pap's theory we should not overlook an important point that arises from the preceding discussion, namely, that we have not avoided the total force of the objection from high predicates by adopting the universal definition of type. As we have just seen, on Russell's theory and for our purposes, the following category principle,

> If *A* and *B* are of different types then no predicate is significantly ascribable to both *A* and *B*,

seems to be of central importance. But, as we have also seen, if high predicates are univocal, this principle is obviously false, so that if we wish to defend the principle, we seem forced to agree with Russell after all that they are ambiguous. Pap rejects the principle and avoids excessive ambiguity, but does so in such a way that type differences are of no importance for our purposes. Russell saves the principle but only by forcing 'thought of,' 'denoted by,' and other high predicates into an unnatural ambiguity. We should try to avoid both of these alternatives and the only way to do this is to modify the principle so that it has the kind of consequences we require, but avoids excessive ambiguity. The most promising way to do this, which as we shall see is the way taken by Sommers, is to make an explicit exception of high predicates in this category principle. Thus:

> For any predicate, *P*, if *A* and *B* are of different types and *P* is not a high predicate, then *P* is not significantly ascribable to both *A* and *B*.

This is something like what Pap seems to be implying when he says that "type predicates are significantly applicable to everything," [12] because type predicates are one kind of high predicate. This modification does not take us very far, however, because we are faced with the task of providing some criterion for high predicates. If we can do this we may be able to return to a modified version of the existential definition of type sameness and thereby avoid the unwieldy universal definition. However, before we pursue this further, let us turn to an examination of Ryle's theory of types or categories because we are particularly interested in category mistakes as discussed by Ryle and do not want to stray too far away from what Ryle means. This might happen, for example, if we pursued Russell's theory along the path suggested by Pap. Let us examine Ryle's theory and then see how it compares with Russell's as we now understand it.

RYLE AND CATEGORIES

Ryle says that "the logical type or category to which a concept belongs is the set of ways in which it is logically legitimate to operate with it." [13] However such a quick characterization is of little help in arriving at a final definition. For one thing, a category is not a set of ways of operating with a concept. It would be more accurate to say that it is a set of all the sentential contexts in which the term can legitimately be used. Another interpretation, closer to the conception we worked with in the discussion of Russellian types, is that a category is a set of all terms which can be legitimately used in the same sentential contexts. Although Ryle does not say anything explicitly about categories more helpful than this, he has made a quite definite statement about category differences, which, of course, is what is essential to category mistakes.

> Two proposition-factors are of different categories or types, if there are sentence-frames such that when the expressions for those factors are imported as alternative complements to the same gap-signs, the resultant sentences are significant in the one case and absurd in the other.[14]

If we let '*A*' and '*B*' stand for what Ryle means by proposition

12. Pap, p. 48.
13. Ryle, *The Concept of Mind*, p. 8.
14. Ryle, "Categories," pp. 77–78.

factors and add the requirement of unambiguity, we can translate this quotation as:

(7) '*A*' and '*B*' are of different categories or types if there is at least one unambiguous sentential context into which '*A*' can be substituted meaningfully, but into which '*B*' cannot be substituted meaningfully, or conversely.

Interpreted this way, Ryle's statement about category differences is like (6), which was our final version of Black's suggestion about Russell's definition, with the one exception that in (7) the entities which are of different types must be linguistic while in (6) the only requirement is that they are one semantic level below the linguistic entities mentioned on the right-hand side. Nevertheless, in order not to blur over the differences between Russellian types and Rylean categories, we should note two things: whereas Russell's original formulation, (1), considered nonlinguistic entities and facts, Ryle's considers linguistic terms and sentences; and although in our final formulation of Russell's definition we found it better to talk of sentences rather than facts, there still remained the nonlinguistic entity–linguistic term difference. This may well be an important difference, because whereas Russell's definition as we revised it requires an inference from a premise about sentences to a conclusion about nonlinguistic entities, Ryle's requires merely an intralinguistic inference. Thus someone might accept Ryle's definition but reject Russell's because, for example, he rejects the implication

If '*A*' and '*B*' are of different types, then *A* and *B* are of different types

on purely ontological grounds.[15]

A RYLEAN DEFINITION OF TYPE

Another difference between Russell's and Ryle's treatment of type difference is that Russell provides a necessary and sufficient

15. A mind–body identity theorist, for example, might claim that 'sensation' and 'brain process' belong to different logical categories, but also want to deny that sensations and brain processes belong to different categories because sensations are identical with brain processes.

condition of type sameness and therefore of type difference, while Ryle states merely a sufficient condition of type difference and thus only a necessary condition of type sameness. Ryle has done enough for someone interested only in establishing category mistakes, but it surely would be preferable if an "if and only if" definition which created no additional problems could be found. What is needed in addition to (7) is:

> (8) If '*A*' and '*B*' are of different categories or types, then there is at least one unambiguous sentential context into which '*A*' can be substituted meaningfully, but into which '*B*' cannot be substituted meaningfully, or conversely.

It might be thought that Ryle rejects (8) because he claims that the converse of what we have interpreted as (7) is false.[16] However, although (8) is the converse of (7), it is not equivalent to what Ryle calls the converse, namely,

> (9) If there is *at least one* unambiguous sentential context into which both '*A*' and '*B*' can be substituted meaningfully, then '*A*' and '*B*' are of the *same* type.

What (7) and (8) give us is

> (10) '*A*' and '*B*' are of the *same* type = df. Given *any* unambiguous sentential context, '*A*' can be substituted into it meaningfully if and only if '*B*' can be substituted into it meaningfully.

Thus although Ryle is right in rejecting (9) with its existential criterion of type sameness, this provides no reason to reject (8) which is equivalent to a universal criterion. Thus if (8) is acceptable we can accept (10) as a Rylean definition of type sameness and can as a consequence define 'category' in the same way 'type' was defined by Russell.

The only situation in which we would find reason to reject (8) would be one in which '*A*' and '*B*' are meaningful in all the same sentential contexts but belong to different categories. But because there would be absolutely no reason to claim they belong to different categories if there was not one context in

16. Ryle, "Categories," p. 78.

which one was meaningful but the other was not, we can eliminate this situation. Thus we can accept (8) and conjoin it with
(7) to give the Rylean definition of type sameness expressed
in (10). This turns out to be the Russellian definition (5), with
the one exception that (10) requires that we talk only of linguistic expressions being of the same type. And, with a different
exception, (10) is equivalent to definition (3) with the addition
of the unambiguity amendment. Definition (3) concerns true
sentences while (10) considers only meaningful sentences.
There is one way that this difference is important. If we use
definition (3), then because we must work with true sentences
we must have some grounds for claiming that the sentences we
work with are true if we are to justify the conclusion we reach
about the categories of '*A*' and '*B*'. For (10) we need only have
reason to think that the sentences are meaningful so that we can
be justified in applying (10) when we are not justified in using
(3), but the converse is false. Consequently (10) is easier to
use and, ceteris paribus, we should use it instead of (3). And,
indeed, there is no difference in the conclusions we reach about
the type sameness or difference of '*A*' and '*B*' because it is irrelevant for the purpose of the definition whether the sentence
we pick with '*A*' or its denial is true. Whatever we can conclude
from substituting '*B*' for '*A*' in a sentence would also be concluded by substituting '*B*' into the denial of that sentence, regardless of which sentence is true. We only need to know that
for any sentence using '*A*,' it has truth value if and only if the
corresponding sentence using '*B*' has truth value. Consequently,
because (10) differs from (3) and (5) in unobjectionable ways
and thus expresses an unobjectionable version of Russell's definition, and because it expresses Ryle's claim with an unobjectionable clause added, we shall use (10) in any future discussion of the views of Russell and Ryle.

Objections to definition (10)

Having seen that (10) is much like (3) and also (5), it is
not surprising that objections to them also apply to (10). In
fact, one of the objections, Smart's, was originally raised against
into 'The seat of the —— is hard' but 'bed' does not, so that
Ryle's claim about type difference. His objection applies to (7)
and thus to (10). Smart claims that 'chair' goes significantly

by (7) we get the seemingly false conclusion that 'chair' and
'bed' belong to different categories. And if, as discussed above,
we can conclude from this that only high predicates are significantly ascribable to both 'chair' and 'bed' then we must also
conclude that predicates like 'heavy,' 'red,' 'large,' and 'wooden'
are either high predicates or ambiguous, which is surely unsatisfactory.

Definition (10), like (5), makes meaningful substitutibility
into all sentential contexts a necessary and sufficient condition
of type sameness, so that it avoids the high predicate objection.
It is, however, open to the objections that it provides a most
unwieldy criterion of type sameness and that it does not help
with the problem of how to determine for any particular predicate whether or not it is significantly ascribable to entities of
different types. Furthermore, we have just seen the problem
generated by Smart's objection as it applies to (7) and therefore to (10). There is also a problem we have not discussed
yet, i.e. the problem of finding a test for sentential meaningfulness and meaninglessness which can be used with a definition
such as (10) to arrive at a conclusion about type differences.
Consequently, although (10) faces no problems not faced by
versions (3) and (5) of the Russellian definition, and is preferable to (3) because it does not require that we know the truth
value of sentences, and is a less vulnerable claim than (5) because it avoids inferences from language to entities, it is still not
a definition with which we can rest content. We must try to handle the above problems.

SOMMERS' CRITERION OF TYPE SAMENESS

We have found no way to state a sufficient condition of type
sameness which both avoids the high predicate objection as the
universal version does, and is a usable criterion as the existential version is. In two recent articles F. Sommers has proposed
such a criterion by concentrating upon the high predicate problem. Sommers, in effect, criticizes the criteria of Russell and
Ryle because they overlook this problem and then he proposes
an amendment to eliminate the problem. For our purposes the
important point of his proposal is that it uses an existential
criterion which, although it allows us to infer the type sameness
of two predicates from their meaningful substitution into one

sentential context, requires that any such context itself contain no predicates which are higher than both the two predicates being tested. Thus Sommer's amendment, in effect, rules out the use of sentential contexts containing high predicates and thus avoids the high predicate objection. What is essential, then, is that he define what it is for one predicate to be higher than another. What he actually does is define what it is for one predicate to be higher than two others.

HIGH PREDICATES AND A CRITERION OF TYPE SAMENESS

We can state Sommers' definition as

A predicate '*A*' is higher than the predicates '*B*' and '*C*' = df. A general sentence (such as 'All *A* is *B*') using '*A*' and '*B*' is meaningful and a general sentence using '*A*' and '*C*' is meaningful, but a general sentence using '*B*' and '*C*' is not meaningful.

Using Sommers' terminology, where he drops the single quotes and uses $U(AB)$ to mean that a general sentence with predicates A and B is meaningful and $N(AB)$ to mean that it is not meaningful, we can state his definition as:

A is a higher predicate than B or C = df.
$$U(AB) \cdot U(AC) \cdot N(BC).^{17}$$

Although Sommers uses this concept in his criterion, we have seen that all he needs is a criterion that requires that the predicate of the sentential context C is not higher than one of the predicates being tested, either A or B. This would guarantee that C is not a high predicate. We can achieve this by using a fourth predicate D which is meaningful with A or B but not with C. Thus we want $U(AD)$ or $U(BD)$ but $N(CD)$. By conjoining this with the basic requirement of the existential criterion that A and B are both meaningful with the third predicate C, and by assuming the nonambiguity amendment, as we shall from here on, we get, using Sommers' terminology,

(11)   If $\{\{[U(AD) \vee U(BD)] \cdot N(CD)\} \cdot [U(AC) \cdot U(BC)]\}$ then $S(AB)$, i.e. A and B are of the same logical category.[18]

17. F. Sommers, "The Ordinary Language Tree," *Mind* 68 (1959): 172–73.
18. Cf. Sommers, p. 173.

It should be noted that (11) provides only a sufficient condition of type sameness. It might be thought that just as we found the converse of (7) to be unobjectionable so that we could arrive at the "if and only if" definition (10), so also we could use the converse of (11). However, the converse of (11) implies

If $S(AB)$ then $N(CD)$,

which states that two terms being of the same type implies that there are two other terms of different types. This is surely dubious and is clearly false for any language with only two predicates or for any language with all its terms of the same type, as is at least possible. Thus we should not use the converse of (11). This is not troublesome, however, if we can continue to use (10) as a definition, for if so, we need in addition only a sufficient condition of type sameness which is usable as a criterion and which avoids the high predicate objection.

We can see how (11) avoids this objection by letting $A =$ person, $B =$ number, and $C =$ thought of. Consequently we get $U(AC)$ and $U(BC)$ which on the original existential definition would have led us to the false conclusion that 'person' and 'number' are of the same logical category. However, to reach this conclusion on Sommers' criterion we also need a D such that

$[U(AD) \lor U(BD)] \cdot N(CD)$.

However, there is no D with which 'thought of' cannot be joined significantly and so the inference is invalid. This is also true of the other high predicates such as 'interesting,' 'denoted by a word,' 'an entity,' 'of some type,' and others. Consequently, because Sommers' criterion is existential and avoids the high predicate objection, it may be what we need to establish type sameness. It can be adapted to result in a criterion for type difference, but there is a question of whether the existential criterion of type difference, (7), requires any amendment. Sommers thinks that it does, however, because (7), which he would state as

$[U(AC) \cdot N(BC)] \supset D(AB)$, i.e. A and B are of different categories,

is, he claims, equivalent to

$[U(AC) \cdot U(AB)] \supset S(BC)$,

and this is falsified by the high predicate examples. These two sentences are equivalent, however, only if $D(AB)$ implies $N(AB)$ which is not obvious. In fact, if we accept (7), that implication is false. Let A = entity, B = number, and C = heavy, so that by (7) we get D(entity, number). But it surely is true that U(entity, number), so that the implication required for Sommers' equivalence is false. Thus (7) can escape Sommers' attack. However, we should not hold (7) with (11) because taken together they produce results which are surely unsatisfactory. We have found that (7) gives us D(entity, number), and we can show that (11) gives us S(entity, number) by letting A = entity, B = number, C = sum of two numbers, and D = heavy. It seems we should then give up either (7) or (11), but which one?

THE REJECTION OF CRITERION (7) AND A NEW DEFINITION
OF TYPE DIFFERENCE

It would seem that (7) should be discarded because numbers are entities so that 'number' and 'entity' should be construed as being in the same logical category. But stones are also entities so that 'stone' should be put in the same category as 'entity' and consequently, it would seem, as 'number.' We can avoid this problem by prohibiting the inference from $S(AC)$ and $S(AB)$ to $S(BC)$, that is, denying statement (e):

If two entities are each of the same type as a third, then they are of the same type,

which was first discussed when examining the first part of Black's objection to Russell's definition. This, in effect, is what Sommers does because he claims that $S(XY) \equiv U(XY)$ and we know that $U(AC)$ and $U(BC)$ do not imply $U(AB)$. He also claims that $D(XY) \equiv N(XY)$ which we have seen is false if we use (7), because it is then false that $D(XY)$ implies $N(XY)$. This, I think, provides the best reason for rejecting (7). There is no reason to establish $D(AB)$ unless we can infer $N(AB)$ from it, and thus establish a method to rule out sentences using both A and B as illegitimate. If the inference from $D(AB)$ to $N(AB)$ is invalid, then there is no value in establishing that two terms are of different categories. Therefore because the inference is invalid if we use (7) we should either amend (7) or give it up altogether.

The problem we must eliminate is that (7) requires us to put two terms into different categories when one, A, is so much higher than the other, B, that A can be used significantly with lower terms not significantly usable with B. This is the problem involved with the three terms 'entity,' 'number,' and 'stone.' As stated, (7) prohibits only one of the terms, either A or B, from being higher than the other. Thus if we write (7) using Sommers' terminology, except for variables instead of C and D in order to emphasize the existential character of (7), we get

(7a) $\{(\exists X)[U(AX) \cdot N(BX)] \vee (\exists Y)[U(BY) \cdot N(AY)]\} \supset$
$$D(AB).$$

Criterion (7a) tells us that if we can find one term that goes meaningfully with A but not with B, or goes meaningfully with B but not with A, then $D(AB)$. According to (7a), then, we can establish $D(AB)$ by verifying either

(12) $(\exists X)[U(AX) \cdot N(BX)]$,

which guarantees that B is not higher than A, or

(13) $(\exists Y)[U(BY) \cdot N(AY)]$,

which guarantees that A is not higher than B. But it is not enough to guarantee that just one term is not higher than the other, because that is compatible with the other being a high predicate. We can remedy this defect by requiring that neither term be higher than the other. We need, then, the conjunction of (12) and (13) in the antecedent of the criterion rather than the disjunction. Thus:

(14) $\{(\exists X)[U(AX) \cdot N(BX)] \cdot (\exists Y)[U(BY) \cdot N(AY)]\} \supset$
$$D(AB).^{19}$$

As before, we have the problem of determining whether the converse of (14) is acceptable so that we can arrive at an "if and only if" definition. In this case the converse seems innocuous, as can be seen by realizing that it is equivalent to

(15) $\{(X)[U(AX) \supset U(BX)] \vee (Y)[U(BY) \supset U(AY)]\} \supset$
$$S(AB).$$

19. Cf. Sommers, "Types and Ontology," *Philosophical Review* 72 (1963): 358, for a derivation of an equivalent criterion. Criterion (14) is implied by criterion (11) as can be indicated by interchanging B and C in (11) and using $D(AB) \equiv N(AB)$ and $S(AB) \equiv U(AB)$.

That is, if either A or B is significant with all the terms the other one is, then the two are of the same category. This is surely acceptable. Let us, then, accept (15) as unobjectionable. Thus we arrive at the definition:

(16) $D(AB) =_{df.} (\exists X)(\exists Y)[U(AX) \cdot N(BX) \cdot U(BY) \cdot N(AY)].$

One result of (15) is that each high predicate belongs to every category, which is also one unobjectionable consequence of (11). In addition, (15), like (11), allows terms like 'individual,' 'object,' 'property,' 'relation,' and 'event,' which are not high predicates, because not significant with everything, to be in the same category with terms not significant with each other. For example, although 'object' is not a high predicate because N(object, brain occurrences), it is significant with everything significant with 'person' and with everything significant with 'square root.' But N(person, square root). Let us call such predicates "relatively high" predicates. This consequence of (11) and (15) is important because it requires that we further amend the category principle previously amended to accommodate high predicates so that it also accommodates relatively high predicates. The following will do:

> For any predicate, P, if A and B are of different types and P is neither a high predicate nor a relatively high predicate, then P is not significantly ascribable to both A and B.

Problems for criterion (11) and definition (16)

Although (15) provides a sufficient condition for type sameness, it is, like (8), a universal condition which is unwieldy to use. Thus it seems we should use (11) as a criterion of type sameness instead. However, although (11) seems to be an easily usable criterion because we need only find two terms, C and D, that meet its requirements, it does not seem that for every pair of terms, A and B, there is such a pair, C and D. Consider the two terms 'dog' and 'cat.' They seem to be of the same category but I do not see how to show this using (11). Consider the following quantified version of (11):

(11a) $(\exists X)(\exists Y)\{[U(AX) \text{ v } U(BX)] \cdot N(XY) \cdot$
$[U(AY) \cdot U(BY)]\} \supset S(AB).$

We need an X and Y such that U(dog, X), $N(XY)$, U(dog, Y), and U(cat, Y); but I cannot find two terms that go with 'dog' and 'cat' but not with each other. Thus it seems that, although where (11) can be applied it can be used as a criterion, it does not apply in all cases. Indeed it seems applicable only where one of the terms is considerably higher than the other. It may be, then, we shall have to fall back on (15) and verify its universally quantified antecedent inductively. This is not a completely satisfactory solution, but we shall have to rest content with it, at least in this book. I want to concentrate here upon category difference now that we have reached a criterion for that which is usable, and, if we can handle the Smart problem, unobjectionable.

The Smart problem is that if we accept (7) as the criterion for type difference, then we must conclude that 'chair' and 'bed' are of different categories because U(chair, hard seat) and N(bed, hard seat). But surely these two terms belong in the same category because both are pieces of furniture. This objection would seem also to apply to (14) and therefore (16) if we take A = chair, B = bed, X = hard seat, and Y = box springs. The only way I can find to handle this objection is to deny $N(BX)$ or $N(AY)$ so the conditions of (14) are not met. This may seem strange but one intuitive way to judge some cases of type sameness is by wondering whether a normal perceiver could perceive something which is B and X, or A and Y. It surely is possible to see a bed with a seat, and a chair made partly from a box spring. However, someone might reconstruct the objection using A = chair, B = rug, X = legs, and Y = 1/8 inch thick. My intuition here is that we should conclude that $D(AB)$ even though someone might claim they are both furniture. Rugs are, however, different from chairs, different enough to belong to a different category. Thus I think it is plausible to reject the Smart objection and to accept (14) and also (16).

CATEGORY DIFFERENCE AND TESTS OF ABSURDITY

I have suggested we may be able to avoid the Smart objection and have relied on my intuition in doing so, but my intuitions about 'chair' and 'rug' are not so clear as those about 'person' and 'square root.' This brings us to one troublesome feature of the whole preceding discussion, a feature we have so far ignored. In discussing each of the various proposed definitions and criteria we have talked about what is meaningful or significant, and what is meaningless or absurd, but we have not investigated what it is to be meaningless or absurd. Ryle, in fact, ends his discussion of categories with the question, "But what are the tests of absurdity?" [20] This question, as far as I know, has not been answered, but let us examine some attempts to find an answer.

Certain kinds of grammaticalness are sufficient conditions of linguistic absurdity. That is, if a certain purported sentence is ungrammatical in certain ways, then it is not a sentence and is consequently meaningless and linguistically absurd. Thus it may be possible to use certain grammatical absurdities to pick out that certain terms belong to different grammatical categories and that certain purported sentences contain grammatical category mistakes. Having done this it may be possible to infer that these purported sentences also contain logical category mistakes of the kind in which we are interested. It is not at all unreasonable to think that grammatical category differences and mistakes will be reflected in logical category differences and mistakes.[21] Ryle might well agree to this, but he would insist that there are certain logical category differences not demarcated by grammatical category differences, so that a grammatical criterion of category mistakes is not sufficient to account for all cases of category differences. He says, for example,

> 'So and so is in bed' grammatically requires for complements to the gap indicated by 'so and so' nouns, pronouns or substantival phrases such as descriptive phrases. So 'Saturday is in bed' breaks no rule of grammar. Yet the sentence is absurd. Consequently the possible complements must be not only of certain grammatical types, they must also express proposition-factors of certain logical types.[22]

If Ryle is right, then no attempt to use purely grammatical devices to discover all logical categories will succeed. If, however,

20. Ryle, "Categories," p. 81.
21. I have briefly discussed a related point, namely, the relationship of grammatical strata and language strata, in *Metaphysics, Reference, and Language*, pp. 227–36.
22. Ryle, "Categories," p. 70.

Ryle is wrong, then we may be able to construct an easily usable
criterion for category absurdity which relies only on investigations of nonsense generated by ungrammaticalness.

D. J. Hillman has attempted to show that Ryle has not made
his point because, in spite of Ryle's claim, the absurdity of 'Saturday is in bed' results solely from a grammatical mistake. It is
not clear whether Hillman thinks that all logical category mistakes can be derived from grammatical mistakes. Although at
one point he says that "if we were now to think of categories
as defined by some (grammatical) context and not in isolation,
we should be in a better position to deal with odd sentences like
'Saturday is in bed'," [23] he never specifies whether he is dealing
with one species of categorially odd sentences which includes
'Saturday is in bed,' or whether he means to include all categorially odd sentences. Nevertheless we can use his work to
test the hypothesis that all category mistakes are grammatically
derived. This hypothesis is worth considering because if, as
Hillman and others think, a theory of transformational grammar
is being developed to provide a way to decide whether or not
a particular group of words is a sentence or a nonsentence, then
we will be able to construct a workable criterion of category
differences and therefore of category mistakes.

A GRAMMATICAL TEST FOR LOGICAL DIFFERENCES

Hillman's approach is to divide Ryle's criterion into two criteria, one for grammatical category differences and one for relating them to logical category differences. They are:

C1   two expression *A* and *B* are of different grammati-
     ical categories if there exists at least one environ-
     ment such that when *A* and *B* are imported as alter-
     native complements to the gap in this environment,
     the resultant expressions are a sentence in the one
     case and a non-sentence in the other.

C2   If two expressions *A* and *B* are of different grammat-
     ical categories then the proposition-factors they ex-
     press are of different logical categories.[24]

23. D. J. Hillman, "On Grammars and Category Mistakes," *Mind* 72
(1963): 233.
24. Hillman, p. 229.

Hillman uses these criteria to prove that 'Saturday is in bed' is absurd because it involves a grammatical mistake. He does so by using 'I went to the cinema this ——' to prove that 'Saturday' which fits grammatically and 'John' which does not fit are of different grammatical and therefore different logical categories. And because '—— is in bed' takes 'John' grammatically, it will not take 'Saturday' grammatically. Therefore, contrary to Ryle, this absurdity derives from a purely grammatical mistake.

One obvious problem for Hillman's criteria is whether the grammatical category differences picked out by C1 do reflect logical category differences as claimed in C2. We can grant that 'man' belongs in a different grammatical category from 'a man' and from 'John' because the first does not fit in '—— is in bed' while the others do. For the same reason we can agree that 'a president' and 'the president' belong in a different grammatical category from 'president.' And perhaps we can also agree that 'man' and 'president' belong in different grammatical categories from 'men' and 'presidents' because the latter, unlike the former, fit in '—— are in bed.' But although the inferences warranted by C1 may be sound, the further inferences warranted by C2 seem faulty. Surely 'John,' 'a man,' and 'man' belong in the same logical category. This is also true of 'president' and 'presidents.' Thus Hillman's criterion is too strong, for it would require that terms in the same logical category be in different categories. Perhaps Hillman can revise C2 so that only certain grammatical categories imply logical categories, for example, so that the grammatical categories of singular and plural are made irrelevant. It is not clear, however, how he would justify such a change without bringing in nongrammatical considerations.

A second objection to the thesis we are considering, however, is that although Ryle picked a poor example to illustrate his point, a simple adjustment in the example is all he needs. If he had used 'Some Saturdays are in bed' he would have an example of a grammatically correct sentence which is absurd. Grammatically, 'Some —— are in bed' can take any plural common noun whether it be 'Saturdays,' 'persons,' 'numbers,' or some others. This is also true of Hillman's other sentence frame, 'I went to the cinema this ——.' But in both cases, and in most others, only some of the grammatically correct sentences are meaningful. Such grammatical-categorial distinctions are not fine enough to catch logical-categorial differences such as those among days of the week, persons, and numbers. It seems that what is needed in addition to grammatical criteria such as Hillman's are criteria which are semantic rather than grammatical.

There is a reply to the second objection. Some of the latest work in linguistics has tended to destroy whatever sharp division there might be between grammar and semantics by incorporating into grammar categories and distinctions traditionally thought to be semantic. Thus Chomsky has claimed not only that the categories of noun, proper noun, and common noun are grammatical categories, but also that the "subcategories" of abstract noun, concrete noun, and human noun are grammatical categories.[25] If such categories are construed as grammatical, then, by limiting the nouns that form grammatical sentences when substituted in 'Some —— are in bed' to concrete nouns, we could show 'Some Saturdays are in bed' is a grammatical absurdity.

It is clear that Ryle, in claiming that 'So and so is in bed' breaks no grammatical rules, was limiting grammatical categories to more traditional ones such as noun, pronoun, proper noun, and common noun. If we construe a grammar as limited to such categories, then 'Some Saturdays are in bed' is not a grammatical absurdity. It would seem to qualify as a semantic absurdity, and the categories relevant to showing it absurd would be semantic categories. Ryle, then, is right as he construes grammatical categories, but perhaps wrong as grammatical categories are widely construed now. We need not debate this issue further, however, because what is important for our discussion is that a grammar, as traditionally construed by Ryle and others, cannot handle such absurdities unless supplemented either by incorporating "semantic" rules and concepts into the grammar, or by developing a separate semantic theory to be applied to the results of using the grammar. For our purposes it does not matter which way a grammar is supplemented. But the supplemented theory that I wish to examine because it con-

25. See N. Chomsky, *Aspects of the Theory of Syntax* (Cambridge: Massachusetts Institute of Technology Press, 1965), pp. 63–83.

tains a clear criterion of absurdity, takes the second approach. I shall, then, assume that approach for the rest of the discussion.

A SEMANTIC CRITERION OF ABSURDITY

Although in talking of *logical* categories we might seem to be considering merely grammatical or syntactical categories, because logic is supposedly a purely formal discipline, we have seen that such categories seem to be related to meaning or significance in ways which take us beyond the resources of what is usually construed as a purely syntactical theory. Because of this it might seem more appropriate to call them semantic categories, and to call category mistakes one form of what are known as semantic anomalies. For this reason an investigation of semantic anomaly as defined in semantic theory seems a likely way to find at least the beginnings of a criterion adequate to distinguish cases of meaninglessness or absurdity which do not seem to have a syntactical origin.

Recently J. J. Katz and J. A. Fodor have been trying to characterize the kinds of components an adequate semantic theory requires. In their article "The Structure of a Semantic Theory" [26] in which they propose certain semantic components, they also provide a criterion of semantic anomaly which uses these components. It is important that this criterion be satisfactory because they claim that any satisfactory semantic theory must be able to distinguish between semantically regular sentences and those semantic anomalies which are not the result of purely grammatical anomalies. Thus our investigation of their criterion of semantic anomaly may have important consequences for the semantic theory they propose.

To understand the criterion Katz and Fodor propose, we must have some idea of how they interpret a semantic theory and what they take its components to be. They claim that a semantic theory is a theory which is designed to account for all the abilities a fluent speaker of a language has for interpreting sentences in ways which go beyond the resources of a grammar,

26. J. Katz and J. Fodor, "The Structure of a Semantic Theory," *Language* 39 (1963): 170–210; reprinted in J. Katz and J. Fodor, eds., *The Structure of Language* (Englewood Cliffs, N.J.: Prentice-Hall, 1964), pp. 479–518.

but which are not dependent upon the nonlinguistic settings or contexts in which the sentences are uttered. This provides a semantic theory with a specific subject matter, bounded on the one hand by the subject matter of grammar and on the other by those interpretative abilities of speakers which depend on non-linguistic contexts. We should, then, distinguish between a semantic theory and a grammar. A grammar provides rules

> which generate the sentences of the speaker's language. In particular, these rules generate infinitely many strings of morphemes which, though they are sentences of the language, have never been uttered by speakers. Moreover, a grammar generates the sentences which a speaker is, in principle, capable of understanding in such a way that their derivations provide their structural descriptions. Such descriptions specify the elements out of which a sentence is constructed, the grammatical relations between these elements and between the higher constituents of the sentence, the relations between the sentence and other sentences of the language, and the ways the sentence is syntactically ambiguous together with an explanation of why it is ambiguous in these ways.[27]

REQUIREMENTS FOR A SATISFACTORY SEMANTIC THEORY

According to Katz and Fodor, there are four facets of a speaker's interpretative ability which are not accounted for by a grammar and which do not depend on nonlinguistic contexts. They are, then, the four facets any semantic theory must account for, that is:

(1) The ability to "detect nonsyntactic ambiguities and characterize the content of each reading of a sentence."
(2) The ability to determine "the number of readings that a sentence has by exploiting semantic relations in the sentence to eliminate potential ambiguities."
(3) The ability "of detecting semantic anomalies."
(4) The ability to use one sentence to paraphrase another.[28]

27. Ibid., p. 172.
28. Ibid., p. 175.

We are interested in the third facet, so let us concentrate on seeing whether or not the semantic components Katz and Fodor propose are adequate for the purpose of constructing a criterion of semantic anomaly which accounts for the ability of fluent speakers to detect the anomalies. Katz and Fodor propose two new components as additions to the components necessary for an adequate grammar: a dictionary and projection rules. The dictionary is to provide us with information not provided by a grammar, and the projection rules tell us how we are to use the grammatical and dictionary information to arrive at conclusions relevant to the four semantic facets of speakers' interpretative ability. In examining the criterion Katz and Fodor propose for semantic anomaly, we shall, in effect, be examining a rule which tells us how to utilize the grammatical and dictionary information to account for the third facet of a speaker's interpretative ability. We must, then, examine the kind of information the dictionary provides if we are to understand how to use this rule or criterion.

According to Katz and Fodor, there are five different kinds of information that any adequate dictionary must provide. Using the word 'bachelor' for illustration, we can list the five kinds of information as follows: first, the part of speech, represented by a grammatical marker, e.g. noun; second, the number of senses of the word, represented by diverging paths each with a distinct set of semantic information; third, the systematic semantic features, represented by semantic markers, e.g. (human) and on one path, (male); fourth, the idiosyncratic semantic features, represented by distinguishers such as [who has never been married] on the (male) path, and on another, [who has the lowest academic degree].[29] This leaves one more dictionary information marker which is called a selection restriction and which is either a semantic marker or a distinguisher which functions to limit the class of semantically acceptable combinations for the term. It is, then, a marker essential to a discussion of semantic anomaly.

A CRITERION OF SEMANTIC ANOMALY

We can best understand selection restrictions and thereby semantic anomalies by examining the way Katz and Fodor dis-

29. Ibid., p. 191.

cuss 'spinster.' They consider the phrase 'spinster insecticide' which is surely anomalous. According to them we establish that this is an anomaly by considering the relevant path of 'spinster' and applying the criterion of semantic anomaly. The relevant path is

> 'spinster' → adjective → (human) → (adult) → (female) → [who has never married]⟨(human)⟩.

Here the parentheses give us semantic markers, the brackets show a distinguisher, and the angles indicate that the semantic marker (human) is a selection restriction. This last means that all and only terms which contain the semantic marker (human) in their paths are semantically acceptable with 'spinster.' [30] Let us use '*A*' and '*B*' to refer to linguistic expressions, '*A* → (*B*)' to mean that *A* has the marker (*B*) in its path, and '*N*[*AB*]' to mean that the expressions *A* and *B* are semantically anomalous when used together. Using this notation we can represent a criterion of semantic anomaly as follows:

1. $(X)\{\{ \{A \rightarrow \langle(B)\rangle\} \cdot \sim\{X \rightarrow (B)\} \} \supset N[AX]\}.$

Thus because 'insecticide' does not have the semantic marker (human) in its path while 'spinster' has ⟨(human)⟩ in its path, it follows that *N* [spinster, insecticide]. The criterion thus works for this case. The question is whether it works for all others as it must if it is to account for the ability of fluent speakers to detect certain grammatical sentences as semantic anomalies.

In the following discussion I shall grant the dubious characterization of 'spinster' as an adjective, and will raise objections to the Katz and Fodor account of semantic anomaly accordingly. It may be that some of the claims I shall make about terms acceptable with 'spinster' will seem odd, because it may seem odd to construe 'spinster' as an adjective. To test my claims, therefore, it may be helpful to use 'unmarried' as well as 'spinster.' Furthermore, I shall assume that this semantic theory is to account for all semantic anomalies and not just those involving adjectives modifying nouns, and so many of the objections I shall make also raise problems for handling other kinds of anomalies, such as in 'Next Saturday is in bed.'

To see a defect in this criterion we need only consider the

30. Ibid., p. 199.

word 'animal' which results in semantically acceptable sentences when used with 'spinster' because 'There are spinster animals' is true. It follows from the premises 'There are spinster people' and 'All people are animals,' both of which are true. But 'animal' does not have the semantic marker (human) in its path, so the criterion must be amended to avoid the conclusion that N[spinster, animal]. ·The following criterion would suffice:

2. $(X)\{\{\{A \rightarrow \langle (B) \rangle\} \cdot \sim \{X \rightarrow (B)\} \cdot \sim \{B \rightarrow (X)\}\} \supset N[AX]\}.$

According to this criterion, it is not enough that (B) is not in the path of X; it must also be true that (X) is not in the path of B. Therefore, because, presumably, the semantic marker (animal) is in the path of 'human,' the above problem is avoided. But there is still the problem that semantic markers such as (inhabitant), (patient), (descendant), (individual), and others are neither in the path of 'human' nor do the corresponding words have (human) in their paths. Nevertheless, all the corresponding words are semantically acceptable with 'spinster.' Here both the criteria fail to distinguish properly. The problem lying behind the failure of both (1) and (2) to be adequate criteria of semantic anomaly seems to be that many terms semantically acceptable together do not have relationships which can be spelled out in terms of the semantic information markers Katz and Fodor provide. The criteria, then, are too strong. The terms 'spinster' and 'descendant,' for example, form semantically acceptable combinations but seem to be unrelated in terms of semantic markers and distinguishers.

It might be replied at this point that the selection restrictions suggested by Katz and Fodor are too specific, and that both criteria (1) and (2) would be adequate if the restrictions were made more general. Thus we might try to broaden the selection restriction for 'spinster' to ⟨(animal)⟩, or to ⟨(living individual)⟩, or perhaps even to ⟨(spatiotemporal individual)⟩. If we broadened it in this way, then, because presumably 'animal,' 'inhabitant,' 'descendant,' and the like would also have (spatiotemporal individual) in their paths, both (1) and (2) could avoid the previous problem. Nevertheless, the previous problem facing (1) can be revived because it is false that N[spinster, individual], but 'individual' does not have (spatiotemporal individual) in its path. We could save (1) by broadening still

more the selection restriction for 'spinster' to ⟨(individual)⟩ and
then to ⟨(entity)⟩, but if we did this, then, because all but syn-
categorematic words would have this summum genus marker
(entity) in their paths, we would be enabled to derive obvious
anomalies such as N[spinster, square root]. The criteria would
become too weak.

We need not go to the extreme required to save (1) from this
objection, because (2) avoids it using (spatiotemporal individual). But there are other problems facing (2) as well as (1).
One is that we have as much reason to put (spatiotemporal individual) in the path of 'insecticide' as in the path of 'spinster,'
and thus we have no way to show on either (1) or (2) that
N[spinster, insecticide]. Another problem arises because of high
predicates, which, as we have seen, are predicates significantly
applicable to anything no matter what its category. Unless selection restrictions are to place limits only on the nouns acceptable
with adjectives, which I assume is not the case, then a problem
arises for "high adjectives" such as 'interesting,' 'discussed,'
'usual,' and 'unique.' These adjectives are significant with 'spinster,' but, because the corresponding markers are not in the
path of 'individual' nor is (individual) in the path of these words,
we would have to conclude they are not significant with 'spinster' if we accepted either (1) or (2). Furthermore, there are
"high nouns" such as 'subject,' 'object,' and 'entity' for which
the same problem arises. For these reasons we should reject
both (1) and (2) even if we broaden selection restrictions to
avoid the original objection. They remain too strong even with
the selection restrictions broadened so far that they also become
too weak.

It might seem at this point that we have been relating semantic information markers to semantic anomalies in the wrong
way. Perhaps we should require a certain kind of semantic relationship to hold between semantically anomalous terms. But
this will not help, as we can see by examining the following proposal:

3. $(X)\{\,\{\,\{A \to \langle (B) \rangle\} \cdot \{X \to (\text{non-}B)\}\,\} \supset N[AX]\,\}.$

This criterion avoids all the above problems because none of
the terms have (nonhuman) in their paths. But there are two
problems with this criterion. The first is that there are very few

terms which would seem to have (nonhuman) in their paths. It seems that neither 'insecticide' nor 'number' nor 'continuity' would have such a marker in its path, and thus this criterion would have the defect of not being able to account for obvious semantic anomalies such as 'spinster number' and 'spinster continuity.'

The first problem shows that criterion (3) must be supplemented if it is to be capable of detecting all semantic anomalies. This objection, which shows that (3) is too weak, is not as serious as the counterexamples raised against criteria (1) and (2), which show them to be too strong. The second problem is more serious however. It seems that for unambiguous nouns, if 'P' $\rightarrow \langle (Q) \rangle$, then all P's are Q's; and if 'R' $\rightarrow$ (non-Q), then all R's are non-Q's. From this we can conclude that no P's are R's and thus it is false that $N[$'P,' 'R'$]$ contrary to criterion (3). A similar problem arises for adjectives. We can illustrate this by assuming that 'robot' has (nonhuman) in its path, so that taking $A =$ spinster, and $B =$ human, and using criterion (3), we get $N[$spinster, robot$]$. But clearly because all spinster entities are humans and, based on the preceding assumption, all robots are nonhumans, it follows that there are no spinster robots. Thus 'There are no spinster robots' is true if 'robot' has (nonhuman) in its path. Consequently criterion (3) is both too strong and too weak.

Although we have not examined all the possible criteria of semantic anomaly that might be constructed using the dictionary markers allowed by Katz and Fodor, I cannot think of one that will be adequate to its job. The problem of trying to construct a criterion using only the semantic information markers, whether semantic markers or distinguishers, allowed by Katz and Fodor is further emphasized by the following dilemma. It seems that any criterion for semantic anomaly will fail if it contains as its sufficient condition *only* that some semantic relationship, describable in terms of the semantic information markers allowed by Katz and Fodor, obtains between two terms. As evidenced by criterion (3), it seems that no terms meeting such a condition are semantically anomalous. Furthermore, if this is true, then any criterion containing such a sufficient condition in conjunction or disjunction with any other will also fail. But a criterion will also fail if it contains as its sufficient condition *only* that some such semantic relationship does *not* obtain. As evidenced by the failures of criteria (1) and (2), some terms that seem to have no relationships describable in terms of the semantic information markers of Katz and Fodor nevertheless form semantically acceptable combinations. The conclusion of the argument is that any criterion will fail if it contains as its sufficient condition of semantic anomaly a statement made only in terms of such semantic information markers. If this argument is sound, then if a semantic dictionary is to provide only the information allowed by Katz and Fodor, and if a semantic theory is to account for semantic anomalies, there is reason to think that the kind of semantic theory they have outlined is not adequate. As yet I have been unable to find reasons to doubt the soundness of this argument.

CONCLUSION ABOUT CATEGORIES, GRAMMAR, AND SEMANTICS

We have found reason to think that a grammar sufficient to determine all clear cases of grammatical anomalies does not provide adequate resources for a criterion to decide cases of meaninglessness. There are also reasons to think that the resources of a semantic theory as proposed by Katz and Fodor are in some ways too strong and in other ways too weak to pick out all and only cases of nongrammatical meaninglessness. This, of course, is not to say that no semantic theory can account for this kind of meaninglessness, but at present it seems we must rely on our unreliable intuitions in applying a criterion to determine logical category differences. Such a procedure is not completely satisfactory. This might prompt someone to deny the assumption we have been making that there are linguistic absurdities which are semantic or at least nongrammatical as traditionally conceived.

Denying that there is a nongrammatical kind of meaninglessness would have the apparent advantage that a semantic theory would not have as one of its adequacy conditions that it account for purely semantic anomalies. This would remove the objections to the theory of Katz and Fodor we have considered. It would not, however, help with the task that led us to consider linguistic anomalies here. This task is to devise a more effective way to apply a criterion of category difference. As we have been construing grammars following Katz and Fodor, sentences such as 'Some square roots are conjunctions,' which involve category mistakes, are not grammatically meaningless. Thus if we adopt the view that there is only grammatical meaninglessness, we must also reject calling 'Some square roots are conjunctions' meaningless. We should, then, call it false. And because the grounds of its falsity do not seem to be empirical, it seems it would have to be an a priori falsehood.[31] But it appears to entail no logical contradiction, so it seems we should conclude it would be some kind of synthetic a priori falsehood. And because intuitions are no more reliable about the synthetic a priori than about semantic anomalies, we would again be faced with the task of devising a test for a more effective application of a criterion of category difference. But, paraphrasing Ryle, what are the tests of the synthetic a priori?

We have found one advantage in claiming there is only grammatical meaninglessness, an advantage which is of little help for the problem that interests us here. There are also disadvantages that may outweigh this one advantage. The first is that a sentence such as 'Some square roots are conjunctions' clearly seems to be meaningless rather than true or false as it would be if there was only grammatical meaninglessness. Therefore unless there is some clear theoretical advantage in this counter-intuitive proposal, we should not adopt it. Second, if we agree that 'Some square roots are conjunctions' is a synthetic a priori falsehood, then this certainly requires some kind of explanation —if not semantic, then some other kind. But no other kind seems to be available. Third, if we agree that 'Some square roots are conjunctions' is false, we are faced with the question of what to do with its denial, 'No square roots are conjunctions.' It would seem that the denial should be called true if the sentence is called false. But, surely, both sentences involve category mistakes because both use the same two terms from different categories. Consequently we would have the counter-intuitive result that some sentences that involve category mistakes are literally true. On the other hand, if we were to call

31. See Pap, pp. 52–54.

both the sentence and its denial false, then we would have a very strange set of sentences which might better be singled out as meaningless so that no one is misled into making unsound inferences using them.

While there are disadvantages to calling certain sentences involving category mistakes nonformal a priori falsehoods, all of them rest on the claim that the proposal has counterintuitive consequences. Such disadvantages can be counterbalanced if we can find good theoretical reasons for the proposal. The only theoretical reason which seems to me to be at all plausible is that if we accept the proposal then we can use the usual two-valued logic in working with sentences involving category mistakes. It is true that if we agree that every such sentence has a truth value, and that its denial has the opposite truth value, then the domain of sentences covered by two-valued logic is larger than if we call such sentences meaningless. I am not prepared to say whether this is sufficient to overcome the counterintuitive features of the proposal. I do not think, however, that it makes any difference for the acceptability of our criterion of category difference whether or not we call certain sentences containing category mistakes semantically meaningless or nonformal a priori falsehoods the denials of which are true. In both cases we can apply the criterion once we have the relevant information of the form $U(XY)$ and $N(XY)$. We have found that at present we must rely on clear cases of $U(XY)$ and $N(XY)$ to use the criterion. We have interpreted 'N' to stand for a certain kind of nonsense or meaninglessness, but there seems to be no compelling reason against interpreting it to stand for a certain kind of nonformal a priori truth or falsity. Nevertheless, because our purpose has been to examine category mistakes and criteria for category difference, and because there seems to be nothing gained for our purpose in being counterintuitive, let us continue to call category mistakes meaningless, at least until there are more forceful reasons to the contrary.

It may be objected that in the context of this book we *must* interpret 'N' to stand for meaninglessness rather than some unique kind of truth or falsity. The reply to the property objection to the identity theory (Chap. 1) depends on showing that principle D does not warrant the inference that sensations are not identical with brain entities. But if certain extentional predicates true of one, result in any kind of false statements when ascribed to the other, then principle *D* does warrant the non-identity claim. The reply to this objection is that principle *D* could and should be revised if sentences containing category mistakes were to be construed as a kind of a priori falsehood. In Chapter 1 we justified the use of *D* instead of principle *C*, because *C*, but not *D*, warranted the unjustified conclusion that gas temperatures are not identical with mean kinetic energies of gas molecules. We should, then, revise *D* if we rule out category meaninglessness, because the same problem that previously arose for *C* would then arise for *D*. And if we were to revise *D* to accommodate temperature–mean-kinetic-energy identity state-ments, it would also accommodate sensation–brain-entity iden-tity statements. Indeed, the following revision will do regardless of which interpretation we give '*N*':

E. $(x)(y)\{(\exists F)\{\mathcal{E}F \cdot [(F$ is true of $x \cdot F$ is non-*N*-false of $y)$
v $(F$ is true of $y \cdot F$ is non-*N*-false of $x)]\} \supset x \neq y\}$.

CONCLUSION ABOUT LOGICAL CATEGORIES

We have concluded that there is a satisfactory definition of category difference, definition (16), which can be used as a criterion with cases of linguistic nonsense to arrive at a decision about category differences and, thereby, category mistakes. And, although we have found neither a grammatical nor a semantical theory which we can use to pick out all cases of linguistic non-sense, this does not affect the correctness of the criterion. We have, therefore, completed the discussion except for one point. Throughout this discussion there has arisen the question of whether or not we could find a category principle warranting an inference from the fact that two terms are of different categories to a conclusion about whether predicates significant with one are not significant with the other. We found first that high predicates such as 'interesting' and 'thought of' and then that other "rela-tively high" predicates such as 'event' and 'object' are significant with terms of different categories. This required us to amend the category principle to accommodate both kinds of predicates. This was important because the category principle finally reached was used in Chapter 1 to refute the property objection to the identity theory. Although I think the use of the amended principle was justified, it would be more satisfactory if a criterion for high predicates and for relatively high predicates were devised. So far I have found no reason to deny that this can be done. If this is devised, then I think that the core of a satisfactory theory of categories will be available. What would remain would be primarily a matter of refinement.

Bibliography

References in this bibliography are classified according to the topics discussed in the book in the order in which they appear. Some duplication is unavoidable. Whenever an article or book is not given full reference, the full reference has appeared previously.

REDUCTIVE MATERIALISM

Historic statements of reductive materialism are to be found in Book III of *De Rerum Naturae* of Lucretius, translated by R. Latham, *On the Nature of the Universe* (London: Penguin, 1951) and in *De Corpore* of Thomas Hobbes, selections from which are to be found in *Body, Men and Citizens,* R. Peters, ed. (New York: Collier Books, 1962). More recent and more detailed statements are to be found in R. W. Sellars, *The Philosophy of Physical Realism* (New York: Macmillan, 1932) and in D. C. Williams, "Naturalism and the Nature of Things," *Philosophical Review* 53 (1944): 417–43.

There are many anthologies of writings both classical and recent that deal with relationships between mind and body: A. Flew, ed., *Body, Mind, and Death* (New York: Crowell-Collier, 1964); G. N. A. Vesey, ed., *Body and Mind* (London: Allen and Unwin, 1964); and J. W. Reeves, ed., *Body and Mind in Western Thought* (Baltimore: Penguin Books, 1958). All are historically oriented anthologies and contain selections from materialists.

Contemporary articles are to be found in S. Hook, ed., *Dimensions of Mind* (New York: Collier Books, 1961); S. Hampshire, ed., *Philosophy of Mind* (New York: Harper and Row, 1966); V. C. Chappell, ed., *The Philosophy of Mind* (Englewood Cliffs, N.J.: Prentice-Hall, 1962); and J. O'Connor, ed., *Modern Materialism: Readings on Mind–Body Identity* (New York: Harcourt, Brace & World, 1969). All of these contain extensive bibliographies. There is also an excellent bibliography of writings pertaining to the philosophy of mind in H. Feigl, *The 'Mental' and the 'Physical': An Essay and a Postscript* (Minneapolis: University of Minnesota Press, 1967). There are many useful references in J. Shaffer, "Recent Work in the Mind–

Body Problem," *American Philosophical Quarterly* 2 (1965):
81–104.

MIND–BODY IDENTITY THEORY

A large number of articles have appeared in the last fifteen
years devoted to defending or attacking the identity theory. Some
of the most important appear in C. Borst, ed., *The Mind–Brain
Identity Theory* (London: Macmillan, 1970). The primary im-
petus is the work of H. Feigl, U. T. Place, and J. J. C. Smart,
all of whom defend a form of the identity thesis. Place's views
are to be found in "Is Consciousness a Brain Process?" *British
Journal of Psychology* 48 (1956): 44–50 (reprinted in Chappell), and in "Materialism as a Scientific Hypothesis," *Philosophical Review* 69 (1960): 101–104. In 1950 Feigl published
"The Mind–Body Problem in the Development of Logical Em-
piricism," *Revue internationale de philosophie* 4 (1950): 64–83
(reprinted in H. Feigl and M. Brodbeck, eds., *Readings in the
Philosophy of Science* (New York: Appleton-Century-Crofts,
1953), pp. 612–26). Later Feigl wrote "The 'Mental' and the
'Physical'," in H. Feigl et al., eds., *Minnesota Studies in the
Philosophy of Science,* 3 vols. (Minneapolis: University of Minnesota Press, 1956–62) 2 (1958): 370–497. He also wrote
"Mind–Body, not a Pseudo-Problem," in *Dimensions of Mind,*
pp. 33–44. B. Aune replied to Feigl's views in "Feigl on the
Mind–Body Problem" in P. K. Feyerabend and G. Maxwell,
eds., *Mind, Matter, and Method* (Minneapolis: University of
Minnesota Press, 1966), pp. 17–39.

J. J. C. Smart defended the identity theory in "Sensations
and Brain Processes," *Philosophical Review* 68 (1959): 141–
56 (reprinted in Chappell, pp. 160–72) and *Philosophy and
Scientific Realism* (New York: The Humanities Press, 1963).
This led to many replies: K. Baier, "Smart on Sensations,"
Australasian Journal of Philosophy 40 (1962): 57–68; J. Mar-
golis, "Brain Processes and Sensations," *Theoria* 31 (1965):
133–38; J. T. Stevenson, "Sensations and Brain Processes: A
Reply to J. J. C. Smart," *Philosophical Review* 69 (1960):
505–10; A. C. Garnett, "Body and Mind—the Identity Thesis,"
Australasian Journal of Philosophy 43 (1965): 77–81; G.
Pitcher, "Sensations and Brain Processes: A Reply to Professor

Smart," *Australasian Journal of Philosophy* 38 (1960): 150–57.

Smart replied in "Brain Processes and Incorrigibility," *Australasian Journal of Philosophy* 40 (1962): 68–70; "Further Remarks on Sensations and Brain Processes," *Philosophical Review* 70 (1961): 406–07; "Sensations and Brain Processes: A Rejoinder to Dr. Pitcher and Mr. Joske," *Australasian Journal of Philosophy* 38 (1960): 252–54; "The Identity Thesis— A Reply to Professor Garnett," *Australasian Journal of Philosophy* 43 (1965): 82–83; and "Materialism," *Journal of Philosophy* 60 (1963): 651–62.

One of the replies to Smart, Jerome Shaffer's "Could Mental Events be Brain Processes?" *Journal of Philosophy* 58 (1961): 813–22, elicited responses from R. Coburn, "Shaffer on the Identity of Mental States and Brain Processes," *Journal of Philosophy* 60 (1963): 89–92; and J. Cornman, "The Identity of Mind and Body," *Journal of Philosophy* 59 (1962): 485–92. Shaffer replied in "Mental Events and the Brain," *Journal of Philosophy* 60 (1963): 160–66. D. Gustafson's article "On the Identity Theory," *Analysis* 24 (1963): 30–32, critical of Shaffer, led to Rita Norton's "On the Identity of Identity Theories," *Analysis* 25 (1964): 14–16.

Other defenders of various versions of the identity theory are H. Putnam, "Minds and Machines," in *Dimensions of Mind,* pp. 138–64; D. Lewis, "An Argument for the Identity Theory," *Journal of Philosophy* 63 (1966): 17–25; D. R. Luce, "Mind–Body Identity and the Psycho–Physical Correlation," *Philosophical Studies* 17 (1966): 1–7; T. Nagel, "Physicalism," *Philosophical Review* 74 (1965): 339–56; R. Rorty, "Mind–Body Identity, Privacy, and Categories," *Review of Metaphysics* 19 (1965): 24–54 (reprinted in Hampshire, pp. 30–63); N. Maxwell, "Understanding Sensations," *Australasian Journal of Philosophy* 46 (1968): 127–45.

Other critics of the identity theory are R. Brandt, "Doubts about the Identity Theory," in *Dimensions of Mind,* pp. 62–70; J. Kim, "On the Psycho–Physical Identity Theory," *American Philosophical Quarterly* 3 (1966): 227–235; R. Brandt and J. Kim, "The Logic of the Identity Theory," *Journal of Philosophy* 64 (1967): 515–37. N. Malcolm's contribution, "Scientific Materialism and the Identity Theory," *Dialogue* 3 (1964):

115–25, in turn led to replies by R. Hoffman, "Malcolm and Smart on Brain–Mind Identity," *Philosophy* 42 (1967): 128–36; B. Gert, "Can a Brain Have a Pain?" *Philosophy and Phenomenological Research* 27 (1966): 432–36; E. Sosa, "Professor Malcolm on 'Scientific Materialism and the Identity Theory'," *Dialogue* 3 (1964): 422–23, with a rejoinder by Malcolm, pp. 424–25.

Other articles on the identity theory are by Richard Routley and V. Macrae, "On the Identity of Sensations and Physiological Occurrences," *American Philosophical Quarterly* 3 (1966): 87–110; P. K. Feyerabend, "Materialism and the Mind–Body Problem," *Review of Metaphysics* 17 (1963): 49–66, and "Mental Events and the Brain," *Journal of Philosophy* 60 (1963): 295–96; W. Sellars, "The Identity Approach to the Mind–Body Problem," reprinted in *Philosophy of Mind,* pp. 7–30; C. Taylor, "Mind–Body Identity, A Side–Issue?" *Philosophical Review* 76 (1967): 201–13; J. Teichmann, "The Contingent Identity of Minds and Brains," *Mind* 76 (1967): 404–415; and, in *Mind, Matter, and Method,* M. Brodbeck, "Mental and Physical: Identity Versus Sameness," pp. 40–58, and M. Scriven, "The Limitations of the Identity Theory," pp. 191–97.

OBJECTIONS TO REDUCTIVE MATERIALISM

PERSONS AS ONTOLOGICALLY BASIC ENTITIES

Strawson stated his view in "Persons," in *Minnesota Studies* 2 (1958): 330–53. This is reprinted with some alterations in *Individuals, An Essay in Descriptive Metaphysics* (London: Methuen, 1959), chap. 3.

Critical comments on Strawson include A. J. Ayer, "The Concept of a Person," *The Concept of a Person and Other Essays* (New York: Macmillan, 1963); J. Cornman, "Strawson's 'Person'," *Theoria* 30 (1964): 145–56; S. Coval, "Persons and Criteria in Strawson," *Philosophy and Phenomenological Research* 24 (1964): 406–09; R. Freed and J. Fodor, "Pains, Puns, Persons and Pronouns," *Analysis* 22 (1961): 6–9; D. S. Mannison, "On the Alleged Ambiguity of Strawson's P-predicates," *Analysis* 23 (1962): 3–5; J. Fodor and R. Freed, "Some Types of Ambiguous Tokens," *Analysis* 24 (1963); T. Forrest, "P-predicates," in Avrum Stroll, ed., *Epistemology*

(New York: Harper and Row, 1967), pp. 83–106; G. Iseminger, "Meaning, Criteria and P-predicates," *Analysis* 24 (1963): 11–18; A. Plantinga, "Things and Persons," *Review of Metaphysics* 14 (1960): 493–519; R. Puccetti, "Mr. Strawson's Concept of a Person," *Australasian Journal of Philosophy* 45 (1967): 321–28; C. Rollins, "Personal Predicates," *Philosophical Quarterly* 10 (1960): 1–11; R. Rosthal, "Ascription of Mental Predicates," *Philosophical Studies* 12 (1961): 20–28; J. Shaffer, "Persons and Their Bodies," *Philosophical Review* 75 (1966): 59–77; D. Pears, *"Individuals* by P. F. Strawson," (critical notice) *Philosophical Quarterly* 11 (1961): 172–85 and 262–77; D. Van de Vate, Jr., "Strawson's Concept of a Person," *Southern Journal of Philosophy* 7 (1969): 9–24; B. A. O. Williams, "Mr. Strawson on Individuals," *Philosophy* 36 (1961): 309–32.

THE PRIVACY OBJECTION

Many articles written relevant to the question of private languages discuss the notion of privacy and various kinds of privacy. Some of these articles are: R. Woolheim, "Privacy," *Aristotelian Society Proceedings* 51 (1950): 83–104; D. Gustafson, "Privacy," *Southern Journal of Philosophy* 3 (1965): 140–46; D. Locke, "The Privacy of Pains," *Analysis* 24 (1963): 147–52; A. Kenny, "Cartesian Privacy," in G. Pitcher, ed., *Wittgenstein: The Philosophical Investigations* (New York: Doubleday, 1966), pp. 352–70; A. J. Ayer, "Privacy" in P. F. Strawson, ed., *Studies in the Philosophy of Thought and Action* (New York: Oxford University Press, 1968), pp. 24–47; A. R. Louch, "Privileged Access," *Mind* 74 (1965): 155–73; Michael Treisman, "Psychological Explanation: The 'Private Data' Hypothesis," *British Journal of the Philosophy of Science* 13 (1962): 130–43; J. Margolis, "The Privacy of Sensation," *Ratio* 6 (1964): 147–53; R. Lemos, "Immediacy, Privacy, and Ineffability," *Philosophy and Phenomenological Research* 25 (1964): 500–15; N. Malcolm, "The Privacy of Experience," in A. Stroll, ed., *Epistemology,* pp. 129–58; N. P. Tanburn, "Private Language Again," *Mind* 72 (1963): 88–102; I. C. Hungerland, "My Pain and Yours," in A. Stroll, *Epistemology,* 107–28; H. H. Price, "Some Objections to Behaviorism," in *Dimensions of Mind,* pp. 79–84; D. Odegard, "Sensations as

Qualities," *Philosophical Quarterly* 17 (1967): 308–16; G. Sheridan, "The Electroencephalogram Argument against Incorrigibility," *American Philosophical Quarterly* 6 (1969): 62–70; D. M. Taylor, "The Logical Place of Pains," *Mind* 79 (1970): 78–91; T. L. S. Sprigge, "The Privacy of Experience," *Mind* 78 (1969): 512–21.

Of the articles already cited on the identity theory, these discuss the objections from privacy: Smart, "Brain Processes and Incorrigibility"; Shaffer, "Mental Events and the Brain"; Routley and Macrae, "On the Identity of Sensations and Physiological Occurrences"; Kim, "On the Psycho-Physical Identity Theory"; Baier, "Smart on Sensations"; Rorty, "Mind–Body Identity, Privacy, and Categories"; Coburn, "Shaffer on the Identity of Mental States and Brain Processes."

THE PROPERTY OBJECTION

One species of the property objection involves the problem of spatially locating sensations. The location of sensations is discussed in the following series of articles: G. N. A. Vesey, "The Location of Bodily Sensations," *Mind* 70 (1961): 25–35; K. Baier, "The Place of a Pain," *Philosophical Quarterly* 14 (1964): 138–50; G. N. A. Vesey, "Baier on Vesey on the Place of a Pain," *Philosophical Quarterly* 15 (1965): 63–64; J. Margolis, "Awareness of Sensations and the Location of Sensations," *Analysis* 27 (1966): 29–32; G. N. A. Vesey, "Margolis on the Location of Bodily Sensations," *Analysis* 27 (1966): 174–76; D. M. Taylor, "The Location of Pain," *Philosophical Quarterly* 15 (1965): 53–62; R. C. Coburn, "Pains and Space," *Journal of Philosophy* 63 (1966): 381–96.

Applications to the identity theory are to be found in: Brandt, "Doubts About the Identity Theory"; Kim, "On the Psycho-Physical Identity Theory"; Stevenson, "Sensations and Brain Processes: A Reply to J. J. C. Smart"; Smart, "Further Remarks on Sensations and Brain Processes"; Shaffer, "Could Mental Events be Brain Processes?" and Routley and Macrae, "On the Identity of Sensations and Physiological Occurrences."

THEORETICAL TERMS AND OBSERVATION TERMS

The classic attempts to distinguish between theoretical and observation terms are to be found in the works of Braithwaite,

Carnap, Hempel, and Nagel: R. B. Braithwaite, *Scientific Explanation* (Cambridge: Cambridge University Press, 1959), Chapter III; R. Carnap, "The Methodological Character of Theoretical Concepts," in *Minnesota Studies* 1 (1956): 38–76, and "Logical Foundations of the Unity of Science," in O. Neurath, R. Carnap, and H. Morris, eds., *International Encyclopedia of Unified Science* 1 (Chicago: Chicago University Press, 1955), Part 1; C. Hempel, "The Theoretician's Dilemma," in *Minnesota Studies* 2 (1958): 37–98; E. Nagel, "The Meaning of Reduction in the Natural Sciences," in P. Wiener, ed., *Readings in the Philosophy of Science* (New York: Scribners, 1953), pp. 531–59, and *The Structure of Science* (New York: Harcourt, Brace and World, 1961), Chapter 5.

Critical of these attempts have been P. Achinstein, "Theoretical Terms and Partial Interpretation," *British Journal for the Philosophy of Science* 14 (1963): 89–105, and "The Problem of Theoretical Terms," *American Philosophical Quarterly* 2 (1965): 193–203; F. Dretske, "Observation Terms," *Philosophical Review* 73 (1964): 25–42; M. Spector, "Theory and Observation," *British Journal for the Philosophy of Science* 17 (1966): 1–20 and 89–104.

Other articles on or relevant to this problem are P. Alexander, "Theory Construction and Theory-Testing," *British Journal for the Philosophy of Science* 9 (1958): 29–38; P. K. Feyerabend, "An Attempt at a Realistic Interpretation of Experience," *Proceedings of the Aristotelian Society* 58 (1957–58): 143–70; M. Hesse, "Theories, Dictionaries and Observation," *British Journal for the Philosophy of Science* 9 (1958): 12–28; W. Sellars, "Scientific Realism or Irenic Instrumentalism," *Philosophical Perspectives* (Springfield, Illinois: Charles C. Thomas, 1959), pp. 337–69; W. Sellars, "The Language of Theories," in *Science, Perception and Reality* (New York: Humanities Press, 1963), pp. 106–26; J. J. C. Smart, "Theory Construction," in A. G. N. Flew, ed., *Logic and Language,* 2d series (Oxford: Basil Blackwell, 1953), pp. 222–42; J. Winnie, "Theoretical Terms and Partial Definitions," *Philosophy of Science* 32 (1965): 324–28; J. Winnie, "The Implicit Definition of Theoretical Terms," *British Journal for the Philosophy of Science* 18 (1967–68), 223–29; and D. Lewis, "How to Define Theoretical Terms," *Journal of Philosophy* 67 (1970):

427–46. In *Minnesota Studies* 3 (1962) there are G. Maxwell, "The Ontological Status of Theoretical Concepts," pp. 3–27; W. Rozebloom, "The Factual Content of Theoretical Concepts," pp. 273–357; and M. Scriven, "Definitions, Explanations, and Theories," pp. 99–192.

PRIVATE LANGUAGE ARGUMENT

Good bibliographies of the numerous articles that have appeared on the possibility of a private language are contained in H. N. Castañeda, "Private Language Problem," in P. Edwards, ed., *The Encyclopedia of Philosophy* 6 (New York: Macmillan, 1967), pp. 458–64; and in J. T. Saunders and D. F. Henze, *The Private Language Problem* (New York: Random House, 1967).
The discussion of this problem stems from Ludwig Wittgenstein. His views are to be found in *Philosophical Investigations,* translated by G. E. M. Anscombe (New York: Macmillan, 1953), and in "Wittgenstein's Notes for Lectures on 'Private Experience' and 'Sense Data'," *Philosophical Review* 77 (1968): 275–320. Many of the articles on private languages have been written to explain or to defend Wittgenstein. Among these are R. Albritton, "On Wittgenstein's Use of the Term 'Criterion'," *Journal of Philosophy* 56 (1959): 845–57; J. Carney, "Private Languages," *Mind* 64 (1960): 560–65; J. Cook, "Wittgenstein on Privacy," *Philosophical Review* 74 (1965): 281–314; N. Garver, "Wittgenstein on Private Languages," *Philosophy and Phenomenological Research* 20 (1960): 389–96; H. Hervey, "The Private Language Problem," *Philosophical Quarterly* 7 (1957): 63–79; J. Hintikka, "Wittgenstein on Private Language: Some Sources of Misunderstanding," *Mind* 78 (1969): 423–25; N. Malcolm, "Wittgenstein's *Philosophical Investigations,*" in *The Philosophy of Mind,* pp. 74–100; R. Rhees, "Can There be a Private Language?" *Proceedings of the Aristotelian Society, Supplementary Volume* 28 (1954): 77–94, and "A Note on 'Wittgenstein's Notes for Lectures on 'Private Experience' and 'Sense Data'," *Philosophical Review* 77 (1968): 271–75.
Among the articles expressing disagreement with Wittgenstein are A. J. Ayer, "Can There be a Private Language?" *Proceed-*

ings of the Aristotelian Society, Supplementary Volume 28 (1954): 63–76; J. Cornman, "Private Languages and Private Entities," *Australasian Journal of Philosophy* 46 (1967): 117–26; C. Ginet, "How Words Mean Kinds of Sensations," *Philosophical Review* 77 (1968): 3–24; C. L. Hardin, "Wittgenstein on Private Languages," *Journal of Philosophy* 56 (1959): 517–28; M. A. G. Stocker, "Memories and the Private Language Argument," *Philosophical Quarterly* 16 (1966): 47–53; P. F. Strawson, "Critical Notice of *Philosophical Investigations,*" *Mind* 63 (1954): 70–99; N. P. Tanburn, "Private Languages Again," *Mind* 72 (1963): 88–102; W. Todd, "Private Languages," *Philosophical Quarterly* 12 (1962): 206–17; C. Wellman, "Wittgenstein and the Egocentric Predicament," *Mind* 68 (1959): 223–33, and "Wittgenstein's Conception of a Criterion," *Philosophical Review* 71 (1962): 433–47.

Other articles on the problem are H. N. Castañeda, "The Private Language Argument," in C. D. Rollins, ed., *Knowledge and Experience* (Pittsburgh: University of Pittsburgh Press, 1963), pp. 88–105; T. Duggan, "The Privacy of Experience," *Philosophical Quarterly* 13 (1963): 134–42; D. Gustafson, "A Note on a Misreading of Wittgenstein," *Analysis* 28 (1968): 143–44; J. H. Kultgen, "Can There be a Public Language?" *Southern Journal of Philosophy* 6 (1968): 31–44; R. M. Lemos, "Immediacy, Privacy and Ineffability," *Philosophy and Phenomenological Research* 25 (1964): 500–15; L. Linsky, "Wittgenstein on Language and Some Problems of Philosophy," *Journal of Philosophy* 54 (1957): 285–93; J. Margolis, "Ayer on Privacy," *Philosophy and Phenomenological Research* 28 (1967): 259–63; C. W. K. Mundle, " 'Private Language' and Wittgenstein's Kind of Behaviorism," *Philosophical Quarterly* 16 (1966): 35–46; R. J. Olscamp, "Wittgenstein's Refutation of Scepticism," *Philosophy and Phenomenological Research* 26 (1965): 239–47; M. Perkins, "Two Arguments against a Private Language," *Journal of Philosophy* 62 (1965): 443–58; D. Pole, "Cook on Wittgenstein's Account of Privacy," *Philosophy* 42 (1967): 277–79; J. T. Saunders, "In Defense of a Limited Privacy," *Philosophical Review* 78 (1969): 237–48; K. Stern, "Private Language and Scepticism," *Journal of Philosophy* 60 (1963): 745–59; J. J. Thomson, "Private Languages," *American Philosophical Quarterly* 1 (1964): 20–31.

Classification of sensation–brain-phenomenon identity statements

There has been very little written on this subject. Some writers, however, have dealt with it in passing: Feigl, *The "Mental" and the "Physical,"* pp. 71–98; J. Kim, "On the Psycho-Physical Identity Theory," pp. 231–35; H. Putnam, "Minds and Machines," pp. 152–58; R. Rorty, "Mind–Body Identity, Privacy and Categories," pp. 37–49; R. Routley and V. Macrae, "On the Identity of Sensations and Physiological Occurrences," pp. 90–98 and 103–06; W. Sellars, "The Identity Approach to the Mind–Body Problem," pp. 24–27.

FOUR VERSIONS OF ELIMINATIVE MATERIALISM

ANALYTICAL BEHAVIORISM

Analytical behaviorism has been defended by R. Carnap, "Psychology in Physical Language," in A. J. Ayer, ed., *Logical Positivism* (Glencoe, Illinois: Free Press, 1959), pp. 165–98; and in "On Belief Sentences," *Meaning and Necessity* (Chicago: University of Chicago Press, 1947), pp. 230–32; H. Feigl, "Logical Analysis of the Psycho-Physical Problem," *Philosophy of Science* 1 (1934): 420–45; C. Hempel, "The Logical Analysis of Psychology," in H. Feigl and W. Sellars, eds., *Readings in Philosophical Analysis* (New York: Appleton-Century-Crofts, 1949), pp. 373–84; C. A. Mace, "Some Implications of Analytical Behaviorism," *Proceedings of the Aristotelian Society* 49 (1948–49): 1–16.

A strong attack against analytical behaviorism has come from R. Chisholm, "A Note on Carnap's Meaning Analysis," *Philosophical Studies* 6 (1955): 87–89; "Intentionality and the Theory of Signs," *Philosophical Studies* 3 (1952): 56–63; "Sentences about Believing," *Minnesota Studies* 2 (1958): 510–19; and *Perceiving: A Philosophical Study* (Ithaca, New York: Cornell University Press, 1957), Chapter 11.

The following are also relevant to this issue: J. Cornman, "Intentionality and Intensionality," *Philosophical Quarterly* 12 (1962): 44–52; J. Cornman and K. Lehrer, *Philosophical Problems and Arguments: An Introduction* (New York: Macmillan, 1968), pp. 242–53; H. Heidelberger, "On Characterising the Psychological," *Philosophy and Phenomenological Research* 26 (1966): 529–36; H. H. Price, "Some Objections to Behaviorism," in Hook, *Dimensions of Mind,* pp. 79–84; P. Ziff, "About Behaviorism," in Chappell, *The Philosophy of Mind,* pp. 147–50.

Verifiability criterion of meaning

The verifiability criterion has played a significant role in attempts to justify analytical behaviorism. Much has been written about it. Extensive bibliographies on verifiability are contained in R. W. Ashby, "Verifiability Principle," *Encyclopedia of Philosophy* 8, pp. 240–47, and in P. Edwards and A. Pap, *A Modern Introduction to Philosophy* (New York: The Free Press, 1957), pp. 756–59.

R. Carnap defends a version of the principle in "Testability and Meaning," *Philosophy of Science* 3 (1936): 419–71, and 4 (1937): 1–40; and "The Elimination of Metaphysics through Logical Analysis of Language," reprinted in Ayer, *Logical Positivism,* pp. 60–81; A. J. Ayer formulates and defends the principle in *Language, Truth and Logic,* 2d ed. (New York: Dover Publications, n.d.); "The Principle of Verifiability," *Mind* 45 (1936): 199–203; "Verification and Experience," in *Logical Positivism,* pp. 228–43. Alonzo Church replied in a review of *Language, Truth and Logic* in the *Journal of Symbolic Logic* 14 (1949): 52–53, a reply which prompted P. Nidditch, "A Defence of Ayer's Verifiability Principle against Church's Criticism," *Mind* 70 (1961): 88–89. This was followed by I. Scheffler, *The Anatomy of Inquiry* (New York: Alfred A. Knopf, 1963), and D. Makinson, "Nidditch's Definition of Verifiability," *Mind* 74 (1965): 240–47. J. W. Cornman replied to Makinson in "Indirectly Verifiable: Everything or Nothing," *Philosophical Studies* 18 (1967): 49–56.

Other defenders of the principle, some of whom give different formulations of it, are C. G. Hempel, "Problems and Changes in the Empiricist Criterion of Meaning," *Revue Internationale de Philosophie* 4 (1950): 40–63; "The Concept of Cognitive Significance: A Reconsideration," *Proceedings of the American Academy of Arts and Sciences* 80 (1951): 61–77; K. Popper, *The Logic of Scientific Discovery* (London: Hutchinson, 1959);

H. Reichenbach, "The Verifiability Theory of Meaning," in *Readings in the Philosophy of Science,* pp. 93–102; W. C. Salmon, "Verifiability and Logic," in *Mind, Matter, and Method,* pp. 354–76.

RYLEAN BEHAVIORISM

Gilbert Ryle has expounded his views in many works. Those most relevant to this topic are *The Concept of Mind* (New York: Barnes and Noble, 1949); "Thinking and Language," *Proceedings of the Aristotelian Society, Supplementary Volume* 25 (1951): 65–82; "Feelings," *Philosophical Quarterly* 1 (1951): 193–205; "Thinking," *Acta Philologica* 9 (1953); "Sensation," in H. D. Lewis, ed., *Contemporary British Philosophy,* 3d series (London: Allen and Unwin, 1956), pp. 427–43; "Pleasure," *Proceedings of the Aristotelian Society, Supplementary Volume* 28 (1954): 135–46.

Critics of Ryle are: J. W. Cornman, *Metaphysics, Reference, and Language* (New Haven: Yale University Press, 1966), pp. 38–45 and 63–70; A. Danto, "Concerning Mental Pictures," *Journal of Philosophy* 55 (1958): 12–20; A. C. Ewing, "Professor Ryle's Attack on Dualism," *Proceedings of the Aristotelian Society* 53 (1952): 47–78; J. Findlay, "Linguistic Approach to Psychophysics," *Proceedings of the Aristotelian Society* 50 (1949): 43–64; A. Garnett, "Mind as Minding," *Mind* 61 (1952): 349–58; W. J. Ginnane, "Thoughts," *Mind* 60 (1960): 372–90; S. Hampshire, "The Concept of Mind," *Mind* 59 (1950): 237–55; M. Mandelbaum, "Professor Ryle and Psychology," *Philosophical Review* 67 (1958): 522–30; H. R. King, "Professor Ryle and *The Concept of Mind,*" *Journal of Philosophy* 48 (1951): 280–96; A. Pap, "Semantic Analysis and Psycho-Physical Dualism," *Mind* 61 (1952): 209–21; T. Penelhum, "The Logic of Pleasure," *Philosophy and Phenomenological Research* 17 (1956): 488–503; J. J. C. Smart, "Ryle on Mechanism and Psychology," *Philosophical Quarterly* 9 (1959): 349–55; J. Wisdom, "The Concept of Mind," *Proceedings of the Aristotelian Society* 50 (1949): 189–204; J. N. Wright, "Mind and the Concept of Mind," *Proceedings of the Aristotelian Society, Supplementary Volume* 33 (1959): 1–22.

POSTULATION ELIMINATIVE MATERIALISM

This version of eliminative materialism stems from W. V. Quine. His views are outlined in *Word and Object* (Cambridge, Mass.: Massachusetts Institute of Technology Press, 1960), pp. 262–66, and in "On Mental Entities," *Ways of Paradox* (New York: Random House, 1966), pp. 208–14. David Lewis expresses a similar view in "An Argument for the Identity Theory," *Journal of Philosophy* 63 (1966): 17–25.

SENSATION ELIMINATIVE MATERIALISM

Richard Rorty's position in "Mind–Body Identity, Privacy, and Categories," *Review of Metaphysics* 19 (1965): 24–54, is best construed as this version of eliminative materialism. Criticisms of his views will be found in J. W. Cornman, "On the Elimination of 'Sensations' and Sensations," *Review of Metaphysics* 22 (1968): 15–35; and R. Bernstein, "The Challenge of Scientific Materialism," *International Philosophical Quarterly* 8 (1968): 252–75. Rorty replies to both articles in "In Defense of Eliminative Materialism," *Review of Metaphysics* 24 (1970): 112–21.

ARGUMENTS FOR THE EXISTENCE OF SENSA

There is an extensive literature on the problem of sense-data. Here only that part of the literature dealing directly with arguments for sensa will be considered. The different arguments are often conflated. Authors fail to distinguish among perceptual relativity, illusion, and hallucination, and confuse the causal argument with the time-gap argument. To help avoid such confusion, references are made specifically to those pages that are directly relevant to an argument.

ARGUMENT FROM PERCEPTUAL RELATIVITY

Explanations or favorable treatments of the argument will be found in A. J. Ayer, *The Foundations of Empirical Knowledge* (London: Macmillan, 1964), pp. 9–11, 32–36; *The Problem of Knowledge* (Baltimore: Penguin Books, 1956), pp. 91–93; G. Berkeley, *Principles, Dialogues, and Correspondence* (New York: Bobbs-Merrill Company, 1965), pp. 108–31; C. D. Broad, *Scientific Thought* (Patterson, N.J.: Littlefield, Adams and Co., 1959), pp. 274–76; P. Cummins, "Perceptual Relativity and Ideas in the Mind," *Philosophy and Phenomenological Research* 24 (1963): 202–14; A. O. Lovejoy, *The Revolt Against Dualism* (La Salle, Pennsylvania: Open Court, 1960), pp. 25–27; G. E. Moore, *Some Main Problems of Philosophy* (New York: Collier Books, 1953), pp. 46–52; B. Russell, *The Problems of Philosophy* (London: Oxford University Press, 1959), pp. 8–12.

Those who are critical of the argument include D. M. Armstrong, *Perception and the Physical World* (London: Routledge and Kegan Paul, 1961), pp. 1–14; W. H. F. Barnes, "The Myth of Sense-Data," *Proceedings of the Aristotelian Society* 45 (1944–1945): 91 and 103–06; R. W. Bronough, "The Argument from the Elliptical Penny," *Philosophical Quarterly* 14 (1964): 151–57; N. Brown, "Sense Data and Material Objects," *Mind* 66 (1957): 180–81; R. M. Chisholm, "The Theory of Appearing," in M. Black, ed., *Philosophical Analysis* (Englewood Cliffs, N.J.: Prentice Hall, 1963), pp. 98–99; Cornman and Lehrer, *Philosophical Problems and Arguments,* pp. 47–51; R. J. Hirst, in G. M. Wyburn, R. W. Pickford, R. J. Hirst, *Human Senses and Perception* (Toronto: University of Toronto Press, 1964), pp. 243, 246–47, 253–55; E. B. McGilvary, "Perceptual and Memory Perspectives," reprinted in R. J. Hirst, *Perception and the External World* (New York: The Macmillan Company, 1965), pp. 199–208.

ARGUMENT FROM ILLUSION AND HALLUCINATION

Defenders of the argument are Ayer, *The Foundations of Empirical Knowledge,* pp. 1–57; Lord Brain, *The Nature of Experience* (London: Oxford University Press, 1959), pp. 11–22; C. D. Broad, "Professor Marc-Wogau's *Theorie der Sinnesdaten,*" *Mind* 56 (1947): 104–07; Sir Roy Harrod, "Sense and Sensibilia," *Philosophy* 38 (1963): 232–34; Lovejoy, *The Revolt Against Dualism,* pp. 28–30.

Among the critics are Armstrong, *Perception and the Physical World,* pp. 14–27; and "Illusions of Sense," *Australasian Journal of Philosophy* 33 (1955): 90–99; J. L. Austin, *Sense and Sensibilia* (New York: Oxford University Press, 1964), pp. 20–32 and 44–103; N. Brown, "Sense Data and Material Objects," *Mind* 66 (1957): 181–94; R. J. Hirst, "Perception,

Science, and Common Sense," *Mind* 60 (1951): 481–89, and in G. M. Wynburn, R. W. Pickford, and Hirst, *Human Senses and Perception,* pp. 251–53; A. Quinton, "The Problem of Perception," *Mind* 54 (1965): 33–39; C. H. Whiteley, "Physical Objects," reprinted in J. V. Canfield and F. H. Donnell, Jr., eds., *Theory of Knowledge* (New York: Appleton-Century-Crofts, 1964), pp. 445–46.

Also relevant are: Arthadeva, "Naive Realism and Illusions," *Philosophy* 34 (1959): 323–30; Cornman and Lehrer, *Philosophical Problems and Arguments,* pp. 51–72; R. Firth, "Austin and the Argument from Illusion," *Philosophical Review* 73 (1964): 372–82; H. H. Price, who in *Perception* (London: Methuen, 1932), pp. 21–54, defends the argument, but later in "The Argument from Illusion," H. D. Lewis, ed., *Contemporary British Philosophy,* 3d series (London: Allen and Unwin, 1956), pp. 391–400, attacks it; W. Sellars, "The Identity Approach to the Mind–Body Problem," reprinted in Hampshire, *Philosophy of Mind,* pp. 16–19.

CAUSAL ARGUMENT

Defenders include Lord Brain, *Mind, Perception, and Science* (Oxford: Blackwell, 1951), Chapter 1; J. Eccles, "Neurophysiological Problems in Perception," reprinted in Canfield and Donnell, *Theory of Knowledge,* pp. 409–10; H. P. Grice, "The Causal Theory of Perception," *Proceedings of the Aristotelian Society* 35 (1961): 121–52; B. Russell, *The Outline of Philosophy* (London: Allen and Unwin, 1927), Chapters 12 and 13.

The argument is attacked by Armstrong, *Perception and the Physical World,* pp. 139–44, and "Illusions of Sense," *Australasian Journal of Philosophy* 33 (1955): 90; R. Firth, "Sense Data and the Percept Theory," *Mind* 58 (1949): 453–56; R. J. Hirst, "Perception, Science, and Common Sense," *Mind* 60 (1951): 491–94; A. Quinton, "The Problem of Perception," *Mind* 54 (1965): 32–65.

ARGUMENT FROM TIME GAP

This argument is defended by Bertrand Russell in *Human Knowledge: Its Scope and Limits* (New York: Simon and Schuster, 1948), pp. 203–09, and *The Outline of Philosophy,* pp. 138–42 and 150–56; and by C. D. Broad in "Professor Marc-Wogau's *Theorie der Sinnesdaten,*" *Mind* 56 (1947): 120–24.

It is attacked by R. C. Henson, "Ordinary Language, Common Sense, and the Time-Gap Argument," *Mind* 76 (1967): 21–33, and by W. A. Suchting, "Perception and the Time-Lag Argument," *Philosophical Quarterly* 19 (1969): 46–56. The argument is also criticized by C. W. K. Mundle, "Common Sense Versus Mr. Hirst's Theory of Perception," *Proceedings of the Aristotelian Society* 60 (1959–60): 75–76; G. E. Meyers, "Perception and the 'Time-Lag' Argument," *Analysis* 17 (1957): 97–102. There is also a symposium: "The Time Difficulty in Realist Theories of Perception," *Proceedings of the Aristotelian Society* 11 (1911–12): 124–87, featuring H. W. Carr, F. B. Jevons, W. Brown, and G. Dawes Hicks.

SELLARS' POSTULATIONAL JUSTIFICATION OF SENSA

Wilfrid Sellars' arguments are presented throughout his writings, the majority of them appearing in three volumes: *Science, Perception and Reality*; *Philosophical Perspectives* (Springfield, Illinois: Charles C. Thomas, 1967); and *Science and Metaphysics* (London: Routledge and Kegan Paul, 1967). Articles on this aspect of his work include B. Aune, "Comments" on the essay "Phenomenalism" by Sellars in H. N. Castañeda, ed., *Intentionality, Minds, and Perception* (Detroit: Wayne State University Press, 1967), pp. 215–85. Sellars' reply appears in the same volume, pp. 286–300. Also relevant are R. Bernstein, "Sellars' Vision of Man-in-the-Universe," *Review of Metaphysics* 20 (1966): 113–43 and 290–316; J. W. Cornman, "Sellars, Scientific Realism, and Sensa," *Review of Metaphysics* 23 (1970): 417–51; G. H. Harman, "Review of *Philosophical Perspectives,*" *Journal of Philosophy* 66 (1969): 133–44; K. Lehrer, "Review of *Science, Perception and Reality,*" *Journal of Philosophy* 62 (1966): 266–77.

TYPES AND CATEGORIES

Bertrand Russell outlined his theory of types first in *The Principles of Mathematics* (Cambridge University Press, 1903) and in "Mathematical Logic as Based on the Theory of Types," *American Journal of Mathematics* 30 (1908): 222–62. Later it appeared more fully in *Principia Mathematica* 1 (Cambridge University Press, 1910). He also discussed types in R. C. Marsh, *Logic and Knowledge* (New York: Macmillan, 1956), pp. 321–44.

Criticisms of Russell will be found in M. Black, "Russell's Philosophy of Language," in P. A. Schilpp, ed., *The Philosophy of Bertrand Russell* (New York: Tudor Publishing Co., 1944), pp. 227–55 (which also contains a reply by Russell, pp. 679–741); R. Carnap, *The Logical Syntax of Language* (London: Routledge and Kegan Paul, 1937); A. Church, "A Formulation of the Simple Theory of Types," *Journal of Symbolic Logic* 5 (1940): 56–68; T. Drange, "The Paradox of the Non-Communicator," *Philosophical Studies* 15 (1964): 92–96; L. Goddard, "Sense and Nonsense," *Mind* 73 (1964): 309–31; A. Pap, "Types and Meaninglessness," *Mind* 69 (1960): 41–54; F. P. Ramsey, "New Foundations of Mathematics," *Proceedings of the London Mathematical Society* 25 (1925): 338–84; J. J. C. Smart, "Whitehead and Russell's Theory of Types," *Analysis* 10 (1950): 93–96; W. V. Quine, "New Foundations for Mathematical Logic," *American Mathematical Monthly* 44 (1937): 70–80; P. Weiss, "The Theory of Types," *Mind* 37 (1928): 338–48.

Gilbert Ryle explains and defends his notion of "category mistake" in "Categories," *Proceedings of the Aristotelian Society* 38 (1938): 189–206. Other relevant writings of Ryle are "Systematically Misleading Expressions," *Proceedings of the Aristotelian Society* 32 (1931): 139–70; *Philosophical Arguments* (Oxford: Clarendon Press, 1945) (reprinted in Ayer, *Logical Positivism*, pp. 327–44); *The Concept of Mind* and *Dilemmas* (Cambridge University Press, 1953).

Articles on Ryle's concept of category include: A. J. Baker, "Category Mistakes," *Australasian Journal of Philosophy* 34 (1956): 13–26; J. W. Cornman, "Categories, Grammar, and Semantics," *Inquiry* 13 (1970): 297–307 and "Types, Categories, and Nonsense," in *Studies in Logical Theory* (Oxford: Blackwell, 1968), pp. 73–97; R. C. Cross, "Category Differences," *Proceedings of the Aristotelian Society*, n.s. 59 (1958–59): 255–70; E. Erwin, "Farewell to the Category Mistake Argument," *Philosophical Studies* 19 (1968): 65–71; E. W. Hall, "Ghosts and Categorical Mistakes," *Philosophical Studies*

7 (1956): 1–6; B. Harrison, "Category Mistakes and Rules of Language," *Mind* 74 (1965): 309–25; D. J. Hillman, "On Grammars and Category Differences," *Mind* 72 (1963): 224–34; M. Thompson, "On Category Differences," *Philosophical Review* 66 (1957): 468–508; J. J. C. Smart, "A Note on Categories," *British Journal for the Philosophy of Science* 4 (1953): 227–28.

F. Sommers states his views in "The Ordinary Language Tree," *Mind* 68 (1959): 160–85; "Types and Ontology," *Philosophical Review* 72 (1963): 327–63; and "Predicability," in M. Black, ed., *Philosophy in America* (London: Allen and Unwin, 1965), pp. 262–81. Articles on Sommers include D. Passell, "On Sommers' Logic of Sense and Nonsense," *Mind* 78 (1969): 132–33; R. B. de Sousa, "The Tree of English Bears Bitter Fruit," *Journal of Philosophy* 63 (1966): 37–46; S. Haack, "Equivocality: A Discussion of Sommers' View," *Analysis* 28 (1968): 159–65; D. Massie, "Sommers' Tree Theory: A Reply to de Sousa," *Journal of Philosophy* 64 (1967): 185–93; R. Van Straaten, "Sommers' Rule and Equivocity," *Analysis* 29 (1968): 58–61.

Also relevant are: *Metaphysics, Reference, and Language*, pp. 63–66; J. Passmore, *Philosophical Reasoning* (New York: Scribner's, 1961), Chapter 7; R. Rorty, "Pragmatism, Categories, and Language," *Philosophical Review* 70 (1961): 197–223; G. J. Warnock, *English Philosophy Since 1900* (New York: Oxford University Press, 1966), Chapter 7.

Index

Abstract entities, 7

Absurdity: as category, 260, 284; tests for, 310–25; grammatical, 312–15; semantic, 315–25. *See also* Meaninglessness

Achinstein, P., 72*n*, 78*n*, 104*n*

Adverbial materialism, 15, 19, 126, 185–90, 255, 257, 279, 281; evaluation of, 267–78

Adverbial sensing: theory, 80, 187, 209, 215, 219, 225, 235, 255, 268, 271; terminology, 178–79, 188, 189; is barbarous, 271, 272

Analysis. *See* Analytical behaviorism; Rylean behaviorism

Analytical behaviorism, 16, 17, 143–51, 266; and analysis, 133, 134, 139, 143, 145, 262; and other eliminative theories, 150, 154, 158, 160, 162, 184, 262

A posteriori: property, 7, 186; individual, 7, 13, 278

Apparitions, 208, 209

Appear words: epistemic and nonepistemic use, 194

A priori: falsehood, 323; synthetic, 323; nonformal, 324

Armstrong, D., 3*n*, 122*n*, 194*n*

Ascriptive: self, 84, 85, 96; other, 84, 96

Aune, B., 229*n*, 237, 238*n*

Austin, J. L.: argument from perceptual relativity, 193, 195; argument from hallucination, 202, 203*n*, 204

Ayer, A. J.: argument from perceptual relativity, 193, 195, 201; argument from hallucination, 202, 203; time gap argument, 218, 220

Baier, K., 37*n*, 38*n*

Basic: particles, 4, 111, 112; level of science, 242, 245, 253–57; entities, 248–49, 252–57

Beetle in box, 92

Behaviorism. *See* Analytical behaviorism; Rylean behaviorism

Berkeley, G., 166*n*, 271; idealism (phenomenalism), 6, 10, 126, 181, 267, 278; on direct perception, 222–26

Black, M., 301; first objection to Russell, 286–90, 307; second objection to Russell, 290–92; reformulation of Russell's definition, 292–94, 301

Boyle's law, 76, 77, 104

Brain: processes, classification of, 106–07; parts, 112–18, 190; colors, 117–18, 274; events and sensings, 185–86, 266–78

Brain, W. R., 201, 202, 208, 209*n*

Brandt, R., 31*n*

Bridge principles. *See* Correspondence rules

Carnap, R., ix, 72, 74, 78*n*, 83, 96

Cartesian: dualism, 6, 10, 23, 32; egos, 24, 32, 33, 240, 249, 255, 283

Categories: logical, 17, 108, 144, 147, 283, Appendix passim; Russell's theory of, 284–94; Pap's theory of, 294–300; Ryle's theory of, 300–03; Sommers's theory of, 304–10; grammatical, 311, 313, 314; sub-, 314; semantic, 315. *See also* Category difference; Category mistake; Category sameness

Category difference, 56, 113, 118, 295, 297, 306–10, 312, 325; criterion of, 55, 56, 107, 118. *See also* Categories; Category mistake; Category sameness

Category mistake, 144, 283, 298, 311, 312, 315, 323, 324, 325. *See also* Category difference

Category principle 55, 56, 57, 110, 111, 299, 309, 325

Category sameness, 285, 286, 295,